gift of
Kornaros

P9-DFD-831

PUBLIC CHOICE IN AMERICA

Theodore Lownik Library
Illinois Benedictine College
Lisle, Illinois 60532

PUBLIC CHOICE IN AMERICA

An Introduction to American Government

WILLIAM C. MITCHELL

University of Oregon

MARKHAM PUBLISHING COMPANY / CHICAGO

JK
274
M163

Markham Political Science Series
Aaron Wildavsky, Editor

Copyright © 1971 by Markham Publishing Company
Second Printing March 1971
All rights reserved
Printed in U.S.A.
Library of Congress Catalog Card Number 70–136626
Standard Book Number 8410–3042–1

For Jim, Waverly, and Jeannine

ACKNOWLEDGMENTS

Writing this book has been a pleasure, not only because of occasional daydreams about substantial royalties but a generous interest shown by many good friends while the writing proceeded. John Applegath, my friend of many years, deserves credit for being not only a good friend, but also a generous publisher willing to assume responsibility for the advancement of risky endeavors.

James Levine and Lawrence Pierce kindly tolerated unsolicited progress reports and my uninhibited glee over matters they could not have found very interesting. They also shared their teaching experiences and their knowledge of American politics, for which I am most grateful. My wife and colleague, Joyce M. Mitchell, permitted me to use countless of her ideas about American politics, teaching, and texts without citations. Her contributions ranged from basic conceptions in the book to minute but important facts about American history. Readers must not fault her, however, for whatever shortcomings they may detect; all of them, including policy stands, are mine.

A number of readers of the first draft of the text performed no less than heroic tasks for they had to patiently struggle through all the shortcomings of a first draft. I would like to thank Aaron Wildavsky, Stephen Puro, Robert Ross, and Donald Strickland for their thoughtful, sympathetic, and detailed critiques. Another colleague, who may prefer to go unacknowledged, contributed an unusually thorough critical analysis and helpful suggestions. His lengthy and detailed critique pointed out many shortcomings, and while painful to read, it was highly valued. Mrs. Jean Ehrhorn typed the various drafts with incredible skill, speed, tolerance, and good spirits. Her self-reliance and intelligence facilitated the tasks of the author, copy editor, and all the others who labored to produce the final copy. Mrs. Eleanor McConnell, of Markham Publishing Company, edited the final draft. Her uncommon skill and sensitive understanding were essential to an impatient author and publisher wanting to finish the work and meet our publication deadlines. I deeply appreciate her contribution.

Eugene, Oregon   W. C. M.
August, 1970

PREFACE

Those who have scanned the table of contents have probably noted that this book bears little relationship with the conventional American government text. Nevertheless, this is a text on American politics and government action. While it consciously attempts to innovate in various ways, the level of analysis is designed to acquaint beginning students with political analysis problems. Simple exposition, plentiful examples, and elementary formulations are the hallmarks of good texts; I hope the book fulfills those qualifications.

The emphasis in this volume is on public choice, which is both the problem to be explained and the source of our explanations. The area of public choice has become a focus for a specialized discipline, and I have therefore treated public choice or policy both as an empirical problem in need of explanation and as a normative dilemma for strategists who would affect policy. Hopefully, the analyses advanced will encourage readers to become more able policy scientists and advocates.

Neither encyclopedic displays of institutional facts nor moralistic preachings about the evils of "power elites" mark this book. Rather, my concern has been with policy outcomes and the processes by which resources are allocated and benefits and burdens are distributed—and how these processes may be improved.

I assume that varying degrees of choice are available to the American people. I further assume that citizens are guided by self-interest in the pursuit of private goals. While economists have long appreciated the analytical and normative power of rational, self-interest models, political scientists have tended to question if not reject these twin postulates for analyzing and prescribing public choice. Advocacy of a more informed self-interest is explicit herein, but it is also qualified and marked, I hope, by some regard for the civilities of a decent public life. I mention these points in anticipation of criticism to the contrary. Not all men who claim to work in the public interest serve us, nor do all men harm others who profess to serve but themselves.

Adam Smith observed that those who work for themselves usually produce good for others, while some who disdain private interests do irreparable injury to countless others. Whatever the balance of private motives and public good in actual life, this book is based on a fine appreciation of the analytical rigor to be derived from treating people as fairly reasonable individuals in pursuit of personal satisfactions. This same logical rigor is highly useful in prescribing strategies and setting forth criteria for public policy.

A writer of a text must, like everyone, pursue somewhat incompatible goals and therefore make decisions about their relative trade-offs or worth. To have more of one value normally entails less of others. I have had to face these dilemmas. Should I write for instructors, professional colleagues, or students? The students seem to want interesting material, style, clarity, simplicity, and ease of reading as well as something called relevance—and even these demands may be somewhat incompatible. In any case, some students want more of some while others want more of others. Professional colleagues are more inclined to judge a book on the basis of scholarly criteria: knowledge, precision, up-to-date materials, completeness, and sophisticated reasoning. Classroom instructors, particularly those with heavy teaching loads, understandably want a text that is convenient and not too demanding of their own scarce resources. At the same time, a book should enable them to prepare adequately for classes without having to memorize it. No text in any field has ever managed to fulfill all these legitimate but conflicting objectives. Certainly this book has not. I have had to make some choices. These goals were uppermost in my mind at the outset:

1. Bring the basic ideas and tools of modern political analysis to the attention of the American government student.

2. Convey these ideas and tools as simply as possible and still be reasonably in accord with their more technical expression.

3. Explain the relevance of our political institutions, not by endless and mindless repetition of legal facts, but through an application of theory (both analytical and normative) to those institutions.

4. Convey just enough facts to be informative but honor the student's well-known aversion to tables and other paraphernalia of scholarship.

5. Analyze our polity as an ongoing system of activity and outcomes, having consequences for both citizen and government.

6. Interpret and pass judgment as well as describe behavior and policies.

I believe these goals are worthy but they impose a variety of costs. For the instructor, the primary cost is a bit of "retooling"; the ideas depart from old-fashioned institutionalism and from behavioralism. They stem from a congeries of traditional political science, modern economics, and business administration with their varying emphases on choice, decision making, conflict theory, and the like. For the student, the chief costs consist of reading that is a little heavier than has been generally demanded by traditional American government texts. I hope I have reduced this price somewhat by not including boring recitations on the formal structure of government. For the sake of students, I hope my colleagues will understand that their technical work must be conveyed in somewhat less elegant terms than they might have chosen themselves. Readers, I hope, will realize that more complete statements are available, and will refer to original sources.

In sum, the approach is designed to present public policy choice as a collection of rational choices made by self-interested individuals.

CONTENTS

Chapter I

ON THE IMPORTANCE OF GOVERNMENT

Throughout this book, one point of view will be pursued. Government and political processes are presented as productive, necessary, and understandable. This approach, introduced in this chapter, consists of viewing the polity—administration of government—as an analog of the economic system: that is, as a set of more or less distinct processes institutionalized formally or informally and performing quite similar functions.

These functions chiefly involve arriving at public choice or public policies having consequences for allocation, distribution, control, and resource mobilization. The questions we will ask pertain to the performance of these functions. Both empirical-analytical and normative questions are suggested and both are dealt with throughout the text. In addition, questions and problems are presented as exercises in analysis of typical situations.

Two themes are presented in this chapter: the extraordinary importance of government in our daily lives and the kinds of questions we think important in studying American politics.

Political scientists may often be inclined to stress the importance of government for obvious reasons of occupational self-interest, but they are more aware than most ordinary citizens of the daily impacts of government on their lives. The citizen often gains clearer recognition of politics and government only when a bureaucrat or a law disrupts the daily routine and leaves him uncomfortable. One such experience is being drafted into the military. Writing a check for an unexpectedly large income tax return is another. Other major or minor annoyances caused by government are citation for a traffic violation or having one's favorite TV program displaced by a political speech.

When governments deal in high-level bargaining, treaties,

or trade agreements, with the UN or a government in another part of the world, politics is dramatic; it occupies the front pages of most newspapers and consumes most of a TV commentator's time. But politics is also of the mundane—the everyday occurrence. Because we take so much of government for granted it may be worthwhile to remind ourselves of its potential significance for us.

Consider what would happen if we were suddenly deprived of government services such as weather reports, subsidized education, free use of streets and sidewalks, clean drinking water, airports, police and fire protection, the municipal swimming pool, a sewage system, and the like. How could we start anew to provide ourselves with these necessities? In attempting to answer such a question we must raise again the age-old question of the origins of government.

Instead of going back to philosophical fundamentals, perhaps something of the extraordinary presence of government can be shown in another way. The 1970 telephone directory in Eugene, Oregon lists the following governmental offices:

CITY OF EUGENE

Airport-Manager	Development Agency	Police Department
City Hall	Eugene Water and	Sewage Treatment
Civil Defense	Electric Board	Plant
Department of Parks	Fire Department (8	
and Recreation	stations)	
(nine separate	Library	
activities and	Maintenance Division	
phones)	Planning Commission	

LANE COUNTY OFFICES IN EUGENE

Agricultural and	Election Division	Parks and Recreation
Home Economics	Fair Board	Commission
Extension	Finance and Auditing	Pioneer Museum
Assessor	4-H	Planning Commission
Circuit Court	General Administra-	Public Works Depart-
Circuit Court Report-	tion-Personnel	ment
ers	Health and Sanitation	Purchasing Depart-
Civil Defense	Housing Authority	ment
County Commission-	Juvenile Department	Sheriff's Department
ers	Medical Investigator	Surveyor
County Clerk	Mental Health De-	Veteran's Affairs
District Attorney	partment	
District Court		

STATE OF OREGON OFFICES IN EUGENE

Alcohol and Drug Section: Regional Office
Compensation Department
Department of Employment
Forestry Department (2 divisions)
General Services Department
Board of Health
Board of Higher Education

Highway Department (4 divisions)
Bureau of Labor (4 divisions)
Liquor Control Commission (3 divisions and 3 stores)
Department of Motor Vehicles (2 offices)
National Guard
Board of Parole and Probation
Public Utility Commissioner

Public Welfare Commission
Sanitary Authority
State Police
Tax Commission
Vocational Rehabilitation
Workmen's Compensation Board

U.S. GOVERNMENT OFFICES IN EUGENE

Department of Agriculture
Agricultural Stabilization and Conservation County Committee
Farmers Home Administration
Forest Service
Soil Conservation Service
Department of the Air Force
Department of the Army
Corps of Engineers Recruiting Station
115th Military INTC Group
Army Reserve
Coast Guard
Department of Commerce
Dellenback, John (Congressman)
Federal Aviation Administration
Federal Telecommunications System Operator

General Services Administration
Department of Health, Education and Welfare
Immigration and Naturalization Service
Department of Interior
Bonneville Power Administration
Bureau of Land Management
Bureau of Commercial Fisheries
Geological Survey
Internal Revenue Service
Judiciary
Department of Justice
Federal Bureau of Investigation
Department of Labor
Bureau of Apprenticeships and Training
Wage and Hour and Public Contracts Divisions

Department of the Navy
Marine Corps Recruiting Station
Marine Corps Reserve
Naval Investigative Service Resident
Naval and Marine Corps Reserve Training Center
Recruiting Branch Station
Peace Corps
Department of Post Office
Selective Service Local Board 13
Department of Transportation
Coast Guard
Federal Aviation Administration
Federal Highway Administration
Department of Treasury
Veteran's Administration

These directory entries add up to some 105 public offices. Countless elected officials and many special governmental districts are not listed. The mayor and city council members are not listed because they do not have full-time positions with special offices. In short, the above list is but a partial listing of governmental offices in Eugene, Oregon, a city of but 70,000 residents. Consider New York City with its more than 1,400 government offices.

Note, too, that the city has fewer offices (12) and apparently provides fewer services than any other level of government. The county lists at least 27 offices, the state has 20, and the federal government has by far the greatest number with 46. The number of military, police, and public service operations is large. Many of the public services and controls denoted by the office titles suggest that more than one—and usually all three—levels of government are involved. Our political division of labor is a vast complex formal structure of offices, but it is hardly neat and orderly. Practically all activities are shared.

No single citizen will have regular contact with these more than 100 offices of government, but he will very likely have periodic relationships with a few, such as tax officials; perhaps an occasional session with a policeman and a court; an even less frequent contact with the military; and no *direct* contact with most of these agencies and politicians. But all of us will be affected by their decisions in some way or another, and more or less continuously. Many of the contacts will be pleasant because they involve decent public servants and free services; some will be unpleasant; and for some people in minority groups will be highly unpleasant. All in all, government is one of the most pervasive and powerful influences in our lives, in spite of our tradition that that government governs best which governs least. The presence of government in Eugene, Oregon seems apparent; much less obvious is the impact or significance of governments at all levels throughout the nation. No sentence or two can possibly summarize the impacts of 521,000 elective officials, 12 million bureaucrats, 90,000 governments, and a total budget of more than $260 billion. We shall need some sixteen chapters to discuss these impacts.

Still we've given no hints as to what information we might want to know about our governments and that, after all, is the most important problem. The history of political science demonstrates that there is no shortage of questions to be posed. This text raises a number of them. Most questions we will ask are very commonplace and ancient; others are fairly novel at this stage of political inquiry.

What Should We Know?

Unlike most texts this one will not define politics in a sentence or two but will indicate some of the questions we will raise and attempt to answer. In a sense, we are begging the question of a definition by claiming that American politics is whatever this author says it is in these pages. If you can answer most of the following 20 questions you need not read any farther; you are already a political scientist. If you cannot answer any of the questions or, worse, even understand them, this book is for you.

1. How can we best account for the fact that during recent years the federal government has paid agriculture five times more money than it has business and about twelve times more than labor?

2. The state income tax burden in Oregon during 1966 was distributed as shown in Table I-1.

TABLE I–1
Distribution of Income Tax in Oregon, 1966

Annual Income	Percentage of Taxpaying Population	Percentage of Total Income Tax Revenue
$ 0–5,000	45.3%	8.2%
5–10,000	35.6	33.4
10–15,000	14.0	27.4
15,000 +	5.1	31.0

How can we explain obvious inequalities in the sharing of these burdens?

3. At least one famous political scientist has asserted that while elections are effective devices for controlling leaders, they are quite ineffective as indicators of majority preferences. Is this true? Why?

4. Almost all Americans believe they are loyal and good citizens, yet only $167,397 was donated voluntarily to the U.S. Treasury in 1969. Why? Is compulsory taxation necessary? Why?

5. If most voters (more than 80%) vote as their parents did, how is it ever possible for different parties to win public office?

6. Under what conditions might a citizen opt for each of the following sets of policy controls?

Restriction of no one's activity,

Simultaneous restriction on every citizen,

Simultaneous restriction on the activity of every citizen but oneself.

7. Consider the fate of a proposal which would send all blacks (in the United States) to Africa and/or all Jews to Israel under the following modes of decision:

Special referendum among American voters with a simple majority rule,

Congressional vote with logrolling (exchange of favors) permitted,

Congressional vote with logrolling prohibited.

8. Suppose that the government had $10 billion to allocate between highway construction and mental health projects and that your marginal utilities for each good are as depicted in Figure I-1, indicate the optimal allocation. Explain your choice.

9. Which of the following federal programs might be substantially reduced if the strict norms of rational resource allocation were applied?

Veterans' benefits,

Agricultural subsidies,

Highway expenditures,

NSF fellowships in social sciences.

10. Which of the following programs are most and which are least sensitive to political demands and why?

Natural resource conservation,

Agriculture,

Public housing,

Foreign aid,

Space exploration,

Veterans' assistance.

11. Are taxes or expenditures more subject to drastic reform? To annual fluctuations? Why?

12. How can we explain the fact that some 425 counties have no federal food aid programs for the poor but do accept considerable sums of agricultural subsidies for their better-off citizens?

13. Some critics say that logrolling in Congress has bad consequences. What are the consequences? Are they all bad? Which ones are? Why?

FIGURE I–1
Marginal Utility Curves of Two Public Goods

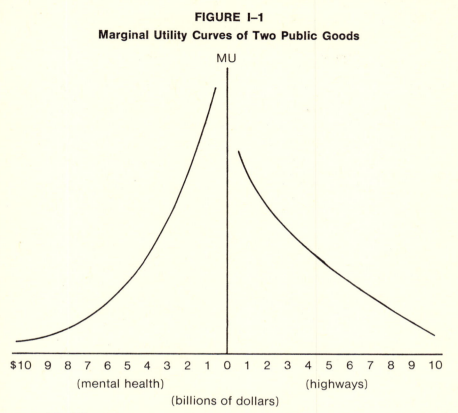

MU

$10 9   8   7   6   5   4   3   2   1   0   1   2   3   4   5   6   7   8   9   10

(mental health)   (highways)

(billions of dollars)

14. What differences will it make for the voters, the candidates, and public policy if we abolish the electoral college and substitute the popular vote in electing our Presidents?

15. Why are such issues as birth control, miscegenation, divorce, treason, drug use, dress codes, fluoridation, integration, nudism, school prayers, immigration laws, and the like so hotly contested at certain times in our history and not at others?

16. How is it that a people who value private property and individual rights so highly have enacted a highly progressive income tax? Why does this tax have so many "loopholes"? Is there any connection between the two ideas?

17. If one wants to reduce the number and intensity of student demonstrations, how can it be done?

18. Of the following activities, which would you have performed by local government? By states? By the federal government? Which would you have jointly managed? Why?

Drug control,
Street maintenance,
Education,
Air traffic control.

19. Under what conditions might you expect to form a successful third party?

20. Why do we devote approximately $377 per capita to defense and only $7 to parks? Can this ratio be changed? How? Why?

If these problems are baffling it is because the writer wishes to illustrate how political reality daily inflicts difficulties on all of us—whether ordinary citizens, practicing politicians, or political scientists. The questions are all real, either in the sense that they attempt to portray aspects of our actual political life and therefore call for explanations, or because they illustrate strategic and policy dilemmas that need solutions. If these questions have been read with some care, the reader may have noted some underlying themes about politics that will pervade this book.

Four Basic Analytical Problems

COLLECTIVE GOAL ATTAINMENT

Perhaps the most noticeable theme or question pertains to the problem of how our political system decides what to do and how to do it. Political systems are man made and not ordained by gods—contrary to the beliefs of some rulers. As such, political systems are designed and used for purposes deemed important by at least some of their members. In short, even the most oppressive polity is productive in that it provides valuable goods and services some men desire and use, although it may be unproductive in the sense that no *new* goods are produced—merely redistributed. Even though one may not favor a particular activity, one can be sure that someone else will profit from its performance.

We will also want to discover why Americans have turned increasingly to government for solutions of their problems. We expect to learn something about the basic dimensions of governmental activity including historical trends, to identify typical kinds of problems and activities that become public, and perhaps even to make some predictions about the future.

WHO GETS HOW MUCH OF WHAT?

Implicit in the above discussion and explicit in Problems 1, 8, 12, and 20 is the question of *who gets what* and *how much* from governmental activity. If governments exist for the explicit purpose of the betterment of citizens we should be able to know who is achieving betterment since, as the figures in Problem 1 clearly indicate, everyone does not benefit equally. Americans may honor political equality in the abstract but they most assuredly do not achieve it in practice, and few acts of our governments produce equal shares of welfare for everyone. Any reader who considers himself a realist will want to explain why this has been the case so far and make some projections about the future.

WHO PAYS HOW MUCH?

Just as some people gain more and others less in the political struggle, so *some people pay more* and *others less* to finance the many activities our governments perform (see Problem 2). We will learn something about the variety of burdens and why taxation is compulsory (see Problem 4). We will learn something about the range of inequalities and why loopholes in tax laws are to be expected under our system (see Problem 16). We will also learn why some governments and administrations rarely balance their annual budgets.

HOW ARE CITIZENS INDUCED TO COOPERATE?

Active governments cannot mobilize people and allocate resources, redistribute income and allocate burdens without also devising effective means of policy implementation. This is no mean task, primarily because we know so little about how to achieve effective, efficient control over human behavior (see Problem 17). There is no science of human control. Most of what is known is highly tentative and is applicable to relatively small domains of behavior.

Control of inflation, for example, involves human behavior. It is a hotly debated issue in large part because we do not really know how best to prevent or control it. Traffic regulation seems a simpler matter. Yet it can be handled in many ways, with consequences we cannot surely predict. Control of drug use among the young is a subject of much concern. Is drug control by government desirable? How can it be accomplished? How do our governments attempt to control the behavior of corporations, interest groups, criminals, auto drivers, parents, and others? Because the field of public control is among the more fascinating areas of social science and political science in particular, we will explore it in considerable detail.

Of course, the facts we will discover have relevance only for the times we specify in our discussions. Things have not always been so, nor will they continue in the same maner with the same results. So we should consider the effects of variations through time. Our political life has changed dramatically in some regards and hardly at all in still others. As we investigate the goals we have pursued, the resources we allocate, the burdens we distribute, and the benefits we share, we always raise the question of trends. Has it always been so? What about the future?

What Should We Do?

This question is supremely important, not only in this book but in the present and future lives of each reader. The chapters in Parts Three and Four confront strategic and policy dilemmas each of us will face in our future roles as voters, administrators, politicians, reformers, and even as political scientists. We will attempt to formulate goals and decide how we can best influence national goals. Thus we can act to increase our influence in distributing the benefits, minimizing the costs, and generally become more effective participants in whatever we decide to do.

The advice advanced, for both strategy and policy, in the following pages will not be enthusiastically received by all readers; many are likely to be highly offended by its Machiavellian character. Indeed, many American intellectuals have expressed considerable animosity toward explicit advocacy of self-interest and the marketplace. Fortunately, many of these intellectuals are now beginning to understand some of the intrinsic failures of public planning, bureaucracies, and even majority rule. (The new left radicals have come to share a profound suspicion of public choice, although for different reasons.) In any event, in Part Three we will explore a variety of strategies for participation in American politics. In Part Four we will advance criteria for the assessment of public policies.

For the moment, I wish simply to offer initial clarification on strategy and policy advice. Misunderstandings about self-interest, exchange, and bargaining impede discussion among students and even political scientists. Hopefully, the reader will be patient enough to read the entire book before deciding that advocacy of these self-interested motives and bargaining institutions is evil. He will then learn that the writer strongly urges the adoption of institutional reforms that should enable these processes to work with far better results for many more citizens.

Finally, the writer is less concerned that readers adopt his policy views than that they become more aware of and sophisticated about their own views and about any changes they may wish to consider. If any single lesson is to be learned from this treatment of American politics it is this: Every existing and proposed rule, institution, process, policy, and behavior has a multitude of good and bad allocative, distributive, and control consequences. It is our task as political analysts to discover those consequences; it is the task of the informed citizen to act as though he understood these implications both for himself and others.

These problems of collective or public choice are universal and cannot be avoided. Americans have answered them in many ways over the past two hundred years and are likely to continue to experiment toward better solutions. There is no single "correct" solution to any of these problems, a fact that makes many impatient but pleases still others. However any single citizen may feel about proposed solutions, he will find others who will disagree and have other preferences. If this were not so we would not need governmental institutions to resolve policy differences. If it were not so some of us would not have jobs as political analysts—there would be no politics to analyze. But since there are differences there are policy problems. The analytic, strategic, and policy questions we noted above are summarized in Table I–2.

Prospects for the Future

Do not be surprised if American politics does not consistently meet the highest standards of perfection. No system can continually and fully satisfy all its members and we should not expect it

TABLE I-2

The Basic Problems: A Summary

What is done	*How can I*	*What is best for me*
Which collective goals do we pursue?	Influence these goals?	Which goals should we adopt?
How are collective goals achieved?	Influence mobilization?	How should goals be pursued?
How are public goods distributed?	Get more of those I want?	How should benefits be distributed?
How are collective burdens allocated?	Minimize my share?	How should burdens be allocated?

to—for many reasons we will explore. Rather than remain at an abstract level of analysis let us offer some preliminary observations on political activities and policy outcomes characteristic of our political life. If some of these statements seem incomplete, they will be further detailed and explained in subsequent pages. In the meanwhile prepare to expect such statements as:

Our governments rarely pursue policies that make some citizens better off without making others worse off.

Very few citizens ever achieve complete satisfaction in their dealings with governments.

We have not been able to achieve either political or economic equality.

Our party system tends to discourage rational choice among voters.

Our governments tend to favor producers more than consumers.

Our party system encourages policies that are alike and vague.

Most policy change, most of the time, is incremental or piecemeal.

Our taxation system tends to be progressive but the benefit system tends to be regressive.

Our governments rarely produce enough public goods to meet demands.

Our governments rarely distribute costs according to benefit principles.

Our governments are rarely able to balance their budgets let alone achieve surpluses.

Our governments do not treat all men equally.

Reform is difficult and costly to achieve.

Large numbers of voters do not vote regularly.

Drastic revisions of the tax laws are very rare.

Governments often devise taxes that conceal incidence.

Governmental bureaucracies are slow, costly, and self-interested.

Politicians make more promises than they can keep.

Pork-barrel legislation is popular among legislators.

Many subsidies go to those who do not need them.

Government spending fluctuates greatly but is still highly predictable.

Some citizens pay a higher price than others for government services.

Passing a law does not always achieve its authors' objectives.

Some states get much more money from Washington than others.

Government acts at times as a protector of some people's civil rights while at other times as the repressor of the liberties of others.

These generalizations about our country's political institutions and performances are not meant to shock. Some readers, we know, may be upset by their rather strong language or assertiveness. Those who complete this book will learn why we make these contentions. They will learn that certain tendencies in all democracies encourage such results and that particular institutions, rules, beliefs, and traditions contribute to specific end results. They can be altered not having been ordained by the laws of the universe. But knowing how to alter them will require considerable knowledge and hard work. Working through political institutions and working to change them is not for the faint hearted.

Our polity, though an imperfect construction of imperfect men, has served some mighty and noble ends and has performed quite well when compared with that of most other nations. We know it has served some men better than others and this inequity is apt to continue for a long time. Rather than discourage, such a fact ought to renew the reader's convictions and willingness to achieve his goals.

Suggested Readings

Dahl, Robert A. *Modern Political Analysis* (Englewood Cliffs, N.J.: Prentice-Hall, Inc., 1963).

Duverger, Maurice. *The Idea of Politics* (Chicago: Henry Regnery Co., 1966).

Froman, Lewis A., Jr. *People and Politics* (Englewood Cliffs, N.J.: Prentice-Hall, Inc., 1962).

Grodzins, Morton. *The American System* (Chicago: Rand McNally & Co., 1966).

Miller, J.D.B. *The Nature of Politics* (Chicago: Encyclopaedia Britannica Press, 1962).

Schattschneider, E. E. *Two Hundred Million Americans in Search of a Government* (New York: Holt, Rinehart and Winston, Inc., 1969).

Policy Outcomes and Public Choice

Part One, consisting of Chapters II to V, presents a variety of materials on certain types or dimensions of public policy during recent years. The emphasis is upon the national goals or policy priorities pursued by the American people through their political system and the implied resource allocations of their choices. In addition, the advantages, privileges, and benefits conferred by these same choices are spelled out in some detail as are the burdens imposed upon our citizenry. We will learn that although everyone benefits to some extent and everyone pays to some extent, all contributions and benefits are distributed unequally. We will also begin to appreciate some of the difficulties public choice poses for people. Contrasts with private choice, especially in the marketplace, are scattered throughout these pages. A much more detailed examination of the nature of public choice is reserved for subsequent chapters.

Chapter II

NATIONAL GOALS AND PUBLIC GOODS: THE AGENDA OF PRIORITIES

"We the people of the United States, in order to form a more perfect union, establish justice, insure domestic tranquility, provide for the common defense, promote the general welfare, and secure the blessings of liberty to ourselves and our posterity, do ordain and establish this Constitution for the United States of America."

These general goals constitute the Preamble to our Constitution. These clauses are used to justify or rationalize most governmental activities; they have on many occasions become battle cries or slogans for conservatives and liberals alike. We do not really know whether the order in which these aspirations are stated indicate either their present importance or the rankings attributed to them by the founding fathers. More likely than not they are of somewhat equal significance, although each of us would probably rank them differently. Such an exercise would force each of us to order his personal priorities, thereby making his political philosophies more explicit.

Budgetary Allocations and Personal Preferences

National goals and their orderings are the concern of every citizen because these goals are really statements about the kinds and amounts of public goods and services we consider important in our daily lives. Grand goals and the rhetoric in which they are cast by our leaders really are made up of very mundane needs like armies, police and fire protection, highways, education, sewage disposal, traffic regulations, weather reports, courts of law, copyright protection, welfare payments, subsidies, and the like. Such goods and services provided by governments are usually labelled *public goods* or *collective goods* by economists and others interested in public choice.

A public good is so identified because it is thought to be one of those peculiar goods or services which once created cannot be readily sold in divisible quantities to a specific person or to a group which may exercise exclusive ownership or control over it. Public goods are thus contrasted to private goods, which can be rationed or made exclusive property by selling in a market for a price. For example, one can buy an auto and claim exclusive ownership, but one cannot buy $3,000 worth of national defense. The amount of defense provided by governments is available to all—including those who do not wish to make use of any defense.

Most of the so-called public goods and services that governments in this country produce and distribute are not pure. When most public goods are divided among the citizenry, some get larger shares than others. For example, trucking companies use public highways more than nondrivers do. Farmers probably use weather reports more than students do. Some people get more police protection than others. In short, many government services are in fact rationed, even though there was no prior intent to do so on the part of the lawmakers. As a result, people demand different budgetary priorities to reflect their own preferences. Government budgets are the outcomes of struggles and exchanges among consumers of public goods with different tastes and political power.

Everyone uses some kinds of public goods. We could not readily carry on our daily private activities without them, because they complement our private goods and facilitate private activities. To drive a car one needs streets and roads. To fly safely requires an airport and traffic control. One who wants his property protected demands the services of a publicly provided police force. If a citizen dislikes certain activities or their consequences, such as air pollution, obscenity, pornography, noisy factories, and violence on campuses, he may wish to see those activities curtailed or regulated. Government can and does provide regulatory services in response to demands of citizens for prohibition or control of the offensive behavior of others.

We turn to governments not only to regulate the obnoxious or costly behavior of others, but to facilitate our private activities and guarantee our safety. Thus we demand education, subsidies, police protection, a monetary system, a legal system and a judicial service, weather reports, free vaccination, and domestic order. Some of us demand that government protect all personal rights and liberties; some demand that government perform this function preferentially. Not everyone can have all the government's goods and services in unlimited and/or preferred quantities. Our political system does not operate as a marketplace providing each person with only those commodities he prefers in the quantities he desires and can afford to pay for given his income.

Public Budgets and Policy Priorities

Political systems provide means whereby citizens or their representatives can sort out countless diverse preferences or demands and rank them in importance so that *scarce resources* can be allocated among competing uses and citizens. Since we cannot honor everyone's policy priorities simultaneously we must establish some ranking system which says, in effect, some people's goals and needs will be met first, others' will have second importance, and so on. We do this in a variety of ways but the end results are symbolized chiefly by numerical, "dollars and cents" entries in public budgets and symbolic statements. The two orderings or rankings may not be consistent. For example, the President, Congress, or a Governor may pay verbal tribute to a goal such as ending racial discrimination yet appropriate or spend very little money to that end in the budget. The rhetoric of public speeches may be used to appease certain demands while the budget is employed to satisfy others.

BUDGETARY PRIORITIES

American public goals can be revealed by looking at a recent annual budget of all our governments. Historical comparison will show whether public priorities have changed very much. The general situation in 1967 is indicated in Table II–1. Complete expenditures are not shown, and some categories are overlapping and ambiguous, but still the table does present a fairly meaningful rough ordering of public budgetary priorities. Surely it is no surprise that "national defense" ranks first. The rest of the table, however, may show a good many surprises. For example, some may be sur-

TABLE II-1

Governmental Expenditure, 1967
(All Governments)

Function	Expenditure (in millions)	Per Capita Expenditure
National defense and international relations	$74,638	$377
Education	40,214	203
Old-Age and Survivors' Disability Insurance	23,919	
Highways	14,032	71
Interest on general debt	13,405	68
Natural resources	10,145	51
Public welfare	9,592	48
Utility and liquor stores	7,351	
Hospitals	6,951	35
Postal service	6,227	31
Space research and technology	5,359	27
Employee retirement	4,584	
Veteran's services	4,425	22
Police	3,331	17
Sanitation	2,523	13
Health	2,506	13
Housing and urban renewal	2,413	12
Financial administration	2,387	12
General control	2,150	11
Unemployment compensation	2,012	11
Local fire protection	1,499	8
Local parks and recreation	1,291	7

Source: U.S. Bureau of the Census, *Statistical Abstract of the United States: 1969* (90th ed. Washington, D.C.: Government Printing Office, 1969), p. 411.

prised to see education in second place—albeit a poor second to defense with slightly more than half as much money. Others, perhaps, will be amazed to note the position of interest on the general debt in fifth place, considerably ahead of all welfare-type expenditures. Public welfare, upon which so many conservatives feel we spend far too much, is far down the list in seventh place. Some radicals may be perplexed at seeing police protection in fourteenth position far below public welfare. All these fascinating bits of information need considerably more explanation. That will be provided in subsequent chapters.

The Rhetoric of National Goals

The "hard data" we have presented in the form of budgets are persuasive. For some critics they are the single most important indicator of those public goals we really value. But to completely ignore the verbal aspirations of a society and cynically observe that they are mere words is to woefully misunderstand man. We live not only on bread but on abstract values, beliefs, and symbols. So it is also of some importance to pay attention to what people say they want, as well as how they say it. After all, a budget is a compromise. It may not be explained or arrived at by means that truly represent the American people. Some goals and groups may be underrepresented, or misrepresented, by our institutions and practices. We shall see in later chapters that that is indeed the case. But the evidence of political rhetoric must still be considered.

What better place to seek the aspirations of 200 million people than in the speeches of their leaders and the programs of their political parties? Presidents and other leaders have always attempted to give expression to the ideals of their people, partly because they believe in them and partly because they want to gain votes and remain in office. Whatever the reasons, they can give us some clues.

One political scientist has analyzed the Inaugural Addresses of our Presidents and documented one fairly obvious conclusion: Presidents do tend to say pretty much the same things despite the changes in times and their own party affiliations.[1] The recurring themes in these highly symbolic speeches include material welfare, unity, equality of opportunity, personal liberty, patriotism, protecting family life, and the like—goals that Presidents, regardless of politics, vow to pursue as they promise loyal service to all Americans. Soon enough, Presidents must become increasingly practical by proposing concrete programs of action with dollar signs attached. Even so, their State of the Union Addresses to Congress, Budget Messages, and specific program proposals contain a surprisingly large amount of emotive rhetoric designed to win adherents for the ideas and reduce potential opposition. Actual budgets and programs make pretty dull reading, so Presidents and other chief executives provide more inspiring declara-

[1] John McDiarmid, "Presidential Inaugural Addresses—A Study in Verbal Symbols," *Public Opinion Quarterly*, 1 (July 1937), 79–82.

tions of intentions, priorities, and actions. No democracy, including our own, could maintain the enthusiastic support of its citizens without such an emotional rhetoric of choice and challenge.

Professor Murray Edelman, in a highly provocative article, persuasively contends that a fundamental function of symbols, especially those found in preambles to legislation, is to induce political quiescence among those to whom great promises are made without the full intention of keeping them.[2] This is especially so in the regulation of business and redistributive activities of governments. Tangible resources and benefits are not distributed to the extent promised in many statutes and the rhetoric that attends their enactment.

Edelman claims that the least important provisions affecting resource allocation are highly publicized while the most important features are not. Tax legislation is frequently of this sort. Reform in the direction of greater equity is usually counted a major goal, yet many loopholes that remain go unnoticed except by those who benefit from them. At the same time, in Edelman's view, the well-publicized verbal symbolic reforms serve to quiet the rebellious demanders, and people are bought off by words. Actually, Edelman is only partially correct.

One example is the tax reform of 1969, in which the rich were not badly affected, yet there were symbolic assurances for those who wanted tax reform. But it is also true that many news media featured continuing series of "exposés" of loopholes and the beneficiaries (sometimes by name) who profited from these laws. Citizens who wished to become informed on the matter could have done so at relatively little cost.

In another area, governmental regulation of business, much symbolic reassurance is given to consumers without accompanying action. Great reforms have been made during the twentieth century to control, reduce, or even outlaw certain private economic activities considered harmful to consumer groups. Thus, regulatory agencies at all levels of government—the Interstate Commerce Commission, Federal Communications Commission, and many others—were originally designed to protect consumers. Some have not always been very zealous in their work, and in fact, the administrators chosen to control certain industries have

[2] Murray Edelman, "Symbols and Political Quiescence," *The American Political Science Review*, 54 (September 1960), 695–704.

frequently become their spokesmen. It is not unusual for representatives of industrial concerns to be appointed to public boards and commissions and "rule" their former and future colleagues. Understandably, their rule is sympathetic.

In still other situations, police have been known to oppress some groups or individuals although it is their explicit task to protect and serve them. The public rhetoric still holds that these servants of the people are supposed to increase the public welfare. Somehow the goal is shunted aside for the welfare of far more limited groups. When this occurs, whose priorities are being realized?

Some Reasons for our Priorities

Why do we do the things we do and not other things? Why do we spend so much on national defense and so little on parks and recreation? There is no simple answer to these questions, since any answer is bound to be a theory of the entire American political process. This kind of theory is so complex we will need two chapters (VI and VII) to discuss it. Some basic considerations can, however, be suggested at this stage.

Political scientists and others, particularly sociologists, are sharply divided on the question of who decides which policies and why. One school of thought maintains that public priorities are set by elites or small numbers of very powerful private persons and groups; another agrees that elites decide, but holds that there are many contending or competing elites. A public budget, both contend, is the result of the values, preferences, and behavior of either competing or unitary elites. Let us have a closer, more detailed look at these theories as they pertain to our public priorities.

THE ELITIST SCHOOL

A political scientist who contends that our budget is a product of a unitary elite is saying that the interests of a few privileged people are reflected in the ordering of our national priorities. He would, in addition, contend that the budget conceals more information than it reveals. The composition of the big general categories, such as highways, does not reveal who benefits from highway expenditures. The same is true in the case of national defense and education.

Elitist critics of our education system, for example, would say it reinforces the status-quo perspective and prepares students to accept and work for the interests of the elites. In addition, the elitist might argue that a budget cannot reflect what is *not* being done that *should* be given high priority, because elites have power to prevent certain reorderings of priorities.

An elite can control society, according to the critics, because of its monopoly control of superior resources. High status, strategic position, wealth, and income give the elite control of top decision-making or policy-making positions in business, government, and the military. Thus they influence public choices and condition or educate the masses to see things and behave in ways that are consistent with the views of the elites. Since they also monopolize coercion—the police and military—they can deal with deviants and rebels.

In this view of society and politics, the ordinary citizen is generally seen as politically passive and loyal to the elites because of ignorance and because his interests are tied to their success.

In short, the elitist would say, the civics book view of government and polity is a totally inaccurate but useful propaganda device for training people into passivity. A national budget of policy priorities sacrifices the real wants of the people in the pursuit of elite interests.

THE PLURALIST POSITION

Pluralists include those political and social scientists who view political power as much more widely dispersed. A pluralist sees a governmental budget and public policy as results of many competing groups striving to achieve their own interests and values, and compromising and bargaining or exchanging benefits as they compete. No one group is so powerful, so united that its policies or priorities are long dominant. Public policy is a compromise made by many people pursuing self-interests; each struggles for his share and supports those who have complementary interests if they will support him. The budget is not decided upon by a self-conscious elite doling out resources, but is a piecemeal allocation of resources resulting from the choices of rational, competing self-interested groups. Whether the result is good for all is an open question which we defer until Part Four.

Pluralists believe that the resources of power are widely if unequally divided. No one group has a monopoly on any single resource, and no group is so unified that it can prevail. Our basic political institutions permit widespread entry and participation in the system for those who can pay the costs. The budget is viewed as a patchwork of settlements negotiated frequently by these competing groups and not subject to enormous, unexpected annual variation. There is, incidentally a great deal of evidence to support pluralist views of the budget-making process.

The specific ordering of budgetary priorities is viewed by pluralists as a fairly good index of relative political power. If national defense has the largest allocation of resources it is because the many groups who profit from such allocations are the most powerful groups. Those with the lowest allocation would be the least powerful.

VARIOUS OTHER CONSIDERATIONS

These two theories will receive much fuller treatment in Chapters VI and VII. For the present we will simply call attention to a number of considerations and questions neither of these theories addresses or provides adequate answers to. Both schools emphasize that budgetary allocations are a result of differing distributions of power or power resources. Neither examines in detail the intellectual resources of various groups or the nature of the expenditure. Defense expenditure is not simply of benefit for some groups and not others. Defense belongs in the category of public goods; it is produced by the government and its support is universal and coerced because some citizens would not voluntarily finance it. It cannot be sold to individual citizens on a market for a price. The same is true of most other items in a budget, but some expenditures can be or are handled by private institutions; that helps to explain why their allocations are less than defense's share. Hospitals and medical care are supported mostly by private persons and groups. For housing, both private and public resources are used. Because housing is far down the list in the public budget does not necessarily mean that housing is unimportant or that its supporters are weak. Rather it may mean that housing has been regarded as essentially a private responsibility. In the future, housing may come to be regarded as a public responsibility, but at present it remains primarily a private task with increasing involvement of the public and government. Another activity Americans have historically preferred to leave to private choice is social security. As industrialization has progressed, government involvement has increased. Thus, such programs as Old-Age and Survivors' Disability Insurance (OASDI) as well as unemployment insurance now rank rather high in the nation's many budgets, and Medicare will soon have high priority.

Another consideration deserves brief mention. Our summary in Table II–1 does not contain the program breakdowns according to levels of government. National defense, for example, is not in local and state budgets; it is the exclusive province of the federal government. On the other hand, the educational budget of the federal government is small compared to its ranking in state and local budgets. A division of labor exists, so to speak, with different priorities for each unit of government. We can illustrate the varying service priorities at each level with a simple table. Table II–2

TABLE II–2

Sample Public Expenditures by Level of Government, 1967

Activity	Federal	State	Local
Defense	53.9%	0.0%	0.0%
Space research	3.9	0.0	0.0
Postal service	4.5	0.0	0.0
Education	4.5	39.8	48.0
Highways	3.0	21.2	7.7
Public welfare	4.0	13.5	6.8

Source: U.S. Bureau of the Census, *Statistical Abstract of the United States: 1969* (90th ed., Washington, D.C.: Government Printing Office, 1969), p. 412.

shows the expenditure percentages for each type of government. Considerable variations can be noted, suggesting different policy priorities at each level. These choices at each level have been influenced by power differentials among citizens and considerations of efficient divisions of labor. The fact that the federal government spends so little of its total revenues on education is hardly the only indicator of education's national importance as testified to by its enormous share at the state and local levels. The latter two levels of government spent over $49 billion as compared to the federal government's slightly more than $6 billion in 1967. Perhaps the future will see a further shifting of burdens toward the federal government. That will depend upon new economic and social necessities as well as political power.

Have Our Priorities Changed?

Obviously, our priorities have changed, but that statement requires some qualification. In 1799 our forebears devoted only 14 percent of the national income to public purposes. That figure has grown to about 30 percent in recent years.[3] In earlier years very little government money was spent on military matters; today this is the largest item by far in the federal budget. In earlier years we spent much smaller amounts on education and highways than current governments do. Yet the percentages spent on these items during the past 70 years have not changed very much. In 1903, for example, educational expenditures amounted to about 16 percent of the total budget, and they are the same today. On the other hand, today's public welfare and health programs constitute about 24 percent of the budgets as contrasted with 6 percent in 1903. The big increases have been in public welfare, schools, and public enterprises. However, even those activities that grew least in importance increased fourfold or more in total expenditures. In not a single activity have expenditures decreased.

While priorities among traditional governmental activities have not always changed much we have added new priorities— new activities and responsibilities. Thus, programs such as space exploration and foreign affairs have become key activities for the federal government. If major programs have not changed in terms of their importance across governmental levels they have within each level. State expenditures for highways have become much more crucial, whereas general control (administrative costs of running the government) have today about one-twelfth as much importance as at the turn of the century. Total expenditures for police, corrections, and interest on bonds have all increased greatly, but as percentages of the budgets, have decreased.

At the local level, expenditures on education have increased as a percentage of the budget, as have welfare payments, health and hospitals, and spending on utilities. On the other hand, police and fire protection, and general control have lower percentages of the funds. So priorities have been altered at each level even when the overall spending has not changed, meaning that we use

[3] Data used here were derived from U.S. Bureau of the Census, *Statistical Abstract of the United States: 1969* (90th ed., Washington, D.C.: U.S. Government Printing Office, 1969), p. 411; U.S. Bureau of the Census, *Historical Statistics of the United States* (Washington, D.C.: U.S. Government Printing Office, 1961), p. 723.

different combinations of governmental units to solve social problems.

Priorities Among Nations

Comparison of budget priorities has always been very difficult, because there are vast differences in the budgetary practices of nations. Actually, few scholars have even raised the question. But in recent years, as interest has arisen in such questions, new and more reliable information has become available.

Nations do spend their monies rather differently. For example, in the early 1960s the United States spent about 12 percent of its total budgets on education as compared to only 5 percent in West Germany.[4] The USSR, however, spent about 9 percent. The United Kingdom spent 13 percent. Defense has seen very large variations among nations. Our country now devotes about 9 percent of the gross national product (GNP) to these pursuits while most other countries devote less than 4 or 5 percent. In the provision of social security Sweden and Germany lead with 23.5 percent and 31.1 percent respectively. The United States apportions only 16.4 percent of its budget. In the field of public health we spend only about half the budgetary percentages that prevail in European nations.

Just why the public expenditures priorities of nations vary is a complex matter, affected by many social, culture, economic, and political differences. We do not, as yet, know which of these factors explains how much of the variance or differences in expenditures. Our ability to account for expenditure variations among governments is limited almost entirely to the level of state governments within the United States.

Priorities Among American States

During recent years a handful of political scientists have been studying policy variations among our fifty states. They hope not only to identify the range of policy choices but also to explain

[4] Richard A. Musgrave, *Fiscal Systems* (New Haven, Conn.: Yale University Press, 1969), p. 41. Also see Frederic L. Pryor, *Public Expenditures in Communist and Capitalist Nations* (Homewood, Ill.: Richard D. Irwin, Inc., 1968), Chapter V.

those variations. Their diligent statistical analyses may be summarized in useful, if fairly rough, terms. A major generalization is this: Most of whatever variance has been found may best be accounted for by differences in economic development among the fifty states. Wealthier states, for example, tend to spend more of their income on public services than poor ones. Equally important is the generalization that states spend very different amounts on the same activities. Illustrations can be found in several areas. On education, for example, 1966 expenditures ranged from $140 per capita in Arkansas to $309 in Alaska.[5] Highways in the same year consumed about $49 per capita in South Carolina and $440 in Alaska. Expenditures on public welfare programs ranged from $15 per capita in South Carolina to a high of $85 in California. Similar wide discrepancies can be found among most other expenditures.

Political scientists hotly debate the reasons for the wide range of priorities in public spending. Some maintain that variations in state economic development is the main cause while others argue that political factors account for at least some of the notable differences. The latter group, however, has thus far not been able to achieve impressive correlations or to prove their thesis under rigorous statistical test.[6] The problem is that political factors that would account for choices made by state governments are not easily quantified and tested. This area needs much study; scientifically-oriented political students may yet make original contributions to our knowledge about comparison of priority choices.

It is not surprising, however, to find striking positive correlations between a state's level of taxation and its "marketbasket of public goods." States that offer lower tax bills have smaller baskets. If more and better public services are sought one must pay more for them. In addition, each taxpayer must pay a different price for the public goods and services he consumes. In fact, we even pay for many we do not want. Moving from state to state to achieve a better payoff is far too expensive and not likely, in any

---

[5] These figures are drawn from U.S. Bureau of the Census, *Statistical Abstract of the United States: 1969* (90th ed., Washington, D.C.: U.S. Government Printing Office, 1969), p. 417.

[6] Some of the political characteristics or variables used include party competition, voter participation, and apportionment. See Thomas R. Dye, *Politics, Economics, and the Public* (Chicago: Rand McNally & Company, 1966), Chapter III; Ira Sharkansky, *Spending in the American States* (Chicago: Rand McNally & Company, 1968).

event, to guarantee receiving the preferred basket. As a consequence, few Americans choose their residence on the basis of budgetary priorities of state or local governments—with one exception. The one public service that does seem to have considerable impact on residency choices is education. Citizens may be said to be "voting with their feet" when they move to those school districts that provide the services they prefer in the amounts they like and at costs they are prepared to pay.

Exercises in Analysis

WHAT SHOULD ALASKA DO WITH ITS "WINDFALL"?

Alaska, the forty-ninth state in the Union, has suffered from financial problems since its admission in 1959. Today, its people and policy makers have found themselves the beneficiaries of sudden wealth and income. About $900 million has accrued already from recent oil discoveries, with the promise of many more millions depending on the supply of oil.[7] What will Alaskans do with this money and the possibilities of still more income? This is a real allocative problem—one that can only be handled by the political system.

Space limitations preclude a full-scale inventory of relevant facts about Alaska's social and economic problems, its resources, and the demands upon those resources, but it must be noted that Alaska has been one of the neediest of states. Although it is the largest state, it is hardly developed, with its vast snow regions and only 2,500 miles of paved highways. Unemployment in 1970 was over the national average. More than 55,000 Indians, Eskimos, and Aleuts still live very primitively. Countless elderly people who settled Alaska during the 1930s are now living on low, fixed incomes while inflation continues to mount. Deep poverty is widespread in the rural areas.

If the $900 million were immediately and equally distributed in cash, it would provide $3,000 per capita. But the decision is not this simple. Here are some of the questions that must be answered. Who should get how much, when, and how? Which goals

---

[7] The following account is based on an article by Kathy Dibell, "Alaska's Problem: Just What To Do with $900 Million," *Eugene* (Ore.) *Register-Guard*, April 2, 1970.

and criteria should be established? What goods and services (public and private) should be produced? For whom? How much of the money should be invested in capital goods the state desperately needs? What kinds of controls should be imposed on the choices?

Many want to spend the money now to make up for past shortages. Others want to insure for the uncertain future. Who wants to do what? Why? The low-income voters, understandably, want to realize some benefits now. The less needy prefer some sort of trust fund that cannot be easily touched. Elected legislators are caught in the pressures of elections and the insistent demands for immediate benefits rather than promises of uncertain future advantages.

Some voters want $250 per month pensions for all those who have lived in Alaska for 25 years or more. That would cost about $400 million to start. Others want a home loan system to alleviate a drastic housing shortage; that would cost about $200 million. Another proposal would have the state make treaty settlement with the natives that would cost about $50 million. The teachers would like to have a $25 million salary increase while the fishermen want to build up the fisheries at a cost of $2 million. Apparently everyone wants airports and schools. Complicating the allocative problem is the basic question of how to handle the oil development, itself, so as to continue high incomes, use good conservation practices, and maintain the environment in an optimal way. What should Alaskans do? If they have not decided by the time this book is being read, how do you think they will decide? Why?

NATIONAL PRIORITIES AND BUDGET CUTS

Many Americans have grown accustomed to seeing ever increasing national income, employment, and governmental budgets. Sometimes, however, depressions and recessions occur, and governmental budgets rise at a slower rate. Under these conditions certain programs, agencies, and public services are cut back as intensive efforts are made to balance the budget. Citizens and policy makers with conservative tendencies opt for achieving economies, while the affected agencies and their supporters rally to save their programs. Our analytical problem is this: When an economy drive is instituted, who shall be cut back and how much?

Our example comes from the efforts of the 90th Congress and President Nixon to reduce the national budget as much as possible

TABLE II-3

Some Appropriations Outcomes, 90th Congress, 2nd Session, 1969

Agency	Requested Appropriation	House Passed	Senate Passed	Final Appropriation
Agriculture	$ 6,923,979,800	$ 5,523,635,500	$ 5,540,550,300	$ 5,531,396,650
Defense	77,074,000,000	72,239,700,000	71,886,893,000	71,869,828,000
Interior	1,432,342,300	1,280,880,300	1,284,372,800	1,284,987,300
Labor	19,301,525,000	17,232,871,300	19,033,346,000	18,566,568,800
Transportation	1,932,032,000	1,353,391,000	1,788,411,000	1,634,266,000

Source: Adapted from *Federal Economic Policy, 4th Edition*, (Washington, D.C.: Congressional Quarterly Service, 1969), p. 89.

in an effort to combat inflation. In Table II-3 we have arrayed a sample of agency requests for appropriations to the Congress and the actions the Congress took with regard to them. Notice that all agencies received less than they requested, although the percentage reductions were unequal. Note, too, that the Senate was more generous than the House in all but one instance—defense requests. One need know very little arithmetic to see that all the final appropriations were compromised by the House and Senate. Readers may wish to make some additional calculations including the percentage size of the final cutbacks for each agency and the compromise figure as proportion of the difference between the two houses. Which house tends to cut most? Which house tends to "win" out in the final compromised or bargained appropriation?

These 1969 legislative outcomes require some explanation. Why was each agency cut back as it was? What factors might assist in devising an appropriate answer? What would we need to know in order to account for the final choices? Is our earlier discussion of elites relevant?

Congress also left the Nixon Administration with the additional task of cutting at least $2.1 billion from its own requests. Budget Director Charles J. Zwick said that the Administration would make the following cutbacks :[8]

Non-Vietnam defense spending	$ 1 billion
Government loan programs	$ 1 billion
Postponing federal highway projects	$200 million
Non-Apollo projects of NASA	$100 million
Army Corps of Engineers projects	$ 49 million
Post Office Department	$ 45 million
Dept. of Transportation nonhighway funds	$ 30 million
Atomic Energy Commission	$ 29 million

An additional $50 million were also to be cut from a number of other undisclosed agencies and programs, according to the Budget Director. Why were these agencies and programs selected by the Nixon Administration to be cut back to the extent shown above? What additional facts would provide an explanation? Is there any way to test alternative theories or explanations to determine which is the more powerful theory?

[8] *Federal Economic Policy, 4th Edition*, (Washington, D.C.: Congressional Quarterly Service, 1969), p. 98.

PRIORITIES ON SEWERS

Sewers are important to individuals in a civilized society. They account for a major expenditure of local governments. One might not think that local governments would encounter allocative problems in providing sewerage service but they do, as this case proves. The county of Washington, Oregon recently adopted a priority schedule for the construction of sewers after the state banned further construction because the limited sewerage facilities had reached capacity.[9] Our problem is to figure out how and why the County Board of Commissioners adopted the priorities they did. While we need much more information than we have perhaps it is still possible to advance plausible alternative explanations and identify the kinds of information required for a full-scale investigation.

Sewer Priorities, Washington County, Oregon, 1970

First	Connections to correct health hazards
Second	Schools and municipal buildings
Third	Dwellings, apartments, and commercial and light industrial buildings for which permits were issued before September 1, 1969
Fourth	New construction of dwellings in approved subdivisions where sewer collection systems were built before September 26, 1969
Fifth	New construction of dwellings in subdivisions where collection systems were built after that date (September 26, 1969), and the same order for apartments, commercial, and light industry.

Variances could be granted if a builder could persuade the Advisory Committee of the United Sewerage Agency.

Among other considerations that make this problem an interesting one is this: Did the Commissioners adopt these priorities because of some perceived set of community needs, apart from the political feasibility or acceptability of the ordering, or

---

[9] Based on "County Adopts Priorities on Sewers," *The Oregonian,* May 20, 1970, p. 14.

did they confine their choices to purely political considerations involving the differential influence of citizens? Or, perhaps, these dual considerations are intertwined. Who would support and oppose correcting health hazards? Schools? Dwellings? Apartments? Why was September 1, 1969 chosen as a qualifying date or deadline?

Suggested Readings

Bauer, Raymond A., ed. *Social Indicators* (Cambridge, Mass.: The M.I.T. Press, 1966).

Dye, Thomas R. *Politics, Economics, and the Public: Policy Outcomes in the American States* (Chicago: Rand McNally & Co., 1966).

Kimmel, Lewis H. *Federal Budget and Fiscal Policy: 1789–1958* (Washington, D.C.: The Brookings Institution, 1959).

Ott, David J. and Ott, Attiat F. *Federal Budget Policy* (Washington, D.C.: The Brookings Institution, 1965).

Sharkansky, Ira. *Spending in the American States* (Chicago: Rand McNally & Co., 1968).

————. *The Politics of Taxing and Spending* (Indianapolis: The Bobbs-Merrill Co., Inc., 1969).

Weidenbaum, Murray. *The Modern Public Sector* (New York: Basic Books, Inc., Publishers, 1969).

Chapter III

ACHIEVING GOALS: THE COMMITMENT OF RESOURCES

In Chapter II we learned of the goals we pursue and the services we demand, but learned nothing about their achievement nor even about the available supply of resources. Our focus will now shift toward our vast and intricate process of mobilizing resources in pursuit of national goals. The dimensions of the task can better be appreciated if we first take a brief backward look to the Administrations of President Washington. During his day governments were small and weak. Our 4 million people, scattered about in 11 states, had a national budget of less than $4.5 million—hardly enough to run a small town today. Most of the revenue was derived from customs, and therefore came from outside the country. The chief activities of the federal government were confined to supporting a small military, paying the costs of previous wars, and paying interest on the public debt. A bit later our governments, and particularly the states, did much to promote and subsidize private enterprise, but all in all the governmental sector remained miniscule in size and scope of activities. We were a newly developing nation.

Today, we are the most powerful nation in the world, and probably in all of history. With more than 200 million people, 3.6 million square miles of territory, and a national product of more than $900 billion we are also the richest people in history. (Our per capita income is higher than every nation but one—Kuwait.) We lead or are among the leaders of the world in the production of most modern industrial products and resources. Many of our states are richer and their governments bigger and more powerful than most nations of the world. We have a governing apparatus of more than 118 million qualified voters, 521,000 elective public officials, 11 million civilian governmental employees, and a military force of 4 million men. Our 90,000 governments own and manage more than 888 million acres of land, or approximately 39 percent of the total land area, with the federal government owning the greatest share—about 33 percent. Our governments own more than 417 thousand buildings, conservatively valued at almost $27 billion.

We are a colossus among the nations of the world. We are the envy of many and the object of hatred and resentment. While we may not be as powerful as some patriots like to believe, we are the dominant fact of international life. We have fought in 19 major foreign wars and currently spend more than $15 billion per year, exclusive of the costs of the Vietnam war, in financing more than 72 defense treaties, pledges, and other agreements. Our immense power influences, for better or worse, the lives of almost every inhabitant on earth.

Public Demands and Private Resources

Despite our immense wealth and military power we must confront the basic and elementary tasks of governing a nation of more than 200 million citizens scattered over a vast territory. Our traditional functions—providing for the common defense, assuring domestic tranquility, and achieving all the modern demands of a restless people—pose organizational and resource problems of the greatest magnitude.

How do we achieve our public goals and satisfy increasing demands for services? How do we mobilize the necessary resources, particularly when they are limited in quantity and quality? How do our governments acquire the needed factors of production: land, labor, capital, and management? Governments, like business firms, cannot produce goods and services without resources. When citizen demand for public goods and services increases so too must the public demand for resources—resources that could otherwise be used for satisfying private wants. Since most of our resources are owned and managed by private persons and organizations, the demand of some citizens to use the resources of others for public consumption is destined to encounter opposition. Because we have strong preferences for private goals the demand for resources to produce public goods is apt to be stoutly resisted by many. Our political parties epitomize that dichotomy: the Republican Party has traditionally represented those who want the public sphere as small as possible, while the Democratic Party has generally represented those wanting it enlarged.

Public Mobilization

Bringing together the efforts and resources of over 200 million people is a vast, intricate, and cumbersome task involving elements of voluntary cooperation, coercion, leadership, rationality, and emotive responses to official pleas for support. While the mobilization effort is most dramatic during great wars, it is normally a continuous series of mundane, ordinary activities. This mostly bureaucratic process is marred by many mistakes and even corruption. Fighting distant wars; putting down internal rebellion; meeting problems of inflation, unemployment, urban renewal, and crime; providing for welfare, housing, medical care, fire protection, and all other routine services pose different and difficult tasks.

We have not always performed these tasks with maximum effectiveness and efficiency. Yet one must marvel at how much Americans have achieved through their formal governments. Our amazing capacity for cooperation would not call for attention were it not for the fact that we so often think of ourselves as an essentially nonpolitical, highly individualistic people. We are, in fact, a highly coordinated society, despite our decentralized decision-making structures. Most countries are unable to achieve high degrees of cooperation without employing dictatorial means. Nations whose citizens do not cooperate usually languish with underdeveloped economies and polities. Cooperation does not come naturally to man. In America it has been produced in several ways —by teaching the child to want to cooperate, by making the benefits outweigh the costs, and by compelling contributions from citizens.

Our governments like to rely on as much voluntarism as possible by opting for suasion, self-enforcing laws, and appeals to patriotic service. Much of a President's time is spent enlisting enthusiasm whenever possible among his cohorts, his allies, and especially the people. The drudgery of administering the budget and public programs is delegated, of course, to the 11 million members of the bureaucracy—particularly those 2.9 million working in the federal agencies.

Since most citizens do not work for government in any direct sense, problems are posed for a government bent on winning our loyalties, support, and resources. Because we work for ourselves in private institutions we tend to see government as "they" rather than "we"—especially around tax time. Still, most Americans are intensely patriotic and a President may assume, under most conditions, that the people will follow his lead, particularly during foreign policy crises. This support cannot be relied on during periods when the nation is deeply divided on crucial policy issues.

At times, certain groups have been known to resist the patriotic pleas of their government. Minority groups such as blacks, students, Chicanos, and Indians are most dissatisfied with our present government and least likely to support it. They feel that governments, and society in general, have failed to fulfill their desires and needs. It is true, however, that our governments have often responded to the plight of these groups with greater speed and humaneness than have many of our private institutions, such as the church, business, unions, social clubs, and the like. Ironically, the military, especially the Army, has been more receptive than any other element of government and society to minorities. Loyalty to a nation, therefore, may be a deeply emotional experience, but it rests on favorable exchanges with governments. A government that only asks but seldom gives is not likely to enlist very many loyal followers. Because American governments have provided for so many of the needs of their citizens they have achieved high stability. In fact they have inspired an almost naive patriotism that sets Americans apart from most other men. Our profoundest loyalties in recent decades have attached to the nation rather than to state or local government, but this has not always been so. In the decades before the Civil War, for example, many citizens asserted primary loyalties to states, regions, and localities.

Under normal conditions American governments do not resort to the intense collective mobilization efforts typical of newly established totalitarian nations. These nations are attempting to modernize at faster rates than western democracies ever attained. Cuba under Castro, China under Mao, and the USSR under Stalin's rule are a few better known examples of governments that have engaged in frenzied, irrational, often economically impossible attempts to achieve modernity and power overnight. Americans have achieved these goals gradually by private effort. We have chosen to mobilize using business firms, cooperatives, and the self-help of barn-raising strategies. During our two great world wars, however, we did—of necessity—centrally organize under government leadership. It was then that we had an inkling of what mobilization is for the ambitious new nation-states.

MOBILIZATION FADS AND SEQUENCES

Occasionally we have mobilization fads—issues that capture the attention of many citizens. By group efforts they work toward solutions of some recently discovered problem. Shortly after this book was begun students across the nation discovered pollution of the environment about them. Within but a few short weeks they had mobilized under the leadership of a few public spokesmen, including two professors, to wage a war against pollution. Slogans such as "Can Man Survive?" were soon made popular. The largest class in the University of Oregon's history—some 2,000—was formed and students were encouraged not only to study but reform society and its policies so that man might survive.

Later, as these pages were being typed, conservation, ecology, and "Can Man Survive?" had been all but forgotten as opposition to President Nixon's war policies captured our interests and emotions. All this happened in but a few weeks. This not-unusual sequence of events is cited as a fairly good example of the American style of mobilization, which we have pictured as a curve in Figure III-1. Typically, great problems develop slowly without much public awareness. A catastrophe suddenly grasps people's attention. Leaders come to the fore to mobilize opinion and finally public action. As the issue becomes popular, its supporters demand concerted mobilization of resources. Politicians and the government join the crusade. The government drafts legislation, and opposition groups gather their own resources in defense of their rights and privileges against encroachment and diminution of income. Eventually, laws are usually passed and a millenium is prophesied. In a hasty effort to amend past errors, funds are appropriated, occasionally more than necessary and poorly allocated; bureaucracies are established; and new vested interests are created. Mobilization becomes routinized and all the old fervent followers with emotions spent settle back into accustomed ways assuming the problem is now being controlled.

Our mobilizations are short-lived combinations of private and

FIGURE III-1
Crisis, Activation, and Public Mobilization

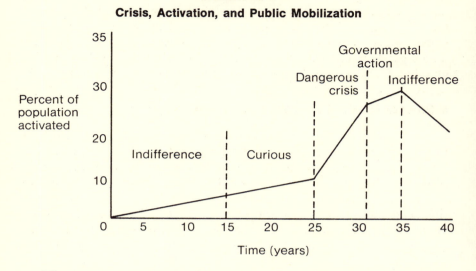

Time (years)

public resources and leadership rather than large, exclusively government-directed efforts as in the totalitarian nations. Ours are more voluntaristic, less nationalistic, and less coercive. They may be less exciting but even the totalitarians have discovered that their "new breed of men" cannot live on a steady diet of patriotic, public, selfless service to a "new society." Man must also pursue his private goals. Perhaps Americans recognize this and do not expect private persons to be so selfless so often nor to listen to Castro-like marathon speeches. Instead, we turn over the great mobilization efforts to impersonal bureaucracies to administer. We have done this during the past decade in exploring the universe and traveling to the moon. The chief role of the ordinary citizen is to provide the taxes and applaud the successful astronauts on their return home. And that brings us to a major role of the citizen: financing the operations of government.

Mobilization and Money

The "business" of public finance might be approached with some trepidation. Some readers and critics of an earlier version of this book asserted that students could not be interested in such concepts as taxes, user fees, bonds, and the like. This may be partially true. Nonetheless, support for and mobilization of the political system and its governments is not only a matter of loyalty but a matter of dollars and cents. The citizen is the one who pays for wars, trips to the moon, and urban renewal. Those who are drafted and must fight for others can appreciate the point. They pay, literally, with years out of their lives, not just with dollars. And although students may not now pay out much of their incomes to support government, they will surely do so in a matter of three or four years. At least one-fifth to one-third of their salaries as wage earners will go to government.

It has been calculated that the average American taxpayer, earning about $9,000 per year, works an average of two hours and 49 minutes each working day to finance government.[1] During recent years he has worked from January 1 to May 9 each year for the government. The "dull" subject of public finance has led to the mobilization of some 2 million Americans in more than 2,300 local and state tax protest organizations during recent years.[2] Tax resentment may cause an estimated 50,000 Oregonians to elude the state income tax.[3] It has inspired countless irrational acts of protest such as sending Band-Aids, shirts, enlarged photos of tax returns, and embittered letters to the tax collectors.[4] It has led to the defeat of thousands of school budgets by irate property taxpayers. The business of financing governmental mobilizations is certainly neither dull nor inconsequential.

How Governments Finance Themselves

American governments, like all governments, have shown a good deal of ingenuity in finding revenue although they habitually complain about insufficient funds. As a result, traditional sources of revenue are constantly being supplemented by new sources, especially by additions to the regular rates on conventional sources. In 1967, for example, as shown in Table III-1, governments on all levels took in a total of $252,532 billion. This represents approxi-

[1] John Cunnif, "Tax Boosts Biggest Cause of Inflation," *Eugene Register-Guard,* May 13, 1970, p. 2.

[2] James P. Gannon, "Taxpayers in Revolt: Citizens Band Together to Fight Levy Boosts at State, Local Levels," *The Wall Street Journal,* May 11, 1970, p. 1.

[3] "50,000 Persons May Be Eluding Oregon Income Tax," *Eugene Register-Guard,* May 4, 1970.

[4] Judy Fowler, "Some People Send in More Than the Money with Their Tax Forms," *The Wall Street Journal,* April 9, 1970, p. 1.

TABLE III–1

Major Sources of Revenue for All Governments (U.S.), 1967

Source	Amount (in millions)	Per Capita
Taxes	$176,121	$890
Charges	30,575	155
Insurance trusts	38,956	197
Utilities	5,246	27
Liquor stores	1,665	8
Total revenues	252,532	1,267

Source: U.S. Bureau of the Census, *Statistical Abstract of the United States: 1969* (90th ed., Washington, D.C.: U.S. Government Printing Office, 1969), p. 409.

mately 32 percent of a gross national product of more than $789.7 billion. About $176 billion came in the form of taxation, and the remaining $76 billion was from a great number of other sources, especially user fees (charges) and insurance trust funds. As we shall note shortly, each level of government resorts to different types of revenue.

A more detailed survey of governmental revenue may be seen in Table III-2, which indicates that for all levels the individual income tax is the major single source and that corporate and sales taxes fall into second and third places. The property tax, which disturbs so many taxpayers at the local level because it is the chief source, is in fourth position as a source of revenue for the entire system.

TABLE III–2

Major Sources of Revenue for Different Levels of Government, 1967

Source	Percentages of Total Revenues		
	Federal	State	Local
Individual income tax	42.7%	8.8%	1.0%
Corporation income tax	19.3	4.3	—
Sales and gross receipts	12.6	40.0	4.6
Charges	9.2	10.3	18.1
Insurance trust	13.6	17.6	2.0
Property	—	2.1	58.5
Utility	—	—	12.8

Source: Ira Sharkansky, *The Politics of Taxing and Spending* (Indianapolis: The Bobbs-Merrill Co., 1969), p. 170.

FISCAL CAPACITY AND TAX EFFORT

In our introductory remarks to this chapter we noted that the mobilization of resources presents a fundamental problem, namely, acquiring sufficient resources to satisfy an almost insatiable demand for their alternative private and public uses. This basic economic dilemma suggests another way of looking at the resource mobilization effort—to ask about the *fiscal capacity* of our governments to raise money and the extent to which they make an *effort* to reach capacity. Although this important concept is a fairly recent one in public finance, it has always been a critical issue in actual political life.

Fiscal capacity is a matter of judgment, not science. However men might differ about the capacity and desirability of governments' raising monies, all would probably agree that capacity refers to the amount of income a state can potentially tap from its citizens. Obviously, the federal government has the greatest fiscal capacity because its boundaries include every citizen, whereas the fifty states and all the other 90,000 governments are constituted of much smaller taxable populations. The idea of fiscal capacity is used primarily to refer to state and local units since they are more easily compared. We will, in subsequent pages, compare our national government's fiscal capacity with that of other nations. For the moment, we are chiefly interested in variations among the fifty states.

Fiscal capacity among the states differs considerably because their citizens' income varies greatly. To illustrate, using per capita annual income as a measure of fiscal capacity, Connecticut led the nation in 1968 with an annual income of $4,231 per capita, while Mississippi was last with $2,057.[5] By the same measure, among the states with greatest fiscal capacity are New York, Alaska, California, Illinois, and Nevada; among the poorest are Arkansas, West Virginia, South Carolina, and Tennessee.

The tax *effort* of a state may or may not be related to its fiscal capacity, depending on the measures being used and public policy in the states. Tax effort means the degree to which this fiscal capacity is utilized—the percentage of income that actually goes into

[5] *Statistical Abstract of the United States: 1969* (90th ed., Washington, D.C.: U.S. Bureau of the Census, 1969), p. 320. See also *Measures of State and Local Fiscal Capacity and Tax Effort* (Washington, D.C.: The Advisory Commission on Intergovernmental Relations, 1968), pp. 3–12; 53–72.

TABLE III–3

Basic State and Local Revenues, Per Capita, 1966

	State + local property taxes	State taxes								
		General sales	Motor fuels	Alcoholic beverages	Tobacco	Motor vehicle licenses	Indi- vidual income	Corpora- tion net income	Property	Death and gift
U.S. average	$125.96	$ 40.37	$23.72	$ 5.05	$ 7.90	$10.66	$21.98	$10.45	$ 4.28	$ 4.14
Alabama	32.99	47.41	26.71	6.62	6.62	1.62	15.15	6.51	6.54	.51
Alaska	68.64	—	24.11	12.33	9.64	16.04	70.73	15.09	.01	.30
Arizona	137.76	59.44	29.58	3.51	7.48	7.80	13.41	8.27	26.56	1.32
Arkansas	48.92	43.18	30.71	3.72	7.44	12.06	14.03	10.66	.26	.36
California	198.34	58.11	29.21	3.67	3.93	9.97	24.01	22.93	9.97	6.57
Colorado	156.23	49.94	27.48	4.15	5.77	10.50	35.55	12.52	1.30	4.26
Connecticut	161.42	47.44	20.84	5.87	11.07	8.60	—	23.64	—	13.91
Delaware	64.69	—	30.54	4.68	10.48	15.20	97.53	25.37	.49	13.20
Florida	98.23	47.64	28.11	12.20	3.14	15.49	—	—	3.63	2.65
Georgia	61.52	50.95	25.67	7.86	8.12	5.15	18.01	13.30	.38	.86
Hawaii	79.12	130.22	16.76	7.53	5.18	.09	65.95	13.86	—	2.01
Idaho	113.43	40.92	26.94	4.44	6.25	16.24	42.08	12.24	1.64	1.32
Illinois	150.23	62.44	16.82	4.48	9.18	12.63	—	—	.17	4.21
Indiana	139.63	57.41	25.32	3.52	7.54	9.76	29.21	2.90	3.87	2.05
Iowa	162.83	41.51	26.82	2.93	8.61	23.80	31.60	2.84	1.40	4.40
Kansas	148.14	50.40	22.14	3.47	7.78	12.51	32.36	10.10	4.03	2.48
Kentucky	$ 51.75	$ 39.86	$25.63	$ 6.04	3.16	$ 5.10	$21.91	$11.39	$ 7.09	$ 3.08
Louisiana	52.84	38.70	21.72	7.75	8.98	5.22	8.45	8.82	5.08	1.49
Maine	124.55	53.22	27.51	3.93	10.64	10.77	—	—	2.27	5.05
Maryland	121.02	35.23	23.67	3.40	6.71	9.12	44.26	9.06	5.89	2.52
Massachusetts	189.59	3.07	20.68	6.64	10.96	5.65	47.17	9.26	.08	6.48
Michigan	135.12	78.54	22.69	6.84	9.15	11.56	—	—	9.10	2.71

	103.20		20.46	6.32	8.70	14.70	21.00		1.66	1.61
Mississippi	50.33	52.02	26.90	3.13	7.80	3.82	4.17	6.81	1.66	.43
Missouri	96.52	54.07	21.02	2.27	5.32	12.55	18.22	2.48	1.19	2.36
Montana	162.46	—	32.59	6.21	8.78	6.90	30.07	9.91	10.45	3.92
Nebraska	177.61	—	33.04	3.69	8.18	5.10	—	—	29.09	.36
Nevada	137.45	51.58	33.68	7.43	11.99	17.73	—	—	7.76	—
New Hampshire	151.80	—	25.26	2.48	12.04	13.93	3.36	—	3.65	4.45
New Jersey	186.00	—	21.04	4.60	11.23	12.41	1.41	6.22	.32	7.65
New Mexico	60.27	65.54	29.15	3.14	7.45	16.94	18.64	—	11.83	1.18
New York	166.82	16.35	14.72	3.63	11.84	11.87	69.61	21.49	.44	7.24
North Carolina	53.99	37.65	26.34	5.74	—	8.22	33.01	18.10	3.64	3.58
North Dakota	129.62	36.25	23.26	5.88	7.92	17.23	14.19	4.70	4.00	.90
Ohio	$125.74	$34.37	$25.37	$3.97	$6.54	$11.95	$—	$—	$4.98	$1.80
Oklahoma	77.72	30.16	30.32	5.64	9.99	19.68	12.34	9.08	.89	5.25
Oregon	141.68	—	24.90	.95	—	17.95	75.38	15.90	.17	4.21
Pennsylvania	87.77	51.75	23.31	5.69	9.50	8.26	—	19.78	—	5.37
Rhode Island	127.84	50.91	22.37	4.04	10.77	10.66	—	16.39	—	7.61
South Carolina	39.59	41.04	25.70	10.87	5.13	4.27	20.47	14.51	.48	.93
South Dakota	153.41	39.46	26.34	5.30	7.99	13.71	—	.86	—	2.14
Tennessee	57.14	45.77	26.42	3.52	7.54	9.74	2.12	9.79	—	2.73
Texas	99.97	22.40	22.52	4.19	12.17	10.48	—	—	4.46	1.96
Utah	117.08	53.35	25.39	1.85	5.13	7.85	37.73	7.94	13.09	2.25
Vermont	115.93	—	26.23	15.21	12.95	22.61	53.27	10.16	.70	3.70
Virginia	75.49	—	25.87	6.24	3.50	10.64	36.65	10.62	3.13	2.24
Washington	104.32	128.98	29.95	9.26	9.88	11.02	—	—	17.56	6.68
West Virginia	54.65	67.20	22.82	2.08	6.41	11.14	13.23	—	.15	2.66
Wisconsin	152.85	22.14	21.64	4.95	10.26	12.53	76.82	22.19	10.47	5.10
Wyoming	169.84	56.46	28.19	2.33	5.13	28.34	—	—	28.15	3.07

Sources: U.S. Bureau of the Census, *Governmental Finances in 1965–66* (Washington, D.C.: U.S. Government Printing Office, 1967); U.S. Bureau of the Census, *Compendium of State Government Finances in 1966* (Washington, D.C.: U.S. Government Printing Office, 1967).

tax payments. Among the states that make a strong tax effort (impose a heavier burden on their taxpayers) are Hawaii, Mississippi, Maine, New York, Oregon, Vermont, and Washington.[6] States that impose a lighter burden on taxpayers include Delaware, Illinois, Kentucky, Missouri, Virginia, Alabama, and Tennessee. A young man seeking employment or a business planning to relocate might want to consider these facts, relating them to the need for low taxes, light burdens, and/or high quality public services.

Regardless of fiscal capacity and tax efforts, we should also note that states rely on quite different mixes of taxes despite their reliance on the same types of general tax revenues. Examples are taxes on property, retail sales, and individual and corporate income, as well as excise taxes on motor fuels, alcoholic beverages, tobacco, and so forth. A potential resident-taxpayer should want to know which kinds of taxes are used and how, because his share of the total burden will be vitally affected by the sources of his income and by his purchases. A man who drinks a great deal might not want to live in Oregon, for example, because the liquor prices and taxes are very high—much higher than its neighbor California. On the other hand Oregon, unlike California, does not have a general sales tax, although it has a stiffer income tax. Hawaii has a heavy sales tax and a light liquor tax on a per capita basis. Table III-3 shows the most recent available figures on the tax packages of the states.

NONTAX RECEIPTS

Nontax sources include revenues from utilities, liquor sales, rents, royalties, interest earnings, special assessments, postal service, school lunch sales, user fees for hospitals, parks, sewerage, education, and countless other items and services which can be sold to citizens. Postal fees brought in the most money— over $4.5 billion dollars in 1966. Educational fees were in second place and monies derived from the sale and use of natural resources in third position. Many states have also successfully invested in the stock market but reliable data is not readily available.

In 1966 receipts from all nontax sources, for all governments, totaled more than $34 billion, an amount equal to the total

[6] Measures of State and Local Fiscal Capacity, pp. 73–86.

of all sales and gross receipts taxes collected that same year.[7] In fact, nontax revenues were second only to the returns from income taxes and are increasing at a faster rate than tax collection. In 1966, nontax revenues made up about 12 percent of income at the federal level, 19 percent at the state level, and 38 percent at the local level.

This brief and inadequate summary of nontax revenues will serve to illustrate the growing dependence of government on the sale of its services. It suggests that governmental goods and services are being distributed in increasing amounts via markets and quasi-markets. What this will mean in terms of changing citizen attitudes toward government is difficult to predict. Surely a very different political system will result if government sells its services rather than distributes them without concern for a price. Would rights be preserved if privilege were for sale to the highest bidder? Would our governments produce the same amount or more of the goods and services they now distribute "free"? Would citizens be more or less pleased with their governments if more user fees were charged? Which goods and services would be among the first to be sold this way? Which would be among the last?

Recall the definition of a public good: Would politicians start campaigning on promises that they would lower prices? Could we achieve greater efficiency by such methods of financing? These are many of the real problems that are arising as we shift more of the financial burden to a fee basis. There are limits, of course, to the types of services that can be sold in markets. Apparently we have not reached those limits.

RECENT TRENDS IN FINANCING

The search for new revenue sources has been unremitting and somewhat successful during the past twenty years. In addition, traditional taxes have been increased by broadening their coverage, increasing their rates, increasing the base on which rates are calculated, or a combination of these. Other means of increasing revenue include more efficient administrative techniques, stricter enforcement of tax laws, increasing the prices of governmentally produced goods and services, and, of course, increased borrowing and inflation. Economic growth has also en-

[7] The following paragraph is based on *Nontax Revenues* (New York: Tax Foundation, Inc., 1968).

abled greater collections because there is more personal and corporate income from which to draw the needed dollars.

Governments at the state and local levels have adopted new taxes. In 1946, 31 states had a personal income tax; today 36 have the tax.[8] In 1946, 24 states used the general sales tax while in 1966 all but Alaska, Delaware, Minnesota, Montana, Nebraska, New Hampshire, Oregon, Virginia, and Vermont made use of that tax. Eleven of the 43 largest cities in the nation have adopted a personal income tax. In 1955 only 370 local units used the tax but by 1965 the number had grown to 1,909.

Perhaps the most significant trend in state and local financing has been the widespread use of user fees to pay for everything to which governments can attach a price. Cities and states charged $22.2 billion in permit and service fees in 1968. This was about $111.04 for every person and provided almost 19 percent of the revenues for these governments.[9] Between 1955 and 1965, user fees rose 183 percent and property taxes—about which nearly everyone seems to complain—rose 120 percent. Some experts have predicted that such fees or charges will rise about 125 percent by 1975 compared with a 75 percent rise in taxes.

Some Comparisons with Other Countries

While few people will go so far as to change their nationality on the basis of a country's tax program, perhaps these matters will take on sharper definition if we take a brief look at other nations as a means of comparison and contrast. A very detailed study is not necessary but a few well-known generalizations should suffice to place our country in perspective.

In terms of total governmental revenues taken from the gross national income, the United States ranked 11th among 40 nations in 1963 and was tied with Denmark at 26 percent.[10] The nations include all the western democracies and a variety of other nations from Latin America and elsewhere. Taxation as a portion of our GNP is 25 percent. This compares favorably with 39 other nations since 12 of them take larger shares. We should observe

---

[8] These data are from Bernard P. Herber, *Modern Public Finance* (Homewood, Ill.: Richard D. Irwin, Inc., 1967), Chapters 11 and 13.

[9] Timothy D. Schellhardt, "Many Local Officials Increase 'User Fees' to Ease Fiscal Pinch," *The Wall Street Journal*, December 4, 1969, p. 1.

[10] Richard A. Musgrave, *Fiscal Systems* (New Haven, Conn.: Yale University Press, 1969), pp. 365–66.

that the amount of revenue and taxation in particular seems to be related to the level of economic development or productivity in each nation; that is, in general the higher the gross national income and standard of living the higher the governmental share of national income; the same is true for taxes as might be expected. If one is concerned with "creeping socialism" he has reason for his anxiety; the government is administering a sizable portion of the national product. Still, many other nations control even greater shares yet successfully manage to preserve individual liberty.

Why Taxation Is Compulsory

If everyone opposes taxes why do we have them at all? Why don't governments rely on other means, such as sales of goods and services or voluntary contributions from individuals and private groups? The answer could be couched historically, tracing how each tax came into being. But that is not what we really want to know.

Our answer should instead rest in the context of the logic of choice. Suppose the goods and services that governments provide were distributed on the basis of individual prices as in a market. How would the government finance and distribute national defense? Is it possible to ration specific quantities of defense to specific individuals and collect a price? We answered this question earlier: Certain "public" goods are "indivisible" and cannot be sold in varying amounts to individuals. Or, suppose the government allowed each citizen to pay according to the value he placed on these indivisible goods. Isn't it likely the citizen would conceal his preferences or lie about them in order to enjoy the service without paying the full amount? Since men acknowledge this "free rider" possibility, they have decided that the only way to attain an adequate supply of indivisible public goods is by coercion. They coerce one another through government into making payments whether each man wants the good or not.

Governments, including our own, acquire resources by making taxation compulsory. Failure to contribute is judged a criminal act, carrying a jail sentence. Therefore, many of the governmentally provided services we take for granted are the products of coercion. We have agreed to *mutual* coercion in order to ensure adequate amounts of public goods and avoid "free riders." No advanced civilization has ever been able to avoid the use of compulsory taxation. Indeed, no alternative method has ever been tried. Voluntary contributions are legal and accepted but no nation could depend on an adequate supply given the "free-rider" possibility.

This element of compulsion affects every citizen. Governmental mobilization of resources reduces his net income, so his concern is quite understandable. Most individuals try to reduce their contributions as much as possible to make them more convenient to endure. Obviously, this requires increasing another citizen's share if we want to retain the same level of services. Consequently, the mobilization of resources provides a focal point for much of American politics.

Some Consequences of Revenue Choices

It is unfortunate that we must depend for information on the consequences of our revenue patterns, on the experts and other men who do not always agree, either on the facts or on their political meanings. Still, we must make some effort to analyze complex sets of consequences of the fiscal policies governments pursue. Fiscal choices pose critical consequences for the individual and society and if we are to act as intelligent citizens we ought to understand them. None of us may choose to become economists for that purpose, but we can advance our understanding somewhat without much difficulty.

The levels and types of revenues we use have profound impacts on many aspects of our lives. For one thing, the level of government services is basically a function of the amount of available revenue. The same is probably true of the quality of those services. The level of government's share of the national income has a great impact on levels of employment as well as on the general price level. Most economists attribute inflation and depression in substantial part to government fiscal and/or monetary policies. When government adds to the private demand for scarce goods and services it necessarily, under conditions of full employment, increases the prices of those same commodities. Every citizen who purchases them competes with the government for short supplies and all must pay a higher price. Likewise, whenever government spends more under conditions of unemployment it tends to increase employment and income.

Whenever government chooses one method of finance and

rejects another it causes some citizens to shoulder a larger burden than they might have under an alternative method. A sales tax, for example, is a heavier burden for the lower-income groups than a progressive income tax is. If a property tax is used, it too can be passed on to lower-income groups in the form of higher rents. If borrowing is used, the bond buyers (wealthier groups) will profit from the interest payments. If liquor and cigarette taxes are imposed or increased, smokers and drinkers will have to shoulder the increased burdens. The point should be clear by now: Fiscal policy choices of governments have an enormous impact on our economic behavior and welfare. Each method will affect our pocketbooks in different ways. Knowledge about these differential effects is likely to influence election outcomes. Voters will tend to reward those who have made life easier and "punish" those who have made it more burdensome. But how do American taxpayers feel about taxation and public finance?

Citizen Views on Resource Mobilization

Given the extraordinary political significance of such phenomena as taxation, borrowing, budgetary deficits, and shortages of public services, how much do political scientists know about citizen attitudes toward them? The fact is we know very little beyond an occasional public opinion poll and a few obscure doctoral theses. Consequently, our discussion will not be as well-informed as it should be. Perhaps more knowledge will be gained in the not-too-distant future.

First, we should note that the American people are not enthusiastic donors to their governments. They rarely make voluntary contributions to the treasuries of the nation they believe is the best in the world and for which many would make the ultimate sacrifice in war. Those who send money to the government make headlines. A little over $167,000 was given the federal government in 1969. Such contributions, it should be noted, are tax deductible. We are told, however, that many more citizens and organizations are now making gifts of large parcels of land to Uncle Sam. According to the *Wall Street Journal,* the incentive is not altogether altruistic.[11] The gifts are made in the hope that the

---

[11] Jerry Landauer, "Some Gifts of Land to Uncle Sam Aren't Altogether Altruistic," *The Wall Street Journal,* January, 1970, p. 1.

federal government will build facilities ranging from office buildings to atomic plants. The donor will benefit in terms of income from rent, increased business, or perhaps tax revenue. The government has been known to accept such offers.

Although citizens have substantial portions of their incomes taken away by government through taxation they seem to know very little about taxes, including the size of their own shares. Various studies have shown that people in all tax brackets do not have accurate knowledge of, and in some instances tend to grossly underestimate, the amounts they pay. Many are unsure of the amount of increase in the rates of personal income taxes they pay as they earn more. Most citizens are unaware of how tax reforms might be structured and handled, are uninformed about tax legislation, and, according to one study, 70 percent of the taxpayers queried did not know of a tax reduction that had occurred earlier during the year of the study. Unfortunately, hardly any research has been done on taxpayer awareness of indirect taxes and of the expected incidence of or burdens of all taxes.

Perhaps it is understandable that the average voter does not pay the high costs of informing himself. He feels there is little he can do to implement whatever views he may form. He seems to be resigned to paying his taxes with only periodic complaints. At best, the taxpayer tries to reduce his federal income tax payments by relying on limited information gleaned from newspapers, friends, and consultations with Internal Revenue personnel or (if he can afford it) an accountant.

Some research has shown that economic position may be a very strong influence on tax preferences and public goods.[12] Lower-income people tend to prefer income to sales taxes while those with higher incomes tend to prefer sales taxes. Property owners apparently oppose the property tax more than nonpropertied persons. A kind of crude sense of the incidence of taxes is apparent but that is all that is necessary to make the decisions voters must make in infrequent elections.

Since voters are poorly informed on fiscal matters generally, they tend to be dependent on official views. Governments can explain mobilization efforts in sufficiently persuasive ways so as to maintain the cooperation of the taxpayers. If voters are not well

---

[12] Elizabeth Likert David, "Public Preferences and State-local Taxes," in Harvey E. Brazer, ed., *Essays in State and Local Finance* (Ann Arbor, Mich.: Institute of Public Administration, 1967), pp. 74–106.

informed about taxes and other means of resource mobilization, governments are much better informed and their preferences are much more explicit and ordered.

Governmental Revenue Preferences

Governments are always in need of more money. One reason is voters always want more services; another is inflation, which has hit government as it has everyone. How they choose and order their preferences in spending this money is the question we will turn to now. Governments do have preferences about amounts and types of revenues. Sometimes they can realize their preferences and at other times they are forced to accept less preferred alternatives. Well, what do our governments like besides more money?

First, governments typically prefer those sources of revenue that bring in the most for the least costs of collection. Thus they prefer the simpler to the more complex forms. This seems an intelligent choice. Second, most governments appear to prefer the surer and more stable sources of funds to the less stable. This desire for assurance or the reduction of uncertainty is also understandable in terms of future planning. Third, a government generally likes to tap the resources of people other than those who vote them in and out of office. For example, cities will often impose a motel and hotel tax, paid primarily by nonresidents. In addition, on college campuses across the land out-of-state students normally pay much more than residents do. Nonresidents, obviously, cannot vote politicians out of office. Fourth, governments select their type of financing according to support. This pertains to the preferences of Republican and Democratic administrations, whose bases of electoral support vary considerably. Democratic administrations usually prefer those revenues—especially taxes— whose incidence falls on the higher-income voters; Republican governments usually shift the burdens downward in the social scale. This is likely because Republicans draw more of their support from higher-income groups than the Democrats do. Neither party can shift the entire burden to other classes, and concessions must be and are made. Economists tell us that some governments (particularly Democratic) may choose inflation as a means of revenue, for two reasons. Inflation enables debtors to pay off their debts in cheaper money. Also, as an indirect means of taxation, it is less likely to directly impinge on many voters. Republicans prefer tighter money policies because their business and banking supporters are expected to profit from such practices. In any case, controlling inflation is a difficult policy choice.

When governments wish to shift the tax burden they generally choose indirect taxes. These make it less easy to identify the ultimate payers, and the burden can be shifted in part or whole. (That is another reason for the popularity of inflationary policies.) In addition, governments will tend to raise the rates of existing taxes rather than impose entirely new or novel forms, because they encounter less opposition. For the same reason a government is not likely to pass a new tax law during an election year, but rather to attempt to reduce tax rates and bases. When it is necessary to impose new taxes, governments soften the blow by pointing to alleged benefits of the increased burden. Beneficial consequences of taxes are indirectly experienced and often must be clearly defined in order to inspire voter support.

We are now in a position to appreciate why mobilizing resources and levying taxes is so crucial a set of policies for governments to choose. Their success at remaining in office is at issue. Accordingly, a government must consider not only the economic consequences of revenue choices but their political implications as well.

We cannot expect governments to commit political suicide; therefore, their problem is like walking a tightrope. They must increase benefits and thereby win the favor of some voters, but not increase taxes so much that they alienate more voters than they benefit. Perhaps that is why governments prefer to distribute benefits widely while confining taxation to the few. And that, of course, is still another generalization about governmental policies. Although governments would probably like to distribute benefits widely and confine the burdens to the wealthy, that policy is not politically feasible. The wealthy, while numerically much smaller than lower-income groups, are able to muster great influence over elections and public policy. (The reasons for this will be given detailed consideration in Chapters VI and VII.)

On the other hand, all governments, including Democratic administrations, are forced to tax the less affluent because the wealthy simply do not have enough money to pay for all the services we demand. Some recent proposals of the Nixon Administration would exempt several million low-income families from any federal income tax. This strategy may have been chosen to broaden the President's electoral appeal among a group that has traditionally supported the Democratic Party. In any case, we should not be surprised if Republicans offer occasional benefits to the poor and Democrats to the rich, because each party draws or hopes to acquire some support from the other end of the social scale.

Our analysis has taken us from the coercive mobilization of resources to achieve wanted goals and services to the question of whose goals and whose services are chosen. While our governments generally prefer to satisfy as many citizens as possible they usually satisfy some more than others. And, as we shall see in Chapter V, the burdens of mobilization are unequally divided among the people just as the benefits are unequally shared.

Exercises in Analysis

PRIVATE MARKETS FOR POLICE AND FIRE PROTECTION

Police and fire protection are publicly provided services financed from general funds—funds to which nearly everyone contributes whether or not he uses these services. In addition, there are insurance companies that insure lives and property and there are private police, including Pinkerton, the classic "private eye," and numerous police employees of private business firms.

These facts suggest some interesting questions. For example, how can we explain the widespread use of insurance, especially fire insurance? Is this use a reflection on the fire departments? Why are so many private police and protection services provided when we have over 458,000 public police employees? Is this a reflection of our insecurity? Finally, consider what might occur if we converted all our public fire and police into private services offered in the marketplace for a price. Some interesting predictions might be made about the price levels for each service, the number of police organizations and firefighting brigades that would form (Would there be more or less than now?), the suppliers of these services, the quality of the services, and who the consumers might be.

VOTER PREFERENCES ON TAXES

Suppose the American voters were given an opportunity to express their views in a national referendum on federal taxes that would become advisory to the government. The referendum would be confined to choices about the proportions of our federal tax dollar that come from the different kinds of taxes. No choice would be permitted on the total size of the tax bill nor on one's own share. The voters would be asked to express their preferences in terms of variations on the present sources or distribution of the tax dollar. The ballot might look like this:

	Present Distri- bution	Your Prefer- ences
Individual Income Taxes (42¢)		_____¢
Corporate Income Taxes (20¢)		_____¢
Employment Taxes (17¢)		_____¢
Excise Taxes (8¢)		_____¢
Borrowing (2¢)		_____¢
Other (to be specified) (11¢)		_____¢
TOTAL	$1.00	$1.00

Would many voters turn out for an election of this type? Most Presidential elections will induce about 60 percent turnout. Who would be most likely to vote? Least likely? Why? How much of a variation from the current tax dollar distribution would you expect? Which taxes would be most and least affected? Why? Which voters would be most likely to prefer the greatest changes for each type of tax? Why?

Suggested Readings

Bator, Francis M. *The Question of Government Spending* (New York: Harper & Bros., 1960).

Davie, Bruce F. and Duncombe, Bruce F. *Modern Political Arithmetic* (New York: Holt, Rinehart & Winston, Inc., 1970).

Davis, James W., Jr. *Politics, Programs, and Budgets* (Englewood Cliffs, N.J.: Prentice-Hall, Inc., 1969).

McKean, Roland N. *Public Spending* (New York: McGraw-Hill Book Co., Inc., 1968).

Mosher, Frederick C. and Poland, Orville F. *The Costs of American Governments* (New York: Dodd, Mead & Co., 1964).

Olson, Mancur. *The Logic of Collective Action* (Cambridge, Mass.: Harvard University Press, 1965).

Schultze, Charles L. *The Politics and Economics of Public Spending* (Washington, D.C.: The Brookings Institution, 1968).

Chapter IV

SOCIALISM FOR THE RICH AND FREE ENTERPRISE FOR THE POOR

Consider these facts: 50 percent of today's college students come from the wealthiest 25 percent of the population while only 7 percent come from the poorest 25 percent. Education will receive about 16 percent of all government expenditures this year and the federal government, alone, will spend more on higher education than it will on public welfare clients.[1] Consider, too, that in 1964, in the State of California, an average family with a child attending the University at Berkeley received an annual average subsidy of $1,700 or a total of $6,800 if the student completed the degree. As a percent of the average annual family income of University of California students at that time ($12,000) this amounted to 56 percent, or 14 percent per year.[2]

How Subsidies Redistribute Income: Examples

THE FARM PROGRAM

In 1969 the federal government spent about $390 million for farm aid to maintain approximately 10,000 affluent American

[1] Richard Harwood and Lawrence Stern, "Students now 'most pampered, cherished beneficiary group,'" *The Oregonian*, September 14, 1969, p. F–12.

[2] W. Lee Hansen and Burton A. Weisbrod, *Benefits, Costs, and Finance of Public Higher Education* (Chicago: Markham Publishing Co., 1969), Chapter IV.

"farmers."[3] The average payment to the 10,000 most favored farmers was $38,610. Some $53 million went to 264 of the largest commercial farmers while the same amount went to 540,000 of the smallest farms. On the average the big farms received $200,-000 while the small farms received about $100. Overall, the government's farm subsidy program gives more than 80 percent to the big operators who constitute only 20 percent of the farm population. Texas farmers were particularly well provided for in 1969 receiving $457 million—more than 15 percent of the nation's total and more than twice as much as its nearest "competitor," Kansas. In the same year 53 Texas farmers each received over $100,000 and 278 received between $50,000 and $100,000. In Lynn County, Texas, 678 farmers received almost $9 million, while 25 percent of the county's residents were regarded as "hard-core poor" (earning less than $1,200 per year). There was no federally-sponsored food aid program for the poor people in this county.

Some recent studies have been conducted by James Bonnen, an agricultural economist, on eight commodity programs of the federal government: sugar cane, cotton, rice, wheat, feed grains, peanuts, tobacco, and sugar beets. The studies show some facts that may startle those who believe in greater equality. They may also startle those who naively believe that farm price support programs are an effective means of redistributing income from the rich to the poor.[4] The results of Bonnen's studies are summarized in Table IV–1. The first six columns should be readily understood; the last one needs explanation. The "Gini concentration ratio" is a measure of the degree of concentration in the distribution of income. The number refers to the extent to which a given distribution departs from a purely equal distribution. Larger numbers indicate greater concentrations, or greater degrees of inequality. In every instance or program the top 5 percent of the beneficiaries receive anywhere from 13.8 percent of the benefits to a high of 63.2 percent (sugar cane). In most programs the top 5 percent

[3] This paragraph is based on a speech delivered in Congress by Congressman Findley of Illinois on May 12, 1969. See "Hunger and Farm Payments in Non-Food-Aid Counties," 115 *Congressional Record*, May 12, 1969, 3531–36.

[4] "The Absence of Knowledge of Distributional Impacts: An Obstacle to Effective Public Programs Analysis and Decisions," in Robert H. Haveman and Julius Margolis, eds., *Public Expenditures and Policy Analysis* (Chicago: Markham Publishing Co., 1970), pp. 246–70.

TABLE IV-1

Distribution of Farm Income and Various Program Benefits: Proportion of Income or Benefits Received by Various Percentiles of Farmer Beneficiaries

	Percent of benefits received by the—						
	Lower 20 per-cent of farmers	Lower 40 per-cent of farmers	Lower 60 per-cent of farmers	Top 40 per-cent of farmers	Top 20 per-cent of farmers	Top 5 per-cent of farmers	Gini concen-tration ratio
Sugar cane, 1965[2]	1.0	2.9	6.3	93.7	83.1	63.2	0.799
Cotton, 1964[3]	1.8	6.6	15.1	84.9	69.2	41.2	.653
Rice, 1963[3]	1.0	5.5	15.1	84.9	65.3	34.6	.632
Wheat, 1964:							
Price supports	3.4	8.3	20.7	79.3	62.3	30.5	.566
Diversion payments	6.9	14.2	26.4	73.6	57.3	27.9	.480
Total benefits[4]	3.3	8.1	20.4	79.6	62.4	30.5	.569
Feed grains, 1964:							
Price supports	0.5	3.2	15.3	84.7	57.3	24.4	.588
Diversion payments	4.4	16.1	31.8	68.2	46.8	20.7	.405
Total benefits[4]	1.0	4.9	17.3	82.7	56.1	23.9	.565
Peanuts, 1964[3]	3.8	10.9	23.7	76.3	57.2	28.5	.522
Tobacco, 1965[3]	3.9	13.2	26.5	73.5	52.8	24.9	.476
Farmer and farm manager total money income, 1963[3]	3.2	11.7	26.4	73.6	50.5	20.8	.468
Sugar beets, 1965[2]	5.0	14.3	27.0	73.0	50.5	24.4	.456
Agriculture conservation program, 1964[6]:							
All eligibles	7.9	15.8	34.7	65.3	39.2	(7)	.343
Recipients	10.5	22.8	40.3	59.7	36.6	13.8	.271

This table presents portions of 2 Lorenz curves relating the cumulated percentage distribution of benefits to the cumulated percent of farmers receiving those benefits. Cols. 1 through 3 summarize this relationship cumulated up from the lower (benefit per farmer) end of the curve, and cols. 4 through 6 summarize the relationship cumulated down from the top (highest benefit per recipient) end of the curve.

[2] For price support benefits plus Government payments.

[3] For price support benefits.

[4] Includes price support payments and wheat certificate payments as well.

[5] David H. Boyne, "Changes in the Income Distribution in Agriculture," *Journal of Farm Economics*, Vol. 47, No. 5, December 1965, pp. 1221–1222.

[6] For total program payments. Computed from data in "Frequency Distribution of Farms and Farmland, Agricultural Conservation Program, 1964," ASCS, U.S. Department of Agriculture, January 1966, tables 3 and 8.

[7] Not available.

Source: James T. Bonnen, "The Absence of Knowledge of Distributional Impacts: An Obstacle to Effective Public Programs Analysis and Decisions," in *The Analysis and Evaluation of Public Expenditures: The PPB System*. A Compendium of Papers Submitted to the Joint Economic Committee, Congress of the United States (Washington, D.C.: U.S. Government Printing Office, 1969), p. 440.

get more than 20 percent. The lower 20 percent of the beneficiaries receive as little as 0.5 percent in the case of feed grain supports and only as much as 10.5 percent under the conservation program. In some states, the concentration ratios are even higher than in Table IV–1; sugar cane growers in Hawaii have an 0.9 income concentration ratio.

VETERAN PROGRAMS

Consider the case of the veterans, a somewhat privileged group in American society. Veteran's benefits became a major item in the nation's budget with the conclusion of World War II and the discharge of more than 16 million men and women who had served during that conflict. A series of laws passed during the war extended previous basic or traditional benefits to veterans and added some highly important new ones. Among the benefits were monthly disability payments; free medical care for service-connected disabilities; pensions for those who may not have been injured but became needy; and low-cost life insurance. To these was added the famous GI Bill of Rights, which included the right to special job placement after the war; college education (allowances for living costs, tuition, books, and fees) ; the right to receive up to 52 weeks of unemployment insurance; and VA-guaranteed home mortgage loans at low interest rates. Similar benefits were later provided for veterans of Korea and Vietnam.

As a result, the federal budget for veterans' benefits has grown immensely. The last payment for a dependent of the War of 1812 was made in 1946, while payments were still being made in the early 1960s for dependents of veterans of the Mexican War. Veteran programs accounted for about $5 billion of the 1968 budget—a total of about four cents of each government dollar. Although it may seem small, this part of the budget is one of those relatively uncontrollable items that a President and his administration cannot affect in significant degree. Of course, the per capita payments and the portions of the budget and of GNP that are consumed by veterans' benefits vary from year to year. In 1948, for example, per capita benefits for veterans amounted to about $57 while in 1953 it came to $31.[5] As wars come and go we should expect similar variations.

[5] Frederick C. Mosher and Orville F. Poland, *The Costs of American Governments* (New York: Dodd, Mead, & Co., 1964), p. 113.

In Chapters VI and VII we attempt to explain why veterans are able to command or obtain the benefits they do. No inference should be made either that these benefits are undeserved or that they are sufficient compensation for those who have fought in the nation's many battles.[6]

OTHER ADVANTAGES

The kinds of transfer payments or subsidies we have cited amount to a considerable sum each year. Over $8 billion of the federal budget went into subsidy payments during 1968; the estimate for 1970 was $9.7 billion. More than $23 billion were spent by the federal government in subsidy payments from 1965 to 1968.[7] However, in spite of these large sums, direct cash subsidies are hardly the major means of assisting various groups in their efforts at making more money. Another powerful aid, which redounds primarily to business, is government licensing and regulation of prized business opportunities. Those who can procure a license to operate a radio or television station pay very little for the privilege but earn a great deal. Those who can acquire a retail liquor license in a state like California, are likely to make a comfortable living indeed. Those who can manage to gain tariff protection, as in the case of the oil industry, can force consumers to pay much more for oil and thereby make themselves wealthy. A taxicab license in New York City now costs the licensee about $20,000. The right to operate a bank or become a plumber, electrician, or barber is a controlled right—one that in fact serves to ration an artificially limited supply of these positions and opportunities. We pay for the granting of these privileges in the form of higher prices. Regardless of their expressed original purposes to upgrade and control quality they do confer substantial differential rewards.

[6] Veterans who may chance to read these pages might be interested to know that the Veterans Administration periodically publishes a "Fact Sheet" which lists all federal benefits for veterans and their dependents. Some recent issues list more than 40 pages of a great variety of advantages one might qualify for as a veteran or dependent, thereof. Veterans Administration, *Federal Benefits . . . For Veterans and Dependents* (Washington, D.C.: U.S. Government Printing Office, 1968).

[7] U.S. Bureau of the Census, *Statistical Abstract of the United States: 1969* (90th ed., Washington, D.C.: U.S. Government Printing Office, 1969), pp. 383–84.

In each of these instances a few people receive a great deal of privilege or monetary gain from governmental actions and policies, while the bulk of the people either pay more or receive a great deal less. These incidents merely illustrate rather than fully describe the enormous importance of governments as distributive agents in American society. Each citizen is subsidized in some manner to some extent by one or more governments and programs. Our governments are not simply neutral referees, confined to providing little more than law and order; they have come to be engaged in producing and distributing a vast variety of goods and services. In some cases provision of these items serves to add to our incomes, status, power, and general satisfaction. In some ways governments directly add to our income while in others they simply facilitate our making money in the private economy. Sometimes they send us checks, as with agricultural subsidies, and sometimes they increase our net income by decreasing our taxes. Sometimes they grease some wallets by granting large contracts with inflated costs—a common practice with aircraft manufacturing firms. And sometimes for some people the grant is a commodity in kind. One such subsidy is the surplus food program now being discovered by students.[8]

Types of Benefits

Few people have a very precise or complete conception of the incredible variety of benefits being distributed by our governments. No exhaustive inventory of governmentally provided services and goods has been compiled. Full appreciation of the politics of distribution can only be attained when we have some idea of the vast array of "commodities" used by the citizen in his everyday life. One way of organizing the endeavor is to classify goods in terms of their major properties. In our case all these goods contribute toward enhancing a citizen's income, social status, power, self-esteem, or affection—his well-being and welfare.

[8] "Use of Food Stamps Grows on Campus," *The Oregonian*, May 13, 1970, p. 6. Students can also qualify for many other subsidies including low cost loans with long-term repayment plans guaranteed by the federal government. It has been estimated that some $35.3 million or about $540 per student was made available in the form of scholarships, grants and loans to college students in the State of Oregon during 1968–69. See Matt Kramer, "Estimated $35.3 Million in Loans, Aid Went to State Students," *The Oregonian*, April 20, 1970, p. 11.

Presumably most men, most of the time, prefer more rather than fewer of these components of his welfare. Presumably, too, as one gains more of them he values each increment less until the point of satiation when no aditional unit will add to his total welfare.

GOODS, FACILITIES, AND SERVICES

Let us look at governmentally-provided *goods*. Actual physical goods or commodities are provided to the citizenry in great quantities. For example, each of us makes considerable use of water provided by government. Some citizens acquire surplus food as part of their public assistance while virtually all make use of sidewalks, highways, and airports. These latter goods may also be appropriately considered as examples of *facilities* that complement private activity. Such facilities include sanitation, parks and recreational areas, public housing, schools, parking facilities, meeting halls, hospitals, libraries, municipal golf courses, and fairgrounds. In addition to goods and facilities, countless *services* are perhaps the single most numerous type of benefit provided by government. The postal service is the most widely known and used traditional service. Others include fire and police protection, employment bureaus, electrical power, information services including weather reports, hundreds of thousands of publications offered by the Government Printing Office at very low prices, health services, research services of the Library of Congress, snow removal, disaster relief, school buses, advice to homemakers and farmers, assistance from official representatives such as Congressmen, legal aid, and education. Additional services involve regulation of behavior through the use of law, police, and the courts. Control of monopoly, sanitation inspections, consumer protection, and land-use zoning are examples of the last, in addition to the obvious quelling of destructive acts.

RIGHTS, PRIVILEGES, AND INCOME

Another type of benefit less obvious than services are *rights* of thought and behavior. Certain rights are granted everyone by virtue of citizenship; they include the basic political rights of the Constitution's Bill of Rights, the right to vote, and the right to hold public office. In general, these rights are political and serve to enhance one's ability or capacity to participate in meaningful and effective ways in public choice. Although these rights have never been enjoyed to their fullest extent by all Americans, they are even more fundamental than goods, services, and facilities. Provision of those benefits is almost entirely dependent on the exercise of individual liberties such as free speech, free press, trial by jury, and all other individual rights. Because of the enormous significance of these basic rights we can expect much political conflict to center about questions of whose responsibility it is to enforce and honor whose rights.

Another class of publicly provided goods that is highly divisible and unequally distributed consists of certain *legally enforced privileges*. Most of these enable their holders to make money, sometimes making direct competition with the holders illegal. Some licenses that governments grant include: accreditation in a profession; Indian fishing rights; permits to graze animals on public lands; privileges such as logging, camping, or leasing a vacation cabin in a national forest; licenses to operate airline routes, radio or TV stations, taxis, or a vending business from a pushcart; protection from foreign competition by tariff laws and import quotas; legal monopolies; and permits to start a savings and loan or banking business or establish a gambling casino or race track. All these economic activities serve to increase one's income as well as status and other perquisites. All of these privileges confers advantages on those who acquire them and probably increases the cost of living for consumers.

The conferring of these advantages is a political act usually made by bureaucratic and appointive boards or commissions. Granting such a privilege to one implies withholding a comparable privilege from others. Defining who gets such privileges, how, and why is part of our task in this chapter and in the book. What criteria are used in such decisions? Which alternatives will finally be selected?

Still another type of benefit is *direct income payments*. These are more frequently known as transfer payments, since they transfer income from one citizen to another through the agencies and choices of government. Physical resources (except for administrative costs) are not consumed in the process, but billions of dollars of income are redistributed by means that differ from those found in private markets—welfare benefits, insurance, subsidies, grants-in-aid, and so forth. The amount of money transferred and the number of recipients have increased greatly during the past 30 years or more and the trend is likely to continue as each citizen and organization attempts to improve its own well-being. In 1929 transfer payments totalled only about 1.6 percent of personal income while in 1965 they had risen to 7.5 percent.[9] Transfer payments are the main source of livelihood for many. Without them some would perish; others would be reduced to mere subsistence without accustomed amenities of civilized existence provided by the government.

Many who do not receive any of these goods, services, income, or facilities can still qualify for other types of benefits. The federal government lists an imaginative array of programs designed to assist small business in the 193-page third edition of *Handbook for Small Business*.[10] Available are low-cost loans, disaster and emergency assistance, management assistance, research and patent aids, information on how to buy and sell to the government, and advice on minimizing taxes. Every department of the federal government offers some aid to small business.

Nor is big business left out. Special tax treatment, contracts that can be easily padded, and low-cost loans are but a few conventional benefits. Special treatment for contractors who are in financial difficulty, as Boeing and Lockheed were in 1969–70, are commonplace. One headline from Washington read *Pentagon Agrees to Bail Lockheed Out of Financial Crisis—Temporarily.* "Bailing out" meant about $641.2 million. The Pennsylvania Railroad Company (Penn Central) did not fare so well when the federal government withdrew its promised loan of $200 million and allowed that famed concern to declare bankruptcy in 1970. Some industries, especially those involved in mining and processing certain critical materials such as nickel, managed to have the government stockpile those materials at considerable cost to taxpayers and profit for the owners. Business, small and large, has done well by the federal government.

So, too, have state and local governments. *A Catalog of Federal Aids to State and Local Governments*,[11] published in 1964, has

---

[9] Ida C. Merriam, "Welfare and Its Measurement," in Eleanor Bernert Sheldon and Wilbert E. Moore, eds., *Indicators of Social Change* (New York: Russell Sage Foundation, 1968), pp. 770–71.

[10] Senate and House Select Committees on Small Business, 91st Congress, 1st Session, *Handbook for Small Business: A Survey of Small Business Programs of the Federal Government* (Washington, D.C.: U.S. Government Printing Office, 1969).

[11] Committee on Governmental Operations, U.S. Senate, 89th Congress, 2nd Session, *Catalog of Federal Aids to State and Local Governments* (Washington, D.C.: U.S. Government Printing Office, 1966).

since had two supplements. Programs have expanded so much during the years since publication that several hundred pages are required to describe them. Most of these aids to state and local governments do not have their ultimate incidence with governmental units, but with the citizenry of the states and local communities. Each aid program tends to benefit a different group. Beneficiaries of the following array of programs sponsored by the Housing and Home Finance Agency can easily be identified:

public works planning	capital grants
public facility loans	grants for relocation payments
college housing loans	special mortgage insurance
housing for the elderly	demonstration grants
urban planning advances	loans for mass transportation
urban renewal loans	low-rent housing

We've made the point that government serves everyone, even if unequally. Each citizen's special concern will be his own individual annual net balance of advantages and costs. Through general fund financing we pay in to support many others, most of whom we do not know. Each of us can be the beneficiary of the payments of others. As we are often unaware of whom we support so most of us are unaware of our benefactors and the extent of our obligations.

Figuring Out Who Gets What

Our many examples have not shown how important government is in the redistribution of goods, services, and income. In fact, everything a government does or fails to do has distributive consequences. No public budget or activity is strictly neutral with respect to who gets what from our society. Having made that assertion, however, we must also admit that identification and measurement of the distributive impacts present unusual theoretical and empirical problems. For a number of reasons these problems are only now becoming manageable.

While our governments may collect a lot of statistical data about governmental operations, most of their research is not directed toward explaining who gets how much of what. Although our national budget allocates a huge sum of money to national defense, nowhere in the President's budget message to Congress is there a discussion of how much additional income various citizens, workers, business firms, localities, and the like will receive from those expenditures. Only after contracts are awarded can economists determine which firms and states will benefit from them. In nondefense expenditures, however, many programs do not lend themselves to a ready identification of beneficiaries. If an urban renewal program were to be initiated in your community could you predict who would profit and who would be burdened by the program? The question has perplexed the most sophisticated scholars. Furthermore, governments do not provide us with much guidance on the subject, for a number of reasons.

First, they simply do not know the distributive consequences of specific policies and activities. The economic processes have not clearly been defined. Second, governments may not want people to know who benefits and who pays. If a large number of voters found out they were supporting a small number of other citizens they might well vote against the party in power. Third, they would face almost insurmountable problems of research because many public goods are such that they are available to all; no one can trace the values each acquires. If government weather reports are broadcast free, then all who own a radio can make use of the service. We cannot readily say that one group gets more radio service than another. Finally, citizens do not always want to know about inequities, because of our tradition that everyone is "equal before the law" and that each man has but one vote. The knowledge that we are not treated equally may be disconcerting to some because it indicates failure to achieve the ideal.

Choosing the Means of Redistribution

Government may produce redistributional consequences deliberately or inadvertently, directly or indirectly. So, too, they may choose to accomplish these ends by interference in the marketplace or by various mixes of revenue and expenditures policies. Interference may include efforts at price control in one or more types of markets, while revenue policies involve decisions about who to make pay how much to government. Expenditures, as we noted in Chapters II and III, specify where the money is going. While all governments employ all of these means each is likely to have certain pronounced preferences and obligations. For example, local governments do not make many deliberate efforts to redistribute income because they do not have the necessary financial power to accomplish as much as the federal government.

The one activity of great consequence among local governments is education—one of the more successful attempts at affecting income distribution. Lower-income groups have profited a great deal during the history of public education. State governments probably have a greater short-run ability to affect distribution than do local governments because their revenues and expenditures are much greater, but they do not typically pursue distribution as a goal. The federal government, on the other hand, does pursue deliberate policies of redistribution as it does regulatory policies. The direction of redistribution, however, cannot be readily determined unless we also know who controls the government. Republican administrations generally favor the better-off while the Democrats, at the national level, have preferred to aid the more numerous lower-income citizens. Republicans have tended to shun too much interference in the marketplace while Democrats have not always been reluctant to exercise control. If prices must be controlled the Republicans will opt for wage control while Democrats favor commodity control. Republicans tend to prefer monetary and revenue policies over the fiscal and expenditures policies chosen by liberal Democrats. Republicans have historically preferred indirect to direct controls, in contrast to Democratic administrations during the past forty years. These preferences are not inflexible or inevitable; given certain economic and political conditions, they could be policies of either type of administration.

How the "Military-Industrial Complex" Profits

Our analysis has focused on somewhat isolated groups of beneficiaries of government largess who have managed to obtain large sums of transfer payments from some level of government. These payments are made in a deliberate sense; that is, the government's policy is to pay these people in order to add to their disposable income. Far larger sums of money, however, are paid to individuals and organizations that are not transfer payments but are the unintended results of pursuing policies that include traditional functions of government. One such function is national defense.

Although the objective of the policy makers is to protect the nation, not to make some people richer than they would be during peacetime, many people profit enormously from defense. We need to look into the distributive aspects of this program because the total amounts spent on defense are the largest part of the nation's federal budget as well as the budgets of all governments. Let us draw a more precise picture of the magnitude of what President Eisenhower made into a famous phrase—"the military-industrial complex."

We now devote about 9 to 10 percent of our gross national product to defense-related activities. During 1948, the year of lowest expenditures on defense since World War II, we spent $11.8 billion. Since then we have increased our expenditures every year except 1955 and 1956. These expenditures are charted in Figure IV–1. In 1968, out of a total federal budget of $135 billion, we spent about $75 billion on defense—about 56 percent of all federal expenditures. So large a portion of the federal budget is bound to have profound distributive consequences. Who gets the money?

Some citizens obviously get vastly greater shares than others do. In addition, some suffer hardship, because these vast expenditures give impetus to an inflationary trend. Inflation always penalizes certain low-income groups, especially those on fixed incomes such as pensioners or old people. But who profits? The first to profit from large defense expenditures, is, naturally, the military—large sums have created more military positions and higher ranks with higher salaries. Extended military stints abroad have provided military families with subsidized world travel since World War II. More important, a defense industry has been created whose main function is to supply military hardware and perquisites. Among the industries most affected by the military budget are aircraft companies, many electronic firms, research and development groups, and to a lesser extent the automotive industry. (This share has dwindled because of extensive changes in weaponry and technology.) This distribution is tabulated in Table IV–2, which lists the 38 largest military contractors, their dollar amounts in military contracts, and the percentages of their total sales derived from that source. This last column, percentage of total sales, suggests rather clearly which industries, workers, and areas of the country are dependent upon the "weapons culture" of the federal government. Changes in the military budget profoundly affect men who derive their living from making weapons;

FIGURE IV–1

Federal Expenditures for National Defense, 1940–68

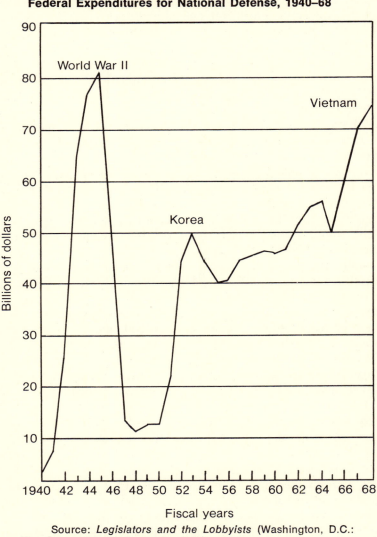

Fiscal years

Source: *Legislators and the Lobbyists* (Washington, D.C.:
The Congressional Quarterly, 1968), p. 51.

also vitally affected are retail businesses who service defense
workers. Loss of a contract can cause economic depression for
an entire city. In 1968, Alaska, Connecticut, District of Columbia, Hawaii, Utah, and Virginia all had from 8.7 to 10.3 per-

cent of their civilian work forces employed in defense industries.[12]

We can also gain a perspective on the distribution of military expenditures by looking at the amounts spent among the various states and regions of the country. In Table IV–3 the states are arrayed according to the amounts they derived from contracts in 1966. In Table IV–4 the states are listed according to the total sums of defense-related expenditures in 1967, these include salaries, rather than defense contracts. And finally, income distribution among regions as it is affected by various government expenditures, including the military, is presented in Table IV–5.

Every section of the country is a beneficiary in some manner or other. This is made quite obvious by the fact that the military and Congress have managed to disperse bases and operations across the nation. One or more installations were found in more than 75 percent of the 435 Congressional districts in 1968.[13] Such bargains, sometimes called "pork-barrel," between Congressmen and the Defense Department make a good deal of strategic sense for both politicians and the military. Whether viewed as efficient or obstructive, the system distributes income widely if not equally. Inequalities in distribution are also suggested by the fact that in 1967 more than half of the defense budget ($39.2 billion) went to 34 companies and one-fourth to only seven companies.[14] Clearly, defense monies are the biggest item in our government budgets. As such, they create an important redistributive mechanism and a vast network of beneficiaries who have powerful vested interests in maintaining these expenditures.

Some Are Less Fortunate

The thrust of the chapter has been to suggest that our governments dole out vast sums of money. That they do, but not all profit equally from the affluence our society has generated. This section will deal with those who have not the political power to gain more from the system. Who are these less fortunate citizens?

The average annual family income of Americans during recent years has been about $9,000. There are, nevertheless, at least

---

[12] *Statistical Abstract of the United States, 1969*, p. 249.

[13] *Legislators and the Lobbyists* (Washington, D.C.: The Congressional Quarterly, 1968), p. 51.

[14] *Legislators and the Lobbyists*, p. 51.

TABLE IV-2

Business Awarded to Largest U.S. Military Contractors Through Defense Contracts, 1961–67 (in millions of dollars)

Fiscal year	1961	1962	1963	1964	1965	1966	1967	7-year total	Per-cent of total sales
1. Lockheed Aircraft	$1,175	$1,419	$1,517	$1,455	$1,715	$1,531	$1,807	$10,619	88%
2. General Dynamics	1,460	1,197	1,033	987	1,179	1,136	1,832	8,824	67
3. McDonnell Douglas	527	779	863	1,360	1,026	1,001	2,125	7,681	75
4. Boeing Co.	920	1,133	1,356	1,365	583	914	912	7,183	54
5. General Electric	875	976	1,021	893	824	1,187	1,290	7,066	19
6. North American-Rockwell	1,197	1,032	1,062	1,019	746	520	689	6,265	57
7. United Aircraft	625	663	530	625	632	1,139	1,097	5,311	57
8. American Tel. & Tel.	551	468	579	636	588	672	673	4,167	9
9. Martin-Marietta	692	803	767	476	316	338	290	3,682	62
10. Sperry-Rand	408	466	446	374	318	427	484	2,923	35
11. General Motors	282	449	444	256	254	508	625	2,818	2
12. Grumman Aircraft	238	304	390	396	353	323	488	2,492	67
13. General Tire	290	366	425	364	302	327	273	2,347	37
14. Raytheon	305	407	295	253	293	368	403	2,324	55
15. AVCO	251	323	253	279	234	506	449	2,295	75
16. Hughes	331	234	312	289	278	337	419	2,200	u
17. Westinghouse Electric	308	246	323	237	261	349	453	2,177	13
18. Ford (Philco)	200	269	228	211	312	440	404	2,064	3
19. RCA	392	340	329	234	214	242	268	2,019	16
20. Bendix	269	286	290	257	235	282	296	1,915	42

21. Textron	66	117	151	216	196	555	497	1,798	36
22. Ling-Temco-Vought	47	133	206	247	265	311	535	1,744	70
23. International Tel. & Tel.	202	244	266	256	207	220	255	1,650	19
24. I.B.M.	330	155	203	332	186	182	195	1,583	7
25. Raymond International*	46	61	84	196	71	548	462	1,568	u
26. Newport News Shipbuilding	290	185	221	400	185	51	188	1,520	90+
27. Northrop	156	152	223	165	256	276	306	1,434	61
28. Thiokol	210	178	239	254	136	111	173	1,301	96
29. Standard Oil of N.J.	168	180	155	161	164	214	235	1,277	2
30. Kaiser Industries	—	87	49	152	219	441	306	1,255	45
31. Honeywell	86	127	170	107	82	251	306	1,129	24
32. General Tel.	61	116	162	229	232	196	138	1,124	25
33. Collins Radio	94	150	144	129	141	245	202	1,105	65
34. Chrysler	158	181	186	170	81	150	165	1,091	4
35. Litton	—	88	198	210	190	219	180	1,085	25
36. Pan. Am. World Air.	127	147	155	164	158	170	115	1,046	44
37. F.M.C.	88	160	199	141	124	163	170	1,045	21
38. Hercules	117	182	183	137	101	120	195	1,035	31

u-unavailable.
* Includes Morrison-Knudsen, Brown & Root, and J. A. Jones Construction Co.

Source: Legislators and the Lobbyists (Washington, D.C.: The Congressional Quarterly, 1968) p. 56.

TABLE IV-3

Allocation of Defense Contracts Among States, 1966

Rank	State	Amount (in millions)	Percent of U.S. total	Rank	State	Amount (in millions)	Percent of U.S. total
1	California	$ 6,689	17.9%	27	Arizona	$ 250	.7
2	Texas	3,547	9.5	28	Colorado	210	.6
3	New York	3,262	8.7	29	Rhode Island	198	.5
4	Missouri	2,278	6.1	30	South Carolina	181	.5
5	Connecticut	1,936	5.2	31	Utah	179	.5
6	Pennsylvania	1,649	4.4	32	New Hampshire	162	.4
7	Ohio	1,602	4.3	33	Oklahoma	158	.4
8	Massachusetts	1,422	3.8	34	West Virginia	142	.4
9	New Jersey	1,235	3.3	35	Arkansas	127	.3
10	Georgia	1,148	3.1	36	Kentucky	124	.3
11	Illinois	1,064	2.8	37	Mississippi	115	.3
12	Michigan	1,034	2.8	38	Nebraska	104	.3
13	Indiana	898	2.4	39	Vermont	100	.3
14	Maryland	868	2.3	40	Oregon	99	.3
15	Florida	799	2.1	41	Alaska	86	.2
16	Virginia	665	1.8	42	New Mexico	81	.2
17	Louisiana	656	1.8	43	Montana	78	.2
18	Minnesota	650	1.7	44	Hawaii	65	.2
19	Washington	606	1.6	45	Maine	57	.2
20	Tennessee	538	1.5	46	Delaware	52	.1
21	North Carolina	448	1.2	47	Wyoming	33	.1
22	Kansas	399	1.1	48	Nevada	29	*
23	Wisconsin	384	1.0	49	North Dakota	17	*
24	District of Columbia	358	1.0	50	Idaho	15	*
25	Alabama	297	.8	51	South Dakota	9	*
26	Iowa	279	.8		U.S. TOTAL	$37,382	100.0%

Source: *Legislators and the Lobbyists* (Washington, D.C.: Congressional Quarterly Service, 1968), p. 52.

TABLE IV-4

Defense Department Payrolls by State, 1967 *(in thousands of dollars)*

States	Military Personnel	Civilian Personnel	States	Military Personnel	Civilian Personnel
Alabama	$ 183,682	$ 233,054	Montana	$ 57,185	$ 10,142
Alaska	166,177	56,368	Nebraska	83,034	30,490
Arizona	139,190	60,744	Nevada	36,524	18,836
Arkansas	57,753	32,759	New Hampshire	29,021	65,271
California	1,149,666	1,327,522	New Jersey	226,565	243,069
Colorado	223,226	115,751	New Mexico	96,162	88,061
Connecticut	19,461	32,195	New York	168,249	313,218
Delaware	49,944	10,497	North Carolina	438,637	87,523
District of Columbia	185,772	209,226	North Dakota	75,829	9,416
Florida	384,402	213,393	Ohio	135,453	354,184
Georgia	531,870	286,579	Oklahoma	209,527	226,097
Hawaii	176,346	170,611	Oregon	20,303	25,057
Idaho	21,974	3,951	Pennsylvania	76,650	527,887
Illinois	303,567	221,233	Rhode Island	44,077	70,632
Indiana	51,928	115,747	South Carolina	242,561	130,139
Iowa	9,269	5,795	South Dakota	37,611	10,135
Kansas	179,409	39,980	Tennessee	89,632	48,534
Kentucky	289,334	109,344	Texas	1,067,477	514,532
Louisiana	198,809	56,816	Utah	28,338	203,417
Maine	61,161	13,248	Vermont	1,392	512
Maryland	326,965	366,331	Virginia	590,139	622,809
Massachusetts	138,941	192,862	Washington	250,093	196,530
Michigan	104,398	103,294	West Virginia	2,947	8,557
Minnesota	26,396	18,067	Wisconsin	17,010	23,170
Mississippi	143,227	49,549	Wyoming	24,108	5,441
Missouri	178,439	165,871	TOTALS	$9,349,830	$8,044,446

Source: *Legislators and the Lobbyists* (Washington, D.C.: Congressional Quarterly Service, 1968), p. 62.

TABLE IV–5
Regional Percentages of Defense Expenditures, 1963

Income level and region	Population	Personal income	Defense expenditure in percentages
Low income	29.7%	22.9%	17.8%
Southeast	21.7	16.1	11.2
Southwest	8.0	6.8	6.6
Average income	36.3	37.7	32.1
Rocky Mountain	2.4	2.3	4.2
Plains	8.3	7.9	6.3
Great Lakes	19.8	21.0	12.6
New England	5.8	6.5	9.0
High income	34.0	39.4	50.1
Mideast	21.4	24.6	22.0
Far West	12.6	14.8	28.1

Source: Adapted from Joint Economic Committee of the 87th Congress, 2nd Session, *U.S. Economic Growth to 1975: Potentials and Problems* (Washington, D.C.: U.S. Government Printing Office, 1966).

9.6 percent (1967) who do not earn enough to escape what the federal government defines as poverty.[15] That makes a total of approximately 26 million people, of whom 32 percent are nonwhites. And the income necessary to avoid being classified as poor is minimal; in 1966 price terms it was $3,335 for a family of four not living on a farm.[16] It does not take much imagination to understand that under conditions of inflation such an income does not provide a decent living let alone provide any amenities or enable saving for the future.

To give these poor just enough additional income to raise them above the poverty level would require, according to one estimate, an additional $11 billion.[17] The poor receive considerable sums of income from government, as we shall see in greater detail shortly, but it is hardly enough ($16 billion for 26 million people in 1966) to guarantee them one dollar above the poverty line.[18]

These poor people are found everywhere, in cities, in towns, on farms, in every section of the land, but they are concentrated

[15] *Statistical Abstract of the United States, 1969*, p. 330.
[16] Merriam, "Welfare and Its Measurement," p. 763.
[17] James Tobin, "Raising the Incomes of the Poor," in Kermit Gordon, ed., *Agenda for the Nation* (Garden City, N.Y.: Doubleday & Co., Inc., 1968), p. 104.
[18] Tobin, "Raising the Incomes of the Poor," p. 104.

among certain groups: Negroes, Indians, Mexican-Americans, small farmers, elderly, fatherless families, Puerto Ricans, iron and coal miners, the ill, uneducated, disabled, migrant workers. Needless to say, these groups are not mutually exclusive; in fact, many are characterized by several of these handicaps. A profile of a poor person might show him as black, uneducated, a rural or ghetto resident, older, ill or disabled, and so forth. The poor who are born into poverty are most likely to be unable to escape it. One handicap leads to another and each reinforces the others in a vicious circle of psychic depression, hostility, hopelessness, and fear.

While many programs are designed to assist in alleviating the malady no combination seems to have had any marked degree of success in reducing the total number of poor. The number of poor has in fact decreased during the last ten years by about 10 million but that is due more to economic conditions than legislation. At best, our policies and not inconsiderable expenditures—a total of more than $100 million during 1966–67[19] for all welfare programs at all levels—have not reached the disadvantaged in such a way as to cure their situation. Much of the $100 million reaches the middle-class rather than the genuinely disadvantaged. At best, one can estimate that perhaps only $26 billion from the federal government went to the various disadvantaged and needy during any recent year.[20]

The range of programs assisting the needy and the poor is very broad including cash payment programs such as Old-Age and Survivors' Disability Insurance (OASDI), aid to families with dependent children (ADC), aid to the blind, and aid to the permanently and totally disabled. All of these are usually summarized as "public assistance." In addition to these traditional expenditures a great variety of other programs have been designed to improve the income earning capacities of the poor. These include the Job Corps, Economic Opportunity Act, adult education, child day care, rural loans, Neighborhood Youth Corps, community action programs, Project Head Start, Vista, and others.

Opposition to these public assistance programs seems to be strongest among the middle-class and working-class citizens. This probably stems from their image of the programs' recipients—millions of able but shiftless people being "coddled" by government. In fact, of the needy who received about $7 billion under

---

[19] Merriam, "Welfare and Its Measurement," p. 771.
[20] Merriam, "Welfare and Its Measurement," p. 772.

public assistance in 1966 about 7 to 8 million *cannot* become productive workers. About half are too young (approximately 3.5 million dependent children), some are too old, some are disabled, and some are blind. Most of the poor outside of these categories apparently want to work and live at the higher standards of the middle-class but they are disadvantaged and cannot easily escape their bondage. Ghetto residents, Indians on reservations, and many of the white rural poor are not being assisted sufficiently to increase their incentives, skills, and assets to become more useful citizens. White middle-class Americans frequently will not live near them or grant them the status, jobs, and income that acted as incentives in their own rise from poverty. Without the promise of a better tomorrow what can one expect from a man? Perhaps a worse aspect of our well-meaning public assistance programs is that they fail the "beneficiaries" in another way: They often breed the conditions they are supposed to relieve.

Another indicator of the nation's concern for its citizens' welfare is found in its expenditures on social insurance such as sickness and maternity insurance, unemployment insurance, work accident insurance, and family allowances, most of whose benefits accrue to wage earners. The United States ranked *last* in its total expenditures on such programs (1962) when compared to eight western European countries. We ranked last on each program except unemployment insurance, in which we ranked second.[21]

Even our position at the bottom of the list does not adequately reflect the situation until one looks at the actual figures involved. Whereas West Germany ranked first with a total of 14.4 percent of its national income on such programs the United States devoted but 4.8 percent. We would need to treble our expenditures in order to achieve parity with most European countries. If we did, we could probably do much to eliminate poverty. We have not made the appropriate policy decision which can only be made in the political process. Instead, we have placed war expenditures in higher priority. For welfare spending, we have relied more on personal responsibility and a philanthropic tradition, along with minimal government participation.

We have partially identified the poor or the disadvantaged and we have described in all-too-brief compass some of the efforts

---

[21] Joint Economic Committee, Congress of the United States, 89th Congress, 1st Session, *European Social Security Systems* (Washington, D.C.: U.S. Government Printing Office, 1965), p. 11.

our governments make to reform and alleviate their situation. We have as yet made no effort to explain why these people are still unable to command the assistance that others who are better off gain from their governments. Some of those who gain the most need it least. And as we have just observed, most of the needy gain the least from political action. Even so, significant portions of their income do come from government; a far larger percentage, in fact, than in the case of the higher-income groups, who may gain more in actual dollars. In looking at the net results of government expenditure and taxation we can see that lower-income groups, while decreasing in number, remain low in income and needy.

One last point needs to be made with respect to the assistance derived by the poor as opposed to that received by middle- and upper-income groups. When the disadvantaged and the needy on welfare buy their food stamps, are investigated by welfare sleuths, and are forced to detail and explain their lives, they are degraded, humiliated, and made to be grateful for their pittances. But when the middle class receives its educational subsidies; the upper-income groups, their tax exemptions; absentee wealthy farmers, their subsidies, and businesses; their tariff concessions; no humiliation is ever experienced. Perhaps we should subject the better-off to the same treatment—or, better, not disgrace those who must have government assistance to barely survive. The psychic costs of poverty and disability should not be multiplied by government.

The Net Results

Our discussions have centered on a variety of aids and advantages provided various elements of the population by government. So far we have made no attempt to sum up these various quantities to analyze who gains how much and at what costs. Ad hoc listings of benefits will never show these net balances; they can only dramatize inequalities. Fortunately, a handful of economists have been active during recent years in estimating the balance sheets of various income groups with government. One of the most thorough studies was done by W. Irwin Gillespie.[22] Although his methods are far too complicated to study here, he was considerate enough to translate his many tables into three compact charts and

[22] "Effect of Public Expenditures on the Distribution of Income," in Richard A. Musgrave, ed., *Essays in Fiscal Federalism* (Washington, D.C.: The Brookings Institution, 1965), pp. 122–86.

figures. These convey his results with clarity. We have reproduced them here in Figures IV–2, IV–3, and IV–4.

The overall results of the exchanges involving expenditures and taxes in Figure IV–2 suggest that the pattern of fiscal incidence is such that in general the upper-income brackets pay for benefits received by the lower-income brackets but that the middle class pays its own way. Losses in transactions with the government are accordingly suffered by the rich and gains are made by the lowest income recipients. Another way of looking at the results is to study the individual expenditures and tax curves because their results differ. The expenditure curves suggest that government actions and policies are "mildly progressive," that is, they favor the poor who earn less than $3,000 per year. If they favored the rich the curves would rise instead of decline. The tax curves are a bit more complicated since they show that taxes work against the poor and favor the middle and upper-income levels. Note that those whose incomes exceed $10,000 are not detailed.

FIGURE IV–2

Taxes, Expenditures, and the Net Budget Pattern, Federal and State-Local Combined, 1960

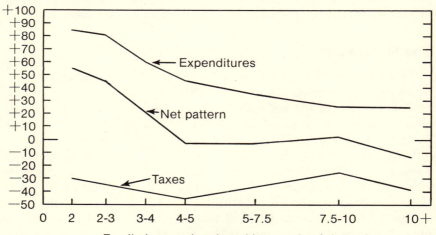

Source: W. Irwin Gillespie, "Effect of Public Expenditures on the Distribution of Income," in Richard A. Musgrave, ed., *Essays in Fiscal Federalism* (Washington, D.C.: The Brookings Institution, 1965), p. 165. Figures IV–2, –3, and –4 © The Brookings Institution. Reprinted by permission.

FIGURE IV–3

Federal Taxes, Expenditures, and the Net Budget Pattern, 1960

Percent of money income

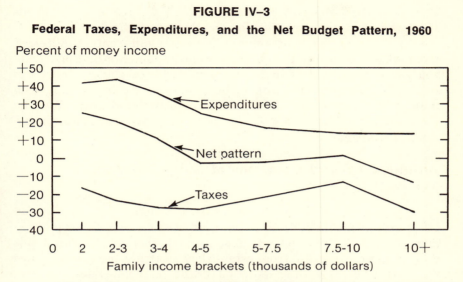

Family income brackets (thousands of dollars)

Source: W. Irwin Gillespie, "Effect of Public Expenditures on the Distribution of Income," in Richard A Musgrave, ed., *Essays in Fiscal Federalism* (Washington, D.C.: The Brookings Institution, 1965), p. 164.

FIGURE IV–4

State-Local Taxes, Expenditures, and the Net Budget Pattern, 1960

Percent of money income

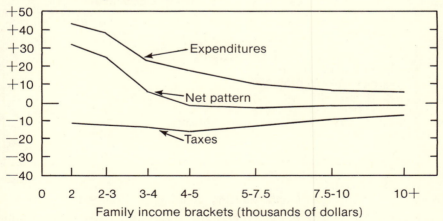

Family income brackets (thousands of dollars)

Source: W. Irwin Gillespie, "Effect of Public Expenditures on the Distribution of Income," in Richard A. Musgrave, ed., *Essays in Fiscal Federalism* (Washington, D.C.: The Brookings Institution, 1965), p. 164.

They constitute about 34 percent of the income recipients. Figures IV–3 and IV–4 are variations on the themes of Figure IV–2 showing that the patterns of relationships are different at different levels of government. If you were wealthy which situation would you prefer: the state and local, the federal, or the combined results? Which situation profits the poor most? Finally, how can these mixed results be accounted for as political choices? Why do we tax and spend the way we do? Hopefully, we will begin to find some partial answers.

Attitudes Toward Government Subsidies and Expenditures

The existence of substantial aid to various occupational and other groups would seem to imply that most citizens favor governmental expenditures and/or subsidies. Whether or not this holds up in practice, it is far from established as truth, because we have very little useful opinion data on grants and subsidies. We can only point to isolated studies and draw rather undependable inferences.

The Gallup Poll provides a few examples of opinion on programs that may be thought of as forms of subsidies. Table IV–6 shows how Americans felt about them during the mid-1960s:

TABLE IV–6
Attitudes of Americans Toward Subsidies

Program	Percent in favor
Federal aid to depressed areas (at present rate or increased)	75%
Retraining the poor	75
Antipoverty programs	70
Head Start	67
Urban renewal	67
Increased construction of nursing homes	66
Low-rent public housing	63
Federal aid to education, including grants to supplement teachers' salaries	62
Low-interest federal housing loans	60
Medicare for entire family	50

Source: Based on Lloyd A. Freed and Hadley Cantril, *The Political Beliefs of Americans* (New York: Simon and Schuster, 1968), Chapter II.

These few programs or policy areas suggest that the American people were quite favorably disposed toward a number of governmental programs which clearly provided subsidies for various activities and groups. We cannot tell how these same citizens feel toward outright well-known subsidies for agriculture and the shipping, gas, and oil industries because of the absence of data. We can speculate, however, that those who would benefit would probably approve. Many others, including those neither directly nor adversely affected, might disapprove of at least some of these subsidies if they were labelled as such.

Exercises in Analysis

SUBSIDIZING CERTAIN POSTAL USERS

Many of the subsidies we have cited as well as countless others go unnoticed by the average citizen. If he is vaguely aware of them, he knows little about their magnitudes, recipients, and means of payment. One possible exception the public is generally conscious of is reduced postal rates for mailers of "junk" or third class mail, and catalogs sent under fourth class. Still, most people are unaware of the dimensions of this activity, or of their own role in supporting it. At least 26.3 percent of the total domestic mail deliveries qualify as third class so the magnitude of the

TABLE IV–7

Financing of Selected Classes of Mail, Fiscal 1968

Classification	Percentage of costs paid by mailer
First class	104.6%
Airmail	107.3
Second class	25.9
Third class:	
Single pieces	104.3
Bulk rate regular	72.6
Bulk rate nonprofit	32.5
Fourth class:	
Parcels	100.9
Catalogues	68.8

Source: Adapted from Frank S. Joseph, "Washington Pressures/Direct Mail Advertising Association," *National Journal*, 2 (January, 1970), 249.

TABLE IV–8

Incidence of Expected Gains and Losses for Typical Public Expenditures

Expenditure	Direct gains	Indirect gains	Negligible gains	Net loss
Public housing	Builders Suppliers Banks	Tenants Buyers	General public	Landlords
Agriculture price supports	Large farmers Processors	Department of Agriculture	General public	Consumers Taxpayers
Urban renewal	Downtown business Financial institutions City government Builders	Tourists Middle class culture Consumers	General public	Dispossessed tenants Slum landlords Criminals
Postal subsidies	Second class users Third class, bulk Fourth class, catalogues		Newspaper subscribers Magazine subscribers	Taxpayers First class users Air mail users
"Impacted areas" program	Children of federal employees Children of defense workers Children of civilians working on federal property	Congressmen Parents of school children in impacted areas Impacted areas	General public	Taxpayers

Program	Recipient			
Interstate highways	Commercial truckers, Tourists, Contractors, Suppliers, Bus companies		Airlines	Businessmen in bypassed towns (motels, service stations), Nondrivers, Taxpayers
Military expenses	Professional military, Defense contractors, Defense workers	Schools, Property taxpayers in impacted areas, Military, Veterans' groups, Military aid recipients		Draftees, Sacrificed civil programs, Taxpayers
National Science Foundation fellowships	Recipient	Universities, Professors	General public	Taxpayers
National parks				
Space exploration				
Sanitation control (restaurants)				
Census				
Social Security				
Old age pensions				
Unemployment insurance				
Patents and copyrights				
Public education				
Foreign aid				
Medicare				
Police protection				

subsidy is apt to be great as we shall soon see. Besides the annoyance caused householders by unwanted mail, those of us who use first class, airmail, and third class single piece rates are required to pay more than our share of the costs; more in fact, than is needed to cover the mailing expenses of these types of mail, as evidenced in Table IV–7.

The question is this: Why are some categories of mail required to pay more than their legitimate share of the costs while others (such as second-class mail used mostly by newspapers) are required to pay only about one-fourth of the costs? And even among the subsidized we note that they are unequally subsidized. Why is this? Further, while the Constitution forbids the government to encourage religious institutions, these institutions profit a great deal through cheaper, "nonprofit" mailing rates—in addition to being exempted from property and income taxes. (Incidentally, many churches have real estate and stock market investments whose profits are not taxable.)

Finding answers to these questions will require some digging for additional facts and the application of some common sense. One hint: first find out who uses which types of mail service. Then attempt to learn something about the political power of these users. Chapters VI and VII will assist in making this inquiry somewhat more manageable.

IDENTIFICATION OF BENEFICIARIES OF PUBLIC EXPENDITURES

The general analysis and cases cited in this chapter suggest that every public program and expenditure has some redistributive consequences. In effect, they make some people better off and others less well off while some are made to suffer net losses. For reasons we have already offered, identification of beneficiaries and losers is an extremely troublesome research problem if one wishes to be thorough and precise. Readers can appreciate the efforts of investigators much more if they will try their own hand at measuring the incidence of public benefits. Accordingly, an incomplete table of commonplace public expenditures is included for readers to inspect and discuss. Table IV–8 provides a set of public expenditures and programs with an illustrative set of probable beneficiaries and losers. The task is twofold: (1) Inspect the sample entries for purposes of modification and clarification; (2) Complete the table for the remaining programs. Explanations of the entries are necessary if the exercise is to be meaningful.

Suggested Readings

Anton, Thomas J. *The Politics of State Expenditure in Illinois* (Urbana: University of Illinois Press, 1966).

Barnet, Richard J. *The Economy of Death* (New York: Atheneum, 1969).

Bazelon, David T. *The Paper Economy* (New York: Vintage Books, 1959).

Chase, Samuel B., Jr., ed. *Problems in Public Expenditure Analysis* (Washington, D.C.: The Brookings Institution, 1968).

Donovan, James A. *Militarism, U.S.A.* (New York: Charles Scribner's Sons, 1970).

Downs, Anthony. *Urban Problems and Prospects* (Chicago: Markham Publishing Co., 1970).

Fishman, Leo., Ed. *The Economics of Poverty* (Englewood Cliffs, N.J.: Prentice-Hall, Inc., 1965).

Hansen, W. Lee and Weisbrod, Burton A. *Benefits, Costs, and Finance of Public Higher Education* (Chicago: Markham Publishing Co., 1969).

Jacob, Herbert. *Debtors in Court: The Consumption of Government Services* (Chicago: Rand McNally & Co., 1969).

Kafolis, Milton Z. *Welfare Economics and Subsidy Programs* (Gainesville, Florida: University of Florida Press, 1961).

Kershaw, Joseph A. *Government Against Poverty* (Chicago: Markham Publishing Co., 1970).

Lydall, Harold. *The Structure of Earnings* (Oxford: Clarendon Press, 1968).

Maxwell, James A. *Financing State and Local Governments, Rev. Ed.* (Washington, D.C.: The Brookings Institution, 1969).

Merriam, Ida C., and Alfred M. Skolnik. *Social Welfare Expenditures Under Public Programs in the United States, 1929–66* (Washington, D.C.: Social Security Administration, 1968).

Musgrave, Richard A., ed. *Essays in Fiscal Federalism* (Washington, D.C.: The Brookings Institution, 1965).

Musolf, Lloyd D. *Government and the Economy* (Chicago: Scott, Foresman and Co., 1965).

Peacock, Alan T., ed. *Income Redistribution and Social Policy* (London: Jonathan Cape, 1954).

Poole, Kenyon E., ed. *Fiscal Policies and the American Economy* (Englewood Cliffs, N.J.: Prentice-Hall, Inc., 1951).

Rothenberg, Jerome. *Economic Evaluation of Urban Renewal* (Washington, D.C.: The Brookings Institution, 1967).

Weisbrod, Burton A., ed. *The Economics of Poverty* (Englewood Cliffs, N.J.: Prentice-Hall, Inc., 1965).

Wright, Deil S. *Federal Grants-In-Aid: Perspectives and Alternatives* (Washington, D.C.: American Enterprise Institute for Public Policy Research, 1968).

Chapter V

THE SHARING OF BURDENS: COMPULSORY INEQUALITY

In Chapter IV we surveyed the means and extent of our collective resource commitments but without considering the question of whose resources or *who pays how much of the total bill*. While voters may worry a great deal about rising government expenditures, increasing tax bills, and increasing indebtedness, they are also greatly concerned about their *relative shares* or burdens. We may each have one vote but we do not pay equal amounts in taxes nor do we share equally in the sense that all contributions entail the same marginal sacrifices. In this chapter we will survey some facts concerning the allocation of burdens as well as governmental and citizen responses to the problem of the equity of burden-sharing. The views of the politicians, other leaders, and voters can be quite different since their respective roles and responsibilities are at odds. For example, economists and treasury officials are apt to regard taxation as an instrument for the manipulation of consumer demand; the taxpaying public, however, prefers to see taxes as a compulsory and inconvenient burden for public services. Since taxes furnish the largest portion of total governmental revenues (69 percent in 1967), the concern of both groups is justified. And since citizens make other forms of contributions, such as military service, we can readily appreciate why questions of equity arise. Who shall pay how much and who shall be chosen to serve are fundamental policy issues.

While few Americans would deny a love of their country, still fewer have ever made a voluntary contribution to any of their governments. When did you last send any money to a government treasury without being required to do so? How many men genuinely volunteer for military service? For jury duty? Under our present system, support of government must be a compulsory activity or government is an impossibility. We explained this paradoxical love of country and the need for compulsory contributions in Chapter IV. For the moment, accept the proposition; then reflect on these "oddities" from American taxation circa 1965–69 —the major form of citizen contributions or burdens.[1]

1. Some 29 persons earned more than $1 million in 1968 and paid not one cent in federal income taxes.

2. A loophole in the federal law allowed oil and mining companies to avoid $100 million yearly in taxes.

3. In 1966 there were 154 individuals with incomes of over $200,000 who did not pay income taxes.

4. Some $79.5 billion in religious property goes untaxed, although it includes income-producing real estate, bonds, and stock market investments.

5. In 1969, some 69 percent of the people said their federal income taxes were "too high." Only 25 percent thought they were about "right," and no one thought they were "too low."

6. Treasury experts estimate that $35 billion of income fails to be reported on income tax returns and that this costs the government about $4 billion a year in taxes.

7. Every year, Internal Revenue Service gets about 20,000 tips about tax cheating from jealous neighbors, disgruntled employees, spurned girlfriends, and the like.

8. Of more than 80 million taxpayers, only 1,324 were convicted of evading federal taxes in 1966.

9. In 1968 some 24 state legislatures made additions to their tax levies but 11 states actually reduced some rates or abolished certain taxes or exempted certain groups from having to pay certain taxes. Total tax revenues, however, increased 8 percent over 1966.

10. The Mobil Oil Corporation would be saved $12 million in taxes under a special exemption to the repeal of the investment credit under the Tax Reform Act of 1969.

11. Lockheed Corporation would be saved $6.5 million under a similar provision.

---

[1] The following statements were reported in Remarks of Senator Lee Metcalf of Montana to the U.S. Senate and published as "AFL-CIO Program Urges Tax Justice and End to $17 Billion Loopholes," *Congressional Record* 91st Congress, First Session, April 14, 1969; and by Senator Edward M. Kennedy, of Massachusetts, as reported in "Kennedy Outlines 14 Instances of Special Tax Bill Provisions," *The Oregonian*, December 8, 1969.

12. The nation's 20 oil giants paid an 8.5 percent average tax.

13. A real estate operator with a total income of $7.5 million paid at the same rate as a $10,000 per year married wage earner with two children.

14. As "farmers," 101 individuals capable of making over $1 million in other endeavors claimed $7.6 million in tax write-offs for farm losses.

15. About $800 million worth of tax loopholes went to real estate operators constructing motels, office buildings, plants, and high-rise, high-rent apartment complexes.

16. In 1965 the petroleum industry as a group paid taxes at an effective rate of 21.1 percent of total net income and other mineral industries at 24.3 percent. At the same time, the average manufacturing corporation paid taxes at the rate of 43.3 percent.

A Few Basic Facts on Taxes

All of us have occasion to be upset over taxation and for good reasons. Taxation is not only compulsory but lowers our income and goes for the support of activities we disapprove of and people we do not even know. Furthermore, each citizen pays a different price for the same public services. A citizen's financial relationships with government on each of these accounts is almost the exact opposite of those occurring in the marketplace. Even so, the total tax burden in the United States is the lowest of the major western democracies. Only Canada and Switzerland have smaller tax burdens, as shown in Table V–1.

Note the considerable range among these countries, a spread of some 18.2 percent. In the United States, 27.3 percent of the gross national product amounted to about $176 billion in 1967, or nearly $890 per capita.[2] Contrast this with the situation in 1902 when the per capita tax bill was about $18, and half of that went to local governments. Of the remaining $9, $7 went to the federal government and only $2 was paid to state governments. It is obvious, of course, that the level of services was not the same then as it is now. Further, only the unsophisticated reader would as-

[2] U.S. Bureau of the Census, *The Statistical Abstract of the United States, 1969* (90th ed., Washington, D.C.: U.S. Government Printing Office, 1969), p. 409.

TABLE V–1

Total Tax Burdens Among Western Democracies, 1965

Nation	Percent of GNP
Sweden	39.0
France	38.5
Austria	35.2
Norway	34.9
West Germany	34.4
Netherlands	34.1
Britain	29.9
Belgium	29.7
Denmark	29.7
Italy	29.6
United States	27.3
Canada	27.1
Switzerland	20.8

Source: Edwin L. Dale, Jr., "U.S. Tax Lowest in Western Bloc," *New York Times,* March 24, 1967.

sume that the value of today's dollar is unchanged since 1902. In large part, the growth of public expenditures and taxation is a product of inflation and should be scaled down or deflated to show the true changes. Still, the average citizen is making more money now and giving increasing percentages of it to government.

The recipients of the tax dollar have also changed. Local government was the chief beneficiary of taxes at the turn of the century, but this has not been true since 1936. While local governments now get far more money than they once did ($141 per capita in 1966), this amount is overshadowed by the sum of $598 that goes to federal government. Even the state governments now get more than the local units ($161 in 1966).[3] We pay more taxes now and pay them in different ratios to the three levels of government.

TAX BURDENS AMONG THE STATES

A tax-sensitive citizen might well want to look into the costs of running government in the several states. For example, state and local tax revenue as a percentage of personal income in the state ranges from a low of about 8 percent in Illinois to a high of

[3] *Facts and Figures on Government Finance, 1967* (New York: Tax Foundation, Inc., 1967), p. 23.

more than 12 percent in Hawaii (1967). Most states are under 10 percent.[4] A citizen who wants to be taxed as little as possible should not, however, catch the next plane to Illinois. Rather, he should study the types of taxes found in the various states. His own personal share will be more affected by the type of tax and its rates than by the general information just provided.

While the general sales tax is the major source of revenue among the states, it is not found in at least eight or nine states. Fourteen states in 1966 did not collect an income tax and thirteen did not have a corporate income tax. In short, different sources of income and activities are taxed and the taxpayer should know not only the source of his income but which states tax which sources, at what rates, with what exemptions. Gaining this information is costly—perhaps even too costly, given the marginal returns.

Curious readers may, nevertheless, want to have some better idea of the general tax burden in the several states. In Table V–2 figures are presented on state and local taxes per $1,000 of personal income. These are averages and not the exact amounts of taxes each citizen pays; the range on either side of the mean can be considerable. The overall range in Table V–2 is from a high of $190.96 in North Dakota to a low of $105.13 in the District of Columbia. The median amount, about $136.14 (West Virginia), is just above the mean for the United States as a whole—$134.51 for each $1,000 of personal income. These are state and local taxes, exclusive of federal taxes. Taxes make up the bulk of state and local revenues—in fact, nearly 70 percent. Of that 70 percent, property taxes constitute the single largest source in most states. No wonder some taxpayers get upset over their property taxes. Those who vote against increases in public expenditures and increases in property tax assessments and rates may be more rational than their academic critics.

Allocation of the Tax Burden

The ultimate question concerning the costs of government is who pays how much. It is not an easy question to answer. We do know a good deal about the incidence of taxation—who pays how much—thanks to the efforts of diligent economists. These econo-

[4] Ira Sharkansky, *The Politics of Taxing and Spending* (Indianapolis: The Bobbs-Merrill Co., Inc., 1969), pp. 131–32.

TABLE V-2

State and Local Tax Burdens, 1968

State	Revenue per $1,000 of personal income	State	Revenue per $1,000 of personal income
North Dakota	$190.96	Delaware	$135.50
Wyoming	185.89	Nebraska	135.38
New Mexico	170.59	Kansas	134.35
Alaska	169.79	Georgia	132.80
Hawaii	165.66	Alabama	130.79
Minnesota	162.69	Maryland	129.96
Nevada	162.19	Massachusetts	129.26
California	160.84	Kentucky	126.25
Arizona	159.26	North Carolina	125.13
New York	158.21	Maine	123.71
Louisiana	157.88	Tennessee	123.57
South Dakota	157.62	South Carolina	123.17
Idaho	156.59	Arkansas	122.93
Montana	155.89	Indiana	122.42
Utah	153.72	Virginia	120.82
Vermont	150.61	Texas	118.74
Colorado	150.12	Rhode Island	118.48
Washington	149.43	New Jersey	114.13
Wisconsin	148.82	Pennsylvania	113.38
Iowa	143.99	Missouri	112.72
Mississippi	143.56	Ohio	111.99
Oklahoma	142.45	New Hampshire	111.59
Oregon	140.66	Connecticut	107.31
Florida	138.13	Illinois	105.40
Michigan	138.13	District of Columbia	105.13
West Virginia	136.14		

Source: "Where Taxes are Highest, Lowest," *U.S. News and World Report* (October, 1969), 77.

mists have found they can study incidence not by identifying specific individual citizens but rather by categorizing people according to income level. We know how much of the total tax revenues are paid by each income group and we know how much of their income goes into taxation. This latter information, as of 1965, is summarized in Table V-3. Although the total amounts may have changed considerably since then, the respective shares have not changed very much.

Three crucial tendencies are apparent in Table V-3. First, the distribution of the total tax burden indicates that taxes at the lower levels of income are regressive; at the middle ranges some-

TABLE V–3

Taxes as Percentage of Income, 1965

Income classes	Federal	State and local	Total
Under $2,000	19%	25%	44%
$2,000–4,000	16	11	27
$4,000–6,000	17	10	27
$6,000–8,000	17	9	26
$8,000–10,000	18	9	27
$10,000–15,000	19	9	28
$15,000 and over	32	7	38
Total	22	9	31

Source: Joseph A. Pechman, "The Rich, the Poor, and the Taxes They Pay," *The Public Interest* 17 (Fall, 1969), 33.

what proportional; and at the high end of the scale, progressive. This means that for the very poor (under $2,000) each dollar they contribute represents a greater sacrifice than is true for those who are somewhat wealthier. Second, the tax burden varies at different levels of government. The federal tax burden is very mildly progressive after incomes of $10,000, while the state and local burden is consistently regressive. There is a good reason for this: state and local governments rely on sales and property taxes, which tend to be regressive, while the federal government relies upon the income tax. Ours is notably progressive among the democracies of the world.

Another way of looking at the incidence of taxation is to reverse the usual perspective. This method asks not what percentage of one's income goes to government, but what part of governments' revenues are paid by which groups. For the nation, little data is available. We do have some data on the situation in Oregon for 1967, which we have displayed in Table V–4. Note that only the $5,000–10,000 group pays about what should be expected if the shares of the state tax revenues were apportioned on the basis of population. The under $5,000 group, constituting over 45 percent of the population, pays only 8.2 percent of the tax revenues. On the other hand, the 5.1 percent earning in excess of $15,000 pays 31 percent of the state taxes. But we are really less interested in population shares than in income shares. Table V–4 suggests that the income tax is progressive in Oregon, which means that the state employs an income tax with considerable effectiveness. (Some would even say a vengeance.) The more progressive tax

TABLE V–4

Tax Burdens in Oregon, 1966

Income level	Percent of population paying taxes	Share of state tax revenues (*percent*)
Under $5,000	45.3	8.2
$5,000–10,000	35.6	33.4
$10,000–15,000	14.0	27.4
$15,000 and over	5.1	31.0

Source: News item in the *Oregonian,* November 10, 1967, 1. Original data provided by Mr. F. H. W. Hoefke, State Tax Commission.

structure is further assured since Oregon does not have a sales tax. Not all states follow Oregon's example.

SOME COMPARATIVE NATIONAL DISTRIBUTIONS

Most people do not compare their own tax burdens with those of other countries. But such a comparison is instructive. It could reassure the dejected average American taxpayer, or convince high-income taxpayers to bank in other, more sympathetic nations. In many other nations, however, things are worse. We have seen that most other democracies charge their citizens more than we do; now we note that each democracy charges different taxpayers differently. The United States, for example, as Figure V–1 shows, is easier on almost all income levels than are Britain, Sweden and West Germany. On the other hand, the United States is tougher on the higher-income groups than Sweden and West Germany are. The graph in Figure V–1 also indicates that rates at which income is taxed change in much the same way for Britain and the United States. Rates in both nations increase at a faster pace than those for Sweden and West Germany do. Paradoxically, Sweden, a socialist country, taxes the lowest-income families much more than the United States, the most capitalist of the four nations. Paradoxically, too, Sweden is easier on the rich than the capitalistic United States and West Germany.

Another way of appreciating our comparatively light tax burden is to ask how much people in other lands would pay if they used the American income tax system. One student did ask that question of eighteen democracies and came up with the not entirely unexpected answer that only the Swiss and Japanese would

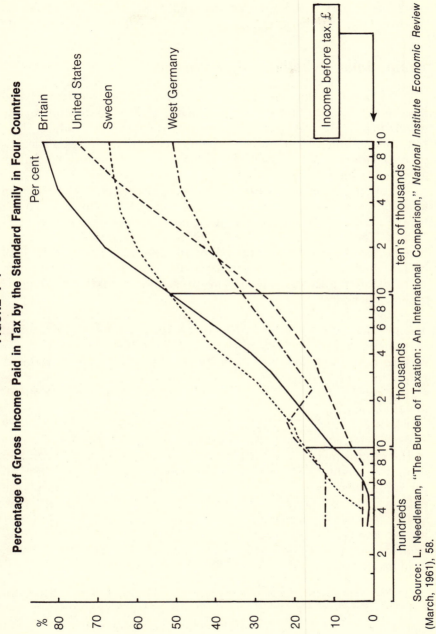

FIGURE V-1

Percentage of Gross Income Paid in Tax by the Standard Family in Four Countries

Per cent

Britain

United States

Sweden

West Germany

Income before tax, £

hundreds   thousands   ten's of thousands

Source: L. Needleman, "The Burden of Taxation: An International Comparison," *National Institute Economic Review* (March, 1961), 58.

pay less.[5] Sixteen other countries would pay more—often much more—if our laws were applied to their nationals.

Exemptions, Evasion, and Avoidance

One's net income can be directly increased by receiving benefits, but it can also be raised by reducing one's contribution to the government. Most American citizens are careful to reduce their tax bills as much as possible through legal exemptions and legitimate avoidance. A few (we do not have accurate figures) actually evade payments. Evasion is, of course, illegal.

How much money is saved by taxpayers in general (or, from another perspective, how much is lost by government) through legal exemptions is difficult to say. One estimate, by a former Assistant Treasury Secretary, Stanley Surrey, places federal revenue losses at more than $40 billion in 1969 and more than $119 billion during the fiscal years 1968–70.[6] Figure V–2 attempts a more graphic although incomplete presentation of the "leakages" and beneficiaries.

Most "loopholes" in our income and property tax laws were enacted deliberately to assist specific groups and even individual taxpayers. These legal exemptions include outright exemption for certain taxpayers, differing definitions of taxable income, reduced rates, tax deferrals, excess depreciation allowances, bad debt reserves for banks, mortgage interest deductions, oil depletion allowances, capital gains, and many more.

The drain of potential resources or tax dollars in Figure V–2 must be viewed from another perspective as well, that is, the size of the groups or numbers of taxpayers receiving each type of privilege. For example, the number of taxpayers who profit from capital gains must be fairly small because most Americans simply do not own enough stock to make any difference in their tax payments. The same observation applies to holders of state and municipal bonds whose interest payments are not taxed, and to beneficiaries of the oil depletion allowances. On the other hand, millions of homeowners have their tax payments reduced by mort-

[5] Vito Tanzi, "Comparing International Tax Burdens: A Suggested Method," *Journal of Political Economy* 76 (October, 1968), 1078–84.

[6] "Lost Revenues from Tax Incentives," in *Federal Economic Policy, Fourth Edition, 1969* (Washington, D.C.: Congressional Quarterly Service, 1969), p. 20; and, "What Is the Impact of Those Tax Breaks?" *Business Week* (February 1, 1969), 62–64.

FIGURE V–2

Tax Privileges and the Drain on the Treasury, 1970

	Amount (billions of dollars)
Capital gains	5.5–8.5
Tax-free municipal bonds	4.6
Income of the aged	2.3
Charity exemptions	2.2
Mortgage interest deductions	1.9
Oil depletion allowances	1.3
Medical expenditures allowances	1.9
Consumer interest deductions	1.3
Farm income and capital gains for lumber	1.0
Bad debt reserves for banks	0.6
Servicemen exemptions	0.5
Dividend exemptions	0.3
Others	16.6

Actual receipts $210 billion

Source: Based on "What Is the Impact of Those Tax Breaks?" *Business Week* (February 1, 1969), 62–64.

gage interest deductions; the same can be said of medical exemptions and consumer interest charges. These provisions for special treatment are as controversial as the degrees of privilege. In any case, the government receives much less revenue and some of us retain more of our income because of them. Three special exemptions deserve special attention in our federal tax structure.

CASE 1. DIFFERENTIAL TREATMENT OF INCOME BY SOURCE

Although our case is outdated in terms of the actual figures, it still illustrates an important consideration in determining the amount of income tax one pays, namely, the source of the income. The federal government does not treat all income as equal, but grants differential privileges depending on how the money is earned. In 1956, for example, a single person with an annual income of $100,000 would pay very different amounts if he earned his money in different ways.[7] Thus, if he had earned his income from salary, his tax would have been $65,928; if he earned it from oil royalties, his tax would have been $42,829; on income from sale of investments (capital gains), his tax would have been $25,000; and income from interest on state and local bonds would not have been taxed at all.

CASE 2. CHURCH PROPERTY

Church-owned property in this country was valued at some $79.5 billion in 1969.[8] None of this property is taxed, as is other private property. The total that would be paid in taxes if the property were taxable is hard to compute. This is because the rates differ so much from one state and locality to another. Obviously, the figure would be very large. Consider the revenue for a city like New York if its $726 million in church property were subject to standard rates!

CASE 3. FOUNDATIONS: REAL AND PHONY

Foundations have an honored position in American life because they provide a means of doing social good with private rather than governmental means. As an encouragement, our governments have not taxed them as private business firms. Needless to say, a great many entrepreneurs have perceived the possibilities of decreasing their tax loads by setting up foundations, ostensibly for charitable purposes, but really for tax reasons. Their donations to charity are miniscule while the tax savings are enormous. Treasury officials say that one dollar in tax money is lost for

[7] Stanley S. Surrey, "Do Income Tax Exemptions Make Sense?" *Colliers* (March 30, 1956); reprinted in Grossman, et al., eds., *Readings in Current Economics* (rev. ed., Homewood, Ill.: Richard D. Irwin, Inc., 1961), pp. 183–90.
[8] "Tax Suit Poses Economic Threat to Churches," *The Oregonian*, November 20, 1969, 24.

every seven dollars of certain payment transactions these "foundations" consummate. In short, the Treasury lost about $110 million annually during 1968 and 1969.[9]

Just why so many loopholes prevail is a debatable issue. One answer is that our highly progressive income tax encourages wealthy taxpayers to exert pressure on legislators by lobbying for special privilege. Their rationale may be that legal loopholes facilitate growth of essential industries such as oil. Another partial answer suggests that in a highly complex society laws must take account of special sets of circumstances that may take precedence over our desire to maintain and achieve greater equality of treatment. Tax laws, because they are so important, are likely to be the targets of demands for special treatment.

No tax reform in our history has managed to eliminate major exemptions and loopholes. Even the last sweeping tax reform in 1969 failed to achieve notable success in that area.

All these tax privileges are legal. We do not wish to suggest that Americans are cheaters and disobey tax laws on any grand scale. In fact, precisely the opposite is true; most Americans are loyal, honest taxpayers—this stands in sharp contrast with those in many other lands. Only 1,324 of 80 million taxpayers were convicted of evasion, cheating, and falsifying returns during 1966.[10] The Internal Revenue Service estimates that it collects well over 97 percent of the taxes due. Treasury experts estimate that $4 billion in taxes are lost yearly because some people do not report all their income; in 1966 unreported income was $25 billion. Each year the IRS gets about 20,000 tips about tax cheating for which the informants are paid if convictions result: in 1965, 792 informants received rewards of $597,731.[11]

Taxpayers in other countries are much less diligent and honest about their taxes.[12] An economist in Spain has said that four sets of books are kept by businessmen: one real set, one for the stockholders, one for the industrial group, and one for the government. Citizens in Italy, France, Brazil, India, and most Latin and South American nations openly cheat and negotiate their tax set-

[9] "Shadow Foundations Shown to be Oil, Mining Tax Dodges," *Eugene Register-Guard*, November 24, 1969, 5–A.

[10] John Pierson, "Most Americans Pay Their Taxes . . . And They'd Better," *Palo Alto Times*, March 20, 1967, 5.

[11] Pierson, "Most Americans Pay Their Taxes."

[12] "At Income Tax Deadline in Other Countries, Evasion Is The Standard Form," *The New York Times*, April 15, 1969, 6.

tlements. The chief means of evasion is unreported income; in India this is said to amount to $4 billion yearly. One reason for the tendency of Americans to be more loyal and honest in tax matters may be that our government has greater administrative capacity for enforcement than many other nations do.

Governmental Tax Preferences and Behavior

Despite much research into policies of taxation, some of which we mentioned in Chapter III, we still do not know very much about governments' preferences or about the reasons for their choices. Most histories of American fiscal policies provide much more detail than confirmed generalizations. In addition, unreliable data supports the generalizations that do exist. Since this is the case we can only list tentative generalizations that have been made and encourage readers to ask why and how they might be further tested and explained.

1. The greater the electoral turnouts the greater the reliance on direct rather than indirect taxation.

2. The more democratic the government the greater the reliance on progressive income taxes.

3. Democratic administrations will accept a higher rate of inflation than will Republicans as a substitute for increased taxation.

4. Our governments rarely know the incidence of any tax with confidence.

5. Drastic reforms of tax practices are rare.

6. Tax cuts are preferred to balanced budgets.

7. A progressive income tax will be used to appease the low-income groups while loopholes are included to appease the higher-income groups.

8. Any government will prefer general fund financing to earmarked taxes (those designated for special use).

9. Earmarking of taxes is a strategic governmental move to gain acceptance of unpopular taxes.

10. Earmarked funds are a popular means for an interest group to remove its benefits from annual legislative scrutiny.

11. Our governments have tended to overestimate their revenues and underestimate their expenditures.

12. Politicians and governments are normally for economy, in general; but not at the expense of their districts.

13. Congress rarely passes a tax increase in an election year.

One need not be much informed to detect a certain self-interested rationale underlying many of the above propositions—obviously, politicians and governments wish to remain in office. Their choice of fiscal institutions and policy and especially of taxes is conditioned by a fine appreciation for the wants and prejudices of their constituents. How else could it be when voters and elections are basic elements of public choice? What alternatives are available with the present distribution of political power resources and the need to bargain over policies? With increasingly larger shares of the gross national product and private or personal income going into the government's coffers we should expect that the politics of taxation will become more contentious. Furthermore, as each taxpayer strives to reduce his own contribution he necessarily threatens to increase that of some other citizen. Perhaps we will become increasingly sensitive to our relative shares as we learn more about them and as equity considerations become more crucial.

Elections, Taxes, and Bonds: The Voice of the Voter

While most governmental financing decisions are not made directly by voters, some decisions are regularly referred to the voters. Such decisions may include school budgets; capital improvements (streets, public buildings, sewerage facilities, police stations, and the like); school bonds for capital improvement; and adoption of taxes, tax bases, and rates. Recent years have shown some interesting general developments. Local school bonds enjoyed a very respectable acceptance from the voters across the country during the period following World War II but the rate of rejection has been increasing during recent years. In 1965, for example, only 25 percent were rejected; in 1966, 28 percent; in 1967, 33 percent; in 1968, 32 percent; and in 1969, a surprising 43 percent.[13] Still, a majority of the bond issues are accepted. In some localities the record is strikingly different. In Missouri, for example, only 6 percent of the total dollar value of bond issues won acceptance in 1969.

Why should this be? A general willingness to support schools is apparent; certain benefits are readily perceived as highly important even though the costs are high. So most bonds and budgets win approval, but under some conditions they do not. Some light is

[13] Item in *U.S. News and World Report* (October 20, 1969), 37.

TABLE V–5

American Opinions on Taxation, 1969

Statement	Agree
"Politicians promise tax relief and then do nothing."	86%
"The big tax burden falls on the little man."	84
"Too much tax money is given to people who don't appreciate it."	78
"Too much tax money is going into wars and defense."	76
"Taxes are set up to give the rich the breaks."	75
"People in power don't know how much suffering taxes cause."	67
"I resent my tax money being spent the way it is."	67
"My standard of living is being hurt by high taxes."	65

Source: "Everybody is Angry About Money," *Life* 67 (August 15, 1969), 25.

shed on the recent "taxpayer revolt" by public opinion polls and it is not a pleasant situation for administrators, especially school superintendents and boards, who are dependent upon the taxpayers' choices. We can better understand these revolts if we look at public opinion, as *Life Magazine* did in 1969 when it commissioned the Harris Poll to study a national sample of citizens to determine their attitudes on public expenditures and taxes.[14] The Harris analysts came to the general conclusion that a deep and bitter national resentment exists toward taxes and government spending as well as inflation.

Before we cite statistics we might illustrate the resentment the Harris group reported in the terms of ordinary people. One man said, "The government is run by the rich. You've never heard of a poor politician. I'd quit paying taxes tomorrow if there were someone to lead the revolt." Another said, "Taxes are too high. The poor person like me is hit the hardest." More of the intensity of the "tax revolt" is detailed in Table V–5. The results do not seem surprising given the conditions of 1969. Cynicism was apparent and complaints about the uses of the tax monies were many. Of course, the proverbial "little man" perspective was evident both in terms of his income and lack of political power. When asked

[14] "Everybody is Angry About Money," *Life* 67 (August 15, 1969), 17–29.

where to cut federal spending first these people named foreign aid (69 percent of the respondents) and Vietnam (64 percent). No doubt they feel we are spending vast sums in these areas with little success. Foreign aid expenditures, however, constituted so small a portion of the federal budget that their complete elimination would have had little or no visible effect on the personal incomes of taxpayers. These findings suggest that while voters are self-interested they are not well-informed about fiscal matters; while they may wish to participate in "taxpayer revolts," they need leadership. On the other hand, few want to reduce the level or quality of public services. The same poll shows that the taxpayers want the federal government to continue education, pollution control, the poverty programs, urban renewal, and highway construction and maintenance. Are we to conclude that they are irrational because they want to have as much as possible but pay as little as they can?

The findings of the Harris Poll have a certain ephemeral interest, but should not be thought of as stable opinion about taxes. More important long-term allocative consequences can be attached to citizen views of the "goodness" and "fairness" of various taxes. On this matter we have the results of a public opinion study conducted in Michigan during 1959.[15] That investigation indicates that individuals do act as fairly rational men, preferring taxes that will minimize their tax bills. Thus, a wealthy man prefers a sales tax to an income tax while the poorer man will have the opposite preference. More than 90 percent of the interviewees were quite consistent in their preferences when asked to rank income, property, and sales taxes. The income tax was widely accepted because respondents said it was "based on ability to pay," a popular norm of taxation. Even the sales tax was defended by some as based on ability to pay.

An indicator of ignorance on the incidence of taxes was found in a belief on the part of some renters that the property tax was good and fair. They seemed not to know that it can be passed on to the renter as a part of his monthly rent. The investigators concluded that self-interest was evident in preferences but that opinions were tempered by education, which serves both to sharpen one's sense of interest and to make the educated more liberal.

[15] Elizabeth Likert David, "Public Preferences and State-Local Taxes," in Harvey E. Brazer, ed., *Essays in State and Local Finance* (Ann Arbor, Mich.: Institute of Public Administration, University of Michigan, 1967), pp. 74–106.

"Little Groups of Neighbors": The Military Draft

Taxation may be compulsory, unequal, and painful and may elicit angry responses. These responses do not compare to citizens' reactions to the draft during some of our wars—particularly during the Vietnam war. Conscription of manpower, especially for an unpopular war, is destined to upset youthful males for it is compulsory, unequal, and painful in the extreme. The conscripted individual is taken from the pleasures of civilian youth at a time when life is most exciting, is forced to fight, and be subjected to injury and even death. Even those who never see combat (most do not) must surrender or sacrifice income that might have been earned, lose promotions in a job or career, and miss educational opportunities that may never recur. All this is in the interests of public goals he may not even share, and in fact, may oppose with deep intensity. So the draft, no matter how it is conducted, is one of the ultimate forms of a politically coerced contribution. It lends itself to study as a prime example of the compulsory sharing of unpopular burdens.

In 1968, of 1.1 million male youths examined by Selective Service, about 57.9 percent were found qualified to perform military duties.[16] Of those found available, some 18.7 percent were fulfilling their obligations, 14.1 percent had fulfilled them, 32.6 percent were deferred, 24.9 percent were disqualified and the remainder were classified under a variety of other categories including "conscientious objector." Reasons for disqualification of almost one-quarter of eligible males included medical and mental deficiencies, limited trainability, and the like. These general, basic facts tell us little about who gets drafted and who manages to remain a civilian—and why. Who serves when not all serve?

The draft is discriminatory. It inducts certain citizens and not others. At present, those most subject to the draft are males under 26 years of age. Further, the draft has tended to select the less-educated and less-advantaged lower-income and lower-status groups. The sons of the middle and upper-middle classes are better informed about the draft and the means of legal avoidance. They have been able to achieve exemption and deferment to continue their educations. Resistance to the draft, both as a private matter

[16] U.S. Bureau of the Census, *The Statistical Abstract of the United States, 1969* (90th ed., Washington, D.C.: U.S. Government Printing Office, 1969), pp. 260, 262.

and as an organized public endeavor, has tended to be centered in the middle-class white population. Most youths and their families have attempted private means of legal avoidance first. Public protest is a secondary step, not taken lightly because of the high costs of achieving any major change. Private action is more directly beneficial because it settles the individual's own case. Public action has little if any direct and immediate benefit for oneself, and in fact may actually damage one's private case. In a few instances protestors of the war have been penalized by local draft boards.

Draft boards are the main agency for mobilizing military manpower and the members, therefore, are crucial policy makers as well as allocators.[17] Although General Hershey has called them "little groups of neighbors," they are in fact not in meaningful contact with their youthful neighbors. They are rarely well-known in the community, often beyond 70 years of age, and their chief obligation is to supply a specified number of persons suitable for military duties on specific days. Distance from the people and inequitable policies have served to make them targets for disgruntled draft-age youth. Their work is one of many factors that has encouraged many persons of all political views to advocate an all-professional, voluntary military. Obviously, aside from other considerations, such a military would further concentrate the military burdens and exempt the vast bulk of the young from one of the more onerous obligations of citizenship. The extent of one's obligations to the public continues to be a question of the highest order of priority.

Is a person who objects to the draft any less loyal than his neighbor who objects to high income tax payments? Is the person who refuses to be inducted any less loyal than the person who cheats on his taxes? Some 50,000 Oregonians manage to avoid the state income tax each year while 18 percent of those receiving draft notices during 1968 refused to be inducted. Is objection to a war any more disloyal than objection to welfare services? Americans must of necessity debate the sharing of burdens just as they must debate and decide upon the distribution of rights, public goods and services, and privileges. Citizenship includes both the benefits and the burdens. And, since no free marketplace solution is in sight, the political system must make the policies and choices.

---

[17] For an excellent analysis of the Selective Service System see James W. Davis, Jr., and Kenneth M. Dolbeare, *Little Groups of Neighbors* (Chicago: Markham Publishing Co., 1968).

Exercises in Analysis

SOME PUZZLING VOTES IN A TAX REFERENDUM

In May and June of 1968 and on May 26, 1970, the voters in Lane County, Oregon, went to the polls to cast their votes on a measure that would equalize the tax burden among taxpayers and equalize educational opportunities for their children. Some 16 school districts constitute the Lane Intermediate Education District and each has a different property tax base and set of tax rates because the taxable wealth in each district is very different. The richest district, with great stands of timber, has a taxable wealth of $105,000 per child; the poorest district has only $18,700 per child or about one-sixth that of the richest district. The measure before the voters would, in effect, tax where the evaluation is and redistribute the money to where the children are. Everyone would pay into the fund but some districts would get back more than they contributed. In 1967, six districts paid in more than they received, while ten districts received more than they paid in, as Table V–6 illustrates.

TABLE V–6
How Districts Voted on Equalization Tax, May 1968

District	Taxes to be paid	Monies to be received	Vote Yes	Vote No
McKenzie	$213,223		223	248
Bethel	196,346		615	1,030
Oakridge	91,551		67	117
South Lane	43,368		453	691
Crow-Applegate	28,722		80	139
Triangle Lake	1,383		44	21
Fern Ridge		$135,223	424	139
Springfield		117,585	2,191	2,686
Creswell		73,480	298	163
Junction City		66,958	388	387
Siuslaw		65,836	233	45
Pleasant Hill		60,611	366	217
Eugene		36,108	6,516	6,362
Mapleton		11,768	151	131
Marcola		3,521	87	131
Lowell		3,277	155	115

Source: "Puzzling Vote Vetoes IED Equalization Tax," *Eugene Register-Guard,* May 7, 1968.

On all three occasions the proposal was defeated, after having been passed for 12 years without a defeat. Can you suggest any general reasons for the recent defeats? Some voters seem to have voted against their best interests. Many voters whose districts would have received money voted against the proposal. In effect, they voted to increase their own tax loads. Note that voters from Springfield, a receiving district, voted down the proposal by nearly 500 votes. In other receiving districts the majority voted as expected but substantial minorities voted against themselves. Why? In districts which would have to give instead of receive we also find some voters seemingly voting against their own "best" interests. Triangle Lake is such a district.

Now some questions about Table V–6: Which school district voted rationally; that is, for the measure if they were to benefit and against it if they would lose? How can we best explain the voting behavior of individual voters who voted against their own interests? What further kinds of information would be helpful in providing answers to the previous questions?

THE POSSIBLE EFFECTS OF MULTIPLE CHOICE VOTING

The Attorney General of Oregon has recently opened the way for possible reduction of property taxes by giving the voters a multiple choice among tax substitutes. One of the Oregon State Representatives has indicated that he will offer a constitutional amendment to limit property taxes. At the same time and on the same ballot he will ask each voter to select which of several taxes he would choose to replace the lost property tax revenue. The tax that receives the largest number of votes (plurality) would go into effect.

Assuming this proposal is constitutional in your state, predict the electoral outcomes; that is, select which taxes would be voted in as substitutes for the property tax? Which taxes are most likely to appear on the ballot? Why? What would happen to state revenues? Would the government like this option? What would happen if the voting rule were changed from a plurality to a majority vote? Suppose a two-thirds majority were required; what would happen? Which voters would vote for which type of tax under any of these rules? Finally, why do we have so few of these types of elections? Would they not better express our views on taxation?

Suggested Readings

Fisher, Glenn. *Taxes and Politics* (Champaign-Urbana: University of Illinois Press, 1970).

Maxwell, James A. *Financing State and Local Government* (rev. ed., Washington, D.C.: The Brookings Institution, 1969).

Mosher, Frederick and Poland, Orville F. *The Costs of American Governments: Facts, Trends, Myths* (New York: Dodd, Mead & Co., 1964).

Olson, Mancur. *The Logic of Collective Action* (Cambridge, Mass.: Harvard University Press, 1965).

Pechman, Joseph A. *Federal Tax Policy* (Washington, D.C.: The Brookings Institution, 1966).

Ratner, Sidney. *Taxation and Democracy in America* (New York: John Wiley & Sons, 1942).

Ripley, Randall B. *Public Policies and Their Politics* (New York: W. W. Norton & Co., Inc., 1966).

Sharkansky, Ira. *The Politics of Taxing and Spending* (Indianapolis: The Bobbs-Merrill Co., Inc., 1969).

Stern, Philip M. *The Great Treasury Raid* (New York: Random House, 1964).

PART TWO

Public Choice: Markets, Exchange, and Bargaining

We now have some idea of the actual outcomes of our political processes. Our attention will shift to the major means by which these choices are produced and implemented. Americans, it will be contended, conduct their public choice through bargaining within a set of fairly stable political institutions (sometimes called political markets). Specifically, the bargainers, their strategies and resources, and the effects of basic political institutions on bargaining behavior and the settlements will be considered in detail.

Bargaining is treated as an activity that involves both cooperative and competitive elements and as such is one type of social exchange. Men seek their advantages by offering to confer advantages on others; in doing so they seek, establish, and attempt to maintain favorable exchanges. We will view most political exchange as essentially peaceful and stable, but we will give special attention to situations in which exchange breaks down and bad bargains are struck. We will attempt to explain why some bargainers do better than others and will illustrate with some typical cases from contemporary politics.

Chapter VI

HOW POLICY IS MADE: BARGAINING AMONG POLITICIANS

Chapters II through V provided some idea of the public goals we pursue, the resources we commit to those goals, who gets what from the government, and who pays how much of the costs of these collective goals and individual benefits. Little has been said about the ways in which we make all these decisions. Some theories were advanced, however, about the "causes" of certain choices, and we attempted to explain why government expenditures have increased. Some scholars, including political scientists, argue that policy-making processes and the institutional structure of the system have little influence on final policy outcomes. With respect we reject that view. In these two chapters we will attempt to depict how policies are initiated, accepted, and enacted.

A major contention is that the chief policy makers are politicians and that they are engaged in a continuous, somewhat mystifying activity called political bargaining. We will show who bargains with whom, how, under what conditions, and with what results. The process of bargaining is basic and pervasive throughout our federal system, although its precise workings are somewhat shaped by the particular circumstances of concrete bargaining situations. Thus, it makes a difference if one is bargaining at or across local, state, or national levels. Further, bargaining in the United States assumes certain styles not always found in other societies, including the democratic nations. Particular reference will be made to bargaining in England and France; for further contrast internal or domestic bargaining is distinguished from bargaining with foreign nations. Finally, political bargaining will be contrasted and compared with bargaining in markets.

The Bargainers

Practically every American citizen bargains politically, if not in the direct and formal sense of being a politician, certainly in the indirect sense of being a voter and voicer of opinion that will mobilize or constrain politicians. Citizens do not engage in continuous bargaining; normally their participation is episodic and not very influential. But some men become more or less professional at the task—as one might expect of politicians. Politicians both in and out of office are the chief bargainers and they are exceedingly numerous.

PUBLIC OFFICIALS

With 521,760 elective officials we have one for every 230 adult citizens. Most of these officials occupy local offices, as shown in the following table.[1]

TABLE VI–1
Distribution of Elective Officials

Level	Number
National	2
State	13,038*
Local	508,720
Counties	74,199
Municipalities	143,927
Townships	129,603
School districts	107,663
Special districts	56,943

* 8,000 state legislators.

In addition to this sizable number of elective officials, in 1968 there were more than 12.2 million civil servants[2] (105 state and 291 local employees per 10,000 people), thousands of appointed officials, two major political parties and almost a dozen minor ones, all of whom bargain at one or more levels and in one or more policy areas. We probably have more bargainers than any other nation because our system is more open to participation than most

[1] U.S. Bureau of the Census, *Statistical Abstract of the United States: 1969* (90th ed., Washington, D.C.: U.S. Government Printing Office, 1969), p. 405.

[2] *Statistical Abstract, 1969*, pp. 395, 431.

others. Not unexpectedly, bargaining costs are very high because the number of persons to be consulted is so great.

Official bargainers come from all walks of life—although, as many political scientists have observed, the more powerful government offices attract a disproportionate number of higher-income and higher-status persons. Few working-class or minority people ever campaign for public office at any level let alone become elected to powerful positions. The office structure thus tends to favor the better-off citizens who have the time, resources, and incentives to enter public life.

The bargainers are well paid in the higher offices but at the local level of government tens of thousands are unpaid. Their compensation must be found in influencing people and policies, in added social status, and perhaps in increased private incomes. This is a favored group, typically better educated, of higher status, more influential, and more energetic than the average citizen.

The official bargainers include governmental units in addition to individual officials or politicians. The fifty states and the nearly ninety thousand other governmental units also act as bargainers for their constituents. States bargain with one another, with the federal government, and with local units within their own boundaries. Local units bargain over such services as police and fire protection, exchange of information, reciprocity agreements on handling criminals, and so forth. New York City, for example, through its Mayor, bargains on a daily basis with the State of New York, just as every large city does with its state, over public services and revenues. Many cities, states, and even universities have lobbyists in the national capital protecting and advancing the concerns of their employers. Since so much of the revenue of state and local governments (about $17 billion in 1968) comes from the federal government it would be foolish, indeed, not to be informed about federal aid and to try to get more of it.

Members of each branch of government also bargain with one another. Presidents bargain with Congress; each bureaucracy bargains with at least some other bureaucracy, and each agency bargains with state legislatures, city councils, and Congress. Practically every agency in Washington has a Congressional or Legislative Liaison Officer who represents his agency, doing favors or services for Congressmen and Senators in the hope that the members will return the favors when the time comes to bargain. The White House maintains an influential lobby to bargain with private persons and interest groups. And, of course, the United States government bargains incessantly and directly with other nations and indirectly through numerous international organizations including the United Nations.

PRIVATE PERSONS AND INTEREST GROUPS

We have described the official bargainers, who are entitled to hold office and make authoritative decisions that other citizens must obey. They are not the only bargainers and often not even the most important; certain private persons and interest groups are always active participants. Frequently they are crucial in particular policy situations at the local, state, or national level.

Citizens form interest groups in order to achieve their policy ends; this makes sense since a group can usually mobilize more resources than a person by himself can. We do, in fact, create an incredible number of organizations to pursue policy concerns. One estimate claims that more than 8,716 national associations operate within the United States. Most of them are not permanent interest groups, although they may become politically active on occasion. Some 5,007 business associations have been counted. Business groups in general are better and more extensively organized than others. They operate at all levels of government and in the polity more widely whenever and wherever their interests are presumed to be vitally affected. Some 224 labor unions, 327 agricultural organizations, and 108 veterans and patriotic organizations are other groups that are well organized, ably led, and well financed.[3]

We can gain some appreciation of the activities of interest groups by simply noting the numbers who register with Congress each year and the amounts they spend on influencing legislation. Table VI–2 presents the figures for some recent years. Note the variations in both the numbers of lobbyists and the amounts spent. In 1950 the amount spent by 430 groups was more than $10 million. Recent years have indicated a diminution from that high point. Further, each group is likely to spend differing amounts each year depending on the number and importance of issues affecting them. The big spenders during 1967 included the United Federation of Postal Clerks (AFL-CIO) with $277,524; AFL-CIO National Headquarters, $165,505; and Record Industry Association of America, Inc., $139,919. The National Association of Letter Carriers (AFL-CIO) spent $133,877. While employee organi-

[3] Murray Gendell and Hans L. Zetterberg, eds., *A Sociological Almanac for the United States* (New York: The Bedminister Press, 1961), p. 51.

TABLE VI–2

Annual Registrations and Spending Totals of Lobbies, 1947–66

Year	Registrations	Spending total
1947	731	$ 5,191,856
1948	447	6,763,480
1949	599	7,969,710
1950	430	10,303,204
1951	342	8,771,097
1952	204	4,823,981
1953	296	4,445,841
1954	413	4,286,158
1955	383	4,365,843
1956	347	3,957,120
1957	392	3,818,177
1958	337	4,132,719
1959	393	4,281,468
1960	236	3,854,374
1961	365	3,986,095
1962	375	4,211,304
1963	384	4,223,605
1964	255	4,223,277
1965	450	5,484,413
1966	332	4,656,872

Source: *Legislators and the Lobbyists* (Washington, D.C.: Congressional Quarterly Service, 1968), p. 28.

zations were the heavy spenders in 1967, business organizations have actually dominated during most years. In fact, in total expenditures business groups have led since 1949 (see Table VI–3).

Interest groups do not attempt to influence all legislation, but specialize in policies they think are most important. During recent sessions 26,000 bills were before Congress. To lobby on everything would be pointless and expensive. *Congressional Quarterly* estimates the 18 bills in Congress most heavily lobbied during 1968.[4]

Airport Development Aid
Central Arizona Project
Civil Rights
Farm Labor Bargaining
Farm Program Extension
Food Stamps
Gas Pipeline Safety
Gun Control
Higher Education
Highway Aid
Housing Bill
Import Quotas
Mutual Fund Curbs
Occupational Safety
Radiation Control
Savings and Loan Revision
Tax Surcharge
Trade Expansion

[4] *Congressional Quarterly Almanac* 24 (Washington, D.C.: Congressional Quarterly Service, 1968), p. 881.

The *Congressional Quarterly* made no attempt to rank the relative importance of these issues nor did they have conclusive proof of their estimates, but this list confirms the opinions of most informed journalists, politicians, and lobbyists concerning the relative importance of issues and bills. Economic interests were primary in this list, although they need not always be. Nor does any single issue have only an economic dimension. The interest in gun control bills, for example, may be economic for sellers, but for buyers is probably noneconomic—the pleasure derived from ownership and use.

All the issues listed involve allocations of scarce resources and distribution of benefits; and some involve the allocation of burdens. Others also involve control of activities and people, as in the case of gun control, gas pipeline safety, civil rights, and radiation control. Of course, all these measures also impose additional costs of regulation or administration on the part of the government and regulated persons. In short, congressional measures elicit considerable interest on the part of all groups lobbying in Washington. They lobby to protect or advance their status, pocketbooks, and general well-being.

It doesn't take a soothsayer to predict which issues will most concern particular interest groups. On occasion, however, prediction is difficult because the impacts of legislation may not be readily apparent even to those most vitally affected. To illustrate: the following groups each took a primary interest in from one to six measures during 1968.[5]

Interest Group and Issue	*Position*	*Outcome*
AMERICAN BANKERS ASSOCIATION		
Revenue and Expenditure Control Act	For	Won
Housing and Urban Development	Against	Lost
Savings and Loan Revision Act	Against	Won
Truth in Lending Bill	For	Won
NATIONAL EDUCATION ASSOCIATION		
$6 billion a year federal school aid	For	Lost

[5] *CQ Almanac* 24, pp. 880, 886, and 888.

TABLE VI-3

Lobby Spending by Category for Selected Years

Category	1949 Groups reporting	1949 Amount spent	1951 Groups reporting	1951 Amount spent	1952 Groups reporting	1952 Amount spent	1954 Groups reporting	1954 Amount spent	1956 Groups reporting	1956 Amount spent	1959 Groups reporting	1959 Amount spent
Business	140	$3,280,278	117	$3,089,742	96	$2,215,591	132	$2,289,538	150	$2,031,933	151	$1,761,556
Citizens	30	1,015,073	36	1,492,309	29	416,134	38	615,582	43	395,865	49	512,607
Employee and labor	17	257,301	30	581,488	22	466,733	21	656,149	30	748,320	34	1,217,361
Farm	11	391,595	10	1,281,785	7	356,614	14	411,629	16	345,093	21	314,552
Military and veterans	5	105,723	5	128,425	4	151,343	5	117,821	7	143,338	9	130,752
Professional	15	1,672,043	18	673,442	18	496,634	15	195,437	18	292,571	16	344,640
Foreign policy	14	718,556	11	581,005	9	195,726	—	—	—	—	—	—
Reclamation	11	374,174	11	412,004	9	317,878	—	—	—	—	—	—
Tax	13	154,967	31	524,896	22	207,328	—	—	—	—	—	—
Total*	256	$7,969,710	269	$8,771,097	216	$4,823,981	225	$4,286,158	264	$3,957,120	280	$4,281,468

Category	1961 Groups reporting	1961 Amount spent	1962 Groups reporting	1962 Amount spent	1963 Groups reporting	1963 Amount spent	1964 Groups reporting	1964 Amount spent	1965 Groups reporting	1965 Amount spent	1966 Groups reporting	1966 Amount spent
Business	171	$1,672,259	170	$1,836,126	153	$1,521,600	148	$1,362,045	154	$1,472,863	155	$1,600,629
Citizens	52	494,175	50	531,002	51	707,333	57	1,065,197	64	836,113	59	801,078
Employee and labor	40	892,569	37	945,206	36	1,130,124	33	945,071	31	1,094,782	34	1,347,279
Farm	22	367,238	22	412,524	21	405,849	23	365,471	25	419,633	20	383,156
Military and veterans	10	133,735	6	141,991	5	140,180	6	154,493	7	167,634	8	147,388
Professional	17	426,120	19	344,455	20	318,519	21	331,616	23	1,493,384	20	377,339
Total*	312	$3,986,096	304	$4,211,304	286	$4,223,605	288	$4,223,893	304	$5,484,409	291	$4,656,869

Figures may not add to totals because of rounding.

Note: Total lobby spending, by type of organization, reported to the Clerk of the House under the 1946 Federal Regulation of Lobbying Act is shown for selected years. Beginning in 1954, the classifications "Foreign Policy," "Reclamation," and "Tax" were eliminated and groups previously in those categories were distributed among the other six categories. The figures were computed by Congressional Quarterly.

Source: *Legislators and the Lobbyists*, (Washington, D.C.: The Congressional Quarterly Service, 1968), p. 36.

AFL-CIO

Occupational safety bill	For	Lost
Expanded NLRB protection to farm workers	For	Lost
Strengthened mine safety controls	For	Lost
Consumer protection	For	Won
Nomination of Justice Fortas to Chief Justice	For	Lost

AMERICAN LEGION

Increased pensions	For	Won
Increased compensation for disabled veterans	For	Won
Penalties for desecration of the flag	For	Lost

These four interest groups regarded each measure shown as among the more crucial actions Congress was deciding. Accordingly, they involved themselves in various ways in shaping the outcomes. No one group got all it wanted nor did any one lose on all its concerns. Usually, the losses and victories were less than complete. At times, an interest group is interested in just one amendment or provision of a bill. Sometimes it changes its position as the main bill is altered. For example, the American Banker's Association apparently opposed the so-called "truth-in-lending" bill but approved the final modification of the bill. Precisely this sort of activity constitutes much of political bargaining. Give and take is necessary to these groups in the interest of minimizing legislation they consider bad and maximizing legislation they consider good.

Elements of Bargaining

When people bargain with one another they hope or expect to end up either having more of something they possess or gaining something they do not already possess or control. One must first, therefore, have something of value with which to bargain or trade. Thus, a bargain is a mutually beneficial exchange, which makes both bargainers better off than they were prior to the exchange. If that were not a distinct possibility bargainers would not have incentives to bargain.

Both bargainers may gain from an exchange but the gains

are certainly not always equal; one person may bargain more successfully than another. It is important, therefore, to consider who gets how much from bargaining. Each bargainer wants to cooperate just enough to conclude a bargain but each wants to do as well as he can; in order to do so it is necessary to compete with the very person one wishes to induce to do good. Because of this aspect of bargaining few people become skilled bargainers. Almost contradictory skills and personalities are required to initiate and conclude bargains.

Political bargaining may be interesting and instructive to observe, but it is not an easy activity to describe or even to explain. It is by nature a highly complex activity, full of deception and intrigue. Furthermore, much political bargaining takes place in private, where it cannot be fully observed. This is especially true in the Supreme Courts of the states and the nation. In addition, where many bargainers are engaged none are ever very certain about the activities of others. The processes are not well monitored. More often than not we learn of the outcomes but not the series of deals, understandings, and misunderstandings that went into the final results. Reporters and historians who attempt to unravel particular bargains have found that participants contradict one another, and "forget" crucial stages and actions that may have either facilitated or hindered the agreements. No politician likes to admit that he may not have done as well as another.

On occasion a bargainer must actually lie or conceal part of the truth in order to maintain his position, especially in international bargaining. Politicians and lobbyists exaggerate the size of their following and demand more than they expect to achieve. Of course, they hope they will not be found out.

When politicians bargain they usually exchange support or votes (logrolling) whose consequences entail the eventual exchange of goods and services among other people—the voters and taxpayers. For example, a Congressman from California might agree to vote for a post office in Kentucky if the Congressman from Kentucky will support the Californian on a dam project. Dams, bridges, post offices, and military installations are the most commonly bartered goods in Washington. Or, a President may offer the support of his Administration to a Senator if the Senator will vote for the President on a particularly crucial policy. In election years, a President may promise a member of Congress a federal judgeship for the Congressman's support. A generous campaign contributor may be awarded with an ambassadorship.

Another typical daily form of bargaining goes on whenever politicians decide to modify provisions in a law or proposed rule for a modification in another part of that law or some other unrelated law or policy. President Nixon was said to have rewarded the southern states for their support in the 1968 election by softening his administration of desegregation laws. His unsuccessful attempt to appoint a southerner to the Supreme Court in 1969 and 1970 and the hiring of a former assistant of Senator Strom Thurmond of South Carolina may also be regarded as payments for previous support. Governor Wallace of Alabama is supposed to have offered not to run against President Nixon in 1968 in exchange for a policy of local options on school desegregation.[6]

Other commonplace exchanges occur during election years whenever national administrations help Congressional supporters in their races by such well-known devices as having federal funds allocated to the Congressman's district and giving him credit for the gain; photographing the Congressman in the White House with the President; allocating campaign funds to the Congressman, and generally suggesting that the Congressman is highly influential with the President and the Administration. Obviously, both tremendous skill and luck are required for successful bargaining. Furthermore, because we do not teach our politicians how to bargain they must learn on the job. That can be costly to the party, the interest groups, and taxpayers. Politicians who bargain on the national level are probably more able than those at other levels because they are usually more experienced by the time they reach that level. Of course, a few elite state legislators and big-city mayors have been bargaining for a long time and are very skilled. Most, however, never achieve sufficient longevity to become experienced, because turnover rates are considerable in city councils and state legislatures.

The Bargaining Situation: An Overview

Politicians and others in many bargaining situations soon learn that, regardless of the specific circumstances, certain elements are common to all and can be identified and thus understood. These are characteristics of bargaining in general.

---

[6] Rowland Evans and Robert Novak, "Wallace Has Intricate Plot to Undermine Nixon," *The Oregonian,* June 1, 1970.

1. The bargainers have goals to be achieved.
2. The goals are partially conflicting and partially complementary.
3. The bargainers possess, command, or have access to different amounts and types of information and other resources.
4. The bargainers are typically somewhat uncertain about the goals and strategies of others with whom they must deal.
5. Bargainers seldom know all the possible alternative strategies.
6. Each bargainer suspects the other's motives and promises.
7. Bargaining itself is a costly process.
8. Some bargainers are more skilled than others.
9. Situational and institutional constraints have a vital effect on the success of each bargainer.
10. Some irrational behavior must be expected, and the skilled bargainer learns to predict and identify it.
11. The rules of the game are not always clearly stated or clearly understood by all bargainers.
12. Bargaining takes time.
13. Much bargaining will be accomplished by implicit exchanges.
14. The terms of the settlement may not be clearly stated nor agreed upon.
15. Only rarely will an agreement be permanent. Settlements are only temporary in nature and subject to renegotiation.
16. Bargainers must give up something in order to gain something.
17. No one achieves all he sets out to achieve.

These features of bargaining will be further discussed, although not necessarily in this order. As we continue to unfold the process and its outcomes all the important points will be touched upon—in subsequent chapters if not this one. See Chapters IX and X, in particular, for more strategic choices.

Why Is Bargaining Necessary?

Although bargaining is approved of in the private and business life of Americans, many entertain a deep and abiding distrust of bargaining as a means of settling public disputes and reaching political agreements. Certainly a part of our ambivalence toward politicians is based on this view of bargaining since the politician is the chief bargainer. While bargaining has its defects we must recognize that it is a fact of life and cannot be readily eliminated. *Bargaining is practiced because men (1) have different policy preferences; (2) are sufficiently powerful not to be ignored; and (3) regard some solution to differences as better than none.* Bargaining could only be eliminated if all men agreed on every course of action; then there would be no need for it. But since differences do exist each must be prepared to give and take. In fact, for one to take requires than another give. If we cherish the individual's right to pursue his choices in the polity, bargaining cannot be avoided. In addition, each group's control of resources enables it to demand that it be permitted to bargain. Only those groups whose political resources are minimal are excluded from bargaining circles, and these circles have been narrowing of late.

Types of Bargaining

Bargaining is a type of interaction in which two or more persons attempt to attain better positions by offering rewards to others in exchange for their rewards or concessions. To understand how bargaining operates in political choice, we must consider two factors: what types of payoffs (rewards) are sought and how do people set out to acquire them. These two factors alone will allow us to make some useful discriminations among types of bargaining situations.

Payoffs are either fixed in quantity or unlimited. When they are fixed, the situation is called "zero-sum" or "constant-sum" because the gains of one bargainer must be achieved at the expense of another. When one man's gains are not at another's expense the situation is termed "positive" or "non-zero-sum." There are examples of each in political life, but perhaps the most prevalent and difficult to analyze combine the two properties—situations in which some payoffs are fixed or zero-sum and others are positive.

The other factor—how bargains are arrived at—is not only fascinating but crucial to an understanding of the payoffs and the generation of difficulties for the participants. Bargaining can be *implicit* or *explicit*. In the latter methods, bargainers make explicit trades; that is, they knowingly discuss exact terms and make concrete offers without embarrassment. Lawyers do this in labor negotiations.

Senator Kerr of Oklahoma, a rich and powerful oil man

turned U.S. Senator, is reputed to have bargained explicitly on most matters. According to a lobbyist who knew him well and dealt with him face to face in negotiating terms for a government contract for North American Aviation, Senator Kerr said, "If you get it (the contract), what can North American do for Oklahoma?"[7] Mr. Black, the lobbyist for North American, replied that he would put plants in Oklahoma to build parts for Apollo or to provide other types of work and relieve unemployment. Senator Kerr may have been more explicit and more selfish than other Senators for he once said "I represent myself first, the State of Oklahoma second, and the people of the United States third, and don't you forget it."[8]

In implicit bargaining, agreements are arrived at without direct reference to the issues or the terms. Instead, somewhat ambiguous cues are issued by each bargainer in the hope that other bargainers will understand and respond in such a manner that agreement can be reached. Politicians, especially in international politics, must negotiate in this slow, costly, and burdensome way. Lovers frequently do the same. Terms that are seemingly clear to one of the bargainers may not be for the other, and discrepancy causes much misunderstanding and belated efforts at clarification and apology.

But there is an even worse case than implicit bargaining—that of *conjectural* bargaining, in which neither partner is even clear about the terms of settlement. Perhaps this type best characterizes relationships between voters and their representatives. Voters may have only a very general notion of a Presidential candidate's policy commitments. They do not know how he will treat specific issues as they arise. Further, the candidate does not know his supporters' preferences; neither the candidates nor the voters sign contracts stating their expectations.

All these considerations involving processes and payoffs of bargaining are set forth in diagrammatic form in Figure VI–1. Readers are encouraged to offer illustrations of some bargaining situations for each of the nine cells. Compare the following: a Presidential nominating convention; a vote on a bill establishing a new tax; an appropriation for a new public building; negotiation with the North Vietnamese over ending the Vietnam war;

[7] Hugo Young, Bryan Silcock, and Peter Dunn, "Why We Went to the Moon," *The Washington Monthly* 2 (April, 1970), 45.

[8] Young, Silcock, and Dunn, "Why We Went to the Moon," 43.

FIGURE VI–1
Types of Bargaining Situations

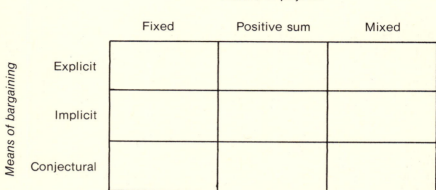

Nature of payoffs

	Fixed	Positive sum	Mixed
Explicit			
Implicit			
Conjectural			

Means of bargaining

President Nixon's decision to invade Cambodia; racial desegregation in a local school system; dress regulations in a local high school. Are these bargaining issues easily typed? When and how can a single issue be converted into another type of bargaining situation? Why should different voters and politicians want to treat the same events in different ways; for example, why might one politician wish racial integration to be accorded a zero-sum status while another would like it to be converted into a positive situation?

EXPLICIT BARGAINS: SOME ILLUSTRATIONS

Explicit bargaining is less prevalent in politics than in the economic system but it is not unknown. Professional politicians have left some rather clear records of bargaining outcomes if not always of the actual bargaining sessions. Our Constitution is a first-rate example of a fundamental set of rules that were bargained over by highly rational men. Many of its major provisions are the compromises of the founding fathers making mutually beneficial exchanges. The Bill of Rights, for example, was appended to the Constitution in exchange for support on its passage.

The federal structure of our government was itself a product of negotiation and compromise. The bicameral nature of our legislative bodies was another bargained agreement. Two of the most famous bargains in American history—the Missouri Compromise of 1820 and the Compromise of 1877—are now remembered chiefly because they were achieved at the expense of a third party, the Negro.

In the former, the issue of slavery was temporarily "resolved" by an agreement between the North and the South that permitted slavery south of the line 36°30′ across the Louisiana Territory but not north of that line. The compromise was intended to maintain equal power between northern and southern states and thus give each a veto power over the other. This bargain governed regional relationships until 1850, when new territories gained after the Mexican War posed a problem for which the old compromise did not have an answer. As the Missouri Compromise became outmoded, the possibilities for conflict increased and tensions culminated in the Civil War.

The Compromise of 1877 ended reconstruction and its hard-line policies. Whites in the South were allowed to reestablish white supremacy in exchange for their support of the reestablished Union and the Republican Party. Whites gained control of any possible claims of labor, western agrarians, and reformers who might have posed a threat to the capitalists and the Republican Party. The Republican Party and Southern Democrats have managed to maintain a fairly effective coalition on the basis of that bargain to this day.

The Etiquette of Bargaining

Bargainers chiefly aim to advance their own interests, but if they do not use means that others feel are legitimate and appropriate, the outcome itself will be viewed as illegitimate. This is especially true in state legislatures and the Congress. Etiquette or norms of fair play are honored among politicians far more often than they are ignored or violated. Honoring rules is itself a resource in bargaining; the bargainer who acquires a reputation for being fair and upholding rules even when they may reduce his payoffs is viewed as highly honorable and dependable.

What are these rules? First, they are informal. The rules are rarely written down and certainly are not enacted into laws; rather they are the gradual accumulation of customary ways of bargaining. Politicians learn them as one learns the rules of etiquette in private life. Since they are informal they may be misunderstood; amateurs, especially, will be prone to inadvertent violations. Some of the more general rules among politicians include:

1. A politician does not threaten the use of violence.
2. A politician keeps his word.
3. A politician shows a willingness to compromise.
4. A politician shares in the workload.
5. A politician respects his elders.
6. A politician honors his office.

More specialized etiquette develops around each type of office and particularly around legislatures. Because legislators engage in collective choice they must have means of regulating and minimizing public acrimony and personal hostilities that are likely to arise on a continuing basis. Most legislators are fully aware of the norms of good political behavior. In addition to the above, which seem to apply to all politicians, the following norms have great significance among legislators.

1. Respect the rights of other members.
2. Remain impersonal in debate.
3. Retain self-restraint in debate.
4. Observe common courtesies.
5. Keep aims open and explicit.
6. Give advance notice of a changed stand.
7. Never campaign against a colleague in his district.
8. Be graceful in defeat.
9. Serve one's apprenticeship.

These legislative norms were found by scholars in at least four state legislatures along with about thirty other norms of good behavior.[9] Not all are equally important nor as important in one legislature as another.

Still more specialized obligations can arise around the committees of Congress, for example. Richard Fenno has written about some norms observed by members of the House Appropriations Committee.[10] According to Fenno some four obligations are viewed as paramount by the membership:

1. Protect the "Power of the Purse" (Congressional control over appropriations).
2. Guard the federal Treasury.

[9] John C. Wahlke, Heinz Eulau, William Buchanan, and LeRoy C. Ferguson, *The Legislative System* (New York: John Wiley & Sons, Inc., 1962), Chapter 7.
[10] Richard Fenno, *The Power of the Purse* (Boston: Little, Brown, & Co., 1966), pp. 95–112.

3. Reduce budget estimates.
4. Serve member constituency interests.

Committeemen who violate these norms have their bargaining power reduced commensurate to the extent to which they violate expectations. A beginner may be permitted a few lapses as he learns; one is forgiven lapses when he is put into an especially difficult position of survival as a politician; but in all other cases one is expected to conform. This pattern should not be too surprising; almost all people comply in organizations they belong to. Conformity is one of the costs we pay for civilization.

Impact of Formal Institutions on Bargaining

Politicians must conduct their bargaining activities within the context of highly legalized or formalized institutions as well as in accordance with the informal rules of etiquette. A politician who sets out to achieve a goal soon learns how incredibly complex the formal structure of our political system is. With our 90,000 governments, 521,000 elective officials, and hundreds of thousands of officials in the bureaucracies a politician cannot expect that achievement of goals will be rapid, inexpensive, and certain. While no politician will have to weave his way through all ninety thousand official governments he will probably have to confront some officials at all three levels, since most activities are shared and not independent. He will also have to deal with other politicians in at least three of the four branches of government: judicial, executive, legislative, and independent regulatory agencies. This process is called "touching bases" or "making the rounds." It obviously involves talking to a great number of officials, private citizens, and groups. The costs in terms of time and energy are apt to be considerable. Demands on his patience will increase as he learns of inevitable delays, unforeseen obstacles, routine "red tape" frustrations, and the obstinacy of opponents.

Each bargainer soon learns that other bargainers have resources based on their constitutional powers and prerogatives, laws and regulations, terms of office, and the resources of their allies. Few politicians are able to run roughshod over many other politicians, because each is able to exercise some degree of veto power. Each can threaten, to some extent, and each can demand a price for his agreements that requires others to settle for less.

We can gain a pretty good picture of what all this means by

TABLE VI–4

Presidential Boxscores: 1954–68

President,	Year	Proposals submitted	Approved by congress	Percent approved
Eisenhower,	1954	232	150	65%
	1955	207	96	46
	1956	225	103	46
	1957	206	76	37
	1958	234	110	47
	1959	228	93	41
	1960	183	56	31
Kennedy,	1961	355	172	48
	1962	298	133	45
Kennedy- Johnson,	1963	401	109	27
Johnson,	1964	217	125	58
	1965	469	323	69
	1966	371	207	56
	1967	431	205	48
	1968	414	231	56

Source: *Congressional Quarterly Almanac, 1968* 24 (Washington, D.C.: Congressional Quarterly Service, 1968), p. 97.

looking at the situation in Congress. Textbooks typically and correctly emphasize that a bill must go through something like 18 formal steps to be enacted into law. No wonder, then, that less than one-twentieth of the bills introduced (20,000 to 26,000 per session) ever win acceptance by the Congress.[11] And, a President cannot realistically expect to see more than 50 percent of his bills successfully passed by Congress. Even those that pass are apt to be considerably revised and amended. See Table VI–4 for boxscores (successes and failures) of some recent Presidents. In only 5 of the 15 years reported has the President scored more than 50 percent.

Congress presents a labyrinth to the bargainer, with 47 committees and 538 pages of intricate parliamentary rules for conducting its business. The House has some 20 permanent or standing committees while the Senate has 16, and the two houses have 11 joint committees—each of these committees has a large number of subcommittees. In the 1960s there were more than 250 subcommittees. Each member had to serve on as many as two major

[11] Of the 26,460 measures introduced in the 90th Congress (1967–68) only 1,002 were enacted, and only 640 of them were public measures; the rest were private. See *Statistical Abstract of the United States: 1969*, p. 368.

committees and a half-dozen subcommittees. Each committee, in turn, has its own administrative staff consisting of both majority and minority representatives.

Consider yourself, then, in the role of Congressman. You must deal with or take into account some 534 other members, each jealously guarding his own prerogatives and the interests of his constituency. You must deal daily with a large number of committees, their staffs, the leadership of the Congress, constituents, lobbyists, bureaucrats, and sometimes the President. You will be faced with thousands of proposals, although you will not vote on all of them. Caught between the pressures, demands, and preferences of party colleagues, the opposition, the Administration, hundreds of lobbies, and hundreds of thousands of constituents, you will be expected to arrive at profitable bargains within a maze of intricate parliamentary rules. In this maze you are expected to keep track of and/or create bargaining possibilities with other members, and to know with whom you can make exchanges on which issues and at what costs. Your little accounting book of deals will be far more complex than any conventional business budget of assets and obligations.

Simply being informed about so many complicated facets of legislative life is demanding and costly. One must know issues, persons, parliamentary rules, and preferences of hometown voters before he can even begin to act like an intelligent bargainer. As a result of these inordinate demands the wise legislator soon learns to specialize in issues and problems pertinent to his district and rely on the advice of leaders about the unknown.

Suggested Readings

Banfield, Edward C. *Political Influence* (New York: The Free Press, 1961).

Blau, Peter. *Power and Exchange in Social Life* (New York: John Wiley & Sons, 1964).

Curry, Robert L., Jr., and Wade, L. L. *A Theory of Political Exchange* (Englewood Cliffs, N.J.: Prentice-Hall, Inc., 1968).

Dahl, Robert A. and Lindblom, Charles E. *Politics, Economics, and Welfare* (New York: Harper & Brothers, 1953).

Domhoff, G. William. *Who Rules America?* (Englewood Cliffs, N.J.: Prentice-Hall, Inc., 1967).

Gergen, Kenneth J. *The Psychology of Behavior Exchange* (Reading, Pa.: Addison-Wesley Publishing Co., 1969).

Hilsman, Roger. *To Move a Nation* (New York: Doubleday & Co., Inc., 1967).

Homans, George C. *Social Behavior* (New York: Harcourt, Brace & World, 1961).

Hoopes, Townsend. *The Limits of Intervention* (New York: David McKay Co., Inc., 1969).

Hunter, Floyd. *Community Power Structure* (Chapel Hill: University of North Carolina Press, 1953).

————. *Top Leadership, USA* (Chapel Hill: University of North Carolina Press, 1957).

Ilchman, Warren F. and Uphoff, Norman T. *The Political Economy of Change* (Berkeley: The University of California Press, 1969).

Kessel, John H. *The Goldwater Coalition* (Indianapolis: The Bobbs-Merrill Co., Inc., 1968).

Kuhn, Alfred. *The Study of Society* (Homewood, Ill.: Richard D. Irwin, Inc. and The Dorsey Press, Inc., 1963).

Mills, C. Wright. *The Power Elite* (New York: Oxford University Press, 1957).

Neustadt, Richard E. *Presidential Power* (New York: John Wiley & Sons, Inc., 1960).

Sayre, Wallace S. and Kaufman, Herbert. *Governing New York City* (New York: W. W. Norton & Co., Inc., 1960).

Schilling, Warner, Hammond, Paul Y., and Snyder, Glenn H. *Strategy, Politics, and Defense Budgets* (New York: Columbia University Press, 1962).

Scott, Andrew M. *Competition in American Politics* (New York: Holt, Rinehart & Winston, Inc., 1970).

Zeigler, Harmon. *Interest Groups in American Society* (Englewood Cliffs, N.J.: Prentice-Hall, Inc., 1964).

Chapter VII

HOW POLICY IS MADE: PHASES AND PAYOFFS

We have considered various aspects or slants on the bargaining situation of the politicians without having touched on the actual processes. We cannot ignore this dynamic element much longer. This chapter will begin with a description of the actual phases of bargaining and conclude with some comments on the payoffs.

Four Phases of Bargaining

Once an issue arises, politicians and other leaders begin the long and tiring process of trying to achieve a mutually acceptable agreement or settlement. That settlement may only be a phase or episode in a longer and wider range of bargaining over many issues. Within its own confines, however, we can detect a variety of quite different activities taking place through time. This bargaining process has four distinct phases: discovering the bargainable, finding areas of agreement, critical bargaining, and presenting results to the public.

DISCOVERING THE BARGAINABLE

In the first phase the parties discover the bargainable issues. At the outset, neither party really knows what the other wants or is fully prepared to trade or exchange. Much of this stage is public ritual, but another, more private, aspect is establishment of actual bargainable objects and definition of the range of disagreement and possible avenues of agreement. Bargainers express hopes for successful negotiations but also issue dramatic claims and counterclaims. A tough stance is an integral element of the ritual.

FINDING AREAS OF AGREEMENT

This second phase comes into being when politicians get down to the "nitty gritty" and hard bargaining begins. These bargaining probes are made easier whenever the objects of bargaining are quantifiable and do not involve basic moral or ethical commitments. It is easier to arrange acceptable compromises when men contend over the number of miles of highways to be built, the rate of an income tax, or the number of persons to be included under social security than it is to set conditions for interracial relationships or loyalty to the nation. Bargainers will attempt a great variety of tactics to ferret out hard and soft positions on both symbolic and material payoffs. They may test sincerity by threatening to walk out or make secret proposals. (President-Elect Nixon used this tactic with the North Vietnamese in 1968.) A bargainer may send somewhat concealed messages to the other side through third parties, as in the implicit bargaining we discussed in the previous chapter. A bargainer may even leave a conference in order to test the other side. Depending on the situation, use of these probing tactics may make conditions worse, but since that isn't known at the outset, they are always tried. That is the nature of bargaining, and only experience can teach men these skills.

CRITICAL BARGAINING

When this third phase begins, bargaining can break down or proceed to a successful conclusion. In the critical phase, actual proposals and counterproposals are offered. By judging reactions, each side learns whether the other(s) will continue to offer concessions. Each side must be careful to offer enough, but not too much. Mutual concessions must be made. Once a concession is offered it can rarely be retracted; each negotiator must live with his proposals. This is the critical period because actual concessions are offered and considered. If an agreement is reached a fourth phase begins in which a wider public is informed.

PUBLIC PRESENTATION OF RESULTS

Not all political bargaining situations entail public presentation of the results, but in a nation that values publicity, many do. Woodrow Wilson expressed the nation's feelings when he said he favored "open covenants openly arrived at." While some bargaining is done publicly, usually only the final agreements are made public. Congressional committees frequently meet in "executive session," at which only the members may be present along with whomever they invite—usually an Administration witness. The news media are barred.

When results are final the followings of the bargainers must be convinced that a good bargain was struck—a difficult task since the inevitable compromises and concessions may disappoint the followings on one or both sides.

The bargainer must satisfy his more vehement and vocal supporters that he did well in the bargaining. Our foreign emissaries, especially, are expected to get the best of all bargains. President Eisenhower had to convince the Rightists of his party that he did not lose or sell out in ending the Korean conflict. President Nixon, had, has, or will have the same dilemma in ending the Vietnam war. Local politicians, to a lesser extent, must also show how much they benefitted the local community. Public presentation of results is an important phase because it may contain the seeds for future breakdown or success of the bargain.

Strategic Considerations in Bargaining

In a previous section we stressed the cooperative aspect of bargaining by describing the etiquette of participation. While bargaining is cooperative in the sense that an agreement is sought, we cannot ignore the equally strong desire on the part of each bargainer to get as large a share of the payoff as possible. This is the competitive element, the strategic nexus. Emphasis is on how to gain larger shares. In this section a variety of actual bargaining situations in recent history are described. The first two cases concern two Presidents; a third deals with Supreme Court Justices; a fourth with the strategies of budget officers in Illinois; a fifth with mayors and city councils in large cities. In addition, examples show national and international compromises. The illustrations may seem offensive because they smack of self-interest and are not in accord with civics book ideals for our leaders.

A PRESIDENT BARGAINS

Because our Presidents are not dictators, they too must bargain with other politicians in order to accomplish their programs and honor pledges made during campaigns. President Nixon found himself in a somewhat weak bargaining position when he first came into office in 1968 without a majority vote and confronted by a Democratic Congress. He played his role with considerable care and caution until he had a stronger base among the American people. He bargained with skill, as this example indicates.[1]

In 1970 Senator Jackson (Washington Democrat and "hawk" on defense), preparing for reelection, found himself opposed by the peace wing of the Democratic Party. Because Jackson feared a major primary election challenge he felt he had to blunt the attack as much as possible. So he requested President Nixon to hold back the expansion of the ABM system as much as possible and especially to delay the construction of an ABM site in his own state.

This request was unusual since Jackson was a strong supporter of military demands and of Nixon's defense policies. Jackson was attempting to develop a middle-of-the-road position to cut the ground out from under his peace opponents. Nixon readily agreed to accommodate Jackson's request, although defense measures would be temporarily set back. He agreed to delay construction activities on the ABM because he feared that if Jackson were defeated it would be a major defeat for a powerful Democratic supporter on defense. It might also, he feared, be interpreted as a weakness of the Administration and would encourage other peace candidates. Jackson was able to unify and stimulate his supporters to greater efforts by employing the threat of opposition.

A PRESIDENT SOMETIMES MISCALCULATES

In our previous case the success of the calculation of strategic advantage was not known at the time of writing. In the present case, the outcomes are history. This case involves a series of Presidential miscalculations rather than astute maneuvering. Although the President eventually achieved his goal, it took far more time,

[1] The case is based on A. Robert Smith, "Jackson Modifies ABM Stand to Mollify Fellow Democrats," *The Oregonian*, March 4, 1970, 24.

and required far more bargaining costs than it would have had he made better calculations. Even worse, the year-long delay in achieving his ends led to bad economic consequences for the American people. Because many discussions of political bargaining leave an impression of continuously clever strategic reasoning and invariable success, it is essential that the possibilities of failure, costliness, and miscalculation be emphasized.

President Johnson, in 1968, pressed for a "surtax"; that is, a 10 percent tax on regular income tax liabilities.[2] He defended his tax proposal with a series of complicated economic arguments intended to show how it could halt inflation. The public could not understand the complicated economic theory of inflation. To compound his error he simultaneously campaigned for additional "Great Society" measures that would entail much greater federal expenditures. For ten months the President resisted efforts to cut his federal spending proposals or to strategically tie them to his surtax.

Some commentators have argued that he should have termed the tax a "war tax" and defended it as providing necessary revenue to conduct the Vietnam war. Congressman Wilbur Mills, Chairman of the Ways and Means Committee, who held up the surtax measure for almost a year, hinted at a press conference that if Johnson would label the bill a "war tax" it could go through Congress easily.

Still another miscalculation of the President was labelling the bill a "ten percent surtax" instead of a one percent tax on income. Although the dollar amounts would be the same for each taxpayer, the ten percent figure sounded ten times as bad as the one percent figure. Once this mistake was made there was no way of rectifying it.

President Johnson was finally able to get his bill through Congress by promising a $6 billion reduction in expenditures. This promise required him to mobilize a vast lobbying effort on the part of big business. At the same time Johnson lost substantial political gains. Not only did he have to give up $6 billion of his Great Society programs but the anti-inflationary effect of the surtax had been substantially vitiated because of the delay. Why President Johnson made these miscalculations may never be en-

---

[2] This case is based on an account provided in "Lobbying by Business Leaders Key to Passage," in *Congressional Quarterly Almanac* 24 (Washington, D.C.: Congressional Quarterly Service, 1968), p. 275.

tirely clear, but the case does suggest that even astute and experienced politicians make stupendous errors.

BARGAINING AMONG SUPREME COURT JUSTICES

Some readers may be shocked to learn that Supreme Court Justices bargain with one another over some of the most important public policies. How they bargain is something of a mystery because their sessions are private, but their public papers often reveal important insights. In any case, bargaining among such a small, exclusive, high-status, highly trained, and intelligent group of men over highly contentious issues must provide some fascinating material for study. Walter Murphy, a distinguished student of the Supreme Court, has made our task considerably easier with his book on judicial strategy.[3] We make liberal use of it.

Justices behave in a rarefied and demanding legal and political universe; their traditions are long and powerful, public opinion is ever present, and their work is endlessly scrutinized by legal demons—the lawyers. To add pressure, the problems they deal with are often highly emotional and important to the litigants and others affected by their decisions. Supreme Court Justices apparently do not bargain in the more exposed and sometimes crass manner of elected officials and bureaucrats. Most of their bargaining takes place not only in private quarters, but through the indirect means of writing legal opinions, briefs, memos, and the like. Since longevity on the Court can be considerable, a justice is likely to get to know his colleagues very well. This familiarity has advantages but also poses some severe constraints on negotiation.

Apparently the justices do not bargain explicitly, in the sense of Congressional logrolling over their votes and positions, but they do attempt to influence the choice of cases to be considered, the language to be employed in decisions, allocation of workloads, and decisions. Leadership is vital in all these matters because nine men cannot resolve disputes in an anarchic manner. In some instances some of the justices actually have intense personal dislikes for certain colleagues, and these must be moderated. Normally the Chief Justice plays a powerful leadership role in the activities of the Court; he tends to be the chief bargainer in arranging the ultimate outcomes of the most significant cases.

[3] *Elements of Judicial Strategy* (Chicago: University of Chicago Press, 1964).

Unlike the Supreme Court, most bargaining in the criminal and civil courts is a highly explicit and very pervasive activity. Lawyers, judges, prosecutors, and litigants engage in a great deal of pretrial negotiation over the charges to be levied, timing of the trial if there is to be one, members of the jury, and actual terms of the settlement whether in or out of court. Of course, an accused person may bargain to turn state's witness in exchange for a shorter sentence; such agreements are commonplace. In most civil cases the objective is to settle the suit out of court. In divorce cases, for example, estranged husbands and wives bargain through their lawyers over the disposition of property, children, visiting rights, and alimony payments.

STRATEGIES IN A STATE BUDGETARY PROCESS

In a unique and illuminating study of public expenditure in the state of Illinois, Thomas J. Anton detected and elaborated upon a set of "rules" or strategies wise budget officers follow in dealing with the state legislature.[4] We cannot know how legislators would respond to public knowledge of these rules, but experienced politicians presumably are fully aware of them and play complementary roles. These are the rules Anton has identified for the strategy-minded budget official:

1. Spend the entire appropriation and, if possible, a little bit more.

2. Avoid any sudden increase or decrease in expenditure.

3. Avoid requests for sums smaller than the current appropriations.

4. Put as much as possible of a new request into the basic budget.

5. When increases are desired, make them appear as small as possible, and show that they grow out of existing operations.

6. Give the Budgetary Commission something to cut.

These rules suggest that the budget officer has a good understanding of voter demands on the legislators. Accordingly, budget men attempt to protect their own budgets by enabling legislators (the Budgetary Commission) to achieve some of their ends. In

[4] *The Politics of State Expenditure in Illinois* (Urbana: University of Illinois Press, 1966). The strategy presented above is on pages 49–53.

addition, careful rationalizations of proposed expenditures serve to convince not only the politician, but also his supporters, of the need for the expenditures.

BIG-CITY BUDGETS AND BARGAINING BEHAVIOR

Many students of American governmental behavior have advocated that administrators allocate resources in the most efficient way. Most students of actual policy making and policy makers have concluded that real processes of choice diverge sharply from the so-called ideal. In short, policy makers typically act as though they were only partially informed about alternatives, unsure about goals or priorities, and more eager to reduce conflict and complaints than to attain optimal resource allocations. One observer,[5] after extensive studies of decision making in Pittsburgh, Cleveland, and Detroit, concluded that department heads (police, fire, parks, and the like) view budget making as a means by which:

1. Their department is assured of funds to carry on existing programs;
2. Their program is made acceptable to the mayor's office; and
3. They receive a reasonable share of any increases in the total budget so that new problems may be met.

The mayor, on the other hand, worries:

1. Whether the budget will be balanced;
2. Whether existing levels of services can be maintained;
3. Whether wage increases to employees will be possible; and
4. How tax increases can be avoided, especially property taxes.

The city councils have other responsibilities and are subject to different demands. Their view of the budget is conditioned by these considerations:

1. They hear only of demands to increase appropriations;
2. They see the budget (usually) after it has already been prepared in detail by the mayor and his administration;

[5] John P. Crecine, *Governmental Problem-Solving* (Chicago: Rand McNally & Co., 1969), pp. 38–40.

3. They have fewer informational sources than the mayor and department heads.

Accordingly, council members tend to treat budgets as a matter of compromising the mayor's requests with departmental requests, which are usually higher. More often than not they find the mayor's view more acceptable, especially if the mayor is of the same party as the majority of the council. The budget is an end product of incessant negotiation among administrators, politicians, and, spokesmen for the more powerful interest groups. Their divergent perspectives ensure competition over the allocation of scarce resources and the need for mutual accommodation.

If the mayor's budget is balanced his budget reviewers do not scrutinize any departmental budget. If, however, the budget promises to contain a large deficit, they seek ways to trim costs. In the search for economies not everyone is cut equally. Budget cuts, according to Crecine, occur in about the following order:[6]

1. Maintenance;
2. Equipment;
3. Operating expenses, supplies, and materials;
4. Nonadministrative salaries and wages; and
5. Administrative salaries.

Each of the above compromises illustrates a type of solution: a cut here; an increase there; a delay in application; an exemption from control; a voice in administration.

CONGRESSIONAL COMPROMISES IN THE TAX REFORM ACT OF 1969

Although our several case studies have illustrated a number of crucial aspects of political bargaining they have not detailed the compromised outcomes as well as they might or as well as they ought to if we are to appreciate the extraordinary and intricate negotiations that take place. Perhaps that has been impossible given the cases. Our present case, however, is well chosen to illustrate the web of compromises. It deals with a money matter (taxes) and with the job of compromising differences that is delegated to Congressional Conference Committees whenever the

[6] Crecine, *Governmental Problem Solving*, pp. 38–40.

House and Senate find themselves in disagreement. Taxes readily lend themselves to compromises because they are quantitative.

We need not detail the history of the Tax Reform Act of 1969; suffice it to say that Congress rather than the President initiated the measure, that it was the single greatest tax reform in our history, and that it passed on December 22, 1969 over the threat of a veto.[7] Perhaps the latter was never really credible given the favorable votes of 381–2 in the House and 71–6 in the Senate. Tax reforms worth about $6.6 billion were coupled with cuts of $9.1 billion. Since the House version of the measure was different from that of the Senate it was necessary for the two houses to come to some agreement and to provide a version that was acceptable to the President. The Conference Committee worked with a representative of the Treasury Department and the President to hammer out a series of compromises acceptable to all parties. The committee began on December 19 and completed its work after a 17-hour bargaining session that ended at 3 A.M.

The major compromises of the conferees were as follows:

1. Dropped the House's across-the-board income tax rate cuts and agreed to a compromise three-stage increase to $750 in the personal exemption.

2. Accepted the Senate's 15-percent increase in basic Social Security benefits.

3. Agreed to a 22 percent rate for the oil and gas depletion allowance (House: 20 percent; Senate: 23 percent).

4. Accepted a modified version of the House's increase in the $1,000 maximum standard deduction. Conferees agreed to the House figures for the increased allowance but stretched it out to a three-year timetable instead of making it immediate.

5. Dropped the Senate's plan for tax credits for college tuition expenses.

6. Agreed to the Senate's plan for a 10-percent minimum tax on sheltered income instead of the House's limit on tax preferences.

7. Agreed to the Senate provision eliminating interest from tax-exempt municipal bonds from the sheltered income subject to the minimum tax. Also agreed to Senate action dropping the

[7] Taken from a complete account in "Tax Reform: Congress Initiates Action on Tax Cuts, Changes," *Congressional Quarterly Guide to Current American Government, Spring, 1970* (Washington, D.C.: Congressional Quarterly Service, 1970), pp. 35–37.

House provision for a subsidy to encourage localities to issue taxable bonds.

8. Accepted the Senate provision retaining the six-month holding period for an asset to qualify as a capital gain; cut the Senate ceiling of $85,000 on the amount of gains that could qualify for the 25 percent rate, however, to $50,000.

9. Agreed to a 4 percent tax on foundation income—a compromise between the House rate of 7½ percent and the Senate's minimal "auditing" tax.[8]

Note the nature of the compromises: in five instances the Senate's position was adopted while in no cases was the House variation completely accepted. However, the Senate's position on a number of matters was considerably modified in the direction of the House and in a few instances, as with the oil and gas depletion allowances, a numerical compromise was worked out. Although the Senate appears to have done better than the House, that conclusion can't be drawn; House conferees may have won on issues that were of greatest concern while giving up lesser positions. This kind of compromising is daily fare in all our legislative assemblies from local councils to the Congress.

BARGAINING AMONG NATIONS

Bargaining with other nation-states continuously occurs. It tends to be more explicit than it is within our governments and perhaps more widely approved. Although the United States is one of the most powerful nations, we are not always able to dictate international decisions. For one thing, our government does not always wish to do so. When it does, our actions may not be appropriate or our resources sufficient to bargain successfully. We must bargain and be satisfied to achieve less than some of us would like.

Instances of international bargaining are so numerous it is difficult to select one for illustration. One instance, however, should be used because all the elements of bargaining are present and the basic exchanges are explicit. The case involved Afghanistan, China, the USSR, West Germany, and the United States during 1967.[9] The United States was vying with the Communist

[8] *CQ Guide to Current American Government, Spring, 1970*, p. 37.
[9] Based on an account by Robert Keatley, "Cold War Payoff, Afghanistan Benefits as U.S., Soviet Union, Red China Vie in Aid," *The Wall Street Journal*, April 19, 1967, 1.

nations for certain benefits Afghanistan could provide. In addition, the two Communist nations were competing with one another. So, through a complex set of international exchanges, Afghanistan was able to play off other nations to her own benefit. At the same time, each of the other nations received something in return. Figure VII–1 shows these exchanges in a diagram. The Afghans appear to have achieved more than any of the others since they occupied a superior strategic position during a particularly anxious period of the cold war. Obviously, small nations can exploit powerful nations under certain conditions. They can at least derive very favorable bargains. Individual politicians can also take advantage of similar conditions when their votes or support are crucial among other competing politicians. The hold-out

FIGURE VII–1

Some International Exchanges, 1967

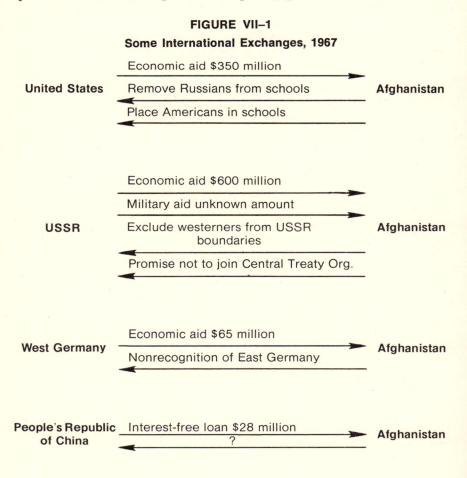

vote in crucial legislative struggles and nominating conventions has a very high marginal utility.

The fact that bargains are consummated does not, of course, mean that they are good bargains, or that all parties are satisfied. For example, did the United States make a good deal in paying Afghanistan $350 million to replace a few Russian teachers with Americans? How did our negotiators arrive at that particular evaluation? Should it be continued? At the same exchange rate? How much are we paying per teacher? Has the exchange rate paid off for each of the nations that made agreements with Afghanistan? Note the nature of the objects exchanged by the five nations: Afghanistan traded off something she had control of—political opportunities—for something she had little of but other countries had more of—economic aid. This is as expected, for the theory of exchange tells us that men exchange that which they have in surplus for that which they want but lack. Each of these nations acted on this premise but whether they could have struck better or more rewarding terms remains unknown.

Why Are Some Bargainers More Successful Than Others?

Of all the questions that intrigue political scientists this one is the most difficult to answer. We will advance a few answers that have been offered and criticize them with equal intensity. The approach we use in this section views public choice as primarily a product of accommodation among individuals and groups who have varying levels of interest in various issues, possess or command varying amounts of differing resources, contest under a set of rules, and interact through various forms of competition, conflict, and cooperation to arrive at public policies which please some and displease others.

THE IMPORTANCE OF BARGAINING RESOURCES

It is perfectly clear that one cannot get very far in the complex web of political bargaining unless he has some "clout" or capacity to drive a better bargain. All are not equal in ability to influence the public policies of communities, states, and national government because each enters the arena with widely varying amounts of the appropriate means with which to influence others. The resources are, for the most part, apparent. For example, it is

TABLE VII–1

Bargaining Resources of Politicians and Interest Groups

Resources	Pres-ident	AFL-CIO	AMA	Sierra Club	American Legion	Communist Party
Social Status	1					6
Votes						
Money						
Group cohesion						1
Group support						
Leadership skills						
Information						
Status of demands						
Incentives						
Command over services						
Authority	1					6

very useful and reassuring if one can have some of each of the resources listed in Table VII–1. It is even more reassuring if one's opposition has fewer, less important capabilities. In Table VII–1 the resources groups need for bargaining are listed in column 1. We've ranked, on a scale of 1–6, some resources of several major individuals and groups. How would you fill in the blanks? How would you rank SDS? The Weathermen? Black Panthers?

These commonly-mentioned assets are not all easily measured although rough estimates are sometimes possible. Conceivably one could even provide an overall "score" for each actor and on the basis of that score predict how well he would do in competition under certain conditions involving various issues. The importance of weighing one group's capabilities against others in specific policy situations cannot be overestimated, since few bargainers can expect to deploy their resources without active opposition. Note, too, the possibilities for coalition formation whenever resources are distributed unequally. Needless to say the group with lesser means may seek alliances with others in order to compensate. The politician or group that can readily and effectively mobilize the greatest amount of these various resources will do better than its opponents.

Most people do not command very much of any one resource, but a few people do have a great deal of all. A President is perhaps the most powerful single individual in the nation because he can command substantial "quantities" of each. Some Senators and Congressmen can also score very highly. Many private individuals and organizations can mobilize vast resources with effectiveness but not on a great variety of issues. Because of this they specialize and economize in order to achieve their most crucial preferences.

The fact that a group can mobilize an impressive array of resources does not always mean they will employ them with a high degree of effectiveness and efficiency. Quite often we learn that unskilled and even skilled bargainers have seriously and disastrously misjudged deployment of their resources—either by an uneconomical overkill or by underemploying them; arriving too late with too little. (Recall the case of President Johnson on pages 138–40.)

Or, they may have used inappropriate resources in a particular situation. For example, bribing officials at the national level is not regarded as ethical; it has, indeed, backfired on a few occasions when it was tried and found out. Also considered unethical is the use of threats or force. Further, it is regarded as wiser, if one wishes to influence policy on nuclear energy, for example, to be advised by experts than by high-status nonexperts. Resources in and of themselves are not always decisive; the skill of a bargainer lies in his good sense—knowing when, how, and how much of them to mobilize, depending on the opportunity, the goals, and resources of one's opponents, circumstances of the issues, and one's own goals. What we mean by good sense is precisely that— having the "right feel"—for no scientific advice is available to handle all contingencies.

A person without command over something another person(s) wants is in a weak position to bargain. An attractive girl has more to bargain with than a less attractive one; a man who has a vote is more valuable than one who does not. A state having a surplus of water is possibly a valuable exchange partner for a state that has little. And for exchange to take place each potential partner must place a different value on his respective goods and services.

Those who have nothing of value are initially unable to participate in the bargaining process. They can become bargainers by offering to refrain from annoying, disturbing, or otherwise harming the better-off. And this is exactly what many reform and radical groups have done throughout American history. When these groups had nothing else to exchange they "blackmailed" the status quo forces by promising not to disturb them in exchange for whatever they wanted. The method seems to work, although at considerable cost to nearly everyone.

Just as a person cannot bargain without exchangeable goods

so, too, a person is not apt to exchange and bargain without an incentive; that is, the expectation of making or protecting a gain by the transaction. Although politics is important in a general sense it may not provide sufficient incentive to induce direct participation for very many individuals very often. Most of our mundane daily activities can be carried on without giving much systematic thought to the impact of public policy even when that activity or impact is of objective significance. The number of issues that interest an ordinary person are a startlingly low percentage of the total available issues. For example, the 90th Congress (1967–68) "considered" 26,460 bills and resolutions and passed a total of 640 public laws, not more than 5 percent of which could have been of any concern to the average person; that total would be 32 laws.[10] Most likely, most of us become interested in not more than a half-dozen issues. And, still fewer would become sufficiently involved to shift their scarce resources from private to public pursuits. Still, it takes but one or two percent of the citizenry to become interested and actively involved in order to make an issue. Or, perhaps just one person—Ralph Nader.

Becoming involved is, of course, more demanding than simply listening to newscasts and reading newspapers. To become involved in political bargaining necessarily requires the sacrifice of limited resources that could be employed on more promising private activities including recreation, making money, or even doing good for others. Given the limited probabilities of successful endeavor in politics the average citizen is more likely to opt for his private pleasures and advancement. Persons who do not must be regarded as somewhat unusual for they have, in effect, decided that a public goal is more important than private ones, that they can influence the outcomes of their public activities, and that the returns are well worth the costs.

The fact that most men respond the way we have described drastically restricts the number of participants in politics and it focuses the responsibility for bargaining more directly on the professional politicians and the professional leaders of interest groups. They are willing to sustain the costs of action because they expect substantial positive payoffs for themselves and/or their followers. Occasionally, politicians find themselves prepared

---

[10] U.S. Bureau of the Census, *Statistical Abstract of The United States, 1969* (90th ed., Washington, D.C.: U.S. Government Printing Office, 1969), p. 368.

to resign or retire because the cost/benefit ratio is no longer rewarding for them and their families. As we all must make a choice between public and private activity so too we must decide among kinds of public activity.

THE DISTRIBUTION OF BARGAINING ASSETS: INTEREST GROUPS, CIRCA 1970

Review of the successes of various groups in the legislative struggle, in Chapters II to V, shows that while some groups do well on some issues and less well on many other issues, most remain uninterested in most social problems. Business, however, seems to do well all the time whether under a Democratic or Republican administration. On state and local levels it may do even better. One reason for this success is that business is in a position to command large shares of almost all assets whereas some other groups, including labor, have notable shares of a few resources but insignificant amounts of many others. And some groups may even suffer from negative status; the Communist Party is one such organization. The KKK, Black Panthers, SDS, and the Weathermen are others with low and even negative status among a wide segment of the population. Business, of course, has money and uses it (Table VI–2 shows it spends more than any other group and more than several other groups combined). Business also has a high level of social status in America, while that status has occasionally dipped, it has rarely stayed low for very long. Polls have shown that labor has a much lower status, despite the fact that there are more wage laborers than any other single group or occupation.[11] Business is also the most thoroughly organized sector of the society. Virtually all of the more than 11 million business firms are members of at least one of the 16,000 business organizations. In 1968 business lobbies in Washington outnumbered all others with 152 of 259 registered organizations.[12] Most of their memberships are overlapping and mutually rein-

[11] In a poll conducted in 1950 in the State of Washington the AFL was accorded a minus 7 score while the CP "earned" a minus 61 from the citizenry as sources of influence over their political choices. Of 13 organizations included in the list the American Legion and Veterans of Foreign Wars scored highest with plus 77 scores. See Howard E. Freeman and Morris Showel, "Differential Political Influence of Voluntary Associations," *Public Opinion Quarterly*, 55 (1951–52), 703–14.

[12] *Congressional Quarterly Almanac* 24, p. 891.

forcing; that is, they do not compete or conflict on basic values, beliefs, and public policies. Some businesses are in conflict about specific pieces of legislation and laws; for example, the trucking and railroad industries. Given the legislative successes of business groups it would be surprising if they had not acquired considerable bargaining skill, a high sense of efficacy in politics, and a great deal of politically relevant information. All these resources —money, status, authority, skill, and information—tend to accumulate and reinforce each other. Accordingly, business has become a powerhouse.

Business is not the only powerhouse in Washington, nor at the state capitals and local court houses. There are 515 national agricultural organizations that have managed to acquire the largest dollar share of federal subsidies, although they comprise less than 9 percent of the population.[13] The farming industry typically does not spend as much on politics as labor or business does, but its other resources make up for any fiscal deficiencies. Among these major assets are formal positions of authority, in state legislatures and in Congress. Our legislative system of representation has long favored rural areas, thus guaranteeing farmers more than their proportional weight in these bodies. In addition, the seniority criterion used in allotting positions of power enables rural representatives to become committee chairmen in much greater numbers than would be expected. This power is less important today than formerly, but is still a highly useful resource. Farm spokesmen have successfully used some powerful traditional cultural themes to justify their demands. This has been important as agricultural populations have decreased. Past successes add up to another advantage. It is important to remember that once a subsidy has been written into law it becomes extremely difficult to remove or even reduce. So agricultural subsidies have, in fact, increased substantially over the past three decades, along with various other benefits.

Another highly favored group, the veterans, have done well for several reasons. They constitute a substantial part of the population (26 million), are highly organized, have powerful al-

---

[13] Charles O. Jones, "Representation in Congress: The Case of the House Agriculture Committee," *American Political Science Review*, 55 (June, 1961), 358–67 and Theodore Lowi, "How the Farmers Get What They Want," *The Reporter*, 30 (May 21, 1964), 34–37. Both articles are reprinted in James E. Anderson, *Politics and Economic Policy-Making: Selected Readings* (Reading, Pa.: Addison-Wesley Publishing Company, 1970), pp. 292–320.

lies in the Defense Department, can lay claim to having served their nation in time of need, have many well-placed members in government, and pursue well-defined interests that are thoroughly understood by the membership. Their many successes are to be expected.

In contrast, countless organizations receive very little in the way of favors or legislation. For example, who ever heard of these interest groups? Bulgarian Claims Committee. Christian Amendment Association. Committee for Time Uniformity. Research to Prevent Blindness. The Voice of the People in Action. Single Persons Tax Reform Lobby. Organizations such as these are not well-endowed, they spend little or nothing on lobbying activities, and their failures to influence legislation are apparent. However, they are not the only groups not doing well on a continuing basis in politics; some well-known civic organizations and, until recently, most civil rights groups, rarely have achieved legislative success. Consumer groups have achieved little effective protection for their clients and members despite the fact that all Americans are consumers. The League of Women Voters, although it labors mightily at all levels of politics, is an essentially ineffectual group. Women's organizations in general have been more successful as social than as political organizations, but this situation has begun to change rapidly. Women are becoming more conscious of their essentially minority role in our polity and our national life. Given their numbers, time, energy, and increased motivation to alter their status we can expect considerably more successful activity during the coming decade. The example of civil rights groups is a powerful incentive and a fitting analogy.

Still another group that has gained great impetus during the current growth of interest in population increases, industrialization, and pollution of the environment are the conservationists. As more people have experienced the costs of these formerly unquestioned activities the demand for control has greatly increased across the land. Conservation groups are likely to become more successful as they acquire more of the resources of power. These groups will probably encounter stiff opposition from profit-minded business, labor, and various minority groups who want more and better employment. The struggle between the middle-class conservation movement and an alliance of the poor, workers, and corporations should be an interesting one; high stakes are at issue.

Every group desires control over political assets, but although allocative outcomes are usually in proportion to the degree and balance of resources we must not forget that victories and gains are sometimes the product of nothing more than good luck. Sometimes events get out of hand and leave some people better off and others worse off. The former cannot honestly assume credit nor the latter blame for their failures. Forces beyond our control have indiscriminately aided some and inflicted deprivation on others. For example, Stalin died shortly after President Eisenhower came into office; that convenient but unpredictable and uncontrollable event alone made the President's task an easier one. Less important but equally unexpected events shape our destinies every day, as the histories of Congress and other decision-making bodies demonstrate. Legislation has been expedited or shunted aside because of unforeseen advantages and obstacles. The politician is not well-advised, however, to depend on such fickle assistance.

The Impact of Formal Institutions

Those who have been reading this book with even the slightest care must realize that our formal rules for bargaining and our political institutions—federalism, separation of powers, bicameralism, the electoral college, and so forth—are fundamentally important to our individual political behavior as well as our collective choice. When a person or group enters the political arena he enters a firmly entrenched set of institutions that he must master if he is to achieve his goals and be successful. Our basic institutions are highly stable and have shown an enormous power to survive; they are facts of political life that cannot be minimized as influences over the political process and policies.

We have alluded to a great variety of institutional impacts on our policies and behavior but we have not summarized them in any particular place. It is appropriate to do so here, after having covered policy outcomes and policy-making processes. Such a summary may also serve as an additional link between Parts I and II and Parts III and IV, which offer advice on how to work within our institutions. Table VII–2 presents a summary of some major impacts of our formal structure of government; it is neither an exhaustive nor detailed presentation. Some of its entries are necessarily controversial because identification and measurement of institutional impacts is both costly and uncertain. Most of the claims, as you will see, are simply conventional wisdom as taught by political scientists.

Bargaining Summarized: Processes and Results

These two detailed chapters need a convenient summary. Perhaps that can best be accomplished by simply listing some of the more important or consequential generalizations encountered in previous pages; a political scientist might call such lists "propositional inventories." Whatever the designation the list is as follows:

BARGAINING AS A POLITICAL PROCESS

1. Bargainers seek short-run gains, especially control of public office.

2. Most bargainers are undogmatic most of the time.

3. The chief search is for agreement.

4. Bargainers operate under conditions of considerable uncertainty.

5. Obstruction, evasiveness, and slowness are among the chief costs.

6. Bargainers attempt to avoid deeply divisive and symbolic issues.

7. There is a high probability that any group can make itself heard somewhere in the process or system.

8. There is no guarantee that any group can make itself politically active and its demands legitimate without paying substantial bargaining costs.

9. No group can succeed for long alone; coalitions are essential.

10. Political parties attempt to honor as many promises as circumstances permit.

11. Every group that is strong enough to cause trouble must be satisfied before agreements can be reached.

STRATEGIC IMPLICATIONS

1. The more resources a group has, the greater the likelihood of its success.

2. No single set of resources is crucial in all issues or situations.

TABLE VII–2

Some Expected Impacts of American Political Institutions

Institution	Beneficiaries and expected benefits	Disadvantaged and expected costs	Comments
FEDERALISM	Southern whites Business 1890–1936	Southern blacks Increased decision-making costs	
	Landlords Local options	Higher external costs Policy conflicts or inconsistency	
	Experimentation		
SEPARATION OF POWERS	Minorities	Increased decision costs	
	Status quo groups Lower external costs		
BICAMERALISM (equal representation in Senate)	Wool and cotton farmers Silver producers Small states Reduced external costs	Densely populated states Increased decision costs	
JUDICIAL REVIEW	Business in 19th century Blacks, accused, unions in recent years	Labor in 19th century Liberal reformers 1880–1937	Same rules can be interpreted very differently by different judges.

SENIORITY RULE IN LEGISLATURES	Legislators from safe districts 22 one-party states	Legislators from competitive districts 19 two-party states	
PLURALITY VOTING AND SINGLE-MEMBER DISTRICTS	Minorities Reduced decision costs	Losers in 3-way electoral contests	
EXTRA-MAJORITY RULES AS IN CONSTITUTIONAL AMENDMENT	Status quo groups and policies Prevents special privileges from being inserted in Constitution	Reformers Increased decision costs	
PARTY SYSTEM	Simplified voting choices for voters Moderates conflict	Vague and contradictory policies Increased decision costs Less stable coalitions Similar policies	Our two-party system is really multiparty.
PRESIDENTIAL ROLE	Populous states Two-party states Urban states	Less-populous states Less competitive states Rural states	
CONGRESS	Less populous states Less competitive states Rural states	Populous states Two-party states Urban states	

3. Resource command tends to be cumulative.

4. Proposals that do not greatly alter the status quo are likely to be more successful than those that do.

5. Proposals that demand changes in behavior are apt to win out over those that demand changes in basic beliefs and values.

6. Those who would demand great changes of any kind must generate more resources than those who defend the status quo.

7. Unexpected events have an enormous influence over the best-planned strategies, sometimes aiding and sometimes ruining them.

8. Inflation has a greater appeal to both voters and governments than taxation as a means of financing government.

9. Public goods and services that serve to complement private activity have a greater chance of being chosen than those that compete.

10. Proposals that promise increases in benefits are apt to be more popular than those that decrease taxation.

11. Social Security proposals will find their chief support among lower-income groups while public works projects are supported most by the middle and upper-middle class.

PUBLIC POLICY OUTCOMES

1. Governments tend to satisfy as many demands as possible.

2. New policies are adopted but only with caution or after crises, in which case they may be adopted without much care.

3. Policies are frequently contradictory across policy areas and among governmental agencies and units.

4. Most policies, once enacted, are likely to enjoy widespread legitimacy.

5. The supply of public goods and services tends to be insufficient.

6. Party policies are generally vague and overlapping.

DISTRIBUTIVE OUTCOMES

1. Producer groups and demands tend to be favored over consumer demands.

2. Relatively little redistribution of income has been achieved.

3. Taxation tends to be somewhat progressive while expenditures tend to be regressive.

4. Present consumption of public goods is preferred to deferred consumption; thus, operating budgets have a better chance of enactment than do capital budgets or investment.

5. To the extent that overall redistribution takes place it is from the rich to the poor.

6. Projects that benefit minorities will be awarded disproportionate shares of the budget.

7. No one group gets all it wants, but neither is anyone completely excluded.

An Exercise in Analysis

BARGAINING AND THE COST OF BEAUTY

In 1965, amidst a hail of publicity, Congress passed a Highway Beautification Act. The Act was designed to improve the appearance of the nation's highways by removal of signs, junkyards, and other eyesores within certain prescribed distances. It encouraged scenic enhancement programs, including new plantings. In this major political effort President Johnson's wife was a major force. Such a seemingly innocuous and potentially beneficial plan apparently appealed to nearly everyone; and the favorable vote was overwhelming in the Congress. One would assume, therefore, that the goals would be pursued with vigor and success.

They were not, as *Life Magazine* showed in its survey in 1970.[14] According to this survey, only 875 of the approximately 700,000 signs that were supposed to be eliminated by July of 1970 were torn down. Only 137 of more than 17,500 junkyards have been moved and but 1,518 have been screened.

The Bureau of Public Roads in reporting on the costs of the Act estimated that the removal of the 1.2 million billboards along interstate highways would take three years and about $559 million; the federal share would be $419 million.[15] The cost of screening and relocation of junkyards would cost in excess of $121 million. Scenic enhancement programs would cost the taxpayers anywhere from a minimum of $991 million to possibly as much as

[14] "The Necessary Law Exists. Here is Why It Does Not Work," *Life Magazine*, July 24, 1970, 34.

[15] For a summary of the Bureau's report see "The Cost of Beauty," in *Congress and the Nation, Vol. II* (Washington, D.C.: Congressional Quarterly Service, 1969), 487.

$2 billion. At a minimum, therefore, the total program would require about $1.6 billion.

Some questions for students of political bargaining: Having noted the obvious failures to implement the laudable goals of the original Act how can we account for those same failures? Why is it, for example, that Congress, after authorizing $325 million to induce compliance with the law appropriated but $150 million during the first two years of the Act and nothing during the next two years? Furthermore the money was spent on landscaping and not on combating junkyards and billboards.

Perhaps it is useful to know that there are 11,700 sign companies and more than 250,000 property owners who lease their land for advertising purposes. If you were entrusted with the responsibility of countering these groups and implementing the law how would you go about the task? How can Congress be induced to appropriate more money rather than just authorizing it? Which Congressmen should one "work on"? What incentives could be provided to induce advertisers to comply? Would the "law of diminishing marginal utility" be of any value in persuading them of the foolishness of more and bigger signs? How? Could taxation be employed as a control? Which groups might be valuable allies in such a struggle? What kinds of bargains could you make with the property owners? The billboard firms?

Suggested Readings

Keynes, Edward and Ricci, David M., eds. *Political Power, Community and Democracy* (Chicago: Rand McNally & Co., 1970).

Brzezinski, Zbigniew and Huntington, Samuel P. *Political Power: USA/USSR* (New York: The Viking Press, 1964).

Leites, Nathan. *On the Game of Politics in France* (Stanford, Calif.: Stanford University Press, 1959).

Rose, Richard, ed. *Policy-Making in Britain: A Reader in Government* (New York: The Free Press, 1969).

Wildavsky, Aaron. *Leadership in a Small Town* (Totowa, N.J.: Bedminister Press, 1964).

PART THREE

Strategy and Public Choice

Here we shift gears from a concern with *what is* to how the politically active can efficiently achieve more of their goals. The orientation is quite frankly Machiavellian. We offer advice to the citizen on how to get more from the "public trough," and we advance strategic and tactical advice for the politician and activist who are interested in shaping public choices and/or its basic institutions. Needless to say the advice is not final and unchangeable. Readers are encouraged to take issue but are admonished to provide reasons for their objections as well as alternative strategies and tactics.

Within this framework, the reader will note that we spend a great deal of time on the situation of voters and politicians since the choice of strategies is constrained by their respective roles and the institutions of policy making. In a sense, one can learn as much about our institutional framework in these chapters as anywhere else in the book. Whether the writer correctly interprets the institutional opportunities and constraints is for readers to decide.

Chapter VIII

BECOMING AN EFFECTIVE VOTER

If our analysis has a strategic implication it is that one must become an effective citizen if he is to protect and advance his concerns. The problem for the average voter, however, is how to be more effective when there are relatively few available courses of action, and those that are available are not particularly impressive or are they likely to produce high payoffs in the short run.

In this chapter we will assess the situation of the typical citizen in terms of his action alternatives given the institutional framework and its constraints on his choices. We will pay special attention to his electoral choices and how they can be improved. We will also offer advice to the ordinary voter concerning (1) how he can better evaluate the performance and promises of politicians and (2) how he can make some preliminary assessment of public policy and its personal impact on him.

What Can a Citizen Do?

The answer to this question is by no means apparent to the typical citizen. Part of becoming a more effective citizen is learning which alternatives can be pursued in American political life, but unfortunately our formal civic education has failed us miserably in this regard. The major goal of the educators seems to be a passive performance of civic "duties" rather than deliberate and rational self-interested participation—we are not taught how to do things politically. Accordingly, most citizens have only the slightest notions of how to proceed in achieving political goals. Hopefully this book and this chapter, in particular, will help to correct the situation somewhat.

Well, what can an average citizen do? He can, if he is willing and able, do many sorts of things:

1. Become aware of political news in newspapers, television, and the like.
2. Conduct political conversations with friends.
3. Attempt to persuade others on how to behave politically.
4. Write to or talk with his representatives.
5. Attend political meetings.
6. Make money contributions to political parties and/or causes.
7. Perform minor tasks for an interest group or party.
8. Solicit funds for political purposes.
9. Campaign actively for others.
10. Vote.
11. Petition.
12. Sponsor test cases in court to assert rights or challenge government decisions.
13. Form an interest group.
14. Run for public office.
15. Participate in street demonstrations and picketing.
16. Destroy public property through arson and vandalism.
17. Show disrespect for public officials.
18. Assassinate public officials.
19. Attempt coups.
20. Refuse to perform legal responsibilities including payment of taxes and service in the military. Symbolize the latter by burning draft cards.
21. Disobey laws.
22. Desecrate cherished public symbols including the flag, government buildings, and monuments.
23. Incite others to riot.
24. Engage in sedition, treason, sabotage, and espionage for other countries.
25. Bribe public officials.
26. Engage in self-immolation. (Unfortunately, this method, if successful, cannot be used again.)
27. Occupy public property.
28. Participate in rebellions.
29. Emigrate.

Even though this list is long, it is hardly an exhaustive set of possibilities, as we are learning daily from the television screens.

Curiously, this generation of American students, which has been so poorly instructed in civic activities, is itself a pioneer in developing new political techniques. But then one should expect that the dissatisfied will be the innovators.

We may observe that these political actions range from the most passive, legitimate, individual responses to the highly active, demanding, and indeed illegal mass activities. They range from the almost costless to some extraordinarily costly choices in which death or imprisonment are the prices to be paid. Most citizens choose the less costly but also less rewarding alternatives. The vast majority chooses the legitimate options, but some people do not. In the year 1968 there were some 435 "civil disturbances" of which at least 26 were "major"; that is, they were characterized by vandalism, arson, looting, gunfire, use of outside police, curfews, involvement of more than 300 active persons, and lasting for more than 12 hours.[1] Some 54 have been described as "serious"; that is, having three of the above characteristics. Eighty-three persons died during these events in 1968. The most profound, unhappy, and costly experience we have had as a nation was the Civil War, obviously an act of secession, rebellion, and, finally, outright war. Some Americans have also chosen to assault and assassinate public officials. The records show that we have had 81 such assaults and deaths since 1835 and that the worst period was the last quarter of the nineteenth century when 43 public officials were killed.[2] Interestingly, some think that recent years have been more violent than earlier years, but the figures do not bear that out since only five assassinations occurred between 1955 and 1968.

A substantial number of Americans have refused to be drafted into military service: in World War II, a highly popular war, the rate of refusal was 11 percent while during 1969 the rate was about 18 percent.[3]

One would suppose that with all these available options the ordinary citizen would be overwhelmed by decision-making dilemmas and costs. In fact, as the above figures imply, very few people choose to engage in illegitimate and costly politics. They make

---

[1] U.S. Bureau of the Census, *Statistical Abstract of the United States, 1969* (90th ed., Washington, D.C.: U.S. Government Printing Office, 1969), p. 138.

[2] *Statistical Abstract of the United States, 1969*, p. 140.

[3] "18% of Oregon Youths Refusing to Be Inducted," *Eugene Register-Guard*, May 23, 1970, 3–A.

this choice not because they have systematically considered all options but because they have been socialized or trained to think primarily in terms of less costly legitimate actions. Most citizens are dedicated loyalists for whom illegitimate political activities are unthinkable. Accordingly, the individual chooses from among a very restricted set of options. He saves on personal costs and the system is saved from having to meet very many serious challenges to its survival. The legitimate alternatives are considered in the remainder of this chapter while advice on the more serious actions is reserved for Chapter X.

The Task of the Peaceful Citizen

The average citizen is likely to be only passively concerned with most political issues and their solutions. Frank recognition of this fact is most important because the amount of time, energy, and other resources he can bring to bear on political analysis is apt to be small. And the probability that he can affect policy is little more than miniscule. Given limited resources, the ordinary citizen is wise indeed who harbors those resources and uses them effectively on limited objectives.

Knowing one's objectives is the first task and it is not an easy one. In any event, the citizen should attempt to discern what benefits him most in his private life. Since we pursue divergent goals we must formulate them carefully. Do we want added social status, power, income, safety, knowledge, affection, or what? Most of us want all of these things and more of them, but all intuitively recognize that they cannot be easily acquired in preferred quantities. We also realize that each goal can be attained in a variety of ways including (1) *purely private individual action*, (2) *private cooperative action with others*, and (3) *cooperative public endeavor*. Each of these alternative means has some advantages, some disadvantages, and some unknown probability of success. If we were purely rational we could probably array our goals into some *ordinal* hierarchy—an order that reflects the comparative importance we attach to each goal. Thus a voter might well decide that he prefers more police protection to more fire protection and more of the latter to more public parks. Or, he might decide that he prefers an income tax to a sales tax and the latter in preference to a property tax. He does not decide just how much more he prefers each to the others; he simply decides the order or ranking of the preferences. And, if he were purely rational, he could then determine how efficiently each alternative means would contribute to achieving his preferences. To do so, he would estimate the costs and the returns or benefits of each alternative under varying conditions. Knowing this cost/benefit relationship he would then rationally decide on a general course of action. Table VIII–1 summarizes this process and illustrates the sort of mental exercise required.

Thus far we have restricted ourselves to noting the general outlines of rational behavior or choice; we have not dealt with the intricacies of all the subchoices entailed in selecting a goal and evaluating the many subalternatives for its achievement. For example, in Table VIII–1, the goal of avoiding the draft has been stipulated along with the three basic means of dealing with the problem. However, each of these basic choices has a number of more concrete or specific alternatives. Private individual action can include such diverse means as burning one's draft card, emigrating to Canada, applying for legal deferment, hiding out within the United States, going to jail, failing to register, or joining the National Guard. No doubt there are other possibilities. The point is that one must not only elaborate on the goals but also on the means; then he must proceed to assess each one in terms of its *expected* benefits, *expected* costs, and *expected* net results or returns. The word "expected" is emphasized because we can rarely predict these outcomes with certainty. Although some results are known it is usually best to state them in terms of probability or the chance that they will be forthcoming. For example, a student might attach a high probability to gaining a legal deferment to remain in college, a 50–50 chance of avoiding the draft by bribing the draft board, and no chance of avoiding it by burning his draft card. In contrast, in assessing the benefits or advantages of going to Canada he might conclude that although he would avoid the draft, the long-run consequences might not be beneficial. In fact, he may decide they would be too costly to endure. Serious investigation of benefits and costs might well convince him to volunteer for service even during a war because the chances of his being wounded or killed are very small indeed. From 1961 to 1970, more than 2.8 million served in the Vietnam war and only 40,000 were killed. He might decide this ratio is small enough to warrant his taking the chance. In his considerations, the prospective draftee ought to add the substantial rewards veterans of active service derive from the nation's public goods.

TABLE VIII-1

The Rational Choice of Action (cost/benefit analysis)

Goals	Alternatives						Expected net results
	Private individual action		Private collective action		Public action		
	Benefits	Costs	Benefits	Costs	Benefits	Costs	
Avoid the draft							
Reduce one's personal income tax							
Reduce the nation's poverty							
End racial discrimination							
Keep blacks out of a neighborhood							
Get a better grade in this course							

No citizen acts according to the rational "ideal" because, paradoxically, it is not rational for him to do so. The costs are too great. Instead of seeking the ideal solution—which requires maximizing returns—he opts for an acceptable or satisfactory solution. The ordinary citizen, in a sense, does attempt a rough approximation of the ideal but he normally does so in a sloppy and not very logical sequence of steps. Typically, he has learned through experience that he prefers some activities to others and some means to others. Most of his goals and values focus around his personal life: getting a better job; having the respect of colleagues; making more money; educating his children; maintaining the loyalty of his family; and experiencing the joys of love, of recreation, of making his house a more comfortable place, and of remaining healthy. So, too, he generally feels that most of these hopes can be best achieved by his own efforts in private life.

Occasionally he perceives that they can only or best be effectively furthered by cooperating with others outside his family and still more rarely he may associate governmental action with furthering his daily interests. He may even recognize that maintenance of a stable society is essential to his achieving his own ends.

It is only when he perceives two or more alternatives that he has a dilemma to resolve. The dilemma becomes a painful reality whenever a friend asks him to assist in some joint venture such as forming a cooperative, signing a covenant, signing a petition, marching in a parade, making a campaign contribution, voting for a certain candidate, canvassing one's district, or running for public office. At this juncture, the citizen must confront his own values and goals, and measure them against his resources of fortitude, money, and time to participate.

Suppose he chooses not to engage in dramatic public actions but only wishes to vote more intelligently in the next election. What should this man do?

The Task of the Voter

Part of the voter's job has already been discussed, namely, clarifying his own situation and interests. Thus, if he is a wage earner in the lumber industry, for example, and he is about to lose his job, it is fairly clear that maintaining an income is his primary objective or interest. Getting another job is usually considered an individual responsibility, except under conditions of extensive unemployment. Policy proposals of governments are relevant to his continued employment and are, therefore, of the greatest significance to an unemployed worker. Policies that are not directly connected to his plight do not concern him. But how can he learn which policies are relevant to or have a bearing on employment. This task is not easy; an economy is an intricate web of interdependencies.

Still, one need not be an economist to sort out the less relevant facts and proposals from the more relevant ones. Interest groups provide assistance on precisely this matter, and one may find literature from such a group particularly instructive. For example, the local chapter of the American Association of University Professors to which the author belongs, recently sent the following newsletter to members. Its meaning and relevance are obvious.

*   *   *

The following is a summary of the actions taken by the Legislature on various bills introduced in the last session which affect our members on the faculties.

1. Salary adjustment fund totaling 10.2 million dollars, to provide an average 6% increase in each of the next two years and adjustments for graduate assistants averaging 15% in 1969–70 and 5% in 70–71.

$750,000 to be used to reward excellence in instruction.

Salary increases at the Medical and Dental School in the amount of 12% during 69–70 and 6% in 70–71.

Salary increases for interns and residents which exceed the Governor's recommendations by $25 per month during 69–70 and an additional $25 stipend during 70–71.

2. HB 1223—Covering retirement contributions out of balloon payments. No longer will the contributions be computed at the lump sum rate but rather on the monthly installments.

3. HB 1854—Actuarily increases the pension benefits for those employees retained in service past 65 years of age.

4. HB 1863—Allows those employees who elected to remain in TIAA-CREF to participate in the PERS Variable Annuity on up to one half of their contributions made on the first $4800 of salary.

5. HB 1756—Removes the Retirement Law double standard

placed on some employees of Federal Extension Co-op programs within Higher Education.

6. Bill passed which would move the offices of the Chancellor and other employees of the State System to Salem. This move to be made upon the completion of the multi-storied office building on the Mall—probably 3 years away.

7. HB 1390—Provides 120-day period after termination of employment on account of illness during which beneficiary may claim death benefits if terminated employee dies from that illness.

8. HB 1515—Revises scope of governmental tort liability; creates immunity from tort liability for public officers, employees and agnts as to claims arising out of certain governmental activities.

9. Legislative Fiscal Committee to study the subject of a State contribution to Medical-Hospital premiums.

As you can see, we have had our successes and our failures. We must now set to work preparing for the next session of the Legislature.

*   *   *

Just as an auto driver does not need engineering knowledge in order to appreciate or even drive his car, so an unemployed person need not be an economist to appreciate employment. In a more general sense, the voter should attempt to estimate the impact of the governing party on his personal welfare. In the language of economics he should be concerned with "maximizing his stream of utility" from governmental action and comparing benefits with the benefit or utility stream promised by the opposition party.[4] If the incumbent's record is positive and outweighs the opposition's promises, he should vote for the "ins." If not, he should vote for the "outs." If they seem to be tied he should introduce new criteria such as past performances of the outs and/or comparison of performances against ideal performances.

Suppose, however, a voter arrives at the conclusion that of all candidates for an office, none will provide any expected benefits and all are expected to inflict harm, injury, or added costs on the voter. In this case, the voter's strategy is fairly simple and straightforward. He should attempt to "measure" or estimate the relative losses he will suffer from each, if elected, and vote for the

---

[4] Anthony Downs, *An Economic Theory of Democracy* (New York: Harper & Brothers, 1957), pp. 36–37.

one who inflict the least losses. In short, choose the lesser of evils. If both are equally bad or the differential between them is minute, he should not vote. It is a waste of his time. Instead of maximizing his expected benefits the cynical voter minimizes his expected losses, surely a rational choice under the conditions as he perceives them.

Implicit in this highly rational approach is the kind of cost/benefit analysis we encountered in Table VIII-1. The alert reader may notice that most of us are in no position to learn much about expected benefits and costs because the costs of becoming informed about alternative policies are substantial. Each voter must ask: How much wiser will my decision be if I seek out one more bit of information and pay another dollar, or hour, or bit of energy to achieve that wisdom? In other words, what is the ratio of expected marginal or additional gain to the marginal or additional costs of becoming better informed? The simple answer is this: For most voters, most of the time, the search for more information on politics, government, policies, politicians, and the like, is not worth the added effort. Such added information will have no appreciable impact on governmental policy choices.

The voter who enjoys reading about politics is another case; he tries to maximize his enjoyment, not his effectiveness in shaping public policies. He should continue to watch television newscasts and read *Time Magazine* or even *The American Political Science Review*. Those who are only casually interested in political activities should rely on their "intuition" and ideology—their fundamental beliefs about society and their personal values—and should make only casual judgments about the performance of governments and politicians. Becoming better informed is more profitable for those whose role in politics is crucial and influential.

We are not advocating that everyone remain ignorant, but rather that each individual decide his own optimal balance of knowledge and ignorance that still allows him to achieve his desired ends. For those who wish to wield influence, especially politicians or lobbyists, it pays to become and remain highly informed; one's position may depend upon that knowledge. A much more modest effort is in order for the typical citizen who is willing to let others make political decisions. One last important point: one should not feel entirely ineffective because of ignorance for there will always be others who are still less well informed and therefore less powerful. All political bargainers labor under varying degrees of uncertainty.

On Evaluating Politicians

Since we vote for candidates much more frequently than for public programs we must have some way of evaluating their past behavior and their future stands and actions on policy. The primary difficulty is that we must assess a representative who deals with countless issues and under unforeseeable conditions. How can we proceed given the difficulties and costs of evaluation?

The least costly means is to note the competing politicians' general ideology and party membership. Since most voters have inherited their party affiliations from their parents they already have a "built-in evaluator." If the symbols a politician uses strike a favorable chord, one should probably vote for him. The voter who considers himself an "independent" and has not made up his mind about his desired policies has a more demanding problem to solve. He will have to look into far more of the activities and promises of the candidates than the ideological or committed voter.

A policy-oriented citizen will want to learn how the candidates stand on several issues. If they are running for legislative offices, for example, the voter could have as many as several hundred roll-call votes to study. Clearly, that task is far too exhausting and costly, and is, in addition, wasteful of time and energy. Instead, he should ask how the candidates promise or have voted on the few issues the citizen considers of the greatest personal significance to him. There are rarely more than four or five of these crucial issues, and occasionally a single issue is paramount. A politician's stand on these few issues will probably indicate his likely positions on many other, lesser issues.

There is no good reason why each citizen should be concerned over everything that happens. Resource limitations preclude consideration of a large number of occurrences. One should attend to the most critical and ignore the least important. Although citizens can do this, the politician cannot, for he must use the less valuable issues for trading purposes as he bargains in the political arena.

Where can one learn about political stands and promises? Obviously one source is the newspaper; many carry articles about the stands of local politicians and often sum up their voting records, particularly at election time. Other sources are interest groups and the politicians themselves. Both are usually more than willing to inform constituents about many current issues. Still more complete accountings are found in the *Congressional Quarterly* and in the *Congressional Record* and state legislative proceedings. These can be acquired through one's representatives. Few citizens are sufficiently concerned to subscribe to or request these sources even though the official ones are free.

Knowing the preferences of politicians is, of course, only one criterion of judgment. Sometimes a choice in a primary election is between two candidates of the same party, both of whom espouse essentially the same philosophy. In this instance we would have to assume either that it makes no difference which candidate becomes the party nominee or that it does make a difference—one could become more effective than the other. A voter might reasonably choose the one who is more likely to run a successful campaign against the opposition and will be more effective once in office. Since candidates recognize this as a criterion they normally campaign against their opponents in terms of personal effectiveness. If a young candidate's opponent has been in office a long time he is criticized on grounds of getting old, less attentive, and less skilled. He, in turn, calls his fresh young opponent inexperienced, unskilled, and without needed political resources such as contacts, seniority, expertise, and the like. (Both candidates may be right.) Incumbents like to cite their successes in obtaining revenues from outside the district (government grants, military contracts, conservation funds, post offices, and various other installations that bring employment and money into the community). They remind voters how they have won some international confrontation; saved the dollar; increased employment; stopped inflation, and so forth. Opponents like to point out the incumbent's failures—something fairly easy to do under most conditions. Rating effectiveness is an extremely perplexing business—one at which most of us are not likely to excel. At the Presidential level it becomes even more complicated because luck and the complexities of official responsibilities all conspire to thwart our efforts at assigning credits and faults. Some newspapermen compile "score cards" for Presidents but most of these wins and losses in getting legislation through Congress are highly misleading. One President may show a high score because he only sends up sure bets, while another may aggressively assume greater risks in the short run for a prospective long run gain. Further, who knows how much credit or blame to give a President or governor when there are so many forces beyond his control? One more consideration: strategy itself is not amenable to empirical testing; we can never experiment to find out whether another strategy would have had any greater success.

If measuring an incumbent's effectiveness is tricky, consider how much more difficult it is to assess a candidate who has never served in public office. How can we estimate his potential? We might turn to political professionals for an estimate, or to people who know him well. They may make some sound predictions on his ability to learn his new job with speed and thoroughness. If we respect the expert we have a solution to the problem. One amusing attempt at assessing political performance is contained in Table VIII-2. We are indebted to the American Civil Liberties Union of Oregon for this imaginative performance rating chart.

In a more serious effort to assess politicians, the voter might compare their promises with their successful fulfillment of them. Few would be willing to attempt this task because politicians have compelling incentives to confuse voters on at least some issues and outcomes, especially when constituents are deeply and equally divided on an issue. Obfuscation, contradictions, vagueness, and the like are typical responses on the part of politicians to cover up uncertainty and further their electoral chances. Since this is true many voters conclude that politicians are always making promises, hiding the facts, and compromising at every opportunity. This judgment may very well be true pertaining to difficult issues, but not all issues nor policy stands are so demanding. When the voters are in substantial agreement, the politician's actions are more clearcut. Politicians do redeem their pledges whenever possible.

Gerald Pomper, a student of such matters, has tested the record of Presidential platform fulfillment and discovered that slightly over half of the 1,399 pledges (1944–64) were honored by either congressional or executive action at the national level.[5] If one relaxes his criteria of keeping pledges nearly three-fourths of the promises are kept, an amazing record given the complex structure of our system and the low estimates most voters hold of politicians and their promises. Pomper also reports that the "in" party, for good reasons, is able to satisfy more pledges than is the "out" or defeated party.[6] It is interesting to note that in specific policy areas, poorest performance was found in labor, government, and civil rights policies; greatest success has been experienced in foreign, defense, agriculture, welfare, and resources

---

[5] Gerald Pomper, *Elections in America* (New York: Dodd, Mead & Co., 1968), pp. 179–203.
[6] Pomper, *Elections in America*, p. 187.

TABLE VIII-2

ACLU Voter's Guide

Performance Rating Chart for Prospective Board Members

Performance	Far exceeds job requirements	Exceeds job requirements	Meets job requirements	Needs some improvement	Does not meet minimum requirements
Ability	Leaps tall buildings with a single bound.	Must take running start to leap over tall buildings.	Can leap over short buildings only.	Crashes into buildings when attempting to leap over them.	Cannot recognize buildings at all.
Timeliness	Is faster than a speeding bullet.	Is as fast as a speeding bullet.	Not quite as fast as a speeding bullet.	Would you believe a slow bullet?	Wounds self when attempting to shoot bullet.
Initiative	Is stronger than a locomotive.	Is stronger than a bull elephant.	Is stronger than a bull.	Shoots the bull.	Doesn't recognize bulls.
Adaptability	Walks on water consistently.	Walks on water in emergencies.	Washes with water.	Drinks water.	Drinks water only in emergencies.
Communication	Talks with God.	Talks with the angels.	Talks with himself.	Argues with himself.	Loses those arguments.

Source: "Voter's Guide," *ACLU Newsletter* 8 (February, 1970), 4.

policies.[7] Just why these differences should appear is left to the reader to explain. Perhaps the analyses of Chapters VI–VII are of some value.

How Voters Choose

Consumers express their preferences by daily purchases in marketplaces, while voters express their preferences chiefly in elections. Since elections provide major opportunities for the voter to make choices it is essential that we attain a thorough understanding of their workings, potential, and limitations, particularly from the perspective of the lowly, lonely individual voter.

While we visit marketplaces much more often than we do the polls (one must if he is to survive), elections occur fairly frequently in this country. Annual elections probably number about 100,000. In the state of Oregon, which may be somewhat atypical, the annual number of elections averages about 2,000. Most of these elections are highly specialized and involve only the voters of such special districts as schools, water and irrigation, sewage, fire protection, flood control, ports, mosquito abatement, and the like. While the total number of elections is considerable, the number for which any specific voter qualifies are really few. But these few elections can differ rather markedly in terms of the types of choices they present for the voters. Let us see how and why and what difference it makes for the voter and public choice.

BASIC ELEMENTS OF ELECTIONS

An election provides a means of making authoritative collective decisions in which individual voters may express some *preference(s)* among *given alternatives*. The electorate's choice is decided on the basis of a *decision rule* such as simple majority $[(N + 1)/2$ or 50 percent $+ 1]$, extramajority (for example, two-thirds or three-fourths), unanimity, plurality, or proportional representation. Modern elections are conducted by *secret ballots* with voters having equal votes—*one vote per person*. Typically, an election is governed by a series of detailed regulations which stipulate the time, place, and conduct of the election. Election watchers from both major parties are present to oversee the administration

---

[7] Pomper, *Elections in America*, p. 189.

of the event and insure its proper conduct. All this elementary description may seem trivial until it is realized that elections are a rather uncommon means of selecting governments and making public policy; most men in history have not participated in the free elections we Americans take for granted. In fact, it has only been in the twentieth century (1920) that full adult suffrage has been extended to women, and it is only now being realistically advanced for black citizens in some parts of the nation.

TYPES OF ELECTIONS

Voters participate not in elections in general but in specific types of elections governed by specific sets of rules and decided by specific decision rules. The nature of the alternatives is likewise apt to differ considerably and thereby impose quite different choice problems on the voter. Elections can be usefully contrasted in terms of decision rules and the nature of the ballot choices or alternatives. The most common election rule in the United States is a plurality requirement, by which the candidate or measure that gains the greatest number of votes is declared the winner. Since we have a two-party system a plurality normally results in a simple majority. However, Presidents have been elected to office with less than simple majorities. Presidents Truman, Kennedy, and Nixon were all minority choices and they shared this fate with eleven other Presidents.

Simple majority rules are found in Congress and state legislatures as well as local governing bodies; these majorities are usually based on those present and voting and do not constitute an absolute majority of all members whether present or not. (Some exceptions are listed below.) The implications of this rule are considerable and fairly obvious: for members of a legislature the task of gaining a majority is easier under this rule than under extramajority rule. The latter rule generally assists the status-quo forces to resist change or reform. In addition, the relative advantages of popular parties tend to be increased under plurality or simple majority rules, because minority groups find it easier and less costly to join one of the two major parties than to coexist without representation. There are few rewards for those sitting in the corridors of politics.

Although plurality or majority rules prevail in general, there are important exceptions. A critical one prescribes how the Constitution can be amended. Article V stipulates that an amendment may be proposed on application of two-thirds of the states or two-thirds of both houses. The amendment will be ratified if it is approved by either three-fourths of the state legislatures or conventions as the Congress may decide. Needless to say, these extramajority requirements have aided in restricting the number of amendments to but 25 in more than 175 years. Another set of extramajority rules are found in the Congress: Presidents when making treaties must secure a two-thirds majority (of those present and voting) of both houses. Impeachment proceedings require a two-thirds majority of those present and voting in the Senate. And a two-thirds majority is required of Congress to override a Presidential veto.

ALTERNATIVES FOR VOTERS

Consider the situation of a voter in a typical Presidential election. He must make a series of choices on candidates for the Presidency, United States Senator, a Congressman, probably several state officials, a state representative, several county and other local officials, various nonpartisan state officials (usually judges), several amendments to the state constitution, special local levies, and perhaps some special district officials. Voters in Lane County, Oregon, in the 1968 Presidential election, voted on 21 different offices (38 candidates), 7 state constitutional amendments, and 3 special county levies. Ballots in other states and elections are often much longer and more complicated than the instance cited in Oregon. In short, a voter has some highly complex dilemmas to confront and resolve.

Electoral choice is exceedingly difficult for a number of reasons, particularly if the voter attempts to be rational in pursuit of his goals. If he attempts to maximize his flow of goods and services from governments he must know how the various parties and candidates might affect his stream of benefits and the price he will pay for them. Will he get better treatment from the Democrats or the Republicans? Where can he get such information? How can he be sure it is relevant and valid information and not propaganda? How much information does he need to make useful estimates? How much time and other resources should he put into this task? The nature of these questions suggests the plight of the typical voter. He is required to resolve dilemmas for which he needs to be informed, but becoming better informed is costly and may not be worth the effort.

Thus far we have analyzed electoral alternatives in terms of parties and candidates; the ballot also demands that we make choices on constitutional amendments, policy proposals, and special levies. Some of these choices are more difficult to resolve than voting for officials, while others are less difficult. Some constitutional questions relate to the basic rules of the game and in effect demand that we take a position on which rule is best for the state and ourselves. Most voters are ignorant of the consequences of such rules and therefore cannot predict their effects on public policies and the personal flows of benefits and costs. Other amendments pertain to or raise issues about the formal reorganization of governmental units; another may ask one to express a preference, for example, on the powers and size of the legislature; still another may ask one to decide whether to allow counties or cities to broaden their debt limitations, or place a ceiling on the rate of the property tax. On a more mundane level voters may be asked to cast a vote on dog control, on a special levy for garbage disposal, or on a local school board's budget. In May, 1970 Oregonians voted on the following state and local ballot measures:

State of Oregon

1. A capital construction bonding issue which authorized general obligation bonds to finance the cost of state buildings and other governmental construction projects, to be repaid from gifts, rentals, parking and other building fees. (Lost)

2. Repeal of the "white foreigner" section of the Oregon Constitution, an archaic section that discriminated against non-white foreigners and tried to give the State of Oregon powers to regulate immigration, something it clearly didn't have and which is in conflict with the U.S. Constitution. (Passed)

3. A revised state constitution for Oregon, which would delete obsolete provisions of the present 110-year-old constitution, increase the size of the legislature, and allow annual sessions if requested by majorities of both houses, in addition to many other new provisions. (Lost)

4. Pollution control bond issue, authorizing issuance of bonds up to one percent of the state's true cash value to provide funds for state and local governments to construct antipollution facilities that must be 70 percent self-supporting and self-liquidating. (Passed)

5. Lower the voting age from 21 to 19. (Lost)

6. A local school property tax equalization measure, giving

the legislature more flexibility in equalizing school tax burdens within a county. (Lost)

Lane County:

1. A five-year garbage serial levy. (Passed)
2. A levy for airport improvement projects. (Lost)

City of Eugene:

1. Decision about whether to allow a religious cross to remain in a city park. (Passed)
2. Proposal to delay construction of an atomic power plant by the city Water and Electric Board. (Passed)

Lane Community College:

1. An increase in the property tax base for the college. (Lost)

These complex issues and many candidates for various state and local offices in a primary election were all on the ballot for voters in one election. The choice dilemmas must be readily apparent.

Each voter was asked to express his personal preferences on policy issues by indicating "yes" or "no" and on future officials by placing an "X" in an appropriate box nearest his choice. His role here is very different from his role as consumer when he enters the marketplace. The consumer can express his preferences much more precisely, because he can purchase more or less of divisible commodities and pay out more or less according to his tastes, his income, and the prices. The voter is rarely able to do this even on tax and expenditure issues. Obviously he cannot divide his vote and "buy" a little more of candidate A and a little less of candidate B. His choices are mutually exclusive; that is he votes for A *or* B. On tax and expenditure issues voters are likewise asked to approve or disapprove the single proposal. They cannot choose from among an array of alternative financing methods (taxes, bonds, inflation, or user fees) nor can they indicate their preferred amounts of expenditures. Consumers normally express themselves on expected benefits and costs simultaneously as purchases are made because expected costs and benefits are presented at the same time for consideration. And they must be if one is to achieve higher degrees of rationality. Of course, the consumer can probably estimate the consequences of his purchases more accurately more of the time than can a voter on a financial proposal.

Another factor in elections further complicates the voter's choice. A consumer chooses for himself and does not force his choice on others, while a voter decides not only for himself but for others. His choice enters into the construction of a collective decision that can be legitimately imposed on the losers. Thus, if a bare majority of 50 percent plus one vote for a sales tax the 50 percent minus one who voted against it will, nevertheless, have to pay the tax. If I purchase a particular make of automobile I do not, normally, impose my choice on others requiring them to also buy that make and model. They can do their own thing and buy or not buy an automobile of their own choice. This decentralization of choice and consequences is one of the great virtues of the market mechanism; since collective decisions entail the imposition of some voters' choices on others, an element of coercion is always present. Since this is true, a voter should consider the impact of his choices on other people as well as the impact of their choices on him and his family. Even a purely selfish voter should consider the probable impacts of his preferences on others because his choices may adversely affect others who may, in turn, cause him trouble. For example, if I vote against a subsidy for certain businesses or ghetto blacks they may react in ways that hurt me. We ought to be aware of such contingencies before we vote.

On Acquiring More Public Services and Income

Our advice has been confined to becoming a more intelligent voter, a role that has its limitations as we have somewhat forlornly learned. Between elections voters must pay taxes, fees, and fines; observe laws; be affected by government rulings and laws; serve on juries and in the military; and perform a host of other roles, all of which are impinged upon by governments. We cannot await elections to alter adverse policies nor can we even expect our individual votes to count for very much in reshaping governmental activities. We must deal with governments daily whether we like it or not. Presumably most of us would like more frequent and more profitable exchanges with our governments, or, at least, fewer unprofitable encounters. How can we achieve these ends in everyday life?

The ingenious and willing citizen can do much to improve his personal relationships with governments through a variety of individual and group activities. Politicians are usually eager to assist the voter if the assistance is not too costly. This kind of service to constituents is a major function or activity of most politicians and bureaucrats. One estimate of the workloads of congressmen indicates that about 27 percent of their time is devoted to constituents and their problems.[8] Most are courteous and helpful. Naturally most governmental activities were not designed to please everyone nor are all public servants pleasant and useful. We should make sure they do not become overbearing or tyrannical and insist that they be helpful. In recent years increasing numbers of *ombudsmen* have been employed by government to seek out citizen complaints and expedite their legitimate demands. Inequities, bureaucratic red-tape, and snafus constitute the majority of complaints, according to some ombudsmen. This is understandable, given the magnitude of governmental operations.

Most local governments provide a wide variety of continual opportunities for the concerned citizen to register his views in council meetings and special public meetings on particular problems such as zoning, tax assessments, highway location, school busing, and the like. Some governments have specialized citizen advisory boards to assist in encouraging the police and other governmental officials to be more responsive and responsible. Their purpose, however effective they are, is to hear about citizen problems and to suggest means of preventing similar difficulties in the future.

Those who object to governmental rulings can usually have recourse to a series of hearings before policies are made final.[9] Although recourse is often highly expensive in our judicial system, many people apparently make use of appeals; the workloads of the courts are beyond belief. Those who are too poor to employ attorneys and appeal procedures may make use of public defenders. This group, however, often seems to lack interest, experience, and ability. Free legal advice is being provided in increasing amounts by lawyer associations and law students.

Our concentration on reducing unpleasant and unprofitable relationships with government has not been without cause. Many Americans continue to view government as a necessary evil. Still,

---

[8] John Saloma, III, *Congress and the New Politics* (Boston: Little, Brown & Co., 1969), p. 186.

[9] Arthur A. Maass notes that *twenty* public hearings and consultations are provided by the Corps of Engineers and Congress in reviewing water resource projects. "Congress and Water Resources," *American Political Science Review* 44 (Sept., 1950), 575–93.

a greater number of citizens believe they will receive more or less equal and serious consideration from governmental officials.[10] Apparently most Americans approach governmental agencies without fear or trepidation, and they tend also to believe in their own effectiveness to correct unjust laws at both the national and local levels. Americans feel competent.

Feeling competent is a necessary condition for effective action in demanding more and better public services. Another condition is being well informed. Unfortunately many citizens are unaware of the vast variety of public services and funds that are potentially available to them. Even local governments are often poorly informed about the types and amounts of federal and state aid for which they might qualify. Since effective action requires each individual citizen to be better informed about programs of potential benefit to himself and his family, these suggestions are offered. He can contact various public agencies and interest groups such as labor unions, veterans' organizations, chambers of commerce, and many others that represent him in the councils of government. Some governmental agencies publish listings of their programs, services, funds, and so forth. Many Americans never take full advantage of their opportunities because of ignorance. Some students of welfare programs maintain that many Americans could qualify for various payments but never apply or exert sufficient pressure to receive higher payments or more services and aids. Many Vietnam war veterans are not taking advantage of some very considerable educational benefits that are theirs for the asking. We hope that none of our readers will miss any such advantages.

Exercises in Analysis

THE IGNORANCE OF VOTERS

Many political scientists (including some of the more eminent) have sadly observed, after reading some public opinion poll, that most voters are not well informed. From this general observation some have concluded that democracy is in danger or may even be impossible or at least irrational when uninformed masses

---

[10] Gabriel Almond and Sidney Verba, *The Civic Culture* (Princeton, N.J.: Princeton University Press, 1963), p. 219.

influence its decisions. These views stem from opinion data such as follows:[11]

Question	Percent answering correctly
"What do you know about the Bill of Rights? Do you know anything it says?"	21%
"How many Senators are there in Washington from your state?"	55
"What is meant by the Electoral College?"	35
"Will you tell me what the three branches of the Federal Government are called?"	19

Is pessimism in order? Why should voters know the kind of information suggested by the above questions? What incentives are there for acquiring and remembering the civics book type of information? What incentives and other reasons for not learning them? For not remembering them? If you really wanted people to learn legal facts how could you induce them to do so? Explain your reasoning.

What other types of information might be more useful for a citizen to master? Readers might think of answering this question in a broader framework: Suppose one had the opportunity and resources to reform our civics education programs in primary and secondary schools. What should be taught that would make citizens more effective participants in the system? What are the chances of persuading our state legislatures of such proposals? School boards?

Now another order of question: Considering these low levels of information how can we explain the fact that our democracy has been functioning fairly well for so long? Suppose twice as many voters knew the correct answers to the above questions; what would happen to our system of government? Would our policies be any different? Why? Would the job of the politician be easier or more difficult? Why?

INCREASING RATIONALITY IN VOTING

One of the problems worrying many educators, editors, and some politicians is the low level of voting participation, particu-

[11] Robert E. Lane and David O. Sears, *Public Opinion* (Englewood Cliffs, N.J.: Prentice-Hall, Inc., 1964), p. 61.

larly in those elections that provide an opportunity for citizens to vote on local school and municipal fiscal policies. Attendance is also extremely low at the many public hearings on municipal budgets, school budgets, and the like. Apparently with this evidence of disinterest in mind the state legislature of Oregon long ago passed a law requiring newspapers to print the entire proposed budgets of local governments and to make free copies of these available on request. Newspapers are reimbursed for their costs of printing and publishing. Presumably the legislature hoped that this requirement would serve to encourage or induce voters to vote in greater numbers and more rationally. Instead, taxpayers take no interest in the proposed budgets as published. In addition, the budgets are not understandable because they do not tell the voter how much he pays and receives. Therefore, the monies the state pays newspapers are wasted.

The problem is this: Is it possible to interest more voters in these matters? If so, how? The analyses in Chapters II to V should be of some assistance. Another question: Why does the legislature keep this law in effect?

INCREASING INTEREST AND PARTICIPATION

In Figures IV–2, 3, and 4 on pages 82–83 we set forth the net exchanges each income group had with its local, state, and national governments. Suppose that either these figures were published or that a simple table showing the same results were presented on the front pages of every newspaper in the country on an annual basis. What consequences might follow? Would the voters appreciate the information? Would they participate more? Why? Would they vote any differently? Why? Would legislators approve of such a plan? Why? Would government work any better? Any easier? Why?

Suggested Readings

Berelson, Bernard, *et al. Voting* (Chicago: University of Chicago Press, 1954).

Buchanan, James M. and Tullock, Gordon. *The Calculus of Consent* (Ann Arbor: University of Michigan Press, 1962).

Campbell, Angus, *et al. The American Voter* (New York: John Wiley & Sons, Inc., 1964).

Cohen, John. *Behaviour in Uncertainty* (New York: Basic Books, 1964).

Downs, Anthony. *An Economic Theory of Democracy* (New York: Harper & Brothers, 1957).

Key, V. O., Jr. *The Responsible Electorate* (Cambridge, Mass.: Harvard University Press, 1966).

Miller, David W. and Starr, Martin K. *The Structure of Human Decisions* (Englewood Cliffs, N.J.: Prentice-Hall, Inc., 1967).

Levin, Murray B. with Blackwood, George. *The Compleat Politician* (Indianapolis: The Bobbs-Merrill Co., Inc., 1962).

Pomper, Gerald M. *Elections in America* (New York: Dodd, Mead & Co., 1968).

Raiffa, Howard. *Decision Analysis* (Reading, Pa.: Addison-Wesley, 1968).

Chapter IX

BECOMING AN EFFECTIVE POLITICIAN

Tradition says that some American mothers believe their sons can one day become President of the United States. If this is so they would be much more realistic to encourage their sons to become local and state politicians; the probabilities of success are far greater. While we have some 521,000 elective public offices, we have only one President, and of the hundreds of millions of Americans who have ever lived to adulthood only 33 have ever actually become President. That is one reason why his status is so high. This high improbability raises some interesting and crucial questions of job availability and strategy for the young Presidential aspirant. In this chapter we will diagnose the situation of the aspiring politician and make some suggestions on how to enter into and succeed in political life.

Opportunities

The American polity is not without opportunities for politicians but most of them are quite a bit less inspiring than a mother's fantasies might suggest. In addition to the more than 521,000 elective offices to be filled there are hundreds of thousands of appointive offices. These should also be regarded as a part of the structure of political opportunities. Many elective officials have also held these patronage jobs at one time or another. The vast bulk of elective offices are at the local level (508,720). Put another way, the average Congressional district elects about 1,200 state and local officers. In terms of sheer numbers most opportunities for the beginner, therefore, are in local governments. Unhappily, it must also be pointed out that the pay in many of these positions is excep-

TABLE IX–1

Annual Salaries of Selected Public Officials, 1969

President	$200,000
Vice President	62,500
U.S. Senator	42,500
Speaker of the House	62,500
U.S. Congressman	42,500
Highest paid governor (New York)	50,000
Lowest paid governor (Arkansas)	10,000
Highest paid state legislator (California)	19,200
Lowest paid state legislator (New Hampshire)	100
State legislators (median)	10,637

tionally low and in some jobs it is zero. Pay scales, however, have been on the increase and in some positions, such as Congress, they are quite high indeed ($42,500), although sometimes hardly enough to meet the responsibilities of a national political and social life. Table IX–1 contains a partial listing of salary schedules for various positions.

Monetary rewards are not the only perquisites; others include a good deal of social status if one holds the right offices. Public officials are now among the most prestigious people in the nation, although they have not always been so treated. Recent polls on such matters indicate that U.S. Senators, big-city mayors, governors, and Congressmen all rank among the top ten occupations. Expense accounts are also of some significance for certain offices; Congressional junkets and the like are for the purpose of carrying out official duties as well as providing travel, recreation, and pleasure. Name politicians are among the highest paid speakers in the land. Of course, politicians are also much in demand after they leave public office; most men who serve for any time at all in high posts will usually have a difficult time deciding among offers from corporations, universities, and lucrative law firms if they have a law degree. The expertise and connections a politician acquires in government are valuable resources for private enterprises that deal extensively with governmental agencies. During 1946–67, 90 ex-Congressmen and 23 ex-Senators were lobbyists for various organizations at various times, usually business and industry.[1] "Knowing the ropes" in Washington or in state capitals is a rare and highly valued skill.

[1] *Legislators and the Lobbyists* (Washington, D.C.: Congressional Quarterly Service, 1968), 45–49.

Another reward of consequence for a politician is the knowledge that he is wielding influence over important decisions affecting the lives of many people. Some people enjoy the exercise of such influence as an end in itself, while others enjoy the resulting public policies and good they may contribute to others. High public office is something most politicians do not like to surrender voluntarily.

Barriers to Entry and Other Constraints

With all these opportunities and rewards politics must appear an attractive job and career. As with all responsible positions there are situational problems, strains, obstacles, and costs that are not subject to much alteration; one must take them as "givens" and work within the legal, political, and cultural limitations.

The first constraint is obvious: A candidate must be able to win a nomination in order to get started as well as continue in office. Politicians do not apply for jobs, as in private business, and, as we shall see, winning elections often requires considerable resources, astute strategies, and some luck. Victorious politicians must appeal to voters, who have been known to be fickle. Stiff competition with other politicians results in an uncertain career. In fact, one normally cannot count on developing a career in the same sense that careers are planned in private life. Politicians do not have much control over their "employers." Still, some positions provide greater security than others. In contrast, some (the President and 13 state governors) are prevented from serving more than two terms by constitutional rules. At least 12 states prohibit consecutive reelection of governors.[2] Among the most secure politicians are southern members of Congress. Most of them have had little or no opposition. Victory is seldom in doubt in more than 300 Congressional districts. All but one-fifth to one-fourth of the House seats are won by larger than 55 percent majorities.[3]

The legal and/or informal tradition of residency in the constituency one hopes to represent constitutes another important constraint on opportunities. Rarely is a politician able, as in Britain, to move about and choose a constituency that will be easy and

[2] Thomas R. Dye, *Politics in States and Communities* (Englewood Cliffs, N.J.: Prentice-Hall, Inc., 1969), p. 157.
[3] William J. Keefe and Morris S. Ogul, *The American Legislative Process* (Englewood Cliffs, N.J.: Prentice-Hall, Inc., 1964), p. 111.

Theodore Lownik Library
Illinois Benedictine College
Lisle, Illinois 60532

economical for him to win. If one wishes to be a Democrat in a Republican state his chances of success are reduced just as those of a Republican are when trying to win office in a Democratic area. Voters tend to prefer representatives who (they feel) can understand them and their problems.

Still another constraint that affects different politicians differently pertains to the nature of their private occupations and the nature of public life. Public office is usually regarded as a part-time job, and most politicians make their livelihood by private work and earnings. The politician's ideal private career, therefore, facilitates and enhances his public life. At the same time, his public life must not greatly diminish his private earning power. The fact that the law profession and some businesses are precisely such occupations is probably a major reason why so many politicians are either lawyers or businessmen. In fact, public life may improve private legal and business earnings. Since lawyers cannot advertise, public office is a legitimate way around that ethical constraint. Other jobs do not jibe as neatly with the requirements of public life. Business, law, and public office are mutually rewarding.

Other constraints on political careers are less in accord with the ideals of American political life. Certain *barriers to entry* must be recognized and dealt with by a politician; that is, if he can affect them. For example, a basic entry restriction for almost all offices of any importance is financial. Running for important offices is usually a highly expensive operation. The 1964 Presidential campaign cost almost $30 million or about 41 cents per vote.[4] A total of $200 million was spent at all levels in the elections of 1964. Table IX–2 shows an interesting cost-per-vote estimate for the 1968 primaries in Oregon.

Even local campaigning can be highly expensive. One successful primary candidate for the city council in Portland, Oregon, spent over $29,000 in 1970. Several others spent in excess of $20,-000. The incumbent governor of Oregon, who had little opposition in his party primary during the same year, nevertheless spent a reported $43,156. Candidates for the state legislature, however, spent relatively little—usually under $2,000.[5] Their general election expenditures will be much higher.

---

[4] Herbert E. Alexander, *Financing the 1964 Election* (Princeton, N.J.: Citizens' Research Foundation, 1965), p. 8. Total campaign costs at all levels in 1964 were estimated by Alexander at about $200 million.

[5] "Goldschmidt's $29,624 Leads Spending for City Council Race," *The Oregonian*, May 26, 1970, 10; "$43,156 Spent for Gov. McCall in Drive to Win Nomination," *The Oregonian*, June 9, 1970, 13.

TABLE IX–2
Costs Per Vote: Oregon Primary, 1968

Presidential campaign	Expenditure per vote received
Democratic	
Senator McCarthy	$2.12
Senator Kennedy	1.95
Republican	
Governor Reagan	1.91
Richard Nixon	1.15
Senatorial Campaign	
Democratic	
Phil McAlmond	2.94
Senator Morse	1.61
Robert Duncan	.53
Secretary of State	
Republican	
F. F. Montgomery	.39
Clay Myers	.25

Source: *Eugene Register-Guard*, June 18, 1968, 12–A.

Other entry barriers pertain not to money but to outright prejudices. Few women or black men, regardless of income, can entertain a reasonable hope of attaining office. While these barriers are slowly being overcome, they persist. No woman has ever served as President, Vice President, or as a justice of the Supreme Court, while only a handful have managed to enter the Congress, hold state governorships, or become mayors of their towns and cities. The exceptions are still sufficiently rare to provide newspaper headlines and television interviews. Slightly more than 1,500 blacks held elective public offices in 1970. With Negroes comprising 11 percent of the population it would take 55,000 black officials to bring them a proportionate share of the positions.

Perhaps one of the more crucial entry barriers at the state and local levels is found in the form of limited or imperfect competition. While the two-party system is firmly entrenched in the nation it is not in the various states and localities. In not more than 16 or 17 states can we say that vigorous competition exists.[6] In a number of other states one might contend that competition prevails for several offices but that one party has a far better chance of winning the elections for substantial periods of time. In nearly one-third of the states one party dominates while the op-

[6] Dye, *Politics*, pp. 95–107.

TABLE IX–3

Patterns of Party Control

Type	Sequences of control	Number of states
One-party system	/D /D /D /D /D /D /D /D	11
One-party predominant	/D /D /D /R /D /D /D /R	16
One-party cyclical	/D /D /D /R /R /D /D /D	8
Cyclically competitive	/D /D /D /D /R /R /R /R	4
Highly competitive	/D /R /D /R /D /R /D /R	9

Key: D = Democratic control
R = Republican control

Source: Based on Joseph A. Schlesinger, "A Two-Dimensional Scheme for Classifying the States According to Degree of Inter-Party Competition," *American Political Science Review* 49 (December 1955), 1120–28.

position remains mostly token. In fact, the situation is sometimes so discouraging that the opposition fails to nominate candidates. Some political scientists, however, argue that more strenuous competition has been evidenced in the southern states during Presidential elections.

The fact that a state is less competitive may make entrance and longevity somewhat easier for candidates in the dominant party if they can please party leaders. Of course, relatively few states are so competitive that all offices are constantly rotated from one party to another. Much more typical are situations in which one party holds state offices for a fairly long period before it loses to the other major party which in turn goes on to win a few elections. At the Presidential level each party seems to win for long periods before being defeated. Long-term cycles seem to predominate in most states and for most offices. Various possibilities are depicted in Table IX–3.

Some Strategic Choices

Thus far we have roughly outlined the situation in which the aspirant for public office finds himself. The outline had to be rather broad because we are depicting the entire system, not just some small corner or detail. The specific situation confronting any specific politician is apt to be filled with a great many variations on our theme and some uniquenesses we cannot anticipate nor easily explain. Still, the situation in all cases poses some hard choices for a politician; these are choices he must make initially and continually make throughout his career if he is to have one:

1. Which party should I join?
2. Which office should I seek?
3. When should I run?
4. When should I announce my entry?
5. Which policies should I advocate? Deemphasize? Ignore?
6. How should I campaign? Strategies?
7. How should campaign money be allocated?

There are no neat answers to these questions, nor is there a science of strategy to which one can readily turn for advice. At best or worst (I never know which), the aspirant should consult veteran politicians or read some of the many handbooks that reporters, expoliticians, campaign managers, and other observers have written on campaigning. Most of this writing is not very reliable, although an occasional attempt is highly thoughtful, perceptive, and even amusing. Some may even be contradictory and very misleading; for example, many works offering conceptions and advice from an advertising and public relations framework. Perhaps, when political science has achieved greater scientific stature we shall be able to advise candidates with greater confidence than is now possible.

Some Tactical Advice or Rules of Thumb

Successful American politicians are rarely reflective about the reasons for their own successes. Defeated politicians have incentives, however, for explaining their failures. As a result, we generally learn more about politics from the latter than from the former group. Whatever the case, politicians do act as though they chose their courses of action on the basis of certain decision rules. In this section we list some of these decision rules or rules of thumb for the politician. We cannot claim that they are well tested and true, only that some men have stated them and/or act as though they followed such rules. Here are a few:[7]

1. Always allow subordinates to announce the bad news and handle unpopular programs.

[7] Most of these rules of thumb were gleaned from James A. Farley, *Behind the Ballots* (New York: Harcourt, Brace & Co., 1938), and J. H. Wallis, *The Politician* (New York: Frederick A. Stokes Co., 1935).

2. Always identify oneself with the good news and popular activities.

3. Cover up mistakes and embarrassing incidents by redirecting popular attention to more favorable events.

4. Hold power in reserve; that is, never threaten prematurely. A credible threat of what one might do under certain circumstances is a better deterrent than a definite statement of what one will do.

5. Never allow adversaries to define the issues.

6. When losing a race, broaden the scope of an issue so as to recruit potential allies.

7. Acquire only as many allies as are necessary to win; to acquire more increases costs and decreases individual shares of the payoffs.

8. Never admit having made a mistake; never confess the truth of anything detrimental.

9. If an action proves injurious to the voters, point out the responsibility of others, unforeseen circumstances, or both.

10. Pick enemies with care—they are valuable targets.

11. Always appeal to self-interests but garb them in the language of the "public interest."

12. Be concerned with future coalitions for the present ones are unstable.

13. Never tell one's friends in private anything you do not want your enemies to hear.

14. To insure the effective spreading of beneficial news tell it "in confidence."

15. Ignore your opponent if you are far ahead.

16. Use subordinates and allies to test the popularity of policies and candidates. *Trial balloons* is the name of the game.

17. Be careful of premature support; the marginal value of one's vote is increased by making it the crucial turning point in a close contest.

18. Never take anything for granted, particularly about the motives of others.

19. Never permit yourself to be placed on the defensive.

20. If a commitment is made, honor it.

21. Never allow opponents to monopolize public attention. If possible, schedule news-making events to divert attention from their activities.

22. Avoid flat statements and commitments about the future. Hedge!

23. Always maintain contact with other leaders—especially potential opponents.

24. Avoid being overly technical and academic.

25. Claim that your policy is relatively unpopular and that you are a courageous statesman willing to pay the costs of unpopularity in the greater interests of the society. In short, portray the opposition as currying the self-interest of the masses.

26. Steal issues and solutions from opponents. Offer policy solutions before they can be offered by the opponents.

27. Never needlessly offend.

28. Be willing to change both strategies and tactics.

The Politician as Policy Analyst and Vote Getter

The previous examples of tactical choices and rules that politicians appear to observe provide a few hints of the role public policy plays in strategic considerations; these hints need to be more fully examined because the politician, especially when in office, is a policy maker. We need to know how he chooses, among policy alternatives, which to adopt, which to reject, which to change, and which to ignore as politically irrelevant. Ordinary citizens and newspaper reporters generally view politicians as being mainly interested in their own reelection. This approach may be somewhat cynical, but is a fairly sound premise on which to analyze the behavior of politicians. We use that assumption in the following paragraphs.

The logic of policy analysis is no different for the politician than for the ordinary citizen. Since the objectives of the politician are vastly different and his resources considerably more plentiful his choices are apt to be both more informed and different from at least some of his constituents. Let us see how.

As the self-interested voter attempts to minimize his dissatisfaction or his utilities, the politician attempts to gain and retain office as long as he can at as low a cost as possible. In order to achieve these ends the politician should support policies and take actions he thinks will please his constituents in sufficient number (normally 50 percent plus one of those voting) to elect and reelect him. In this sense the politician plays an equivalent role in the polity to that of a businessman in the economy; that is, he benefits others in order to profit himself. As a businessman must know about his products and those of his competitors, so the politician must know his issues, public policies, and whatever alternatives may be offered by the opposition. He must also know the "demand curve" or preferences of the voters (consumers), how their preferences might be affected by advertising, and how he can persuade and mobilize them to vote for himself. Such information is costly to acquire and use. But information based on past experiences is not always likely to ensure survival; political demand curves may be altered rather rapidly under some conditions. Unless one is adaptable and, on occasion, innovative, he may be defeated by a new competitor with new proposals. The job of the politician consists—in part—of learning crucial characteristics of his constituents. Such crucial matters include:

1. Voter preferences and distributions thereof.
2. Party identifications.
3. Perceived impacts of public policies on different groups according to race, occupation, sex, age, social status, residence, and religious affiliations.
4. Which and how many voters can be mobilized, how, and when.

Figure IX–1 is a pictorial representation of some informational needs of the politician. Needless to say it is a gross oversimplification. The politician must know not only the objective consequences or impacts of policies on various constituents but (more important) *their perceptions* of these impacts for it is the latter that, in the shortrun, will most sharply affect voting.

Figure IX–1 is incomplete. The politician must sketch lines among and across all the categories of policies, groups, and their most likely voting responses; in short, he must arrive at estimates —or "guesstimates"—for every element in the diagram. Had all these lines been inserted they would only obfuscate the major point. The informational problem is obviously overwhelming if we insist on complete information; such data would also be prohibitive in terms of costs.

Perhaps the situation depicted in Figure IX–1 can be described in somewhat different terms so as to better convey the politician's perspective. Suppose we begin with a Presidential candidate some years ago as he might have surveyed the coming 1968 campaign. He might have seen it this way: Of the more than 200 million population there were about 118.5 million citizens of vot-

FIGURE IX–1

Predicted Impacts of Alternative Policies

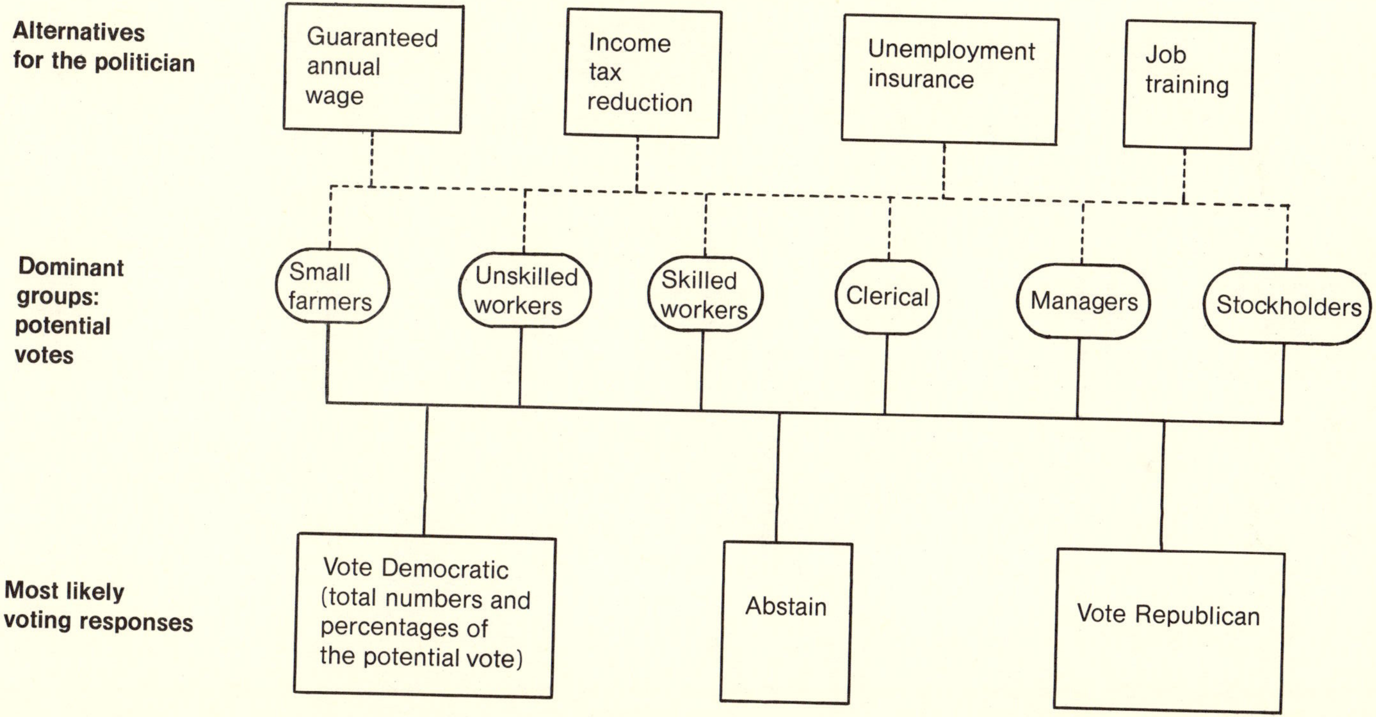

Alternatives for the politician

Guaranteed annual wage

Income tax reduction

Unemployment insurance

Job training

Dominant groups: potential votes

Small farmers

Unskilled workers

Skilled workers

Clerical

Managers

Stockholders

Most likely voting responses

Vote Democratic (total numbers and percentages of the potential vote)

Abstain

Vote Republican

ing age.[8] These potential voters constituted a vast pool of "possible" supporters. The emphasis should be on the "possible" because the pool gets much smaller as one investigates its actual size and composition. In Figure IX–2 we can quickly observe the attrition process and note the constraints and advantages that confront a candidate seeking votes. In the first place the potential pool of voting age persons is reduced by about 21 percent because 20 percent are not registered and another one percent do not seem to know whether they are or not; that reduces the number of voters to around 93 million. Of those who are registered, some 32 percent did not vote. This figure cannot be predicted for certain, although most politicians know that anywhere from 30 to 40 percent abstain in most Presidential elections. Those who stayed away may be viewed as more likely losses for the Democrats than Republicans because they come from groups whose previous political affinities would be with the Democrats.

So now there are about 73 million to think about. Of these, a Democrat should count on at least 42 percent—the lowest a Democratic candidate has ever acquired since 1956. The Republican can count on at least 39 percent, Goldwater's percentage in 1964.[9] In 1968 the Democratic candidate received about the minimal vote he could have expected. The 10 million votes garnered by Wallace might have gone to Nixon and Humphrey in different proportions, depending on the assumptions we make about Wallace's supporters. Traditionally, more should have gone to Humphrey but 1968 was not a traditional year, and Nixon won by only .3 percent.

The point we are making is that a politician must not assume that voters are all alike; they vote at different rates in different groups. The intelligent candidate attempts to "decompose" or "disaggregate" the blocs found in Figure IX–1 into even smaller blocs in order to derive a clearer picture of the situation. For example, in 1968 some 83 percent of the professional and technical people voted while only 54 percent of the manual laborers cast votes.[10] Farmers and farm managers also turned out in large numbers—81.6 percent—while about 44 percent of private household

[8] The above figures were derived from the Bureau of the Census, *Statistical Abstract of the United States, 1969* (Washington, D.C.: U.S. Government Printing Office, 1969), pp. 355–71; and Bureau of the Census, *Current Population Reports*, Series P., No. 192 (Washington, D.C.: U.S. Dept. of Commerce, December, 1969), 10–22.

[9] *Statistical Abstract, 1969*, p. 355.

[10] *Current Population Reports*, Series P, No. 192, p. 22.

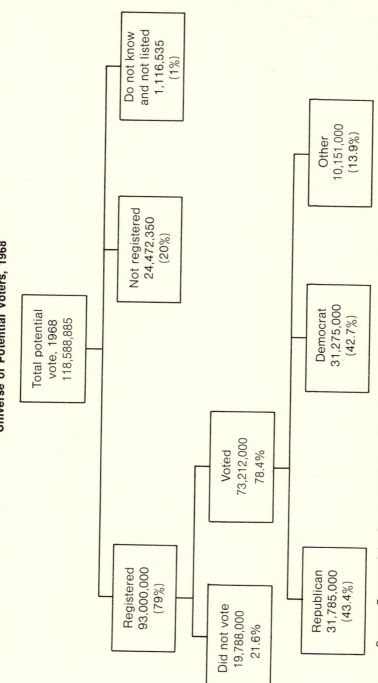

FIGURE IX–2

Universe of Potential Voters, 1968

Total potential vote, 1968
118,588,885

Do not know and not listed
1,116,535
(1%)

Not registered
24,472,350
(20%)

Registered
93,000,000
(79%)

Did not vote
19,788,000
21.6%

Voted
73,212,000
78.4%

Republican
31,785,000
(43.4%)

Democrat
31,275,000
(42.7%)

Other
10,151,000
(13.9%)

Source: Bureau of the Census, *Statistical Abstract of the United States, 1969* (Washington, D.C.: U.S. Government Printing Office, 1969), pp. 355–71; and Bureau of the Census, *Current Population Reports*, Series P, No. 192 (Washington, D.C.: U.S. Department of Commerce, December, 1969), pp. 10–22.

TABLE IX–4
Social Groups and Policy Preferences

Group	Favorable	Unfavorable
Wage earners	Minimum wages Unions Unemployment insurance Medical care Progressive income tax Price controls Public education	Sales tax
Blacks	Job quotas Free public facilities Voting rights Public housing Guaranteed annual income Black police Remedial education	Poll tax Separate facilities Voting requirements Restrictive covenants Union job control
Farmers	Crop subsidies Low cost loans Crop insurance Conservation payments Agricultural colleges Surplus commodity programs	High interest rates Sales taxes on food Minimum wages for agricultural workers Property tax

servants stayed home.[11] Each segment of the population, whether based on race, sex, occupation, income, geographical area, status, or similar factors, has a different potential vote and each has a quite different actual vote. Rational candidates take these kinds of information into account in devising strategy for winning office.

Fortunately for the politician, scientific information on preferences is not necessary. Long residence in his constituency provides him with a vast background of information about his people. He knows their work, sources and levels of income, typical aspirations, and voting traditions. Since the typical politician normally has far more formal education than his constituents he also tends to have more knowledge of policy alternatives and their impacts on various voters. Longevity in public office serves to further enlighten him since much of the activity of public officials is the gathering of policy information reactions to policy options from

[11] *Current Population Reports,* Series P, No. 192, p. 22.

interested persons. On the matter of likely impacts of policy see Table IX–4 in which three typical groups are identified by their most likely responses to a variety of public policies.

Once a politician has identified issues, alternative proposals, and relevant voting groups he is in a position to make some estimates of their likely responses to the benefits and costs of those proposals. If the issue involves money the rational politician estimates both the additional votes to be gained by added expenditures and the votes to be lost from different methods of financing the expenditures, since all programs create burdens or cost money. The rational politician supports additional expenditures up to the point at which the added favorable votes equal the unfavorable votes. Figure IX–3 shows how this works in geometrical terms.

Figure IX–3 tells us that for each additional dollar spent a certain number of votes will be acquired; each dollar creates beneficiaries while each additional dollar of financing becomes increasingly painful to increasing numbers of voters. The more more tax-

FIGURE IX–3
The Calculus of Votes

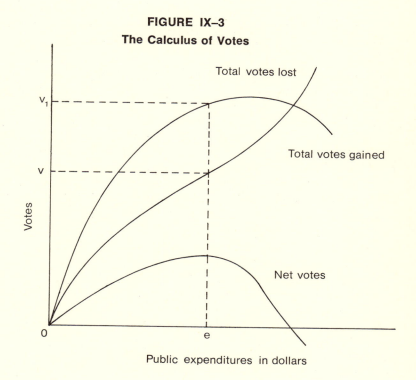

Public expenditures in dollars

payers must pay the unhappier they become. The exact number of voters affected is dependent upon the slopes of the curves. If the same number were affected by each dollar spent and/or taxed the curves would be perfectly straight lines. It is not likely that politicians would encounter many such linear curves or straight lines. Curves that are variants of the ones we have drawn are much more likely possibilities. In the case of the total votes won curve we suspect that the rate of increase in votes will be more than proportional at low levels of expenditures (highly elastic) while as the spending mounts it will become less than proportional (less elastic), as each additional dollar brings in fewer votes. At a very low level of expenditure, for example, each additional $100 may bring in, say, 1,000 votes but as expenditures mount the number of votes added per $100 decreases to say, 900 votes; then 600 votes; then 200 votes, then, finally, zero votes.

On the other hand, as taxes increase, the number of votes in opposition will probably increase at an increasing rate. Thus, the first additional $100 of taxation stimulates say, 200 opposition votes while the last $100 of added taxes creates 1,000 negative votes. A rational politician balances the marginal or incremental values of these two opposing tendencies. That is, he should continue to advocate spending as long as each added expenditure brings in more votes than it loses (0e in Figure IX–3).

While the logic of this choice is fairly clear, the facts of the matter are much less so. We do not have good empirical evidence concerning the position and slopes or elasticity of the curves in Figure IX–3. We have, in fact, constructed the curves on the basis of some dubious assumptions about citizen behavior as it relates to the enjoyment of public goods and the pain entailed by their costs. It might well be that we must draw different curves for different public goods rather than one curve for expenditures in general. Also, we would need different curves for different methods of financing. Surely, financing a program by a steeply progressive income tax will provoke fewer voters than a sales tax will. Of course, financing includes different instruments, rates, and methods of collection.

Another problem faces the politician who tries to measure citizen preferences and objections, in that the acts of consuming and paying for public goods are not coordinated. The goods are paid for, and votes are cast by, other than the consumers of the goods. This problem, however, refers to the empirical facts that produce the curves, not to the logic of the choice situation. In any case, beginners need not worry about methodological problems involved; they can be handled by the professors.

More crucial is the applicability of the marginal calculus to issues that are not strictly budgetary. For example, a politician's dilemma in supporting or opposing such measures as anticommunism, prayers in the school, Sunday Blue Laws, public art and monuments, fluoridation, sex education in schools, opposition to a war, desegregation of races, divorce laws, traffic control, and a host of constitutional issues present calculations that cannot readily be reduced to public expenditures, taxes, and votes in two- or three-dimensional graphs. In these emotional choices the politician has to decide how many votes will be won and how many lost according to his public positions on the issues: strongly opposed or in favor, mildly opposed or in favor, or neutral. Strong positions usually elicit strong reactions. This is probably not desirable unless everyone in the district takes a similar stance. Issues that divide voters more or less equally are more difficult to take a stand on. For every vote gained by some position, another will be lost.

Politicians have devised a number of ways of handling these tough policy questions. One way is to obfuscate the issue and one's position by appearing to support all sides. This can be accomplished by clever phrasing of speeches, lying, casting votes on different sides as the issue winds its way through the political process, delaying a choice until the heat dies down, or any combination of the above. Politicians have been known to take a vacation or to be unavailable when demanding questions are asked.

At other times they will try to avoid potentially hot issues by having them sidetracked in the committee system of a legislature. Pigeonholing a bill is one tactic Congressmen have been known to use for tax and certain labor bills during election years. Highly popular measures that would bankrupt the treasury are handled in this way because no legislator could possibly vote against them. The use of unrecorded voice votes was a traditional device among legislators until 1970, when the House of Representatives abolished the practice. It is still widely used in state and local legislative bodies. Still another time-honored means of avoidance is turning the problem over to a study commission for further analysis and recommendations. Such studies deflect issues, sometimes for a long time. Needless to say, these policy recommendations need not be accepted, nor are they often accepted, since most of these advisors do not' take political consequences into account. Those are reserved for the politicians to assess.

Presidential Campaigning: A Case Study in Decision Making

Presidential aspirants are much in need of advice, but usually receive far more than they need. This unsolicited brief is less intended for the President than for would-be Presidents. Since it is future-oriented, all suggestions run the risk of being outdated as institutions and opinion change in unforeseen ways. Should a national nomination primary be adopted, much of our advice will be highly dubious. Still, some gains are to be derived by analyzing a typical situation faced by campaigners for the office.

Our first consideration may well be on its way out as a major fact of Presidential politics, but it is still true in 1970: Candidates from the two major parties have different strategic problems. Republican candidates since 1932 have had to contend with being minority nominees while the Democrats have benefitted from a majority status. Their respective strategies have reflected this fact in all cases except that of President Eisenhower, who was a special case. However, if the Republican Party is about to become the majority party, as some theorists contend, then party strategies may be reversed.

Majority status automatically confers an advantage. In the case of the Democrats this has meant that the Democratic Presidential nominee could count on a substantial predisposition among the electorate for his candidacy. During recent years that has meant a three to two advantage in party registrations. Since the Democratic edge stems from popularity among the lower-income and lower-status voters, their problem has been to mobilize these more numerous but less active segments of the population on election day. Much of the Democratic paper advantage, therefore, is dissipated or more apparent than real. What Democratic candidates have had to do is reinforce the masses with economic appeal sufficient to convince them to vote.

In contrast, the Republicans, while operating with a smaller pool of sympathetic voters, are able to mobilize a much larger percentage of them. All behavioral research into the matter has shown that the higher-income and status groups who affiliate or identify with the Republican Party tend to vote in far larger numbers than do lower-status people. The Republican Presidential candidate has had three tasks as contrasted to the Democrat: he has had to *reinforce* the faithful, *convince* the independents, and even *convert* some soft Democrats in order to win. Only General

FIGURE IX–4
The Distribution of Partisanship, 1964

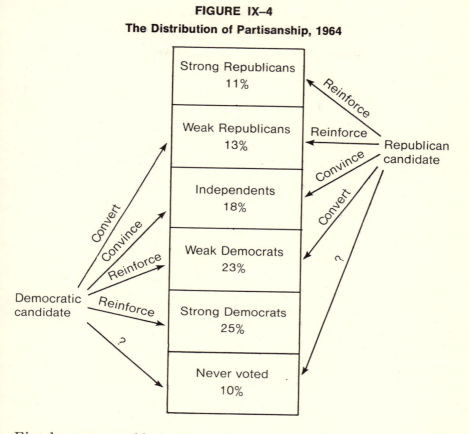

Eisenhower was able to successfully perform this set of contradictory acts. These basic considerations are all summarized in pictorial fashion in Figure IX–4.[12] The percentages in each block or cell refer to self-designated party affiliations. These figures change somewhat from year to year but have been quite stable during the past thirty years or more. Given these facts one wonders how a Republican could ever win office. No doubt some Republicans have asked that question as they went down to defeat.

But the answers are well known: Presidential elections are not decided solely on the basis of popular votes in the election. Rather, they are decided on the basis of electoral college votes and the distribution of the voters throughout the states. Presidents

[12] William H. Flanigan, *Political Behavior of the American Electorate* (Boston: Allyn & Bacon, Inc., 1968), p. 38.

can be elected without majorities among the voters, as 14 have been. We should also observe that those who win pluralities usually have a much larger margin of victory in the electoral college, because winning a state by even one vote gives the winner *all* of the electoral college votes of that state. This rule has given the Democratic candidates an advantage because so many of their adherents live in the highly populous states of the North and East. New York's body of 43 electoral college votes outweighs a combination of most other smaller states. (A state's electoral vote equals its number of Senators and Representatives in Congress.) While the value of an individual vote of each citizen differs among states that consideration is not relevant in this context. What a Presidential candidate wants are electoral votes; at present, he wants 270 because this provides the bare majority for election. These 270 votes can be logically attained in a great variety of ways but in the real world they are constrained by many forces far beyond the control of candidates.

Before proceeding we should illustrate a couple of our previous points with reference to President Nixon's 1968 victory. The following figures represent the electoral outcomes of 1968.

Candidate	Percentage of popular vote	Electoral votes (Total = 538)
Nixon	43.4%	301 (55.9%)
Humphrey	42.7	191 (37.3%)
Wallace	13.6	46 (6.8%)

If the electoral vote were proportional to the popular vote, Mr. Nixon would have received 43.4 percent of 538 electoral votes or 233 votes rather than the 301 or 55.9 percent he did receive. With majority rule prevailing in the electoral college he would not have become President so easily and his fate would have rested with the House of Representatives and, perhaps, George Wallace. At the time, some commentators felt that was indeed the Wallace strategy—to throw the election into the House where he could bargain with his 13.6 percent of the popular votes and 46 electoral votes.

Presidential candidates face a great many "givens" that limit their impact on the outcome. As we have seen, they include some fairly stable party preferences among the electorate, their distribution among the states, the electoral college and its decision rules, resource limitations, party traditions, being "in" or "out" of office, unforeseen political and economic events, and the fight for the party nominations. More than one Presidential nominee has probably wondered if he could do anything to affect his own fate.

Let us amplify the impacts of constraints other than the distribution of party influence and the electoral college we have just surveyed to see if we can further specify the strategic room a candidate has for maneuver. A man who wants to win the highest office in the land will find his chances are better if he has already held office, especially if he performed successfully. A man in high office can capture public attention with his activities if he wishes. He can confer substantial advantages on supporters through his appointment power (6,000 federal offices) and control over many policies of government. If he has not obviously failed in his conduct of the office many voters will be inclined to be loyal to him as a "known" commodity rather than opt for highly uncertain leadership capacity and a set of promises.

In addition, the President also has the opportunity of doing good for many voters, a power which the "outs" cannot provide since they do not have the authority to make policy and distribute benefits. About the only time the opposition can realize advantages occurs when adverse events make a President look bad. The opposition can and should take advantage of that opportunity by blaming the "ins." The problem of the "outs" is finding suitable issues—something the Democrats were less able to do when President Eisenhower was in office. Suitable issues for the opposition means anything that can be blamed on the incumbents, regardless of their responsibility. The optimal strategy is to keep the other party on the defensive as much as possible. Incumbents, however, face a serious problem whenever policies are pursued that place some voters at a disadvantage, and few policies are without that consequence. Just as a President may confer benefits so, too, he may and does impose costs. He cannot avoid it. The goal is to spread benefits widely and confine costs to as few as possible and especially to those who cannot retaliate. Better still, confer benefits that are readily perceived and costs that are concealed from or unknown to the payer.

Candidates, whether in or out of power, must also contend with the fact that their party traditions confine their policy choices. Consistency is still of some value in politics, and a sudden, radical change in policies is destined to upset the traditional following of a party. The nomination convention of the Democrats in 1968 was a party catastrophe of the first order because the entire range of policy positions was openly battled out by the participants. It was especially divisive because of nationwide, immediate news media coverage.

A party in power must also worry about such large-scale events as wars, depressions, and the like, that vitally affect their survival in office. Many critical events are beyond the immediate control of a President but he will be blamed or praised just the same. Most Presidents worry more about how they will respond in the highly visible short run than about how they can shape future events. The American President is a powerful figure but he is not omniscient nor omnipotent. (One or two have apparently thought they were and perhaps a few have been so regarded by their personal staffs. It is not wise for us nor Presidents to become so confident. The Presidency can be a vast learning and humbling experience.)

On a more mundane level, Presidential candidates go where the electoral votes are. Although token appearances are permissible, they should stay away from states they cannot win. On the other hand, time spent in sure states, especially those with few electoral votes, is wasted. The most fruitful time is spent in cultivating doubtful states with large blocs of electoral votes. A simple cost/benefit calculus will support this statement.

Both political parties spent nearly $50 million in the 1968 Presidential election, although many political scientists and others doubt that campaigning has any appreciable effect on the outcome of elections. Some observations about party affiliation can easily lead to such conclusions. For example, more than 80 percent of the electorate identify themselves with one major party or the other. At least one-third view themselves as strong supporters of one major party.[13] About one-third of the voters have made their choice before the party conventions. Another third usually decides during the conventions (mostly in favor of their traditional affiliation) and the remainder decide during the campaign. Again, the latter tend to return to their traditional choice. What can either party do under such circumstances?

The course of action a party and its Presidential nominee will take to influence a favorable electoral decision will depend on what conditions prevail. When a nominee is far in the lead at convention time he may as well assume that he will not win any more votes. He has only to hang on to the margin he has by avoiding terrible

[13] Flanigan, *Political Behavior*, p. 34.

mistakes. The expected loser of such a race can do very little except hope for a miracle; that was the plight of Stevenson in 1956 and Goldwater in 1964. But if the voters have not made up their minds before or during the convention, the race to win the election will be much stiffer. Here the party strategists have their work cut out for themselves, as they did in 1948. Party nominees and their staffs must see to it that their strong supporters are continually reinforced in their allegiances, that the weaker supporters are encouraged to participate, and that unaffiliated voters are courted with finesse. Other things being equal, the turnout and the direction of the votes of the last group is crucial to the outcome. Another tactic is for each party to attempt to reduce the turnout of the opposition voters. This has been especially important to the Republican Party for reasons we have alluded to above. A party may accomplish this end by convincing the opposition voters that the prospect of a win by that party is not frightening. The "me-too" strategy of several Republican nominees during the 1940s was partially based on this strategic assumption.

Except under relatively rare conditions parties cannot alter the basic political configuration or alignments of the nation. At best, parties must confine their activities to finding and developing issues with appeal to the heterogeneous groups that follow their leadership.

An Exercise in Analysis

A PRESIDENT CALCULATES HIS NEXT MOVE: NIXON AND THE CAMBODIAN DECISION, 1970

Our discussion has focused on the domestic situation of politicians because that is the immediate environment of choice and the source of the politicians' problems, opportunities, and resources. For many, however, and especially for Presidents, foreign relations is a major problem demanding quick resolutions. Our discussion problem involves a significant foreign policy choice on the part of President Nixon in 1970. The problem, as he understood it, was whether some action should be taken in the late spring of 1970 involving an invasion or as the military termed it, an "incursion" of Cambodia, during the Vietnam war. President Nixon was noted as a deliberate, calculating, and—according to some—"crafty" politician who carefully weighed the pros and cons of

TABLE IX-5

A Cost/Benefit Calculation of a Major Policy Choice

Options	*"Pluses"* Expected advantages	*"Minuses"* Expected disadvantages
1. "Any action at all" now	1. "Time running out"—weather conditions worsening, movement of enemy, weak Cambodian forces. 2. Discourage Communists from attacking capital and installing puppet government.	1. Military aid to Cambodia could only be minimal and ineffective.
2. Commit American ground forces in "Fish Hook" area	1. Would buy time for Vietnam to take over war. 2. Would speed up removal of American troops from Vietnam. 3. Might lead Hanoi to more serious bargaining in Paris talks.	1. Create deep divisions among Americans 2. Communists might attack Cambodian capitol. 3. Might break up Paris peace talks. 4. May provoke Communist attack in demilitarized zone.
3. S. Vietnam attack in "Parrot's Beak" area	1. Do little to speed Vietnamization of the war. 2. Not a major military area.	1. Less division in U.S. 2. Lessen probabilities of #2, 3, 4 above.

Source: Based on Stewart Alsop, "On the President's Yellow Pad," *Newsweek* (June 1, 1970), 106.

every choice in rather explicit terms. Stewart Alsop, the noted commentator, claims that Nixon actually wrote a kind of cost/benefit analysis of various options available to him at the time. The President's definition of the situation and clarification of the worth of his options is set forth in Table IX–5, in a language quite similar to that which Alsop informs us was used by the President on a yellow legal pad.[14]

The point of this discussion problem is less one of assessing the worth of President Nixon's ultimate choice, which in fact included options 2 and 3, than it is to gain some insight into the problems of rational choice under conditions of considerable uncertainty. For example, did the President state all the options? Were those he expressed stated as completely or accurately as might be desired? Have the "pluses" and "minuses" been placed in the right columns? Are all the relevant assumptions underlying the various advantages and disadvantages made clear? Have any probabilities been assigned to any of the possible consequences of each action? If the answers to these various questions are negative why is it that so intelligent and cautious a President did not make a more detailed outline on his legal pad? Could anyone?

Suggested Readings

Alexrod, Robert. *Conflict of Interest* (Chicago: Markham Publishing Co., 1970).

Banfield, Edward C. *Political Influence* (New York: The Free Press, 1961).

Bullitt, Stimson, *To Be A Politician* (Garden City, N.Y.: Doubleday & Co., Inc., 1959).

Cotter, Cornelius, ed. *Practical Politics in the United States* (Boston: Allyn & Bacon, Inc., 1969).

Kessel, John H. *The Goldwater Coalition* (Indianapolis: The Bobbs-Merrill Co., Inc., 1968).

Kingdon, John W. *Candidates for Office* (New York: Random House, 1966).

Lamb, Karl A. and Smith, Paul A. *Campaign Decision-Making* (Belmont, Calif.: Wadsworth Publishing Co., Inc., 1968).

Leuthold, David A. *Electioneering in a Democracy* (New York: John Wiley & Sons, Inc., 1968).

Rose, Richard. *Influencing Voters* (New York: St. Martin's Press, 1967).

Schattschneider, E. E. *The Semisovereign People* (New York: Holt, Rinehart & Winston, 1960).

[14] Stewart Alsop, "On the President's Yellow Pad," *Newsweek* (June 1, 1970), p. 106.

Chapter X

STRATEGIC CHOICES FOR ACTIVISTS

The past two chapters have dealt with the choices individual voters and politicians must make within the existing system. We have not yet considered how major system changes are made, or under what conditions they are considered necessary. That will be our concern in this chapter.

We have observed that a great many eligible voters do not vote at all, but accept decisions made in elections by the voting majority. Their reasons may vary: they may be satisfied (or not particularly dissatisfied) with the status quo or they may believe that their vote cannot affect the decisions being made. Politicians, on the other hand, believe that they can either affect the status quo or profit from it. They choose to become full-time bargainers in the political arena, rather than limit their bargaining power to a few days each year when elections are held.

Although most Americans are "middle of the roaders" who are reasonably content to be either Republican or Democrat, some are highly dissatisfied with existing institutions and policies. This group is composed of private citizens who are political activists. They are anxious to change the status quo and they believe change is possible. They attempt to influence both politicians and voters to use their bargaining power in order to make major changes. These activists may be called reformers if they seek to work within the system to change public policy, usually in such areas as the power structure and the allocation of resources. Another group is more revolutionary. They see the system as destructive and seek to change it radically. The strategic problem of these political activists, or deviants, will be our immediate concern.

What should a political deviant do? Leave the country? Compromise and join a major party or ally with a major party? Form a new party? Join a revolutionary movement? Drop out and become cynical or apolitical? A deviant may choose a course of action from among these major paths. He can choose irrationally and never reevaluate his position or he can choose rationally and proceed to a reasonably intelligent course of action. He may choose violent or nonviolent means.

Those who are dissatisfied with an existing situation have a number of general options. They can attempt to (1) change human nature in the preferred direction; (2) alter the rules of the game or institutions; or (3) alter specific policies. Policies can be changed either by substituting new leaders for old or by changing the attitudes of existing policy makers. Legal and illegal means can be used to pursue these options; at different stages of the political process both kinds of tactics are used. The most difficult of these options is changing human nature; this is the most difficult because we really do not know what behavior patterns are products of nature and what are products of society.

Furthermore, this option may also be the least desirable one, since it is hardly necessary to change fundamental patterns of belief and action. Some political activists have opted for the less demanding and more promising alternative of changing the rules of the game. Their costs will be commensurately higher, however, if the objects of reform are the more basic rules such as a constitution. This far-reaching change in institutions understandably disturbs people because they are not sure of what the consequences will be. Even if allocative consequences could be predicted, the alteration of as basic a document as a constitution (in a democracy or republic) is naturally of great concern to those who will be affected by proposed allocative changes.[1]

Less threatening and less costly is the reform of less basic rules than a constitution. Just how demanding this will be is difficult to predict, because the reform must first be specified. Its scope will depend on the depth of changes desired. The most likely areas for successful reform are the third group—those of leadership and policy. Leaders are difficult to defeat and governments may

[1] A proposed revision of the entire Oregon Constitution was soundly defeated by the electorate in May, 1970, primarily because a number of privileged programs would have been eliminated and made subject to legislative scrutiny and decision. Among the interest groups who feared this possibility were the Oregon State Grange; Veterans of Foreign Wars; Automobile Club of Oregon; Associated General Contractors of America, Inc.; Oregon Trucking Association; and State Highway Department officials. In each case one provision was the basis for rejection of the entire Constitution.

be slow to change but governments do change policies—witness the thousands of new laws passed each year, which make it difficult to keep up with the ever-increasing flow of new governmental decisions, regulations, ordinances, executive orders, and so forth. In this area, too, reform is easier where policy implications are narrower. Rational reformers of policies, therefore, attempt to alter policy incrementally and to keep consequences visible and in control. Instead of rewriting an entire law or constitution they seek to change specific provisions of existing law.

Each of these grand-scale alternatives has its *expected* (not certain) advantages and disadvantages or costs and benefits. Anyone contemplating serious reform must carefully calculate his strategies and tactics, because his opponents—the status quo forces—surely will and they normally have superior resources.

Only six strategic options are available to activists, but not all are mutually exclusive. Any activist group may pursue different strategies at different times. These are the six strategies available:

1. Leave the country.
2. Instigate revolution.
3. Employ small-scale demonstrations and limited violence.
4. Form a new political party.
5. Take over a major existing party.
6. Form interest groups and coalitions.

The first option and the last three are peaceful; the second and third entail varying levels and types of violence and disruption of the existing system.

The violent methods are the most costly. Even conventional interest groups will occasionally employ violence and deny services to other citizens. Labor unions and some civil rights organizations periodically have practiced violence or become involved in the destruction of property and the harming of people. Farm organizations have dumped milk or burned produce as means of decreasing the supply and dramatizing a market plight in the hope of gaining income supports. Generally peaceful, well-mannered, intelligent middle-class students have participated in campus violence to further educational and social reform. Some of the same youth who fought Chicago police during the 1968 Democratic Party convention had earlier campaigned peacefully for Senator McCarthy. Sometimes we deliberately choose certain strategies.

At other times they are imposed by forces beyond our immediate control, and, according to the historians, we merely act them out.

Leave the Country

Some patriots periodically offer two mutually exclusive alternative relationships to America—"love it or leave it"—as they proclaimed on bumper stickers throughout the late 1960s. Neither of these alternatives is clearly stated, for the former is nebulous, while the latter is incomplete; it does not tell us where to go or what to expect. Which of the following choices is more patriotic: Voting Republican or voting Democratic? Voting or not voting? Becoming a hippie or remaining square? Paying taxes or making voluntary contributions? Waiting to be drafted or volunteering for service? What constitutes "loving" one's country? If a set of criteria could be elaborated, how would they be enforced or applied?

Very few people consider leaving this country as a rational choice of action. Most Americans view their lives here as infinitely better than elsewhere. In this they are confirmed by two facts: immigration into the country must be limited by law and few Americans emigrate. Until 1969 the rate of emigration was only around 12,000 a year.[2] The figure increased considerably after 1969 because of draft evaders fleeing to Canada. This still does not approach the rate (in terms of percent of total population) of dissatisfied Tories who fled the country in our eighteenth century Revolution.[3]

The activist who finds the United States intolerable must consider the prospects of other lands. The price of leaving is high; it includes forgoing the possible chance of changing the United States. For highly uncertain rewards elsewhere one must leave close friends and sometimes a good job and income. Then, too, leaving means beginning life over in an alien society whose politics may be "good" but whose culture, language, and social institutions are strange and "unAmerican." One's standard of living is likely to diminish almost anywhere else in the world. But the most criti-

[2] U.S. Bureau of the Census, *Statistical Abstract of the United States, 1969* (90th ed., Washington, D.C.: U.S. Government Printing Office, 1969), p. 92.

[3] R. R. Palmer, *The Age of Democratic Revolution: The Challenge* (Princeton, N.J.: Princeton University Press, 1959), p. 188.

cal element in the reformer's cost calculations is the fact we mentioned first: the sacrificed opportunity for reform. While being a deviant at home is costly, being a foreigner in a new land will surely not increase one's political resources and influence in the United States. Therefore, leaving the country is not a good prospect under most conditions although it may be necessary for some to avoid the penalties of law. Countless draft evaders and dissenters during the Vietnam war apparently learned of the high costs the hard way. Emigration is not recommended for those interested in radical goals.

Instigate a Revolution

Without question, this alternative is the most demanding and the least likely to succeed. Those who choose to revolutionize basic institutions and policies assume an enormous task, and they can expect to observe the harshest of reactions. Few countries tolerate attacks on basic institutions especially if the attacks are violent. Furthermore, revolution cannot be successful in a nation whose citizens are patriotic supporters of the status quo.

Students of revolutions inform us that certain preconditions must prevail in sufficient degree before a revolution can even begin. The revolutionist cannot create these preconditions, he can only take advantage of them; that is precisely what a good revolutionist does. The preconditions of revolution have not been tested and measured with scientific exactness, but the following seem to find their way into many such lists.

1. Widespread fear that recent gains will be lost or at least significantly lessened.
2. Governmental inability to rule or solve outstanding social problems.
3. Disintegration of the ruling elites.

The immediate question before the rational revolutionist is whether these preconditions exist in sufficient degree. Revolutionary action is not a rational choice if this is not true.

How good are the chances of a successful revolution in the United States? The answer to this straightforward inquiry is not at all as direct and simple as the question itself. Opinion polls repeatedly reflect the fact that Americans remain the most optimistic people on earth concerning their expectations and aspirations, both economic and political. They have also realized more of their hopes than most people. Probably, only the occurrence of a major depression or some other social catastrophe would create more of these preconditions for revolution. Accordingly the probability of revolutionary activity would increase in that case. Polls also show that Americans, as contrasted with English, French, Italians, Germans, and Mexicans, have a very high regard for their political institutions.[4] Such regard stems in part from effective government. Studies dealing with the plight of governments in less-highly-developed nations strongly suggest that they cannot govern effectively and have little respect from their people. United States governments, without maintaining an authoritarian power structure, are surely able to provide most of the basic goods and services governments are expected to provide and in a manner deemed appropriate.

If government's problems and promises outstrip her resources and performances, revolutions and civil wars become a possibility. During recent years violent protests have involved students, ethnic groups, and blacks. These suggest considerable unrest, but hardly enough for a successful revolt. On such occasions the authority of government has been unsuccessfully challenged by groups with revolutionary aims. The Civil War was our major revolutionary challenge, but the South was defeated, and in the lesser rebellions, riots, and demonstrations, of our history the dissatisfied groups have been effectively if not always honorably contained. Scores of newly-developing nations have not been so fortunate as a succession of ineffectual governments have paraded across the scene.

Some theorists claim that revolutions are facilitated when the ruling elites disintegrate or fail to live up to their promises—when they exploit rather than serve society. When this disintegration is attacked by the intellectuals the regime is in danger. Ability to disseminate their views vividly and rapidly gives intellectuals an unusually influential position for encouraging dissenson.

Are American intellectuals fomenting trouble? Are American elites in disarray? The answer to the former question is a qualified yes; to the latter, an emphatic no. Some intellectuals are engaged in serious active opposition to the existing system but so far they have confined themselves chiefly to words. Rarely have

---

[4] Gabriel Almond and Sidney Verba, *The Civic Culture* (Princeton, N.J.: Princeton University Press, 1963), p. 102 and *passim*.

they engaged in any sustained kind of violent attacks. These intellectuals are a small and unrepresentative sample of the intellectual world. Most intellectuals work within the accepted framework and defend it, often with great skill and effect. From the perspective of the radical dissenters, this willingness of the conventional intellectual to labor in behalf of the status quo—and be handsomely paid for it—is far worse. Countless professors advise our governments and our private institutions, clearly aligning themselves with the Establishment.

Most Americans remain unconvinced that revolution is necessary to correct even the gravest of our social ills. They generally have confidence in their nation and in its political institutions, even when an apparent challenge to the system arises. The 1964 Presidential election was a struggle between two opposing main stream viewpoints. A strong New-Deal liberal, Johnson, ran against a strong conservative, Goldwater. Opinion polls showed only 8 percent of the people were worried about "national disunity and political instability"; 5 percent about "lack of law and order"; 5 percent about the election; and 8 percent over "socialism and big government." War was their biggest fear.[5] In short, the fears of Americans at that time were not about the vitality of the nation or its political institutions. Americans have traditionally been highly optimistic about their personal and national progress. Even the Great Depression failed to dim the American dream very much. Thus leftist revolutionaries are not likely to find many converts among the ordinary people.

Although the conditions for revolution do not seem to be present some present-day revolutionists have decided that gains are to be made and that their activity will have a positive impact on eventual outcomes. Anyone who seriously considers promoting revolution should carefully calculate a cost/benefit ratio for his actions. He should also study the works of revolutionists on strategy. He will probably discover that the lessons to be learned must be considerably modified to fit the American scene. Techniques of peasant warfare in Southeast Asia or Latin America are not applicable to our highly urban and suburbanized lifestyle. Strategies and tactics must reflect this condition. It is our belief that less violent strategies than total revolution are more appropriate.

[5] Lloyd A. Free and Hadley Cantril, *The Political Beliefs of Americans* (New York: Simon and Schuster, 1968), p. 105.

Employ Small-Scale Demonstrations and Limited Violence

Would-be revolutionists and rebels must continually assess the worth of such dramatic tactics as mass demonstrations, calculated violence, and killing. These drastic actions have consequences that are serious, if difficult to measure, and should not be undertaken unless the actors can be assured that the payoffs ultimately justify the choice of means. Societies are complex and resistant to experiment, and therefore we are seldom able to decide the cost/benefit results of different strategies and tactics. Many rebels have, however, prematurely concluded that peaceful demonstrations and moral pleas have not had high payoffs. They have decided that the established community will only respond favorably when highly threatening gestures are made against it. Indeed, many facts serve as evidence to suggest that threats and violence have produced useful reactions from the government and its supporters. The drawback for the rebels is that the response includes negative as well as positive policies and behavior. Reactionary movements may and have gained greater power by virtue of the "backlash" phenomenon. On the other hand, it is difficult to deny that during the past decade much legislative progress has been made in the interests of disadvantaged minority groups. Enormous programs and expenditures have been initiated. There is no doubt that the political tactics of activist groups have made white middle-class Americans and governments aware of the plight of one-fifth of the nation. Whether all the well-meaning intentions and programs of government have served to alleviate the difficulties is far more questionable. Some maintain that whatever improvements have been made during the past fifteen years resulted from the workings of forces far beyond the immediate control of government.[6] Uncontrolled population movements, the growth of the economy, and long-term shifts in social attitudes may be far more significant contributory factors than all the government programs. If this is so we might well conclude that the violence employed by radicals and others has been ineffectual and even counterproductive; the gains would have come about in any event or perhaps even sooner. A few historians have even suggested that economic conditions would have caused slavery

[6] Edward C. Banfield, *The Unheavenly City* (Boston: Little, Brown & Co., 1970).

to die out rather rapidly if the Civil War had not occurred; the animosities generated by the war would have been avoided or considerably reduced.[7]

Although we cannot determine the precise utility of violence in promoting good social ends, we must concede that violence does sometimes have certain useful consequences, particularly for individuals who need to bolster their self-esteem and sense of efficacy. Participation in revolutionary movements strengthens one's sense of importance and the bonds of comradeship among its members. The unmet need of disadvantaged groups to gain a heightened sense of personal worth, dignity, and self-confidence, is a need that the rest of "middle-America" cannot appreciate because they have not suffered significant deprivation. These characteristics have seen phenomenal growth among the blacks during their revolt, and the Chicanos and Indians now seem to be gaining that same sense of self-regard and efficacy. It is tragic if in a land of freedom revolutionary activity is the only way available for them to restore these long-lost qualities. Can we afford the cost?

Form a New Political Party

Many abortive attempts have been made to form new political parties. Most have been sponsored by loyal Americans who chose not to revolt, but tried to change policy by peaceful means. In theory, it is possible to alter public policies and leadership. The Republican Party, for example, was founded in 1856, and managed immediately to become one of the two major parties. It has held the Presidency for at least 62 years since its founding. Most new parties are listed on the ballots for at least one Presidential election but rarely attain more than 10 percent of the popular vote or more than 5 percent of the vote in the electoral college. A number of parties remain on the ballots for long periods of time (Socialist, Prohibitionist, and Socialist Labor parties), but their members and candidates rarely delude themselves as to their electoral power. Many minor parties have based their appeal on single policy issues but some formulate general platforms and appeals.

Occasionally a party suddenly appears that dramatically

[7] See, for example, James Randall and David Donald, *The Civil War and Reconstruction* (Boston: D. C. Heath & Co., 1961), Chapter 3.

challenges the major parties in one or two Presidential elections. Among the challengers in recent decades were the Progressive Party under the leadership of Henry Wallace in 1948; the States Rights Party led by Senator Thurmond, also in 1948; and the American Independent Party of Governor George Wallace in 1968. Leaders and supporters of all three parties believed that neither of the major parties adequately represented their ideals. They were primarily issue oriented, although each was led by an interesting and popular figure. None gained more than the 46 electoral votes Wallace received in 1968. Henry Wallace gained only 2.4 percent of the popular vote and no electoral votes, while Thurmond achieved the same number of popular votes and 39 electoral votes. The largest number of popular votes ever received by a third party candidate was gathered by President Theodore Roosevelt as the Progressive Party candidate in 1912. He achieved some 27.4 percent of the popular vote but only 8 percent of the electoral vote. In 1924 Senator La Follette tallied 13 electoral votes on the basis of 16.6 percent of the popular vote. These figures suggest that, historically, third party hopefuls have not done too well, and Figure X–1 illustrates the point. Their political value, however, lies in the ability to influence the policies and strategies of the major parties, especially when their share of the popular vote exceeds 12 percent. An incumbent President who has won by a small margin cannot afford to ignore these voters if he intends to remain in office.

If an activist plans to form a new party, he must be aware of the reasons for their past failures. Among the discouraging circumstances and obstacles third parties face are (1) the enormous costs of mounting a campaign; (2) an incredible labyrinth of state election laws; (3) the need for powerful issues and grievances; (4) the need for a dynamic candidate; (5) massive failures on the part of the major parties; (6) an essentially indifferent electorate; and (7) the electoral college. A new party, by definition, must literally begin from nothing and in a short period, perhaps not much more than a year, form a national organization, train workers, raise huge sums of money, schedule a campaign, get on the ballots of as many states as possible, and convince traditional major-party voters that they ought to trade a lifetime of party allegiance for new and often untried leaders.

The single most significant event that would influence third parties would be abolition of the electoral college. If that happened it is quite possible that we would have a somewhat different

FIGURE X–1

Percentage of Total Presidential Vote Polled by Minority Candidates, 1884–1960

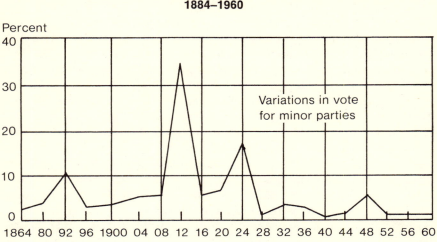

Source: V. O. Key, Jr., *Politics, Parties, and Pressure Groups* (5th ed., New York: Thomas Y. Crowell, 1964), p. 279.

list of Presidents and that third party strategies would change. Without the electoral college, some of the fourteen Presidents who did not win majorities in the popular vote might not have become President. Hayes and Cleveland are two Presidents who did not even win pluralities in popular votes. However, even without the electoral college, the mere existence of a third party is no guarantee of its strength. Its major power would probably be to influence the outcomes by decreasing the votes of one or the other of the leading candidates. Scholars and politicians still wonder whether Nixon owes his 1968 election to Governor George Wallace and the American Independent Party. Since we have no definitive tests, the argument cannot be settled conclusively.

Take Over a Major Existing Party

This useful strategy has been successful, as in the case of Senator Goldwater's Presidential nomination by the Republican Party in 1964.[8] Success, however, is not guaranteed. A notable

[8] For an excellent analysis of the matter see John H. Kessel, *The Goldwater Coalition: Republican Strategies in 1964* (Indianapolis: The Bobbs-Merril Co., Inc., 1968). A more general analysis of Presidential electoral

failure was Senator McCarthy's attempt to win the backing of the Democratic Party in 1968. Wendell Willkie, the Hoosier business-man, stampeded the Republican Convention and won the nomina-tion in 1940 only to go down to defeat against Franklin Roosevelt in his bid for a third term. Perhaps, we can also include General Eisenhower's defeat of Senator Taft in a close nomination contest in 1952 as a somewhat successful protest within a party. In each major party, front-runners have been defeated and "dark horses" nominated for the Presidency. In at least one other case, an in-cumbent President—Lyndon Johnson in 1968—was displaced by challengers within his own party without a formal contest; he resigned before the apparent inevitability occurred. And, where such challenges have failed to win a nomination they have served to affect the candidacy of the man who won, sometimes to defeat him, as might have been the case with Vice President Humphrey in 1968.

Each of the minority candidates mentioned gained his nomi-nation in a dramatic manner and all but Eisenhower then went on to suffer defeat in the general election. The very drama of their unexpected convention victories left deep scars in the party and this no doubt contributed to their subsequent defeats. A nomina-tion may be won but the chances of winning an election have been minimal, except in the unusual cases of Eisenhower (1952) and Franklin Roosevelt, who in 1932, was able to wrest the nomina-tion from a party stalwart, Al Smith. Both Eisenhower and Roose-velt, especially Roosevelt, were able to remake their parties into far more liberal organizations than they had been theretofore.

Form Interest Groups and Coalitions

A fifth strategy for the discontented is to form an interest group that neither engages in violent action nor attempts to take over a political party and seek election for public office.[9] An inter-

---

strategies is advanced by Nelson W. Polsby and Aaron B. Wildavsky, *Presi-dential Elections* (2d ed., New York: Charles Scribner's Sons, 1968).

[9] There are countless books on interest groups. Two of the better more recent ones are Harmon Zeigler, *Interest Groups in American Society* (Engle-wood Cliffs, N.J.: Prentice-Hall, Inc., 1964), and Harry M. Scoble, *Ideology and Electoral Action* (San Francisco: Chandler Publishing Co., 1967). The latter volume is unique and particularly valuable because of its imaginative attempts to devise quantitative measures of the electoral and legislative power of an interest group.

est group, while difficult to organize and maintain, is still a much less costly endeavor than the other four strategies. Unless the goal(s) are unusual its chances of legislative success are much higher.

An interest group is an organization that pursues a relatively narrow range of political goals, and does so by influencing rather than joining political parties and governments. An interest group is generally easiest to organize when the goals are fairly specific and material or occupational in nature. The most powerful interests in the nation are the huge producer groups in business, labor, and agriculture. Groups that pursue nonmaterial objectives seemingly have a more difficult time achieving their ends. Apparently most people are most consistently sensitive to their producer roles and interests. There is some hope for other roles, however, but they seem to rest on the assumption that one's income is more or less secure. Thus, conservation and consumer organizations appear to be gaining more power. Time will tell, however, whether such recreational and consumption-minded groups can win out against the big combines of lumber companies, oil and gas firms, various manufacturers, and the labor unions whose members depend on the income of these companies. As the costs of fighting pollution, stiffening zoning laws, preserving the natural resources increases we should observe the big producer groups waging a tough campaign against the conservationists.

Interest groups can gain influence by forming coalitions with groups having similar purposes. Coalition-building is an important political strategy; under current conditions, political success is highly unlikely without it.

There are situations, particularly in local communities, in which single interests can dominate without resort to support from others. But as our society has grown more complex, political monopolies have decreased. Now few groups are in a position to call all of the political tunes all of the time. Accordingly, those interested in shaping public choices have had to acquire allies; in so doing they have had to both accept less and pay more.

BUILDING COALITIONS

One who opts for coalition building must be willing to share his gains with allies and pay out higher bargaining costs. The more partners one needs, the greater the bargaining costs; the lesser the shares of any given set of advantages or gains. A group interested in finding allies must also be prepared to seek allies in peculiar places. It has been maintained that "Politics make strange bedfellows," but that seems true only to people who do not understand coalition formation. Coalitions are not formed by groups that share every basic value and belief, but by those whose shared or complementary interests can be advanced by common courses of action. For example, the distinguished conservative economist Milton Friedman and the well-known radical and pacifist leader Sanford Gottlieb formed a Council for a Volunteer Military in 1967. At a press conference announcing the coalition Mr. Gottlieb said "I've never appeared on the same platform with a Goldwater man . . . . This is a unique issue with us. It's the one thing we agree on."[10] Mr. Gottlieb recognized the basic requirement of coalition formation—having a *single common concern*, sometimes regardless of the reasons. Coalitions can be formed by people who hate one another on all things but one; if that single concern is strong enough they can work together. Coalition builders should seek out persons and groups whose interests are complementary to their own, and not waste time trying to find partners who agree on everything.

The size of a coalition is a critical consideration. Common sense suggests that a vast number of allies is not always desirable. Numbers increase costs and decrease each one's share of the gains.[11] Oversized coalitions are sometimes recruited because success seems uncertain, but if the uncertainty is not overwhelming one should acquire only enough allies to win. If an alliance becomes too large leaders find it increasingly difficult to please everyone and manage. Defections may be expected because the gains of some are usually made at the expense of other members. The grand New Deal coalition of 1932–68 disintegrated, in part, because various coalition partners saw their gains being nibbled at by other groups in the same coalition.[12] White workers and blacks seemed unable to make common advances to be paid for by noncoalition citizens.

As long as a coalition can make nonmembers pay for their benefits it will flourish. Labor and industry have often been able

[10] Neil Sheehan, "Draft is Uniting Right with Left," *The New York Times*, May 21, 1967, 1.

[11] William H. Riker, *The Theory of Political Coalitions* (New Haven, Conn.: Yale University Press, 1962), pp. 32–33.

[12] Samuel Lubell, *The Future of American Politics* (New York: Harper & Brothers, 1951).

to make the customers pay for increased profits and worker benefits by coalescing in the market as well as in public policy-making.
For at least three decades John L. Lewis' United Mine Workers,
the railroad companies, railroad unions, and the coal industry
managed to form an effective coalition for their collective advantage; it was maintained, however, at the expense of coal consumers as well as those who might have profited from other forms of
transportation. Among their successful common efforts was the
lengthy postponement of the St. Lawrence Seaway. Countless millions who would have benefitted from that development paid external costs for many years.

Government officials play a leading role in mobilizing support. It is usually believed that most businessmen would not be
likely to support a Democratic President's policies and his possible reelection. But in 1967 President Johnson organized one of
the more imaginative coalitions, and many came to the active support of his Great Society programs.[13] Prestigious bank presidents,
utility officials, and department store executives were all recruited
by Administration leaders to lobby with Congress for various em-
battled Johnson social programs including the Job Corps, low-cost
subsidized housing, rent subsidies for the poor, and other proposed governmental activities. Johnson was able to gain their
support because business perceived both potential benefits from
and costs for failure to support the programs. In Pittsburgh, for
example, some 24 banks and other businesses lobbied for subsidized rent for the poor—not because they liked the poor, but to
ward off public housing. Other businesses supported the Job Corps
against the wishes of unions because they wanted more trained
minority workers in their organizations. Still others supported
various parts of the Great Society program because although they
thought they could not prevent them from being approved, they
wanted to claim a right to shape their provisions and administration. Among those who lobbied for rent subsidies and the Model
Cities Program were lifelong Republicans from banking, the lumber industry, paint and wallboard industries, transit companies,
real estate, and other fields. All had financial interests at stake in
rehabilitating core areas of cities and/or preventing what they

---

[13] The above account is based on Alan L. Otten, "New Allies for LBJ:
Varied Motives Impel Many Firms to Support Great Society Programs," *The
Wall Street Journal*, April 19, 1967, 1, 9.

regarded as worse governmental programs, a not uncommon motive for political action. Johnson and his associates had, at times, to educate these groups as to their own gains and possible losses. Self-interest is not innate nor always apparent, even to sophisticated businessmen; coalition builders should be prepared to explain the benefits of their coalitions to the less well informed.

Another apparently improbable coalition formed for a brief period during Eisenhower's second administration illustrates the instability of some coalitions and the use of implicit bargaining among or between the members. While many reformers have dreamed of a Farmer-Labor Party on a national scale none has ever been formed that was effective and stable. In 1956, however, the AFL–CIO came to the temporary support of several farm organizations in Congressional struggles over the maintenance of high price supports for many farm commodities.[14] Ordinarily, city workers and unions oppose rigid high price supports because they increase the cost of living. In this instance, the labor union leaders came to the support of farmers on the grounds that (1) some of the farm supporters would reciprocate when the minimum wage increase proposal was to be voted on a month or two later in the session; (2) unions were worried that unless farm income was maintained at higher levels, unemployed farm workers would move to the cities and compete; and (3) decreased farm income leads to the layoff of thousands of farm equipment workers in the cities. These were not bad reasons for forming an alliance. Later, the minimum wage was raised from 75 cents to $1.00 an hour, and high price supports (90 percent of parity) were restored, but vetoed by President Eisenhower.

Farm policy issues in particular pose some interesting problems for the student of coalitions because it is difficult to account for the votes of some individual Congressmen on these matters. Most, however, behave as expected. During much of the period following World War II, Congress split into a remarkably consistent regional and party pattern of voting whenever certain agricultural issues arose.[15] One bloc, for example, has favored and another opposed high rigid price supports. The former group

---

[14] See Joseph A. Loftus, "Farm-Labor Bloc Upsets the GOP," *The New York Times*, April 10, 1956, 1.

[15] "The Politics of Agriculture: Congressional Voting Patterns and Major Votes," *Congress and the Nation: 1945–1964* (Washington, D.C.: Congressional Quarterly Service, 1965), pp. 673–77.

has also voted for stricter controls over production while the latter has favored minimal or weak controls. The members of the two coalitions and their votes are depicted in Table X–1. The table informs us that neither political party in the House of Representatives is united (a not uncommon observation) nor are the farmers whose incomes and farm operations are at stake. Not all farmers have identical interests; in fact, some have diametrically opposed interests as is the case between the feed-growers (corn and grain) and the farmers who use those feeds to raise beef cattle, poultry, and dairy cows. Higher price supports for the growers mean higher prices for the feed users. Some cattle growers, however, do not worry about commercial feed because they graze their cattle as is done in the Western states. Also smaller and less prosperous cattlemen tend to support the Democratic Party whereas their larger and more prosperous colleagues tend to support the Republican Party. The three major general farm organizations reflect their constituents' interests as do Congressmen. The American Farm Bureau Federation and the National Grange tend to be conservative while the National Farmers Union tends toward the liberal view. In addition, two dozen specialized commodity organizations and special groups represent the diverse and often conflicting positions of cooperatives, milk producers, meat packers, fruit and vegetable growers, canners, poultry farmers, sugar beet growers, and several other producers. Coalition building among these many groups is a never-ending activity, subject to changing configurations as the demands and conditions of agriculture change.

SOME ALLEGED MYTHS OF COALITIONS

The problems of coalition politics are admirably analyzed and extended by a controversial and brilliant black civil rights leader of the 1960s, Stokely Carmichael, and a well-known black scholar, Charles V. Hamilton. In a book entitled *Black Power: The Politics of Liberation in America*,[16] which was designed to provide an ideology and strategy for black liberation from the tyranny of white institutions and rule, they argue that the black man cannot expect to achieve his ends within the traditional political processes of peaceful competition and bargaining. In their quest for

[16] Carmichael and Hamilton, *Black Power* (New York: Vintage Books, 1967).

TABLE X-1

Typical Congressional Voting Blocs on Price Supports and Production Controls

High price supports and stricter production controls		Low or no price supports or controls	
Group	Estimated number of votes	Group	Estimated number of votes
Majority of southern Democrats	100+	Northern urban Republicans	
Majority of western Democrats		Northern Suburban Republicans	
		Midwestern rural Republicans	150
		Northeastern farm Republicans	
Some midwestern farm Republicans	6–50	A few urban Democrats	20–50
Some northern urban Democrats	30–70	A few southern and western Democrats	12

Source: Adapted from "The Politics of Agriculture: Congressional Voting Patterns and Major Votes," *Congress and the Nation: 1945–1964* (Washington, D.C.: Congressional Quarterly Service, 1965), pp. 673–77.

"new forms" of politics they dismiss certain types of coalition building with whites as a possible alternative. In attempting to show the futility of these coalitions, they contend this strategy is based on these three myths:

1. The interests of black people are identical with certain liberal, labor and reform groups;

2. Effective coalitions can be established between the economically secure and weak groups;

3. Coalitions can be based upon friendly sentiments and moral grounds.[17]

The authors go on to discuss each of the alleged myths and find them wanting. They also establish four preconditions for effective coalitions. The list, not dissimilar from the analysis of this chapter, serves as an effective summary to our chapter. These conditions include: (1) Mutual recognition of self-interests; (2) Mutual belief that each coalition partner stands to benefit; (3) Acceptance of the idea that each partner has an independent power base or set of resources; and (4) Mutual recognition that goals must be specific and not general.[18]

Exercises in Analysis

THE CONSERVATIVE COALITION IN CONGRESS

We have analyzed coalitions on both an abstract and a concrete, illustrative level; we have not attempted to provide a history of major coalitions in America nor even to document current powerful coalition efforts. There are, of course, strong coalitions of varied interests and durability at all levels of our political system. But the most powerful and interesting one is found at the national level working primarily in Congress. That coalition, consisting of Northern Republicans and Southern Democrats, has for several decades influenced the course of national policies. Its level of influence varies from time to time, and although its interest covers most issues, the economic issues seem predominate.

Some of the more relevant facts concerning this coalition are presented in Table X–2. The column headed *coalition appearances* refers to the percentage of rollcall votes in which the ma-

[17] Carmichael and Hamilton, *Black Power*, Chapter III.
[18] Carmichael and Hamilton, *Black Power*, pp. 77–81.

TABLE X-2

Conservative Coalitions in Congress

Year	President	Senate Dem.	Senate Rep.	House Dem.	House Rep.	Coalition appearances	Coalition victories Senate	Coalition victories House
1961	Kennedy (D)	65	35	263	174	28%	48%	74%
1962	"					14	71	44
1963	Kennedy/ Johnson(D)					17	44	67
1964	Johnson(D)	67	33	258	177	15	47	67
1965	"	68	32	295	140	24	39	25
1966	"					25	51	32
1967	"	64	36	247	187	20	54	73
1968	"					24	80	63
1969	Nixon (R)	57	43	243	192	27	67	71

Source: "Conservative Coalition Remains Potent In Congress," *Congressional Quarterly Weekly Report*, January 16, 1970, 161.

jority of Northern Republicans and Southern Democrats voted alike. *Coalition victories* refers to the percentage of those appearances that was won by the coalition. While the coalition has obviously won important victories each year we should not overestimate its power. Winning half of the 14–28 percent of the issues voted on does not suggest overwhelming political muscle. A number of exceedingly interesting features of Table X–2 call for our analysis, but in order to conduct that analysis one must have information and some logical skill. Although insufficient information is presented, perhaps the following list of questions will highlight what can be said about coalition formation and influence, as well as suggest additional kinds of information to seek for the solution of the problems. The questions and their answers should also provide some hints about the difficulties faced by reformers and radicals in reordering our policy priorities through the legislative process. What factors might influence the annual variations in coalition appearances? Why are the numbers of victories so different in the Senate and House? Why are there such great variations in victories within each house of the Congress? (The range in the Senate is from a low of 39 percent in 1965 to a high of 80 percent in 1968 and from a low of 25 percent to a high of 74 percent in the House of Representatives.)

Two Democratic and one Republican President served during the period covered in Table X–2; does that make any difference in coalition appearances and effectiveness? Why? Does control of either or both houses of Congress make any difference in the success of the coalition? Does the size of the majority party in either or both houses have any significance?

THE POSSIBILITIES OF A COUP D'ETAT

The troubles of the past few years have stimulated a number of novelists, commentators, political theorists, and others to speculate about the possibilities of a *coup d'etat* in the United States. Among those who have written knowledgeably about that seemingly far-fetched event is Edward Luttwak. His small book entitled *Coup d'Etat: A Practical Handbook*[19] was later applied to the United States in the pages of *Esquire.*[20] Luttwak contends

---

[19] Luttwak, *Coup d'Etat* (New York: Alfred A. Knopf, Inc., 1968).
[20] "A Scenario for a Military Coup d'Etat in the United States," *Esquire* 74 (July, 1970), 60–65; 138–41. A modern fictional illustration can be found in Edwin Corley, *Siege* (New York: Stein & Day, 1969).

that, to make possible the sudden takeover of a governmental apparatus, these three general conditions must exist:

1. The social and economic conditions of the target country must be such as to confine political participation to a small fraction of the population.[21]

2. The target state must be substantially independent and the influence of foreign powers in its internal political life must be relatively limited.[22]

3. The target state must have a political center. If there are several centers these must be identifiable and they must be politically, rather than ethnically, structured. If the state is controlled by a non-politically organized unit, the coup can only be carried out with its consent or neutrality.[23]

Consider these questions: Is the United States in such a state or does it show signs of movement toward these three conditions? What is the evidence? Are these three preconditions sufficient to produce a coup? If not, what additional ones are required? Can a small group of conspirators produce such preconditions? Why?

Suggested Readings

Graham, Hugh Davis and Gurr, Ted R., eds. *Violence in America* (New York: The New American Library, 1969).

Gregg, Richard B. *The Power of Nonviolence* (2d. ed., New York: Schocken Books, 1966).

Leites, Nathan and Wolf, Charles, Jr. *Rebellion and Authority* (Chicago: Markham Publishing Co., 1970).

Lipsky, Michael. *Protest in City Politics* (Chicago: Rand McNally & Co., 1970).

Luttwak, Edward. *Coup d'Etat* (New York: Alfred A. Knopf, Inc., 1968).

Phillips, Kevin P. *The Emerging Republican Majority* (New Rochelle, N.Y.: Arlington House, 1969).

Polsby, Nelson and Wildavsky, Aaron B. *Presidential Elections* (2d ed., New York: Charles Scribner's Sons, 1968).

Riker, William H. *The Theory of Political Coalitions* (New Haven, Conn.: Yale University Press, 1962).

Roberts, Adam, ed. *Civilian Resistance as a National Defence* (Baltimore, Md.: Penguin Books, 1969).

[21] Luttwak, *Coup d'Etat*, p. 24.
[22] Luttwak, *Coup d'Etat*, p. 32.
[23] Luttwak, *Coup d'Etat*, p. 45.

PART FOUR

Public Policy and Policy Making: Some Criteria

The remaining chapters of the text consider a variety of matters pertinent to the improvement of our policy-making processes and public choices. In the first few chapters we will consider some very general guidelines for dealing with social problems. Our approach is to offer decision premises for students of policy and for policy makers. Among the questions in Chapters XI to XIII are what kinds of problems can be usefully handled by public choice processes and what sorts of activities are best or most appropriately handled by which governments in our division of labor. A number of fairly specific but abstract criteria are advanced in Chapter XIV for achieving better allocations of our scarce resources. The same type of advice is extended to problems of individual welfare in Chapter XV. Problems of control and how governments can improve the attainment of their goals are considered in Chapter XVI, while suggestions for improvement of the conditions of public choice more generally are raised in Chapter XVII, the final chapter.

Chapter XI

PRIVATE MOTIVES AND SOCIAL GOALS

These next few chapters attempt to provide guidelines for a variety of public choices—appropriate activities for government, efficient division of labor among our governments, fairer allocations of societal resources, wider distributions of income and services, more efficient allocations of the costs of maintaining government and providing for the people, and greater governmental efficiency in all its workings.

We begin these inquiries by raising some fundamental questions concerning the role of self-interest in achieving a better society. We end with a discussion of certain problems involved in improving the conditions of choice among self-interested citizens. While all these questions are ancient in their origins they remain perennial; we do not expect to find final answers that apply to all peoples. Answering these questions is not only an academic pursuit but is the work of citizens and politicians in everyday political life. What makes them so problematical is the impossibility of reconciling scarcity of resources with a multitude of conflicting demands. These demands stem from men's desires to have more income, status, power, and general well-being.

This last statement and its consequences for political life and public policy in the United States will be our immediate concern. The basis of our approach is Adam Smith's contention that the pursuit of private gain can and frequently does have beneficial social consequences. We will try to identify the necessary conditions for effective social use of self-interest and at the same time will name those conditions under which "doing your own thing" is detrimental to social organization and public policies. We make no claims for or defense of unbridled pursuit of self-interest or for pursuit of income over all other goals. But we will set out purposely to make a case for a kind of constrained or tolerable self-interest. The best protection against exploitation is countervailing power exercised by self-reliant individuals who will not brook unfair competition. Some will wonder why we must defend competition and self-interest in public policy at all, for despite a profound belief in capitalism many Americans think that our democracy can and should be run by selfless individuals. Businessmen and consumers are expected to be selfish but voters and politicians are not.

A Preliminary Note

Anyone who attempts to explain behavior must make some basic assumptions about motivations. His choice of assumptions ranges from pure self-interest to its opposite—pure altruism. If a political scientist must choose one extreme he should opt for self-interest, since that assumption enables him to account for a far wider range of behavior than its opposite. Fortunately, we need not make a choice between these extremes nor must we assume that self-interest is innate. Societies shape the contents of self-interest, prescribe its most appropriate realm or boundaries, and provide codes to govern its application in daily life. Americans, for example, tend to honor self-interest most in the economic system and least in the family. The political system is somewhere in between. Self-interest ("I have my rights") is viewed as a basic right of individuals and interest groups but at the same time citizens are expected to be patriotic and self-sacrificing. Whatever the precise areas, they are socially conditioned.

We can further defend self-interest as an explanation of behavior, perhaps, if we put it this way: To explain a person's behavior or choices we must *pay attention to the structure of incentives and costs and his perception of them in his situation.* If we want to alter his behavior in any way we must reshape the structure of these perceived incentives and costs—by increasing the incentives and/or decreasing the costs of the desired behavior so as to produce a net profit. Such modifications can be produced by restructuring either the *actual* payoffs or the affected individual's *perception* thereof. We can look on the problem as one of accounting—in the very broadest sense, not just in terms of monetary rewards. We can take advantage of existing incentives and/or create new ones for the other person. The purpose is to make life, or some aspect of it, more attractive to our citizens; what could be more democratic or appealing?

Some Virtues of Self-Interest

While few ordinary Americans need to be persuaded that self-interest normally promotes the interests of others in the economic arena, most American voters are highly dubious about self-concern in the polity. We frequently honor the resourceful, energetic, hard-working entrepreneur but we invariably distrust the resourceful, energetic, and calculating politician. The reasoning behind this double standard is not without some merit. In the economy, self-interest is supposed to provide incentives for people to make *mutually profitable exchanges*. If an exchange makes two people (buyer and seller) better off without making anyone else worse off, so much the better for society. Economists call this type of exchange Paretian optimality, after the Italian economist Vilfredo Pareto, who first formulated the norm early in this century. Since the economy provides many opportunities of this sort we tend to think well of self-interest in economic affairs.

Self-interest in the polity is viewed rather differently. Exchanges among politicians are viewed with suspicion because it is assumed that while the politicians and some interest groups may become better off, they pass the costs on to others or to third persons who have had no opportunity to shape the decision or are unable to avoid its worst consequences. Furthermore, deals concluded by politicians necessarily affect others because government has the authority to coerce. When two politicians exchange votes on a tax proposal and a public expenditure, the immediate political benefits go to the politicians, the economic benefits go to the recipients, but the taxes must be paid by voters who did not participate in the making of the decision.

These external costs are not the only costs of such deals. This kind of logrolling among legislators results in the adoption or rejection of policies on grounds other than the merits of the proposals. On issues in which legislators have little or no interest they trade votes to the highest bidder.

While American voters perceive this process in crude and inarticulate ways their intuition is basically sound. They miss some factors, however, in their assessment of the benefits of making policy by logrolling techniques. They view the method as bad, but neglect the beneficial consequences. And such consequences must be evaluated against those of alternative ways of making policy.

The pursuit of self-interest in politics is both worthy and necessary—worthy, because it is consistent with democratic values; necessary, because it provides the motive power to make democracy work. Democracy can only be "for the people" if the people are allowed to decide for themselves what is good and if our policy makers honor these individual preferences. Democracy is worthy only to the extent that it does, in fact, adopt policies and practices that are consistent with individual choices. While no society may be able to accomplish this completely, the effort must be made. The results can then be judged against the performance of other systems. We should honor political self-interest as we obviously honor consumer sovereignty in the market. "The customer is always right" is basically a democratic norm.

That self-interest is consistent with basic democratic values is not its only justification in policy making. Almost equally important is the necessity of self-interest as an incentive to political action. Division of labor in our democracy requires politicians, voters, bureaucrats, party workers, and the like. How can we induce people in our society to fill these political roles and perform jobs that need to be done? In general, we can recruit people by (1) force or threat; (2) appealing to their sense of civic duty and doing good for the public; or (3) promising them private rewards. Actually, we use all three means to recruit personnel but we depend on different incentives for different jobs or, more accurately, on different combinations of inducements for each job.

For example, we draft men into the military but we also pay them salaries and award them medals and social status as additional contingent compensations. In addition, their leaders assure them they are contributing a valuable service to their country. We recruit jurors by a lottery system but compensate them for lost income. We sometimes recruit politicians by draft, but more often by promises of status, power, opportunities for public service, and salaries. We attempt to induce voters to participate by appeals to "duty" and by providing opportunities to shape policies and select officials, satisfactions for having performed a civic duty, and the possibility of improving one's returns from the public sector.

Note that all of these inducements are potential rewards and not threats or deprivations. And when deprivations are unavoidable, as in the case of the drafted soldier, we try as often as conditions permit to compensate for them. We implicitly recognize the need to reward the people we ask to participate in the political life of the nation. In fact, we must, inasmuch as all other institutions and activities offer substantial competing rewards or promises of rewards. All institutions—religious, economic, family, recreational, and the like, compete daily for the attention, resources, services, or other contributions of each citizen. Political institutions must also compete—and they do. Whether they compete successfully is debatable, at least. The most powerful inducement is that of rewarding self-interest.

These rewards not only induce citizens to participate but also tend to improve the quality of their performances. Gradation of rewards—the promise of increased rewards for superior performance—is as much a necessity in polities as in economies and among students taking college courses. (The control implications of this claim are explored in Chapter XVI.) It is doubtful that any polity or society could be successfully operated with absolutely equal rewards for the differential sharing of burdens and responsibilities. Rewards need not always be monetary. Social status and influence are among the most powerful inducements in all societies. Most Presidents of this country did not campaign for office because they wanted the salary; in fact, the presidents of most large corporations make more money than the President of the nation; several Presidents took salary cuts when they assumed public office.

Rather, Presidents are men who prefer status and the exercise of influence and power. They enjoy their work and hope the history books will treat them well. Some want to be loved by the people. These are the basic psychic rewards; we could cut the President's salary by half and not lose one by resignation. But deprive him of his expected status, adulation, and influence and he will likely not seek office again.

The Dangers of Unbridled Self-Interest

We have pointed out some substantial advantages of self-interest in our democracy but so far have said little about its limitations and dangers under certain circumstances. The pursuit of self-advantage does not automatically redound to the benefit of others. What are these limitations and dangers?

EXTERNAL COSTS

The most apparent danger of purely self-interested behavior is the insensitivity of the selfish to the costs endured by others—the external costs. This is especially likely whenever resources or payoffs are limited, as they are in many situations. The incidence of such insensitivity is likely to increase as a political system increases in size because larger size encourages both greater impersonality and ignorance about the secondary or external effects of one's own interests and choices. In general, we tend to care less about people we do not know than those we do. We can be exceedingly callous toward abstract and distant groups. The harm a policy may inflict on other citizens in other sections of the land is of little immediate concern to the selfish.

PEOPLE AS MEANS

Under the norms of competitive behavior people tend to treat others as means to their ends. But no one wishes to be treated as the means. We prefer to be regarded as "ends" about whom others care. Most of us, most of the time, want to be treated with affection and respect, with warmth and understanding; but these, too, are selfish desires. The impersonal marketplace does not make room for generosity and affections; instead it honors the rational calculator. If a political system could be run on pure marketplace considerations we would find citizens treating one another in the more impersonal ways of markets. We would make our agreements by explicit trade and rule out emotive displays of patriotism, loyalty to party and friend, and the willingness to bear unusual burdens. Every man would have his political price and every policy would be the result of such calculations. Few of us could long tolerate that extreme atmosphere.

Indeed, few of us really want our market economy operated on a pure profit basis. That is why advertisers spend so much money to create brand loyalties and to convince the public that their companies have a "heart"; that they are not bloodless monsters preying on the consumers but are working for the betterment of all. And that is also partly why politicians try to act warm, friendly, concerned, generous, and sensitive. The image of a purely rational, self-interested political man frightens most Americans. Voting studies have shown that the "personality" of the politician and particularly at the Presidential level is of extraordinary importance to voters.[1] Because voters find it costly to be rational themselves, they rarely want impersonal politicians. Accordingly, the rational politician will take every opportunity to appear emotional and personal.

SACRIFICE OF SUBSTANTIVE REASONING

Aside from the demands of impersonal selfishness most of us are also aware of the policy implications of pure selfishness. We have already described logrolling and its tendency to reduce reliance on substantive criteria for policy making and to resolve issues on factors other than their merits. But that is true only to a limited extent. While politicians may trade votes across issues, debates among the concerned and affected political opponents will be about the substantive merits of alternative solutions. Congressmen may exchange promises of votes in private but they always publicly discuss issues in terms of effects on people, such as the expected social as distinct from political advantages and disadvantages of the proposals. A great deal of energy, time, and expertise is put into these public debates. And, of course, not all votes are a function of trades, for many legislators are never called on for support. Those who are not are certainly freed for substantive reasoning about policies[2] that concern them.

IMPACT OF RULES ON SELF-INTEREST

The pursuit of self-interest in and of itself is difficult to assess in the abstract; that is, without knowing the institutional framework or context within which it is to operate. In this sense, political behavior is not dissimilar from economic choice. Whether self-interest works and has social benefits depends upon the type of market within which the motives and behavior are channeled. Thus, economists tell us, self-interest produces beneficial consequences in competitive markets but much less beneficial, perhaps even harmful, ones in less competitive or monopolistic markets.

Analogous situations can perhaps be found in politics. For

[1] Angus Campbell, Gerald Gurin, and Warren Miller, *The Voter Decides* (Evanston, Ill.: Row, Peterson and Co., 1954); James David Barber, *Citizen Politics* (Chicago: Markham Publishing Co., 1969), Chapters III–V.

[2] The point is well made by Lewis A. Dexter in Raymond Bauer, Ithiel de Sola Pool, and Lewis A. Dexter, *American Business and Public Policy* (New York: Atherton Press, 1968), Chapter 30.

example, Buchanan and Tullock contend that simple majority rule produces some undesirable consequences while unanimity rules have some powerful virtues.[3] Self-interest is at work under all rules so it is the rule and situation, more broadly, that is responsible for good and bad policies. Therefore, the best way to moderate or control the worst aspects of selfishness in politics is by changing the rules, rather than by attempting to eradicate the "beast" from man's soul.

Constraints on Self-Interested Behavior

In our earlier discussion of the external costs of self-interested behavior, we failed to note that the best guard against unreasonable external costs is the alert, informed, self-interested person who will inevitably endure the costs. Who has a better motive to prevent or reduce a cost than the person who will have to pay for the advantages others are expected to derive?

A constant problem, as we shall observe throughout these pages, is making certain that our institutions protect and advance genuine competition, and that some rough equality exists in terms of political resources so that men may compete effectively against one another. Adam Smith has observed that men will try to reduce competition whenever it threatens to affect them adversely. There is nothing paradoxical in this behavior. We all appreciate the benefits of competition among others since some of those benefits normally accrue to us. But we also recognize—perhaps more readily—that competitors of ours can only serve to advance the interests of themselves and others but not ourselves (in the short run, at least, which is all that really concerns most people). So it is that politicians and businessmen are heard to sing the praises of competition among others while at the same time working assiduously to reduce the influence of their competitors.

Thus, while we advocate public recognition of self-concerned behavior as useful in running our political system, we need not encourage unbridled acquisition. Our own self-interest can lead us to impose some constraints on other people and in return to accept some constraints on our own activities. And that Americans have done in a host of ways.

---

[3] James M. Buchanan and Gordon Tullock, *The Calculus of Consent* (Ann Arbor: University of Michigan Press, 1962), Part III.

One limitation Americans have inadvertently placed on potentially harmful pursuits of self-interest results from some religious beliefs that temper if not discourage selfishness as immoral. Once inculcated in an individual such beliefs serve as policing devices over self-seeking. The same might be said about the social functions of our political culture which emphasizes self-denial among officials, sacrifice, obedience to the law, equality of treatment before the law, and the concept of the public interest. All these ideas and ideals tend to constrain the individual who wishes to plunder or exploit others.

In addition to religious and social norms, we also place a variety of other constraints on selfishness. Legal penalties are imposed to discourage such unwanted behavior as bribery and corruption. Americans have also institutionalized a complex set of public constraints that provide opportunities for citizens to compete with and question the choices and behavior of others, especially public officials. While political competition is hardly as keen as it should be, many opportunities exist for competition in the electoral system as well as throughout the entire policy-making process.

Paradoxically, self-interest may sometimes best be furthered by seemingly moderating one's self-interest. A politician wishing to be elected must perform services for others in order to win out in competitive struggles; if he wishes to continue winning he must continue to serve. By doing good for his opponents and offering some form of compensation to the losers, he may, in some degree, win them over to his side. Outright selfishness leaves no consideration for other people, particularly the defeated, but a tough-minded politician will attempt to win the future support of his opposition by generous actions toward them. In short, rational self-interest requires some awareness of the possibilities for *exchange* of *mutual advantages*. One's own self-interests may lead him to do good for others, saying, in effect, "If you do good for me I will do good for you."

Effects of Self-Interest

We are urging that more concern be shown for the *effects* of self-interest than for the motive, itself. If the effects benefit more people than they harm then self-interested activities are good;

FIGURE XI–1
Consequences of One's Behavior

Impact on others

	Beneficial	Harmful	Neutral
Beneficial	Best	Next to the worst	Not bad
Harmful	Saintly	Worst	Dumb
Neutral	Second best	Stupid	Poor calculation

Impact on self

if they harm more people then they are bad and those consequences should be controlled. Perhaps we can illustrate the problem with a simple box diagram such as Figure XI–1. The more direct impacts of one's behavior can be of three general types: beneficial, harmful, and neutral, and note these impacts may be quite different for different people. Were that not the case we would not have a problem to discuss nor would society have a problem to resolve. As the diagram illustrates, the most useful exercise of self-interest occurs when the self-interested person and many others benefit; the worst occurs whenever many suffer while the self-interested individual profits and the most saintly when a person sacrifices for others. The most difficult of all occurs when the number of people benefitted equals that made worse off. What kind of situation would fit the category "dumb"? We will have more to say about these consequences in Chapter XV. In any event, the crux of the matter is found in the consequences of action.

It is difficult to convince people of the rightness of this concern for the effects, rather than the motives of an action or inaction because our political culture values the motive. If a politician manages to win reelection because he has skillfully designed and helped enact a piece of legislation which benefits others he should be honored for both achievements and not condemned because he relates his reelection to a policy proposal. If a politician supports positions that guarantee his defeat, what public good is served? Bankruptcy in business is of no value to anyone; why should it be in politics?

Apparently many view self-sacrifice as a more heroic motive even when it harms others. Curiously, too, the idea that "doing good" for others necessarily produces good for others is widespread. "Doing good" for others almost always produces good for the person advocating the norm but the good that may result always comes at a cost (external cost) to still other persons. When the more liberal voters lend their support for increased educational expenditures they may do good for some students but they also increase the property tax of low-income elderly pensioners. When the more conservative voters opt for more defense expenditures which presumably aid society they also serve to increase my federal income tax to support a policy I do not approve. Perhaps we should attach some seriousness to the constitutional amendment proposed by Milton Friedman: "Everyone should be free to do good—at his own expense."[4]

The Public Interest

One of the more cherished ideas in political science as well as daily political rhetoric is that of *the public interest*. As everyone believes in motherhood, so everyone is in favor of advancing the public interest. The difficulty begins, however, as soon as we begin to put some policy content into the term and not just intone pleasant sounding noises. The public interest is not something apart from the declared interests of the individuals who constitute a society. This is not to say that individuals cannot hurt themselves knowingly or unknowingly, or that they never make mistakes; rather it is to say that the public interest is not some Platonic or abstract ideal apart from the expressed preferences of individuals. I may not like what others have chosen; in fact many choices that others make in politics, art, wine, style of life, social science, and the like, are unattractive to me and I often complain about them to my wife and, on rare occasions, to the "offenders" directly. But we should not deceive ourselves that *our* personal

[4] Reported in Jack Rosenthal, "Free Enterprise Radicals Score Federal Control," *The New York Times*, May 28, 1970.

views are *the public interest*. Unfortunately social science is still unable to guide us confidently in selecting the most appropriate ideals and public policies.

Some scholars have suggested that we abandon the term "public interest" and they make a persuasive case for it—if only to avoid the unfortunate connotations of the concept. No doubt we will continue to use the term; the public interest is still worth striving for, but only if we understand that it is but a summary term for individual preferences. There is no such thing as a public apart from the people who constitute that aggregate. So understood, the public interest means that one policy is better than another if it contributes more satisfactions to more people than its alternatives.

The problem, as we have seen and will repeat ad nauseam, is in the summation of preferences. That we cannot readily sum them does not mean we should avoid thinking about it, because we must and do "measure" such things every day in political life. At present we have only crude indicators and indices. The task confronting scholars is to perfect the indicators.

WHY WE HAVE A PROBLEM

Readers might well ask why we have a problem; surely what is in the best interests of all Americans is readily apparent. It is only apparent to two groups: to innocents who assume that the values and interests of others are identical with their own and to fanatics who want everyone to adopt their own preferred solutions. Those who are neither innocent nor fanatical see a very real problem in finding institutional means to enable diverse and conflicting individual preferences to be "summed" or aggregated into a collective decision or public policy.[5] If people differ how is it possible to reconcile their differences? Are there any rules that facilitate the operation? To be concrete, consider a situation typical of the Vietnam war when the public was fairly evenly divided over various alternative ways of handling the situation. In this hypothetical public opinion poll, S_1 = immediate withdrawal, S_2 = gradual withdrawal, and S_3 = intensified warfare.

[5] The classic formulation of the problem was provided by Kenneth J. Arrow, *Social Choice and Individual Values* (New York: John Wiley & Sons, Inc., 1951). Also see Duncan Black, *The Theory of Committees and Elections* (New York: Cambridge University Press, 1958).

Strategy	Percent in favor
(S$_1$)	33%
(S$_2$)	33%
(S$_3$)	33%

How can these apparently conflicting policies be reconciled into an acceptable policy to the American people? No matter what is done two-thirds of the people will not like it. No course of action can attain a simple majority. Which alternative is in the public interest?

HOW WE CAN DEAL WITH THE PROBLEM?

Two means have been suggested for dealing with the problem: have voters express (1) their order of preferences ("first," "second," and "third") or (2) their intensities of preferences. The first procedure merely states the order of priorities while the second indicates the exact differences or distances among each citizen's preferences. Thus, a voter might say he likes policy A twice as much as policy B instead of merely saying he prefers policy A to B. What happens to our policy problem when we apply these additional means of seeking out the public interest? Consider this revised situation, when presented to three groups of citizens with differing attitudes toward war:

Rank	Doves	Crows	Hawks
1st Choice	S$_1$	S$_2$	S$_3$
2nd Choice	S$_2$	S$_1$	S$_2$
3rd Choice	S$_3$	S$_3$	S$_1$

No matter how one reads the table of preferences no policy alternative can gain a majority. If we adopted the doves' first choice of immediate withdrawal (S$_1$) we would discover that both the crows and the hawks prefer other alternatives. If we tried to enact the first preference of the crows (S$_2$) we find that both the doves and hawks have a different set of preferences. There seems to be no way out of this curious and painful dilemma.[6] If

[6] Kenneth Arrow named this logical dilemma the "General Possibility Theorem." Other scholars, for perfectly good reasons, have labelled it "Arrow's Impossibility Theorem."

citizens, in preferring A to B and B to C, also prefer A to C we cannot achieve a solution.

One possible solution, or so it seems, is to ask the voters to weight their preferences; that is, to put a number next to each of the policy alternatives. We would then select the policy with the highest number. In theory, this is possible. The first problem, however, is getting people to agree to a weighting system; the second problem is determining how individual voters would decide how much weight to attach to each policy. How would one distribute ten points, for example, among the above alternatives? Would he be honest and express his views (if he knew them)? Or would he engage in a little or a great deal of deception in order to alter the final outcome? Voters would have a powerful inducement to set the number as high as possible for their preferred policy if they thought the first preference of others would win out otherwise. Everyone will exaggerate their first preferences. Can we attain the public interest in this manner?

The cruel fact of the matter is that we cannot devise a foolproof scheme of voting that will enable voters with conflicting preferences to produce a set of public policies such that everyone achieves his first preferences. At best, we can, through our representative system, fashion rough approximations to personal preferences through bargaining. Inequality will prevail and no one will consistently get the policies he wants. He will have to trade off less-desired policies for more desired ones. The results are nothing more than acceptable or workable compromises among the interested and active citizens but that is a major achievement in itself.

Fortunately, issues can be handled over time in such a manner that most people will come to accept a solution even though that issue may have once provoked the most intense feelings. Some readers may be surprised or amused to know that such widely accepted policies as women's suffrage, social security, and the income tax were once hotly contested issues. Issues that disturb us today will one day be resolved although we will have never voted directly on them. And, perhaps, that is wise; experienced politicians bargaining over issues provide a better means of solving social problems than daily referendums among the people. And this may well be the best meaning of the public interest: the devising of political processes that enable workable compromises to be made and reassessed.

Suggested Readings

Banfield, Edward C. *The Unheavenly City* (Boston: Little, Brown & Co., 1970).

Buchanan, James M. and Tullock, Gordon. *The Calculus of Consent* (Ann Arbor: University of Michigan Press, 1962).

Hayek, Friedrich A. *Individualism and the Economic Order* (Chicago: The University of Chicago Press, 1948).

Heidenheimer, Arnold J., ed. *Political Corruption* (New York: Holt, Rinehart & Winston, Inc., 1970).

Lindblom, Charles E. *The Intelligence of Democracy* (New York: The Free Press, 1965).

MacPherson, C. B. *The Political Theory of Possessive Individualism* Oxford, England: Clarendon Press, 1962).

Polanyi, Michael. *The Logic of Liberty* (Chicago: University of Chicago Press, 1951).

Schubert, Glendon. *The Public Interest* (Glencoe, Ill.: The Free Press, 1965).

Smith, Adam. *The Wealth of Nations* (New York: The Modern Library, 1937).

Wallich Henry C. *The Cost of Freedom* (New York: Collier Books, 1960).

Wicksteed, Philip. *The Common Sense of Political Economy* (London: Routledge & Kegan Paul Limited, 1957).

Chapter XII

PROBLEMS IN COLLECTIVE CHOICE

Anyone advocating the explicit use of self-interest in political life is obligated to show how such motives can be usefully employed to solve social problems. The problem is not new. Centuries ago in England both John Locke and Thomas Hobbes gave it lengthy and detailed consideration. Although it seems to be contrary to common sense, self-oriented men can and do agree on common courses of action or public policies and even to mutual deprivations and coercion. They do, say Locke and Hobbes and modern economists, because they find it is mutually rewarding.

Our task in this brief chapter is to continue developing a setting for the following chapters on policy. Those chapters and the advice they offer will make more sense if their intellectual sources are made somewhat explicit in advance. In the previous chapter we portrayed man as a basically intelligent but not always well-informed being, motivated primarily by a desire to achieve more satisfactions from life, confronted by other persons with similar concerns and potentialities, and highly interdependent with other men in a world of scarcities. Needless to say, people in such circumstances inevitably create problems for one another and for themselves—problems of collective choice. In short, how can self-interested but interdependent men live together? How can they achieve the good life?

The Problem of Producing Agreement

As individuals we face the recurrent problem of making optimal use of our limited supplies of time, money, and energy. This is not an easy choice or set of choices, but we somehow manage to make decisions, although all of them may not be optimal. An individual faces conflicting desires when he tries to put together a "market basket" of goods based on his own disposable income. Imagine the difficulties encountered in assembling a "market basket" of public goods when millions of people are allowed some influence in the making of public choices. How can a public decision be made when people differ, often intensely, about what goods to produce and in what amounts? If this is a decision problem for an individual, it is of far greater magnitude for a society.

Scholars use models to illustrate how society chooses. Some of these models treat society as though it were an individual—as if disagreement were absent. In reality, the actual decisions are not unanimous and their consequences are not always predictable. Further, many of the consequences will not occur immediately, but in the distant future to affect people still unborn. How can we devise a decision process or set of rules that will enable more than 100 million adults to achieve as many of their diverse and conflicting personal preferences as possible? Is it possible? Are there any rules or norms we can offer the people and government to improve their choices?

Let us translate these ideas into a simple model that reflects all the above problems and dilemmas. For simplicity's sake, suppose we agree that the federal government will spend $100 million during some given period of time, say one year. To further simplify the model let us assume there are only five public goods on which to spend the money and that we can learn only of each voter's first preference on amounts to be devoted to each of the five goods. A tabular presentation of the choices of five voters in our model is shown in Table XII-1.

The table has a number of notable features. First, the only

TABLE XII–1

Citizen Preferences on Budgetary Allocations

Citizen	Public Goods (in millions)				
	Defense	Law and Order	Highways	Welfare	Education
Able	$20	$20	$20	$20	$20
Baker	60	25	10	0	5
Charlie	5	8	12	15	60
Donald	40	15	18	2	15
Elmer	15	15	30	10	30

agreement on allocations is between Donald and Elmer on law and order; each prefers an expenditure of $15 million. There are no other agreements. Note, too, that the range of disagreement on each allocation varies but in all cases it is considerable. On defense, for example, Baker wants to spend about 60 percent of the budget, while Charlie would allocate but 5 percent. On the other hand, Charlie wants to give 60 percent to education and Baker only 5 percent. These arbitrarily assigned allocations, oversimplified for purposes of our model, may seem unrealistic. Whether they are or not, their function is to illustrate the problem of attaining an agreement that will yield the most satisfaction—or perhaps the least dissatisfaction—among the citizenry. Aside from the practical problems of devising optimal rules and arranging agreements we still must decide which set of allocations is best. That will be done in Chapter XIV.

Some economists contend that resources ought not to be allocated on the basis of personal preferences, especially inconsistent ones, but rather on the basis of the most efficient use of resources, even though these criteria may be at odds with citizen views as expressed in the political system. Governments, the theorists say, should follow the advice of economists with respect to efficient allocations in the market and economy at large. In brief, and in the simplest of terms, they suggest that monies should be allocated among the five activities listed in Table XII-1 in terms of their marginal worth; that is, the last dollar spent on each activity would produce the same amount of utility. (The logic is detailed in Chapter XIV.)

DIFFICULTIES IN COLLECTIVE CHOICE

While a private consumer can approximate optimal allocations of his own money according to his preferences, the citizen cannot achieve this goal with the same relative ease in the public sector. Some rules, however, may facilitate the process more than others. Public goods and their value to the citizen are not readily measured primarily because the goods are indivisible, and not consumable in the sense that private goods are. For example, a storeowner surely profits from police protection for his store. How much value can he assign to protection? How much is it worth in dollars? How much would he stand to lose in theft? Perhaps more difficult is determining how much value we should attach to a national park. And even more important in the present context is a problem that collective choice presents that does not exist in market choice. The five members of the political system presented in Table XII-1 must make a single authoritative decision on the allocation of its resources. Abel, Baker, and the others cannot each have his choices or budget respected and enacted as he can in the market. One budgetary allocation will have to be arrived at, by compromise, arbitrary decision, or other method, and enforced on all members. If personal preferences are highly valued, public choices are arrived at with considerable difficulty. A nation can have but one budget at a time, not millions as in the market.

How can all five voters have their preferences honored under a single choice? The fact that individual preferences vary not only makes actual policy making more difficult than market choice but poses special problems for those who would prescribe political solutions—who decide which allocations are superior and which inferior. These difficulties in the nature of public choice have led some highly logical minds to conclude that no rules of the game can produce a collective choice consistent with the diversity of individual values.[1]

Equity and Envy

We have now become acquainted with the problem of agreement in social choice and optimal resource allocation in a simple model. Perhaps we should add some further complicating details on our way to solutions. Many Americans say that whenever we try to formulate public policy we should attempt to advance the well-being of as many citizens as possible. In fact, we should adopt any change that will benefit at least one citizen while not harming another. This norm (Paretian optimality), however, is not applicable to our political conditions because it covers so few circumstances encountered in large-scale democracies such as ours. Rarely can a policy be adopted that does not harm someone while benefitting others. We can better appreciate this limitation by listing the logical outcomes of a change in policy as follows:

1. All citizens will be better off.
2. All citizens will be worse off.

[1] Kenneth J. Arrow, *Social Choice and Individual Values* (New York: John Wiley & Sons, Inc., 1951).

3. Some citizens will be better off, while others remain un-affected.

4. Some citizens will be better off, while others will be worse off.

5. Some citizens will be better off, some worse off, and some unaffected.

Most readers would agree that the first state of affairs in which everyone benefits is the superior state. A moment's reflection, however, will convince them that such a state is highly unlikely. The second state, in which everyone is worse off, is unquestionably the least desirable, but it is perhaps a somewhat more likely prospect than the first alternative. In wartime conditions, for example, governments demand public sacrifices from all in the short run as the price of survival. But the most probable conditions are the third, fourth, and fifth, with the fifth most likely of all. Of course, these general conditions or consequences do not reveal specific instances and cannot guide us in selecting policies. We must gather additional details about the exact proportions of the population being affected, how, and to what degree. For example:

Proportion of Population

Policies	Better Off	Worse Off	Unaffected
P_1	$\frac{1}{3}$	$\frac{1}{3}$	$\frac{1}{3}$
P_2	$\frac{2}{3}$	$\frac{1}{3}$	0
P_3	$\frac{1}{2}$	$\frac{1}{4}$	$\frac{1}{4}$
P_4	$\frac{1}{10}$	$\frac{1}{5}$	$\frac{7}{10}$

P_1 through P_4 represent four policy alternatives, each with a different distribution of payoffs (costs and benefits). Which policy is best? Many readers will opt for P_2 because a greater number of citizens will benefit than under any other policy and twice as many will benefit as will be hurt. The same ratio holds for P_3. On the other hand, P_4 is the least desirable because it rewards the smallest number. Even worse, under P_4 twice as many are made worse off than are improved.

The decision here seems relatively clearcut and unambiguous. But suppose the best solution were one in which the same number of people benefit and are hurt? Should we consider a policy change or retain the status quo?

In this case, we should identify the people involved. It may be necessary to advance the concerns of some at the expense of others—perhaps because the former have been hurt for a long time and deserve some redress. Some Americans believe that is the case with Negroes, Indians, and minority groups in general. Some white Americans, however, fear that these concerns can only be advanced at their expense. If that is so, should whites pay the price?

The problem underlying our discussion must now be made explicit. It is usually assumed that each citizen is the best judge of his own welfare and that what he says is an honest disclosure. On this assumption, the white southerner's fears that he is being downgraded as blacks are being upgraded must be accepted at face value. On the basis of a historical perspective, however, critics maintain that the white is deceiving himself. The situation is not "zero-sum"; that is, raising a black man's status does not necessarily diminish that of a white man, nor should an increase in the income of one automatically decrease the income of others. In fact, under some conditions increasing the income of one enables others to add to their incomes. What should we do when some benefit and others do not? Let us look at another aspect of the situation.

Is it possible for one or more citizens to become better off without affecting others? If one man's income or status is increased but mine is not (remains the same) is it true that my position relative to that man has not changed? Certainly my absolute level has not changed, but we do not always live with absolute levels, more often we are pleased or disturbed because of the relative rankings. We choose to assess our well-being in relationship to others; that is the primary meaning of social status and stratification. If two political scientists in the same department at the same university are promoted at different rates and receive salary increases at different rates it is not necessarily at one another's expense; still the one who moves at a less rapid rate is likely to be envious and dissatisfied because he is being rated less able by whatever qualities or performances are being ranked. If a professor feels himself to be worse off in comparison to a faster moving colleague, is he worse off? In this sense of invidious comparison there is no such thing as a policy alternative which leaves no one unaffected. However, we do not know many other citizens so we probably do not make as many invidious distinctions. If farmers are given more subsidies most of us do not automatically complain. Still, there are occasions when we do. For example, a good many poor whites have complained in recent years about the apparent favoritism of the federal government in advancing the interests of poor blacks. And many middle class whites complain that blacks now have employment advantages that are not accorded to the whites. The other aspect of this vexatious problem pertains to the fact that a historical wrong that was committed by now deceased generations has to be paid for by presumably innocent individuals.

Since distributive justice or equity is a persistent and unavoidable problem some scholars have suggested that one way of getting around it is to ask or even require the advantaged to compensate those who gained less or actually lost out in the scramble for greater shares. The idea is attractive in the abstract but not in practice since the actual administration of such further redistributions would be extraordinarily difficult to implement. Of course, some form of compensation is actually paid out in the real world of American politics whenever the less advantaged groups are afforded gains. Bargaining power is necessary, however, to ensure that one will indeed be compensated.

Meeting Public Choice Problems: Cautions

We have treated public choice in a relatively abstract manner as entailing two basic and inevitable difficulties: how to achieve some kind of agreement reasonably consistent with the preferences of citizens and how to allocate resources and distribute benefits and costs equitably. We have summarized the logic of these problems but have offered no solutions; they are reserved for subsequent chapters.

The abstractions of the previous pages may have led readers to believe, mistakenly, that magical solutions to these policy problems are possible. To offset any such misunderstanding, we offer next a set of observations about the reality of public choice in America. Perhaps these observations will help provide a kind of "mental set" appropriate for policy makers as well as for those readers of daily newspapers who find our political life baffling and unrewarding. Public choice is a messy activity but it is important and can be exciting to study.

There is a hint here of the way we have treated social problems in this book; that is, we've taken a somewhat cautious but hopeful view of the capabilities of individuals and societies to manage their lives for the good. As men solve problems of agreement and justice so they create them; indeed, they often appear better at the latter task than the former. In any event, the treatment and advice advanced in these pages tends to stress the problems, pitfalls, obstacles, unanticipated difficulties, crises, the obstreperous and sometimes treacherous quality of men. Some will find this uninspiring if not revolting; others will wonder how a person who emphasizes rationality can entertain such a pessimistic philosophy. Both interpretations are erroneous. The challenges that social or public choice pose for men serve not to discourage but to inspire, for the very nature of the problems is so great as to demand the most of whatever resources of rationality individuals and collectivities may command. The ideas set forth in these remaining pages are not the counsel of a weary writer, tired of man's foibles, and resigned to some predetermined fate; rather they are the counsel of one who believes that Americans have heads on their shoulders and that they are capable of using them in better and worse ways.

Those who aspire to a more rational interpretation of life, whether at the personal or societal level, prefer to face up to the difficulties imposed on them as individual and collective choice makers. We have profound limitations as biological-psychological beings. We have profound limitations when acting or deciding as groups. And, we have the fact of scarcity everywhere about us. Accordingly, the need for intelligent choice is manifest and imperative. But there is little to gain in citing obstacles unless one really desires to overcome them and unless they can be effectively dealt with. Our private and public lives can be vastly improved by both private and public means. Although we shall always make mistakes, we should strive to decrease their number and their magnitude; in short, we can learn about ourselves and the nature of social problems and then begin to take action.

Americans are inveterate believers in the solvability of social problems and the possibility of continual progress; in fact, the very choice of the word "problems" suggests that "solutions" can be devised if we only have enough motivation and good will. Differences arise primarily with respect to the agents of solutions: that is, whether problems are best handled by private individuals in private life or through such collective means as voluntary organizations or governments. Many people now contend that cooperative effort among these agents is the best way. We shall have more to say about this matter in subsequent chapters. The point to make now is that Americans are almost unique in their faith and capacity to handle large-scale social problems.

INTERDEPENDENCE THROUGH TIME

Social problems are rarely discrete and independent in the sense that they can be isolated from other problems; since causes and solutions are highly interdependent and frequently in conflict, to solve one problem may be to make another worse. Furthermore, few if any great social problems are limited in duration; they have roots in the distant past and continue to manifest themselves, if in somewhat altered forms. Racial hostilities in America, for example, have always been with us and are likely to continue for a long time to come. They, as other problems, are without final solutions. If we believe in ideal solutions, our biggest problem may be frustration that others do not share our ideals. But while, as members of society, we cope with problems, we will find more or less useful means of alleviating the worst and we will find new ways to assist in promoting something better. Goals such as bringing an end to labor-management problems and racial bigotry, easing community strife, and the like are not very precise; before solutions can be sought we must have better definitions even at that level of generality. There is no single solution to such ambiguous problems as ending some ill-defined condition or promoting an equally ill-defined goal.

TIME LAGS AND CONSTRAINTS

But suppose we are able to specify conditions and goals with some exactitude. What then? One caution worth noting pertains to the time needed to work out solutions. Most of us are rather impatient, particularly when other people stand in the way of our goals. We often hear others complain about the slowness of change ("Why can't the government do something?") but we just as often hear them grumble that the government is interfering in too many things. Governments cannot alter societies overnight. Precisely how much time is required for a policy to take effect is a practical question of substantial policy relevance. Expert advice and policy debate can assist in resolving the question but only experience will decide how much time is necessary, desirable, and available. Patience, unfortunately, is normally not taught as a civic virtue nor is it notably American; perhaps it should be.

UNINTENDED CONSEQUENCES

It is bad enough that governments cannot remake the world without incurring unbearable costs. What is even worse is that governments frequently produce results that are diametrically opposed to desired ends. Our farm policies have probably made the agricultural situation worse, as welfare policies have contributed to unjust welfare administration. Racial integration policies are currently producing more rather than less demand for segregation, as evidenced in the recent, rapid establishment of private schools in the South.

Perhaps one of the more conspicuous failures has been seen in the federally sponsored urban renewal programs and the highway program. Federal highways are often located in low-income areas, thus destroying the only available rentals for slum dwellers. If corresponding urban renewal plans made it possible for the displaced low-income persons to be relocated in better low-rent housing that would help solve the problem. In fact, these slum dwellers are simply "renewed" out of one slum and into another, and the costs they bear are highly disproportional. For example, the federal highway program in Baltimore destroyed the equivalent of 21 percent of all the housing of low-income blacks during 1951–64 and displaced about 237,000 blacks. Had they been compensated for their losses they would have received, according to one estimate, from $812 to $1,194 per household.[2] This compensation, however, would have increased the cost of the highway program 14 to 21 percent. The bulk of that increased cost would have been borne by higher-income groups who are the most likely to vote and protest higher taxes. If a major objective of the urban renewal program is improvement of blacks' housing, that objective was in conflict with highway priorities. Clearly, priorities that please the white middle class population were substituted

[2] Anthony Downs, "Urban Highway and Urban Renewal Programs," as abstracted in *Economic Analysis and the Efficiency of Government*, a Report of the Subcommittee on Economy in Government of the Joint Economic Committee, Congress of the United States, 91st Congress, 2nd Session (Washington, D.C.: U.S. Government Printing Office, 1970), 42. Also cited in Downs, *Urban Problems and Prospects* (Chicago: Markham Publishing Co., 1970).

for housing when the two goals were in conflict. We fully expect that solving social problems will engender conflicting priorities. What is so intriguing is how the goals of one program can be subtly and persistently subverted by the goals of another program and by another set of people.

PRESENT CHOICES AND FUTURE GENERATIONS

Another difficulty in grand-scale social problem solving arises whenever one generation attemps to plan the fate of succeeding generations. A difficult philosophical dilemma lurks here in the sense that it would seem wrong for one generation to impose its conceptions and priorities on another especially since we cannot possibly know what their lives and values are likely to become as conditions change. If we like suburbs can we assume that they will also? This is a real problem because our choices necessarily impose constraints on their choices. Each generation inherits both good and bad conditions from its parents. The environment we live in was created by those who preceded us. How much of that inheritance can be changed is highly questionable, as each of us knows.

We cannot avoid making choices that will constitute basic conditions for others. What we can do is attempt to control those extreme conditions whose subsequent worth or burden is already apparent. For example, the consequences of failure to plan for abatement of various kinds of dangerous pollution are inescapable. But there may be other areas in which our best plans impose real costs on the next generation. Such areas may include the expression of taste as in architecture and landscaping. Whatever we build to endure will be part of the next generation's heritage, and we cannot anticipate their views and tastes. The moral path lies in not persuading ourselves that we automatically do good whenever we plan for the future. The rhetoric of planning is, however, full of assumed good for the future.

SELF–RESOLVING PROBLEMS

Another caution requires explicit attention although some readers may find our explicitness irritating. The point is this: Some social problems do not require costly, grand-scale governmental action because the changing society will, in due course, eliminate the problem without vast expenditures and authoritarian decisions. As the marketplace and other private institutions record and direct changing values, they simultaneously solve some concurrent problems. When, for example, the newly-invented automobile began to displace the horse an entire industry was made obsolete. It did not take long to convert from one mode of transportation to another, as history records, nor was the shifting of workers and resources to other pursuits a lengthy and difficult process. The role of government in this transformation was not important—we did not embark upon a vast governmental program to assist the harness-makers, carriage manufacturers, and horse dealers. Few persons were seriously hurt by this development, and in fact some carriage makers successfully established new businesses as part of the automotive industry. Whenever possible, problems that need government intervention should be distinguished from those that might better be handled by private decisions. It is not the case that if government is not immediately involved we have committed a moral wrong. On the contrary, the intervention of government may well prolong problem-solving and create undeserving beneficiaries of subsidies who will not wish to surrender their plums.

Many agricultural subsidies are cases in point. They assist the already wealthy and do not improve the state of farmers or consumers. Agriculture is changing more because of changing markets, technology, and population trends than because of governmental actions. As several Congressmen and others have noted, there are more governmental bureaucrats now working on the problems of fewer farmers than was the case in the late 1930s.

IGNORANCE AND THE OBSTREPEROUS CITIZEN

In attacking social problems we should constantly remind ourselves that people will not behave exactly as we wish, and that they will have persuasive reasons for not doing so. Private profit, ignorance, opposition to authority, inconvenience, ambiguous directives, and the like all work against compliance with the most careful plans of administrators. We should expect these responses and not always complain about the stupid masses. Laws will be violated. An everyday example is the income tax. During the first eleven weeks of 1970, Oregonians filing their state income tax returns made 2,503 errors in recording their Social Security numbers. Some 4,157 failed to sign their names, while 6,890 made arithmetical errors, and 4,328 had used the wrong tax table.[3] These many mistakes and oversights were all made on a form that tax officials have been simplifying for many years and which is, in fact, fairly simple. Imagine the errors and oversights on federal income tax returns! Once more a moral: Do not expect large-scale programs or activities to proceed without a flaw; the best of intentions and planning will usually produce their share of commonplace shortcomings.

ORGANIZATIONAL DIFFICULTIES

Ordinary citizens are not the only ones who do not fulfill expectations. High-ranking public officials and organizations have their failures, too, as reported in the columns of that sound Republican newspaper, *The Wall Street Journal*.

Before the Nixon Administration took office, the expectation was that the Republicans would be well-organized and efficient, that their proposals usually conservative and economical, would be carefully worked out in advance.

It was a nice theory. In practice, though, it just hasn't worked out that way.[4]

The author, Alan L. Otten, goes on to describe several important organizational failures of the Administration in precisely those areas where President Nixon was anxious to do better than his Democratic predecessors. The point is not to indict the President but to illustrate how unmanageable the operations of government can be even for cautious conservatives. Presidents may order others about and reorganize as all do but the same sorts of problems persist. There are no magical organizational solutions to social problems.

OBSTREPEROUS OFFICIALS

Even the best-planned policies can be ignored or badly administered and, on occasion, completely subverted by unsympathetic governments and administrators. Administrative history,

[3] Editorial, *The Oregonian*, April 14, 1970, 8.
[4] Alan L. Otten, "According to Plan," *The Wall Street Journal*, June 18, 1970, 12.

for example, is replete with well-documented stories of how the many regulatory commissions established during the Wilson and Roosevelt years to control industrial abuses have become spokesmen for those they are supposed to control. Even more notable is the tendency of state and federal administrations not to enforce certain laws either because they disapprove of them or because powerful interests stand in the way of enforcement. A good illustration of such practices is found in the reluctance of the Nixon Administration to enforce the new and stringent mine safety laws passed hurriedly by the Congress in 1969 after a particularly disastrous mine accident in the coal fields.[5] The incident suggests a number of peculiarities about collective choice in addition to the power of certain groups to resist control.

Proposals that are drafted in hurried fashion are rarely sound pieces of social legislation. They are designed specifically to prevent further occurrences of whatever is being controlled, and usually do not take account of the difficulties faced by the controllers and the time needed to organize effective administrative bodies. Mine inspection, to continue this example, requires hundreds of highly trained and experienced inspectors; they are not easily found and cannot be readily trained. The demands made upon the mine industry apparently cannot be satisfied overnight, even if the Nixon Administration were enthusiastic about enforcement. Is the solution, then, to ignore problems or fail to pass laws? Clearly, it is not. The solution is to think these things out more carefully and over a longer period of time, including all the relevant parties in discussion and formulation so that some of the more thoughtless provisions can be eliminated before they become law. Likewise, we should not await disaster before acting and once we act we should not create unrealistic hopes. Frantic action followed by apathy does not resolve important issues.

CONTROLS AND MORE CONTROLS

This litany of difficulties in coping with great social problems through collective action is hardly complete. Another problem that grows out of the very effort to control is the powerful inducement to add still more controls. As plans or policies are implemented the planners learn that those whose actions are controlled will

---

[5] Ben A. Franklin, "U.S. Not Pushing New Mines Law," *The New York Times*, April 4, 1970, 36.

exercise considerable ingenuity in evading or getting around various provisions. So the planners add new rules to close off the escapes and violations. Planners are not the only ones at fault, however. The controlled will by their very actions and demands seek additional clarification of their duties and rights. In doing so they automatically encourage further rules clarifying the old. Laws are rarely repealed; rather, one control generates others. And each control imposes administrative costs as well as costs of compliance. The controlled group must learn the rules, keep records, inform the government, and in general change its behavior in ways that add to its operational costs.

A Closing Note

Life is difficult enough without our making it worse. Having set forth a variety of problems to be encountered in collective choice perhaps we should now attempt to show how we can intelligently approach these same difficulties and even make some of them work in our interests. The remainder of the text assumes a more positive posture by advancing a number of rules for coping with collective choice.

Suggested Readings

Banfield, Edward C. *The Unheavenly City* (Boston: Little, Brown & Co., 1970).

Baumol, William J. *Welfare Economics and the Theory of the State,* (2d ed., Cambridge, Mass.: Harvard University Press, 1965).

Boulding, Kenneth E. *Principles of Economic Policy* (Englewood Cliffs, N.J.: Prentice-Hall, Inc., 1958).

Hirschman, Albert O. *Journeys Toward Progress* (New York: Twentieth Century Fund, 1963).

Walker, E. Ronald. *From Economic Theory to Policy* (Chicago: University of Chicago Press, 1943).

Chapter XIII

APPROPRIATE ACTIVITIES FOR GOVERNMENTS

The preceding chapter provided, in a sense, some generalized guidelines (or, more accurately, a state of mind) for understanding and coping with social problems. This chapter continues that analysis but with emphasis on the appropriateness of governmental action. We will note some triumphs, some total failures, and many less-than-optimal performances. We will advance some reasons for the varying successes of our governments in coping with outstanding social problems and issues. These reasons are important in deciding whether to reform and improve government or to abandon it and allow private efforts to meet the problems of our times. Statements made in this chapter will have important consequences for attaining better resource allocations and distributions of benefits and burdens. In addition to considering the appropriateness of governmental action, we will comment on the most suitable levels of government for its many diverse activities.

The Basic Calculus of Choice

There are a number of specific areas considered appropriate for governmental activity. We will present some popular rationales for deeming these areas fitting governmental concerns. Careful readers may detect a common thread throughout the analysis. This is because our recommendations are guided by a "basic calculus." It can be stated very simply as a systematic effort to assess the expected costs and benefits that result from alternative ways of doing things.

Almost all our goals may be achieved in a variety of ways.

We may pursue them by private individual or collective effort and public endeavor. Or we may employ a combination of activities and divisions of labor depending on our goals and the expected net returns. They can be measured by constructing a cost/benefit table:

PRIVATE		PUBLIC		
Individual	*Collective*	*Local*	*State*	*Federal*
Costs/Benefits	Costs/Benefits	Costs/Benefits	Costs/Benefits	Costs/Benefits

The expected consequences of each proposed activity and solution can be gauged in terms of costs and benefits for oneself and others. In the first column, for example, the costs of private, individual action to construct and maintain streets can be measured against the benefits of such action. Then, calculations can be made for each column to find out which solution is most effective. Other activities of society can be similarly measured; for example, unemployment insurance, air pollution control, weather reporting, drug control, alcoholic beverage control, and postal service.

This analysis, applied here to the substantive problems of choice involved in deciding which activities should be left private and which should be made public, is much the same as that used by voters (see Chapter VIII). The same applies to the calculus of deciding which level of government to use if one decides that public activity is preferred.[1] In brief, then, the calculus says that each of us should estimate what he will gain for himself and others (if he chooses) by doing things in different ways. What will be gained is obviously affected by what one must pay in the way of taxes, fees, bargaining, external costs, and the like. When we opt for exclusive use of private individual action we surrender the gains to be derived from some other means, such as public action at the federal level. These sacrifices are known as "opportunity costs" because we have lost or forgone some opportunities. Likewise the opportunity costs of public action are the losses suffered from not doing things privately.

Calculation of net returns from alternative organizations is a highly complex operation. It cannot readily be performed by the busy or disinterested citizens who are not well informed. Since

[1] The most important book on this question is undoubtedly that of James M. Buchanan and Gordon Tullock, *The Calculus of Consent* (Ann Arbor: University of Michigan Press, 1962).

most people fit into one category or the other, we usually do not make the calculations even when we have the opportunity. But since taxpayers do have an interest in the disposition of public choice, each individual should inform himself sufficiently to decide whether he ought to participate in the collective decision. This is not a difficult choice to make. We learn rather early about some of the consequences of alternative schemes of choice. And if we really care we can become acquainted with fairly serious analyses of organizational costs and benefits.

For example, we should realize that if we opt for private action to solve the problem we will have a greater range of discretion than under collective choice, because the impacts are more likely to be confined to the individual. Private choice has the further virtue of lower decision-making costs since it involves a smaller number of decision makers. For the same reason, private choice tends to increase external costs and benefits. If lower decision-making costs are a goal, private institutions should be employed, but public institutions should be chosen to reduce the externalities. Public choice, since it involves many persons attempting to choose a single policy applicable to all, is much more apt than private choice to increase a feeling of conflict among participants. One person's preferences in public choice become the object of other people's concerns because those preferences may become dictates over their behavior. If a bare majority chooses policy A when I preferred policy B I must adjust my behavior to conform to their preferences. Public choice in government, unless it is unanimous, necessarily and always entails coercion. As we have seen, a *free market* does not, since the purchases of one consumer are not necessarily forced upon other consumers.

These general observations are probably only dimly perceived by many Americans. During public debates, however, partisans will make every effort to detail consequences of different means of choice. The important point is to become better analysts of the good and bad but in terms of expected returns over both the short and long runs. The best decision apparatus for the former may not work as well for the longer haul and vice versa. Determining long-run effects is far more demanding and less certain than specifying and measuring shorter-run consequences because there are many more factors and unexpected events to disrupt predictions. One should also assume that the same difficulties confront others insofar as they too strive to reduce ignorance.

With these considerations in mind we should make some reasonable progress in assessing the appropriateness of various public processes for handling social problems and achieving personal policy preferences. First we will review some of the typically noted costs and disadvantages of government. Then we will consider which activities should be handled by government; in so doing we reflect on the costs and shortcomings of private processes.

Frequent Complaints about Government

Many scholars explain and justify governmental intervention in social life, especially in the economy, as a necessary means of (1) overcoming or reducing externalities, (2) improving upon the imperfections of the economy, (3) correcting certain unintended social consequences such as business cycles, and (4) providing those public goods and services the private enterprise system fails to provide because it lacks a profit incentive or the capacity. Thus, Adam Smith in *The Wealth of Nations* suggested that government should be confined to providing internal and external protection, justice among citizens, and certain public works (public goods) that facilitate private activities. Smith, like most modern conservatives and even hippies, had a profound doubt about the efficacy, efficiency, and appropriateness of governmental control. As Thoreau and others have said, that government governs best which governs least. Whether our governments attempt too much is debatable but the federal government, today, probably performs more than 7,000 distinct activities.[2] Although socialist and totalitarian traditions of the twentieth century have encouraged the growth of government as a good thing, there does seem to be a growing amount of skepticism about government and an increasing appreciation of decentralized private and public decision making. Complaints about governmental action generally include the following:

1. Government rarely innovates.
2. Government is inefficient.

[2] Alfred de Grazia, "A Classifiable Inventory of Faceted Operations of Government," *Hearings Before the Subcommittee on Executive Reorganization of the Committee on Governmental Operations, United States Senate* (Washington, D.C.: U.S. Government Printing Office, 1968), p. 609.

3. Government is insensitive to voters.
4. Governmental errors are excessively costly.

Let us give brief consideration to each of these charges or observations. The wording of the criticisms used here may not do justice to those who have made them in other terms. We should also be aware that what appears as a complaint against government in general may actually be a complaint about a particular form or a particular rule rather than government. If that is so we should change the rule and not attempt to abolish government for that is both impossible and undesirable.

GOVERNMENT RARELY INNOVATES

Complaints about the inventiveness of government are usually backed with illustrations about the traditional loyalties of bureaucracy rather than statistical evidence comparing the innovations of various types of government and private organizations. The fact of the matter is that we really do not have any first-rate studies of this phenomenon and cannot, therefore, arrive at conclusive statements. Such studies are exceedingly difficult to conduct because defining and measuring innovations are treacherous statistical operations. Both private and public employees may be working simultaneously on the same problem or the government may be financing experimental work by private companies. Who should be credited with innovative virtue?

Critics normally approach the matter by noting that bureaucracy is traditional; since government is bureaucratic, they maintain, it cannot invent anything of worth. They conveniently forget that private institutions are also bureaucratic but are somehow able to overcome bureaucratic lethargy. Common sense seems to suggest that very few large organizations are innovative for it is intellectually demanding and costly and it depends on individual thinking. Nevertheless, research and development funds constitute substantial portions of departmental budgetary requests, particularly at the federal level. Some of this research is done by the agencies themselves while increasing amounts is contracted out to advisors and research organizations, universities, and private scholars. One estimate claims that at least a hundred private research organizations are supported largely by governmental funds.[3]

[3] Stephen Enke, "Think Tanks for Better Government," *Executive Reorganization Subcommittee Hearings*, p. 79.

Among the better-known are the RAND Corporation, Hudson Institute, Stanford Research Institute, and Operations Research Organization (at Johns Hopkins University). Many of these institutes have worked primarily in defense research although some are now turning toward domestic peacetime projects of urban renewal, population control, crime control, and other areas of public involvement.

Probably the most widely known type of research activity the federal government has sponsored include "blue ribbon" commissions Presidents appoint. These groups investigate troublesome social problems and devise policy proposals for their effective solution. Recent years have seen the formation of a number of these commissions (101 during 1965–67) and the publication of their reports including special studies of crime, civil disorder, military draft, and civil rights.[4] Several of these reports have received intense publicity and have served to focus serious attention on alternative policy proposals. In addition, Congress conducts and sponsors a great deal of scholarly research. Most Congressional hearings are earnest inquiries into important social problems and governmental policies which eventuate into public debates and the adoption of new laws and policies. The testimony at such hearings normally comes, for the most part, from highly experienced and expert witnesses. The final committee reports and studies are often among the best inquiries social scientists have at their disposal. This has been especially so with regard to the research sponsored by the Joint Economic Committee of the Congress on such diverse economic problems as state and local public finance, fiscal and monetary policy, Soviet economic growth and military strength, and other problems of current import. The Committee on Government Operations of the Senate and the Hoover Commission have also issued impressive studies of governmental policy making and policy suggestions for its improvement.

Nonetheless, the several states and local institutions are not equally committed to innovation and not all administrations and agencies willingly change their habits. The few states that are innovative have gained a certain fame for it; others are notoriously insensitive to change and its control. Wisconsin and Oregon have sometimes been among the former, while some southern states are among the latter.

---

[4] The Library of Congress, Legislative Reference Service, "Presidential Commissions, Boards and Advisory Groups Established Since 1965," *Executive Reorganization Subcommittee Hearings*, p. 102.

Forces for change at the state and local levels include associations of public officials such as the Municipal League and The Council of State Governments. They search continuously for administrative improvements, but not always for the drastic political innovations that might upset the power balance. Understandably, the major constraint on innovation at all levels is the fear of major alterations of constitutional rules and social forces. Those who think they will be disrupted by change represent the status quo and are likely to resist strongly. The same is true throughout life; such responses are not confined to government.

Finally, we should note that while many critics focus on resistance to change in government they also pride themselves on the fact that the United States has the oldest continuous constitution, two-party system, and democracy in the world. We are no longer as innovative with the fundamental rules but are inventive with respect to the implementation or administration of policy.

GOVERNMENT IS INEFFICIENT

Although government may be powerful it may also be inefficient. We may spend too much on some activities and not enough on others. In a more technical sense, government is alleged to be unable to equalize the marginal returns between private and public resource uses and among the countless public goods and services it sponsors. Governments, it is said, cannot achieve efficient resource allocations because they are motivated neither by the possibility of profit nor by the fear of bankruptcy. Governments are also said to be poor performers because decision making is based on very imprecise calculations of the costs and benefits of each program or activity. How much is a police department worth to a community? Of how much worth is national defense? What is the worth of a public swimming pool? How can policy makers decide such questions? How can they rationally decide how many resources to put into any particular program? Without the guidance of market signals (prices) policy makers are in the unenviable spot of making policy on the basis of very limited information about conflicting preferences. Policy makers do not know the demand curves for their goods and services. Accordingly, they cannot achieve a high degree of efficiency.

There is much to be said for this charge *if* we place a high value on efficiency in resource allocation. Fortunately, many concerned economists and public administrators are showing considerable ingenuity in devising market substitutes that enable more rational choices. We will consider these analytical aids in subsequent chapters and will attempt to evaluate their potential payoffs and current use in government circles.

Political processes and rules are more or less efficient in resource use but so are private markets. Only perfectly competitive markets are supposed to attain high efficiency whereas the imperfect market in which elements of monopoly obtain can be highly inefficient. Most markets are not very competitive. So we must not judge the inefficiency of government against the abstract perfect market but against the realities of countless imperfect markets.

GOVERNMENT IS INSENSITIVE TO VOTERS

Although radicals and some liberals accept this observation as a fact conservative critics take an opposing view, namely, that politicians are far too sensitive to voters and continually cater to and encourage their alleged irrationalities and fads of the moment. Actually, critics ought to refine their argument to state that different types of political institutions or rules encourage more or less sensitivity to voter preferences. If this is the case we should adopt those institutions that best reflect our personal demands and preferences. As things now stand, American politicians and public administrators are prevented from reflecting the views of their constituents by two limitations. They find it difficult to discover those preferences and also to devise policies consistent with divergent individual values and preferences. Most politicians undoubtedly prefer more sensitive institutional arrangements but they are hard to invent given the nature of the problem. Elections are not precise indicators of individual or collective choice, as we saw in Chapter VIII.

The arena in which governmental insensitivity is greatest and most directly felt by the average citizen is not with elective officials but the nonelected bureaucrats and bureaucracy. Citizens come into contact with government primarily through the offices of bureaucrats who are authorized to administer controls and inflict penalties and costs. Given such a situation we should not be surprised if citizens complain about the impersonality, inflexibility, and inefficiencies of government. Bureaucracies employ men and women with a great range of abilities and desires to serve others. They, too, may wake up on the wrong side of the bed or take offense at the irate citizen who thinks that government exists to hound him. Each of us can recount some unpleasant or frustrating incident involving government although reflection will show that most of our relationships with our governors are quite pleasant and rewarding. The normal relationship between the American citizen and his officials is one of courteous informal service without the arrogant authority of officials in many other lands. Research on the public's image of public servants suggests that large segments of population have a fairly generous predisposition toward them and particularly regarding the federal government. Honesty and a sense of public dedication are the two characteristics most admired; in fact, public servants are ranked higher than businessmen in these regards. On the other hand, the people tend to favor private enterprise with respect to ability and initiative. These findings of the Brookings Institution should occasion no surprise among us.[5] Most of us are employees of private business and like to think of ourselves as superior to governmental employees in terms of our abilities and drive even though we are familiar with powerful marketplace incentives to cheat and be self-serving.

One last unobtrusive indicator of our government's concern for the citizen is suggested by the incredible lengths to which the bureaucracy goes to please the citizen or at least not offend him whenever it contacts him concerning his responsibilities. The Internal Revenue Service, for example, writes gentle reminders that quarterly payments are due; the Selective Service and the President address the draftee with "greetings"; the policeman normally approaches the traffic violator with almost excessive courtesy; the local tax assessor patiently explains why and how he is assessing your property; the Veterans Administration advises its clients on how and what to apply for in the way of benefits. Not all citizens are so treated but the vast bulk of the middle class can expect just such treatment.

GOVERNMENTAL ERRORS ARE EXCESSIVELY COSTLY

Just as our governments have enormous power and capacity to do good, they also have enormous capacity to do evil and frequently to go unpunished. One of the virtues of decentralized de-

---

[5] Franklin P. Kilpatrick, Milton C. Cummings, Jr., and M. Kent Jennings, *The Image of the Federal Service* (Washington, D.C.: The Brookings Institution, 1964).

cision making is that, under normal circumstances, the cost of making errors tends to be lower and to redound to the person making the error. The larger the scale of operations, however, the greater the cost of an error and the greater the number of people likely to experience those costs. Most Americans concede that our entrance into the Vietnam war was a mistake. Clearly, the costs have been enormous and they are likely to be with us for many years to come.

Because error is costly and responsibility unpleasant, politicians, administrators, and governments are prone to cover up mistakes if they can. And there are more ways of doing so than we may care to admit. In the first place, the ordinary citizen may be distant from the operation. In the second place, he may not have the expertise to understand or note an error. In the third place, as a party member or a patriot he may not wish to admit errors. Many Americans refused to believe that the massacre at My Lai in South Vietnam occurred or that Americans were guilty of this horrible mass murder. When President Kennedy failed with the Bay of Pigs invasion of Cuba in 1961, he was not criticized by many Americans; in fact, his popularity reached an all-time high among Presidents. Apparently errors will be forgiven if they are not perceived as being immediately and personally felt, or can be explained away or blamed on a vicious enemy. Many a politician has sensed this and turned his own errors into electoral victories.

When Should We Resort To Governmental Activity?

We began the chapter with a series of questions about the appropriateness of political and governmental solutions to social and personal problems and then considered a number of complaints about governmental performances. These complaints are more or less justifiable but they do not, in themselves, inform us much on the kinds of problems for which government may provide a better or worse solution than private persons and institutions. In this section we face up to this question. Needless to say, our point of view is but one view and may not be regarded as persuasive to others. The advice consists of reasons for supporting additional governmental activity. The question of when to resort to governmental activity is posed somewhat negatively because the burden of proof should rest on the one who advocates extensions of government.

MAINTENANCE OF "LAW AND ORDER"

Perhaps the most basic function of a government is to maintain some semblance of domestic peace so that citizens may raise their families, develop their potentialities, and enjoy life rather than be miserable and fear every stranger. Writers of the Constitution called this "domestic tranquility." It is not always easy to attain as the often violent traditions of the American frontier and and metropolitan life have shown. A government that cannot guarantee domestic peace is not a government. In maintaining peace or tranquility, order is provided; that is, individuals, upon awakening each day, can predict and expect certain conditions to prevail. No one need provide his own protection by strapping on a revolver.

In addition, by supporting its own laws and gaining respect for them among the populace, a government can ensure survival of order. Laws and popular regard for them are more important than coercion in providing long-term order and peace. If coercion is necessary to meet unusual challenges to law and order, especially when basic rules are being challenged, the wise use of force is imperative. Both too little and too much force are equally harmful—although in quite different ways because they affect different groups. In Chapter XVI we will attempt to specify how the use of force is appropriate in maintaining order as well as achieving other lesser goals.

MONEY AS A PUBLIC GOOD

Money and monetary institutions are among the greatest inventions of mankind. Consider for a moment how our present economy might function if money were suddenly declared illegal. The results would be absurd; our economy could not function.

Because the monetary system is so crucial it is highly important that our government protect and improve its workings. A badly functioning set of monetary institutions and/or a loss of faith in these institutions and the value of money can have disastrous economic and social consequences. As a primary means of communication money serves to facilitate exchange. It also acts as a store of value and a means of deferred payments. In order to fulfill these functions well it must have a degree of stability. While government cannot completely control the supply and demand for money, it does have a primary role to play that requires considerable intervention. Finally, let it be noted that a government must maintain a single monetary system; economic activity is impaired when we use several monies, as our founding fathers discovered under the Articles of Confederation. If one doubts the convenience of a single monetary system consider what must happen when travelling across state boundaries. The costs of conversion would be prohibitive.

COLLECTIVE CONSUMPTION AND FREE RIDERS

Each of us makes use of public goods and services for which we do not pay directly and in some instances do not pay at all. A sidewalk, for example, is a public good that would be difficult to induce private enterprise to produce. Their use cannot be readily sold or rationed among users nor can a profit be realized. Such services as flood control, police and fire protection, highways, education, a monetary system, defense, lighthouses, parks, and similar goods and services are more or less typical public goods. If we depended upon the private entrepreneurs to supply us with these types of goods they either would not be produced at all or would be produced in insufficient amounts. Since we value the convenience of public services, we have agreed to employ government and coercion to provide them.

A special problem arises in the supplying of public goods. Since there is no market to express consumer evaluations of public goods it would be necessary to devise some other institutional means to arrive at prices for each public good. Whether these means were voting or answering questionnaires citizens would be induced to conceal their preferences. Since they know that the public budget will not be affected by their replies and that to give an honest evaluation may produce higher taxes they will be strongly tempted to be dishonest and claim that they do not place a high value on whatever public good is at stake. Even if they were honest they would have difficulty in attaching a value or price to the good because they have not had experience in purchasing public goods. Because of these problems we tend to agree to coerce ourselves into making tax payments. In short, we wish to reduce the number of citizens who will be dishonest and thereby become "free riders." Most of us try to be free riders whenever possible and most of us will attempt to prevent others from freeloading. Compulsory contributions or dues to labor unions are a good illustration of an attempt to prevent freeloading. Our tax system is based on the same idea.

CONTROL OF EXTERNAL EFFECTS

Suppose one is asked to provide a solution to a pollution problem which has been disturbing many citizens in a typical small town. A national fertilizer manufacturing firm has built a plant on the edge of the town and near an interstate highway. Most citizens originally welcomed the company and even made tax and other concessions to attract it to the area since the company would hire 100 employees and be placed on the tax rolls. Unfortunately, in their enthusiasm to get the business they forgot to ask about the environmental pollution potential of the plant. Now that the plant is busy five days a week and at least eight hours a day the citizens have found that the air is polluted with obnoxious odors, that the plant is unsightly, and that some older residents are bothered by the smoke and fumes. What should be done in terms of alleviating the situation?

A number of alternative solutions are available: (1) remove the plant; (2) reduce production levels; (3) install antipollution devices; and (4) compensate for damages and harm inflicted but allow the plant to continue. If we opt for the first alternative we eliminate pollution but also eliminate 100 jobs and salaries. We might also make it more difficult to recruit other businesses. If we opt for the second we will reduce pollution but also reduce job opportunities since the plant cannot continue all its employees. If option 3 is chosen, pollution remains, but presumably at a lower level; jobs will be retained but at the cost of higher prices on the fertilizer. Of course, local citizens will pay little if any of the price increases because they use so little of the product; other Americans will sustain that cost. If the fourth alternative is chosen, the level of pollution will be constant and jobs will continue but at least some of the inconveniences, annoyances and other damages must be paid for by the plant. Of course, the fertilizer users will finance the compensation.

This problem illustrates a number of difficulties in public policy. First which goal should we strive for? Note that we cannot simultaneously obtain all we want of each goal—full employment and no pollution. Note the opportunity costs of each. In option 1 we regain unpolluted air but at the cost of 100 jobs and their wages for 100 families. Local businessmen may not like the cost. The costs of option 4 are continued pollution while the costs of less pollution in option 2 are increased numbers of unemployed or only partially employed workers. The cost of reduced pollution in option 3 is an increased fertilizer price and, eventually, higher food prices. In short, consumers in the rest of the country must pay so that our local residents can breathe a little better air.

Option 1 seems too costly for most citizens in this small town, and 4 seems too difficult for the town and/or company to administer, because it is difficult to measure damages to intangible values in dollars and cents. Since the company is not apt to reduce production voluntarily when it has a good market and since workers will surely not want less work, option 3 will probably be favored by most people. Positive reasons for the choice include the fact that the additional costs can be transferred to others, most of whom are likely to live in other states. Pollution can be reduced, work maintained, production continued, and residents will be at least somewhat happier than before.

In resorting to option 3 we have, in effect, chosen to extend governmental activity because we have decided to require the company to install expensive antipollution devices that add to its administrative costs and the price of its product, fertilizer. The reduction of a widespread externality, pollution, provided the reason for extending governmental operations and intrusion in the private economy. We might have attempted to persuade the company by private means but we would not be as likely to succeed since there is no positive incentive for the company to comply nor authority to enforce compliance. In fact, for one company to fight pollution would be irrational for both the company and the public. The problem is usually so large that the effects of one company's actions would have no perceptive effect yet that company would bear all the costs. When external costs are high and broadly shared, governmental action spreads these costs more widely.

LONG–RANGE CAPITAL INVESTMENT

What should we do to acquire the benefits of very large-scale investments that pay off only in the very long run? For example, how can nuclear power, hydroelectric power, great irrigation projects, exploration of the universe, and certain transportation facilities be provided? Private business is not rushing to organize such

280 Public Choice in America

vast undertakings because (1) they require huge capital outlays and (2) they yield a relatively small profit in the short run. We cannot reasonably expect private organizations or individuals to finance and manage such socially valuable but privately unpromising endeavors. If we value these activities it will be necessary to involve the vast resources of a government. Of course, it is also possible to include business as we do in COMSAT, or whenever government purchases goods and services from business. The billions of dollars expended for the moon shots could hardly be provided by private investors. Resort to government is understandable and desirable. Besides, many of these projects have considerable spillover effects or external benefits that could not be anticipated at the origins of the project.

Useful long-range social investments are not made by private persons and organizations because they are not currently profitable or do not offer a promise of future returns. Our previous example of air pollution devices suggests the rationale. Perhaps an even better illustration is found in the field of natural resources conservation. A lumber company, for example, that plans only for the short run, with no thought for future stockholders, may find it highly profitable to denude entire forests and not plant seedlings to ensure a more permanent supply. While every lumber company and citizen would admit that this practice has bad long-run consequences few would have an incentive to engage in costly individual efforts at reforestation. Besides slaughtering trees the costs include ruination of recreational areas of natural beauty and the greater possibilities of floods since denuded forests cannot control water. The most obvious way to reduce these costs is to employ governmental control or intervention. To prevent one firm from making a profit at a social cost it is necessary to treat all firms in the same industry equally.

UNEMPLOYMENT AND INFLATION: THE BUSINESS CYCLE

To prevent or defeat unemployment, modern economists tell us, we must encourage spending on consumption and/or investment; to prevent or defeat inflation we must restrict spending on consumption or nonproductive activities. Each of the above solutions requires getting individual citizens to behave in ways that may be contrary to their short-run individual interests. In the case of a depression the prudent individual saves his money. He expects further price drops and knows he will need his income to survive.

So he delays or reduces his spending, but unknowingly furthers the deflationary spiral. In the case of inflation, individuals tend to spend immediately because prices may be expected to continue to increase. To do otherwise is to act against one's own short-run interests. This tendency, however, encourages inflationary forces. That is the rationale that allows the government to take counter-cyclical actions that work against individual interests in the short run but further them in the long run. While the money one individual saves or spends would be but a drop in the bucket, the force of all individuals' similar actions is decisive. Governmental control over free-market activity seems desirable in this case.

CONTROL OF MONOPOLY

Americans have been firm believers in the virtues of competition yet have to admit that monopoly and varying lesser degrees of imperfect competition exist throughout our economy. Monopolistic corporations are usually considered bad because they reduce supplies, charge high prices, have disproportionate political influence, and thus put consumers and citizens at their mercy. Some public regulation of monopoly practices is usually considered necessary.

Control can be exercised by any of three means: (1) direct regulation of prices, quantities, and qualities of the monopolistic products, (2) attempt to prevent or break up monopolies so that competition may take place, or (3) governmental operation of its own businesses, especially utilities. The first alternative may defeat our purpose by actually limiting the supply of goods, and perhaps ultimately creating a black market. The second choice has not resulted in any conspicuous gains although we maintain and occasionally apply laws that are supposed to accomplish that end. Instead we resort to public control of natural monopolies as in the public utility field. The third method is used far more than is generally realized. Electrical power, water production, and liquor sales are among the prime businesses owned and operated by government.

REDISTRIBUTION OF INCOME

Although the national income generated by our capitalist economy is the largest in the world, it continues to be unequally divided by a wide margin. (Even so, it is not divided as unequally as the smaller incomes of newly-developing nations.)[6] In general, those who benefit from this unequal distribution of income and wealth oppose alteration of the basic pattern. Nevertheless, many individuals at all income levels feel that government ought to redistribute income and wealth in order to achieve greater equality. Government already intervenes through the use of highly progressive income taxes, inheritance taxes, subsidized programs for lower-income groups, free public education, and minimum wage laws, and these measures have altered the original market distributions. The precise extent of this redistribution is debatable, but students of the problem agree that it is small. Still, if one believes in greater income equality he should support more vigorous governmental intervention in the economy. Whether government can succeed given American economic and political conditions is an important strategic question. We will consider it in greater detail in Chapter XV.

CIVIL LIBERTIES AND RIGHTS

Our political system is entrusted with the responsibility of producing and administering the basic rules by which the entire society operates. In this role, governments both coerce and protect individuals in their interactions with government and one another. This may seem paradoxical but no other institution in society is capable of providing the necessary order. While government is hardly the only institution that takes an interest in civil liberties and personal rights, it is the major one. In fact, government properly has a monopoly on force, and therefore is capable of inflicting great harm as well as good. Our history can be usefully studied as a cycle or process involving the extension and retrenchment—even episodic repression—of liberties. The decade of the 1960s, for example, was one of considerable expansion of individual liberties while the decade of the 1920s was not. Powerful governments can be used for diametrically opposed ends; they are two-edged swords.

Liberties and rights need not always necessarily be expanded for some at the expense of others. In general, however, the granting of a right entails an obligation on the part of others to respect that right. And in some instances the extension of a right

---

[6] Simon Kuznets, *Modern Economic Growth: Rate, Structure and Spread* (New Haven, Conn.: Yale University Press, 1966), Chapter 4.

to some does impose a restriction or added cost on another. The rights of the criminally accused do, in fact, add to the burdens of their accusers, just as collective bargaining rights of employees have added to the costs of decision making and of wages for employers. As students have their rights expanded, professors and administrators will have to adjust and learn to make cooperative rather than authoritarian policies; it will not be an easy learning experience. The power and status of one group has been increased vis-à-vis the other group. That is why public policy on these issues is likely to stimulate heated passions.

Resorting to politics and government to protect and expand liberties is necessary but it is also treacherous since the extension of rights to one group may encourage others to demand the same rights. Likewise, government coerces some groups (usually majorities) in order to advance and protect liberties of others (usually minorities). Those who would assume a strict libertarian position should be constantly aware of these qualifications. Expanding the liberties of free speech, for example, may well bring groups into the political process whose major intent is to restrict or coerce another group. Liberals have learned that the expansion of the economic rights of laborers during the 1930s was no guarantee that these same men would be fervent defenders of the economic and civil rights of blacks, Chicanos, Indians, and academicians during the 1960s. Despite these paradoxes, one must be consistent in allocating basic political freedoms or rights. If one man is to have the guarantees of free speech, press, and assembly, all men must have the same guarantees if citizenship is to be worthwhile.

A GENERAL CONCLUSION

A citizen should consider political means and governmental solutions as possible alternatives if he is unable to further his own ends by private action—either individual or collective. Whenever a problem occurs in daily life the least costly and most promising possibility is to settle the matter on an individual basis. Sometimes it is necessary to involve others in the action—either because they too are affected or because their additional resources are required to win a more favorable result. For the assistance of others we must pay the cost; a cost that stems from more complicated decision making and (possibly) reduced shares of whatever "winnings" may be attained. Coalition partners will want some of the booty, too. Some collective action is appropriate in the private sector. For example, persons may form a cooperative to buy or sell food. Or, one may wish to organize a school, an arts and crafts program, or a neighborhood association for any number of purposes. But, suppose we wanted to prevent a person or a group from infringing on our civil rights, damaging property or reducing our income, power, or social status—to prevent a roving gang from looting our homes, for example. We would quickly learn that we cannot safely or effectively accomplish this by private individual or even cooperative action; public action involving governmental policy would be imperative. A change in the zoning ordinances might solve some neighborhood problems; reorganization or mobilization of governmental agencies might offer greater protection. And such actions might entail going all the way to the federal government in one or more of its branches.

Given the great costs of political action, detailed in Chapters VII to IX, one should be very careful before embarking on extensive political action. And, given the shortcomings of political processes and government we should be even more cautious about the types of activities we choose to turn over to public choice and governmental administration. Despite these cautions there are conditions under which a citizen should become politicized and want government to control and even coerce citizens and even oneself. We have elaborated on these conditions in this and previous chapters. The problem, now, is deciding which level of government can best perform whatever we have decided should be done.

Most Appropriate Level of Government

Once the decision to take government action has been made, further choices must be made concerning the most appropriate level(s) of government at which to conduct these activities. Appropriateness implies a set of standards and some goal(s) to be achieved. It is impossible to make the choice without using such yardsticks. What measures should we keep in mind?

Some objectives and measures immediately suggest themselves. One example is the highest possible level of technical efficiency in operations. Another is the desire to afford citizens the widest possible opportunities to participate in decision making— or possibly to reduce certain types of costs such as decision costs. Another desirable goal is to develop a sense of community, or, in contrast, to reduce alienation. We might choose to further certain economic objectives such as growth, stability, or equity. Our choice of levels of government must then depend on the goal or goals we have set and the type of activity we are considering. Local government is not invariably superior or inferior to the federal government. Since our goals and activities can be mixed and inconsistent as well as complementary and consistent, our decision process will be relatively complex. Lack of adequate information and applicable theory will cause further impasses. We will probably discover that an optimal system consists of cooperation between several levels of government. Each will engage in some specialization while other tasks will be shared. Still other activities will probably best be handled by some suitable cooperation between private and public sectors. When all these general questions have been answered, the questions must become more specific. We can progress in this direction if we review some of the historical strengths and shortcomings of our various governments.

LOCAL GOVERNMENTS

Because local units are the smallest they are apt to permit a greater degree of individual rationality in the sense that the citizen will perceive the relationships between costs and benefits more clearly than in larger units. On this level citizens can be well informed about local politicians, decisions, and future possibilities. Exceptions, of course, are local units such as New York City, which are larger than some nations and thus decrease the individual's impact on and understanding of decisions and processes.

If many activities are on local levels a greater range of options is available for the citizen-consumer. He can "vote with his feet" or move to a local unit that provides the public services he wants in the quantities he prefers. This is only true, however, to a certain extent. Actually the citizen-consumer cannot so easily acquire a desired "market basket" because so many public goods are indivisible. Worse, along with the public "goods" he must also accept the "bads" he does not like. Residents of Ann Arbor, Michigan, for example, must endure poorly maintained streets in order to enjoy a fine educational system. Voting with one's feet is still possible; those who want better education, for example, tend to leave the core areas of cities and flock to more stable suburbs that provide higher quality education. But along with education they have to accept the blandness of suburban life. Thus, despite somewhat limited mobility, citizens in pursuit of certain public goods do act as though they are taking advantage of whatever degree of choice is available. A greater diversity in lifestyles is therefore possible than is the case in more centralized polities. Typically, the result is a wide variation in quality, supply, and price of public goods. For example, expenditures on such items as public education range from an estimated per-pupil high of $1,140 in New York to a low of $432 in Alabama (1969).[7] Equally wide variations may be found for almost every expenditure of local government. Anyone who has traveled across state lines has seen sharp differences in the quality of highways.

A third advantage often attributed to local governments is capacity for experimentation and innovation. Costs of ventures undertaken on a smaller scale are likely to be lower in case of failure and therefore incentive to experiment is increased. This experimentation on a manageable scale has one obvious advantage. Successful experiments can become models for other governments. Local officials try to keep abreast of developments in other communities through written reports and on-site inspections. Professional associations inform their members of new alternatives and their results.

But local governments have severe limitations, too. For one thing, their fiscal capacity is not usually adequate for major undertakings. The desperately low per-capita income in many states does not appear to have much chance of showing significant growth in the near future. To solve this problem, many of the units rely increasingly on state and federal resources. A further impediment local governments must contend with is that they must often depend on personnel who are not highly qualified and are all too often corrupt. Many community power studies confirm the cynical citizen views that local officials are inept at public service but highly skilled at protecting the status quo and their own financial interests. Some of the worst autocracies in the nation are found at the local level. A great deal of reform during the past 40 years has been sponsored not by local or state governments but by a persistent federal government. If the power of local satraps has been reduced it has been primarily a result of federal financing on the basis of federal standards and federal power. It appears the hope for clean-up of the local governing bodies lies in their own desires for federal aid.

---

[7] U.S. Bureau of the Census, *Statistical Abstract of the United States, 1969* (90th ed., Washington, D.C.: U.S. Government Printing Office, 1969), p. 116.

One of the more impressive arguments against decentralizing public activities arises from the complications a strong federal system introduces into decision making. When each unit has some autonomy, as local ones do, their problems include poorly coordinated activities, duplication of services, inconsistent policies, and vastly higher decision-making costs. The latter are further increased because some means of adjudication must be made available to governments that are in conflict. Some 25,683 cases involving diversity of citizenship and governmental jurisdiction were commenced in 1968 in U.S. District Courts.[8]

These costs may not be excessive or disturbing if one values local self-determination more than saving on decision-making costs or the costs of bad policies, or both.

Decentralized policy making has not prevented our governments from acting to overcome the shortcomings of decentralization while attempting to maintain its advantages. Our governments and component agencies engage in far more cooperation than conflict as testified by the vast numbers of interstate compacts or agreements, federal grants-in-aid to states and local units, legislative uniformity codes, cooperative working agreements among agencies, and professional associations of officials. Nearly 200 federal grants-in-aid programs covering 50 policy areas were enacted between 1803 and 1962.[9]

Use of local institutions has gained a certain appeal among both radicals and conservatives during recent years for two major reasons. These groups have been motivated partly by apparent shortcomings of federal programs and partly by a desire to pluralize power and make community life more meaningful (for radicals) and more profitable (for some conservatives). Those who wish to achieve more of these ends should recognize that they can be achieved only at a cost—but that is also true of policy making at any and all levels of government.

ACTIVITIES AND THE SIZE OF GOVERNMENT

Now that we have considered the basic strengths and weaknesses of local political institutions we are in a better position to determine which activities they should perform. Our rules necessarily assist in specifying activities for other levels of gov-

---

[8] *Statistical Abstract, 1969*, p. 150.
[9] W. Brooks Graves, *American Intergovernmental Relations* (New York: Charles Scribner's Sons, 1964), p. 933.

ernment. A simple list of miscellaneous activities would be point-less. Instead, we will attempt to write a few basic rules for division of labor that can be applied to whatever policy problem may arise.

Rule 1. *Use local institutions to regulate activities if those who are to be regulated cannot escape by moving to another unregulated unit.*

An obvious way out for a person or organization about to be controlled or, say, taxed, by a local government is to consider moving to a more favorable or less "hostile" area. While there are distinct and apparent limitations on movement, businesses do threaten to leave whenever regulation is proposed. Some threats are unrealistic; a mining company cannot mine where ore does not exist and the Ford Motor Company cannot pick up its enormous plant in Michigan and move to Nebraska. However, in less dramatic cases these options of mobility and threats are realistic. Many householders are, in fact, escaping higher taxation in the core areas of cities by moving to outlying suburbs and rural localities. They take advantage of core area benefits but do not pay for them. Or, a small business may escape controls on pollution by relocating in a nearby unregulated area. Some localities entice businesses by granting such substantial concessions as tax exemptions, free sites, lower wage rates, a more docile labor force, fewer regulations. The areas which do not offer these inducements cannot compete as effectively for new enterprise.

Rule 2. *Practice economies of scale whenever possible.*

Economies of scale—the relationship between the average cost of producing a good and the size of the producing unit—must be considered whenever a public project is contemplated. Efficient use of resources can only be attained when we consider the costs involved at different levels of activity. A great many activities are well within the scope of efficient production by local units but some are not. Any activity that has an expensive indivisible product such as national defense should not be the responsibility of local governments. State and local boundaries are political and not economic but we cannot overlook economic costs. Assigning responsibilities beyond capacity leads to higher production costs and insufficient supplies of public goods. Not to take advantage of economies of scale is to produce at higher costs and therefore waste precious resources.

We cannot supply a neat and exhaustive list of activities that should be entrusted to localities because we do not know enough about economies of scale—that is, the effect of the size of governmental units on the costs of producing public goods and services. Besides, as activities change and new techniques of control evolve, our judgments will also have to recognize altered circumstances and institute new divisions of labor. What was once an efficient activity for the federal or state governments may now be better performed by local units and, of course, vice versa. However, if we wish to also acquire some of the noneconomic advantages of participation, meaningfulness, community, and the like, we should always opt for the smallest governmental unit capable of performing the activity in question. Again, we must be aware of competing goals because the price of wider participation and the like may be increased costs or decreased efficiency.

Rule 3. *Rely on the federal governments to redistribute income.*

This observation is based on both history and logic. States and local governments in the aggregate may spend and tax more than the federal government but no single unit has a large enough fiscal program to significantly affect the distribution of income. In fact, as we noted in Chapters IV and V, even the federal government does not achieve a great deal in this regard. Logically, if local units embarked on such a program, it would encourage the rich to leave the locality and avoid the extra taxes involved in supporting the poor. And, if community power studies are correct, most communities are run by elites who would not often undertake to redistribute income by taxing themselves and redistributing funds to the poor. Only at the national level could such a program have any support and only at the national level would it be impossible for the rich to escape the burdens. The regressiveness of state and local taxation stands in sharp contrast to the progressive rates of the federal government. We should note, however, that the major activity of local government, education, has been a major long-run force for income redistribution.

Rule 4. *Public activities should be assigned on the basis of the geographical range of the external benefits and costs.*

The point of this rule is to include all and only those persons in a governmental unit who are affected by the activities of that unit of government whether the consequences or spillovers are beneficial or costly. Those who benefit from a service should pay for its provision; those who are harmed and those who must support an activity ought to be included in the decision making concerning the activity. In other words, given the unit of government we should tailor its activities so that no spillovers occur; given the range of any spillovers we should tailor the size of the governmental unit to fit that range.

This rule suggests that different activities should be performed by different sized governments. There is no good reason for uniform size governments in the division of labor. Our recognition of this political reality is testified to by the existence of more than 21,000 special districts and, of course, the federal system itself.

Needless to say, we have not based our units of government on efficiency principles alone; political considerations are also important. The task of adjusting the scope of activities and the size of governments is especially difficult because the measurement of external effects is itself in a rudimentary stage. How can we decide the extent of external benefits in the case of education? Are they purely local? Statewide? National? If national, how is it that the local communities have the major responsibilities for it, not the federal government?

Or consider the somewhat imprecise external effects of functions of the communication media. Regulation of television and radio, for example, should not be a prime responsibility of states or local governments. To assign regulation to these units would complicate the operations of the business unnecessarily. Even worse, it might lead to a great deal of conflicting attempts at regulation and censorship. Conceivably some states might wish to block reception of television programs considered offensive or subversive in their areas. A moralistic local community, for example, might attempt to prevent programming about sex from being presented to their children. A highly conservative state might "jam" the broadcasts of a well-known liberal commentator. Most citizens agree that matters of personal preference should be left to individuals, not governments. If regulation is deemed wise, however, they feel it should be done at the national level since the effects appear to be national in scope.

One way of conceptualizing the range of external effects is to construct a simple scale that can also be thought of as a simplified representation of a map. The ranges of external effects can be placed on a single plane. The scale represents geographical distance or space and therefore the boundaries of governmental units, including the individual, family, block, city, state, region, and nation. The individual is at the left end, and purely localized effects are portrayed at the left side of the scale. The farther we move to the right end of the scale the more distant the effects; accordingly the larger must be the unit of government. In real life, it becomes especially difficult to measure the point at which the effects become minimal. This is particularly marked with intangible effects, such as education. The effects of flood and disease control are comparatively easy to detect.

Still, we have found no hard and fast rules that allow us to assign responsibility. Perhaps we can clarify the situation by listing a variety of activities carried on by various governments that are usually thought to be appropriate activities for them. Such a list is presented in Table XIII-1. Note that some overlapping exists although the table has nothing to say about the nature of the shared actions. Beneficial spillovers or effects have been included but not the costs, as this would excessively complicate the table. Note that the effects of very few activities are confined to local areas (only fire protection, streets, and sewage disposal); for better or worse, most activities in a highly interdependent modern society have serious consequences for large segments of the population. As a result, shared functions or activities are the order of the day. Defining the external effects as precisely as possible enables us to adjust the size of government appropriately.

TABLE XIII–1

Public Activities and Their Effects

	Major Effects			
Activities	*Local*	*State*	*Regional*	*National*
Fire protection	x			
Police protection	x			
Parks and recreation	x	x	x	x
Public libraries	x	x		
Water distribution	x	x	x	
City streets	x			
Interstate highways	x	x	x	x
Air and water pollution	x	x	x	
Sewage disposal	x			
Airports	x	x	x	x
Education	x	x	x	x
Disease control	x	x	x	x
National defense				x
Disaster relief	x	x	x	x

A few readers may have spotted one serious omission among possible units of government and effects—international governments and international externalities. The effects of many American policies are felt the world over. (Some foreigners even claim they should be permitted to vote in American national elections since the results are so consequential for them.) We do recognize the existence of external effects and we attempt to control them in several ways. We join international organizations such as the United Nations; we sign international agreements. If world government has a chance at all, it will only come when peoples recognize the high external costs they endure as separate nation-states.

Exercises in Analysis

THE STATE OF DISUNION

The proliferation of governmental units is a favorite target among journalists, as the following editorial illustrates.

> Want to guess which state has the most units of local government?
>
> The dubious honor goes to Illinois, where, at last count, there were 6,453 separate political entities—about one for every 1,700 residents of the "land of Lincoln."
>
> A special Illinois study commission has looked into this absurd proliferation of tax-levying public corporations and decided that it does not really promote local government of, by or for local people. Instead of gaining strength in numbers—Illinois' local units are being easily divided and dominated by the state and/or the federal government.
>
> That's hardly surprising, especially in view of the trend toward state governments' and the federal government's becoming better-streamlined organizations of centralized authority.[10]

Consider the following questions: 1. Why does the writer assume that one political entity per 1,700 residents is an absurd proliferation? 2. Is the assertion valid that proliferation can only lead to greater domination by the federal government? 3. What values are sacrificed by reducing the number of special districts? 4. What is the meaning of "disunion"?

[10] Editorial, *Eugene Register-Guard*, March 30, 1970.

COSTS OF FEDERALISM

Our discussion of the political division of labor has centered about the advantages and disadvantages of performing various tasks or providing public goods at different levels of government with special reference to local units. We have not questioned the federal system, itself—America's major contribution to the art of governing. Among scholars who have is William H. Riker. In the final chapter of a unique little book, *Federalism: Origin, Operation, Significance,*[11] he asks, "Is Federalism Worth Keeping?"

We cannot use a cost/benefit analysis, Riker contends, because there is no precise means by which to make the calculations. Instead, he suggests that we ask what federal systems actually do and determine which minorities benefit from such systems. This in itself is a somewhat less sophisticated kind of cost/benefit analysis in that it does not assign specific amounts to specific groups. Riker's conclusion is not entirely unexpected: federalism in this country favors the Southern white racists, capitalists, and landlords.[12] He also baldly asserts that if you favor racism you should also favor federalism. Of course, federalism can produce other results that are beneficial.

Must we abolish or abandon federalism in order to reduce or eliminate racism? Is racism the only result of federalism? Can racism be reduced through other means, public or private, within a federal system? How does federalism protect and advance the interests of racists? Capitalists? Landlords? Can the latter two groups be controlled within federalism? How? If not, why not?

Suggested Readings

Elazar, Daniel J. *American Federalism: A View from the States* (New York: Thomas Y. Crowell Co., 1966).

Fesler, James. *Area and Administration* (University, Ala.: University of Alabama Press, 1949).

Heller, Walter. *New Dimensions of Political Economy* (New York: W. W. Norton & Co., 1967).

Lockard, Duane. *The Politics of State and Local Government,* (2d ed. New York: The Macmillan Co., 1969).

[11] William H. Riker, *Federalism* (Boston: Little, Brown & Co., 1964).
[12] Riker, *Federalism*, p. 155.

Maass, Arthur, ed. *Area and Power: A Theory of Local Government* (New York: The Free Press, 1959).

Thompson, Wilbur R. *A Preface to Urban Economics* (Baltimore, Md.: Johns Hopkins University Press, 1965).

Wildavsky, Aaron, ed. *American Federalism in Perspective* (Boston: Little, Brown & Co., 1967).

Chapter XIV

BETTER ALLOCATIONS OF OUR RESOURCES

Reordering our national priorities has been one of the more vocal and insistent calls of the young during recent years. In addition, mature citizens complain that we spend far too much on war—they demand that much more be spent on improving the quality of life here at home. The ordering of priorities and therefore the allocation of resources is always an important goal for the simple reason that even as our resources expand, still they are scarce relative to the growing demands made upon them. The impatient, intolerant, and ignorant are apt to see no problem; they either admit of no goals other than their own or they deny the scarcity of resources. But problems exist and they must be understood and dealt with if efficient use of resources is to be accomplished.

How can we get the most from these scarce resources? Is it possible to achieve more of our diverse individual preferences with some different political ordering of priorities and commitments of resources? Although there is advice to offer on solutions, this chapter will be primarily concerned with clearly stating the issues in a form that will enable further study toward solutions.

The Allocative Problem

Whether we consider goals of the nation, of the states, or of local governments we confront the same general problem: How can we best achieve all the desired goals? The resources at each level are far too limited to satisfy the many conflicting demands made upon them; therefore, some goals will have to be sacrificed for others. Whose goals and whose resources will be sought and whose sacrificed is a fundamental political choice. Whose goals should be sought and whose resources should be commanded are other questions we are about to consider. Figure XIV-1 presents a minute sample of the allocative choices facing the American people—in a vastly oversimplified form.

Let us say that each year the nation begins with a certain amount of resources in the form of its expected national income and known capital assets. In 1967 this amounted to $790 billion. These assets and income can be used in a variety of ways. The first choice we make through our basic political institutions is an allocation between the private economy and the public economy. In 1967 we allocated about 32 percent to the latter; the remainder stayed in the private economy and therefore was divided according to private choice. A recurrent question is whether that division was the best possible one. Other nations have made different allocations as, indeed, our own country has at various times.

Once we choose, and we do not do this in one distinct decision for all levels of government, we must then decide at which levels how much will be spent and for what purposes. Since our policy-making system is not dictatorial or highly centralized, these choices are made by countless people in highly independent ways. Our state and local systems are not told what they must do by a national planner. Within certain cultural and economic constraints and certain political conditions set by the federal government including policy guidelines and grants-in-aid, the local units decide for themselves. In 1967, for example, about 63 percent was administered by the federal government, another 19 percent by the states and finally, 18 percent by local units.[1] Current allocations are not much different.

Were these appropriate amounts or allocations? Perhaps we can better discover an answer by referring to the actual activities for which such monies are spent at each level. This information is found in Chapter II, Tables 1 and 2.

If we had a very different political system—a highly cen-

---

[1] U.S. Bureau of the Census, *Statistical Abstract of the United States, 1969* (Washington, D.C.: U.S. Government Printing Office, 1969), p. 407.

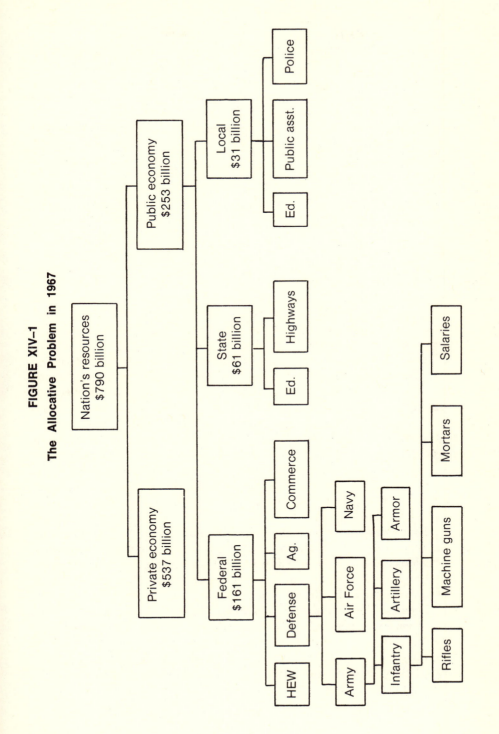

FIGURE XIV-1

The Allocative Problem in 1967

tralized one, for example—some planner or planning board would make all choices for us. Beginning at the top with the broadest allocations the planner would work down through a sequence to the lowest levels, even to such technological choices as the best kind of surfacing to apply to a new highway or the kind of rifle to adopt for the infantry. The planners, in this case, would not have to consider the personal tastes or preferences of the citizens and could, in principle at least, allocate resources among public activities in such a way as to satisfy the demanding criterion of efficiency. They would thus derive the greatest possible return from public investment. What is efficient use of resources in the public sphere?

Efficiency as a Criterion of Public Policy

The concept of efficiency is a most important one among economists and conservative citizens, although the former may have a much more precise notion of the meaning of the concept. Citizens, however, surely have some sense of what is involved in saying that one way of doing things is more or less efficient than another. While all may agree that efficient use of scarce resources is a highly desirable standard by which to judge political systems and administrations, we must not assume that it is the only worthy end. In fact, efficiency may be far less important than equity, a sense of community, or widespread participation. Like any other goal, efficiency can often be attained only at the cost of other goals. We will discuss this problem at greater length in subsequent chapters, but for the present let us view efficiency as our main goal.

Efficiency means gaining as much value as possible within certain resource constraints, or, given some goal, with the least use of resources. In other words, it involves getting as much as one can from whatever expenditure is made. Achieving greater efficiency is seldom simple. It is least simple of all in the public sector, because the costs and benefits of alternative programs are not as easily measured as in the private sector. When costs and benefits cannot be directly and readily measured we have no standard for judging whether we have achieved more or less efficiency. Slow progress is being made in this regard while we continue to make choices.

Optimal Allocation of Resources:
Public and Private Uses

The first question of public policy, as we noted in the intro-
duction, involves allocation of society's resources between public
and private uses. In an intuitive sense we probably all recognize
the desirability of achieving as much return as possible in this
allocation—what some scholars have called a "social balance."
How to do that is a question that has occupied economists for
years. Some of their answers are discussed in the following paragraphs.

EQUALIZING MARGINAL RETURNS

In a general sense a government is considered wise if its
leaders decide to allocate resources between the private and public sectors in such a way that the marginal values of or last dollar
spent on goods in each sector is equalized. By this yardstick, *the
last dollar of expenditure on public goods and services yields the
same satisfaction as the last dollar devoted to private goods and
services. At that point total satisfaction will be maximized.*

According to some well-known theorists and critics the ideal
of equalized marginal returns does not obtain in the United States.
John Kenneth Galbraith is one economist who claims that "social
imbalance" exists; that we typically spend too much on private
goods and far too little on public goods.[2] He maintains that we
spend too much on cigarettes, alcohol, cosmetics, and other personal luxuries, and not enough on city libraries, parks, antipollution measures, and cultural matters in general. Perhaps an even
better illustration of social imbalance is in the ratio of private
automobiles (far too many) to adequate public highways and
roads (too few). Since we cannot have all we want of both public and private goods we must be willing to sacrifice one for the
other. Under this theory of equalizing marginal returns, we should
do this only to the extent that our satisfactions from each are
equal.

It must be said that other theorists are less disturbed by
imbalances; they see them not only as facts of life but as yield-
ing positive benefits. Albert O. Hirschman, for example, thinks

[2] *The Affluent Society* (Boston: Houghton Mifflin Co., 1958), Chapter
XVIII.

FIGURE XIV–2

Public-Private Resource Allocation: The Ideal State

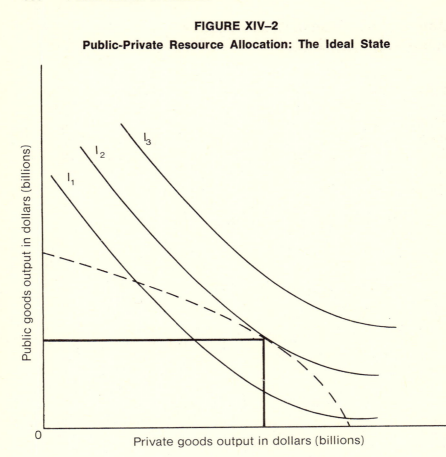

that imbalances can act as spurs for one sector to catch up with another.[3] His position seems to make a virtue of reality. Still, he would agree that the ideal final state is one of balanced allocations.

This ideal final solution is graphically shown in Figure XIV-2, which shows a series of "indifference curves." Each of these, I_1, I_2, and I_3, depicts a set of preferences among public and private goods; that is, combinations of these two sets of goods that are of equal value to a given person or to society. Because any point or combination along any single curve yields the same level of satisfaction, the curves are known as indifference curves; the person is indifferent among these combinations. The farther away

[3] Albert O. Hirschman, *The Strategy of Economic Development* (New Haven, Conn.: Yale University Press, 1958), especially Chapter 4.

the curve from the point of origin the higher the level of satisfaction. For example, I_3 yields more satisfaction than I_2 and I_2 more than I_1. That seems reasonable since it is better to have more of both goods or at least more of one good while the other remains constant. As we move along a single curve, however, we must give up some of one good in order to get more of another. To gain more private goods requires a sacrifice of public goods and vice versa. The rate at which an individual or a society is willing to do this is known as the "marginal rate of substitutability." At times a person may be willing to surrender or trade a lot of private goods in order to get a little more public goods. That would occur when one is blessed with a great supply of the former and very little of the latter. That, too, seems reasonable and consistent with most human behavior.

The other important curve in Figure XIV-2 is the dotted line that goes by several names: "transformation curve," "production possibility curve" and "resource curve or constraint." Unlike the indifference curves, this curve does not describe people's preferences, but delineates the combinations of goods that can in fact be produced by the public and private sectors. The curve tells us that, given scarcities of resources, we can only produce certain total amounts of each good. The farther this curve is from the point of origin the more goods can be produced. Note that here, also—because of scarcity—one must give up private goods to produce public goods and vice versa. The shape and slope of the transformation curve tells us the rate at which these production trade-offs can be made.

We have drawn the curve so that the point of intersection of the transformation curve and the second highest indifference curve describes the current situation in the United States: about 32 percent of the nation's output is public and the remaining 68 percent is private. We can express preferences about that ratio, as Galbraith and others do. Galbraith might like to see a combination of, say, 40 percent public and 60 percent private goods. He would also, like most people, advocate pushing out the production possibility curve so that we could get to a still higher indifference curve.

PUBLIC OR PRIVATE ALLOCATIONS AND TAXATION

The analysis presented in Figure XIV-2 is not entirely consistent with the concept of burdens in Chapter V because it does not include a direct statement on the role of taxation in deciding an optimal mix of public and private goods. Some citizens' indifference curves would be sharply affected or altered by added knowledge of the tax bill for public goods. The ability to pay will surely be a consideration for many if not all taxpayers. In addition, taxpayers will resent paying taxes for public goods they do not receive or are unaware of; to the extent they do resent it they may be said to be suffering some disutility or dissatisfaction. Their disutility must be subtracted from the utility or satisfactions they and each other person derive from use of the public goods. Using the marginal calculus, a person should demand additional public goods as long as the marginal utility is greater than the marginal disutility. When the two factors are equal he should stop. The same would be true for an entire society if we could make the questionable assumption that it is possible to add and subtract the utilities and disutilities of different citizens. Figure XIV-3 shows this choice in geometric terms.[4] Observe that as one chooses more units of public goods (moving toward the right along the horizontal line) the marginal or added utility diminishes. That means each additional unit provides less utility than the previous unit, while the marginal disutility of having to pay more for goods offering less satisfaction increases. So long as the marginal gains of additional public expenditures are greater than the marginal disutilities it seems desirable to produce more public goods. The point of equality (e) where the horizontal line and the middle line or the net marginal utility curve intersect is the point at which to cease production. The middle line merely results from subtraction of the distance between the disutility curve and the horizontal line from the marginal utility curve. Marginal utility is equal to marginal disutility (MU = MDU) at Oe quantity of public goods. To go beyond that point would produce more disutility than utility; to produce less would mean that potential utility was not being realized.

The optimal production of public goods cannot be determined by reference to taxation and preferences alone; a more complete explanation would consider such additional facts as the distribution of the tax load. A citizen who is required to pay out more taxes might not (and usually does not) want as many goods produced, while citizens whose tax bill is small may demand more

    [4] For a detailed exposition of ideas involved in Figure XIV–3 see Richard A. Musgrave, *The Theory of Public Finance*, (New York: McGraw-Hill Book Co., Inc., 1959), Chapters 4 and 5.

FIGURE XIV-3

Taxation and Resource Allocation

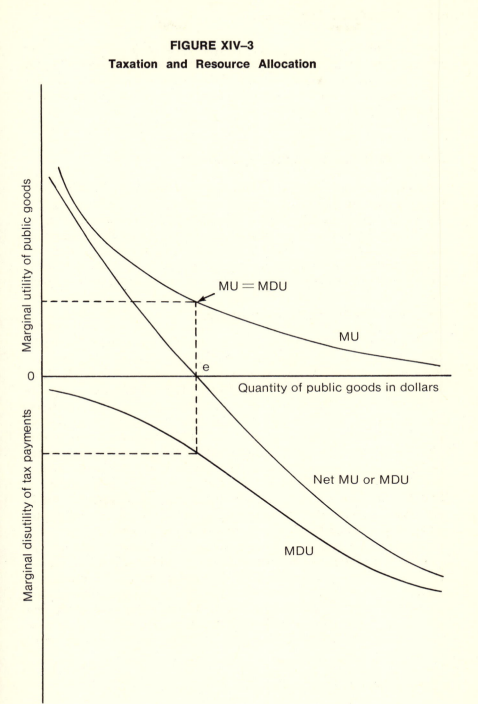

public goods. The question of relative shares is so crucial that we must deal with it at greater length elsewhere (see Chapter XV). Instead, let us take up a perplexing complication in our policy advice—whether we are producing too little or too many public goods.

Some Theories of Social Imbalance

With this image of the ideal abstract solutions in mind perhaps we can again ask why we never seem to achieve the proper balance of public and private allocations. There are almost as many theories as there are theorists. Some claim that there are too few public goods to complement our wealth of private goods, while others claim we simply spend too much on public goods. Each theorist has his own explanation of these conflicting results.

TOO FEW PUBLIC GOODS: GALBRAITH

Professor Galbraith is undoubtedly the most widely known economist on the problem of social imbalance; in fact, he apparently coined the term. According to Galbraith, the output of public goods is deficient because of three factors or forces at work within our society: advertising, tax considerations, and inflation.[5] With respect to the first factor, Galbraith maintains that private enterprise has an advantage over the public sector in that it can support a vast advertising campaign for its products but that the governments are prevented from doing this for their goods. Private enterprise does spend a lot of money in this manner. In 1967 it amounted to nearly $17 billion.[6] Obviously government is at a disadvantage. The second force concerns payment for public goods. Most public goods are financed by tax payments that are unrelated to the use of those goods. Most citizens perceive tax issues as unrelated to the satisfactions provided by public goods. In addition, many citizens believe that governments are inefficient or waste a great deal of money. Thus, we minimize our tax bill and thereby also minimize our supply of public goods. As to the third factor, inflation contributes its share to the imbalance in the sense that the wages of public employees rise less rapidly than

[5] *The Affluent Society.*
[6] *Statistical Abstract of the United States, 1969*, p. 775.

those of private workers thus drawing off the more talented servants to the private jobs. Deterioration in the quality of public
services is one result. Inflation also increases the prices governments must pay in their market purchases. And, citizen views of
government reflect these unfortunate developments.

TOO FEW PUBLIC GOODS: DOWNS

Anthony Downs maintains that our governments produce too
little because their budgets are too small; they are too small because citizens are more ignorant of cost/benefit considerations in
the public sector than in the marketplace.[7] The benefits of private
goods are much more apparent to the ordinary person because
they redound to him in a much more immediate and direct sense
while the benefits of public goods are generally less immediate,
less visible, and more indivisible. On the other hand, the costs of
public goods are readily apparent insofar as they are income,
sales, and property taxes. The average uninformed citizen quite
rationally reacts by being against big budgets. Then, too, many
government services are essentially repressive or regulatory. Doing good for one citizen usually entails the control of another's
behavior and welfare. We protect workers, for example, by forcing employers to bargain with them through unions. We attempt
to protect the general citizenry by using police; obviously the criminal is unhappy with this situation. One inevitable result of this
confusing cost benefit situation is an inadequate supply of public
goods and services.

TOO MANY PUBLIC GOODS: BUCHANAN

The theories of Galbraith and Downs have not gone unchal-
lenged. A number of economists, particularly James M. Buchanan,[8]
have contended that governments normally overproduce and therefore misallocate resources. The reason again relates to the idea
of citizen views of costs and benefits. Buchanan feels that citizens
demand more public goods because they do not know the cost
side and think that someone else will be paying for them. Poli-

[7] "Why the Government Budget is Too Small in a Democracy," *World Politics* 12 (July, 1960), 541–63.
[8] *Public Finance in Democratic Process* (Chapel Hill: University of North Carolina Press, 1967).

ticians "unknowingly" abet this tendency by logrolling (see Chapters VI, VII and IX). Each politician is induced to vote for more expenditures because trading his vote for support on legislation beneficial for his own district is mutually profitable for himself and his constituents. The entire nation pays for the local post office. "You vote for my post office funds and I'll vote for yours," makes sound political sense. Paradoxically, everyone underestimates costs and the budget goes up, even though no one wants that end result.

Optimal Allocation Among Public Goods

Just a scarcity is a persistent fact that conditions our choices between public and private uses of resources, so too is it a fact within each sector. While we know a great deal about achieving more efficient uses of private resources in markets, we do not have as solid and extensive knowledge about achieving optimal resource allocations among public goods. Here, again, we must face the fact that we cannot have all the public goods we might wish and so we are encouraged to be as economical as possible in using whatever level of resources we decide to employ. We should want to get as much as possible from alternative uses.

For reasons already discussed, this is a far more difficult problem in the political system than in markets. The relevant factor, of course, is how choices are expressed. To show the logical dimensions of the choice dilemma, we will oversimplify with an abstract illustration. Then we will discuss the political difficulties of achieving efficient solutions.

AN OPTIMAL CHOICE BETWEEN PUBLIC GOODS: HIGHWAYS AND DAMS

Suppose our goal is constructing highways and dams. We have $12 billion to spend. How much should we allocate to each? The answer will be found in their respective utilities or satisfactions for society. To acquire as much utility as possible from dams and highways we must first know how much utility each produces. This in turn enables us to "compute" their respective marginal utilities—the additional value derived from an additional expenditure on each project. Because this is an important notion, we have visualized it simply in Table XIV-1. Columns 1 and 3 list

TABLE XIV–1

Hypothetical Marginal Utilities of Public Goods

Highways		Dams	
Resources (in billions)	MU	Resources (in billions)	MU
$1	80	$1	60
2	72	2	58
3	64	3	56
4	28	4	54
5	48	5	52
6	40	6	50
7	24	7	48
8	8	8	40

the successive quantities of resources for each use and columns 2 and 4 indicate the assumed marginal utilities for additional expenditures on each good. Note that these utilities are different— no two goods are likely to produce the same utility for any individual. These different valuations are important because they permit exchange, which is crucial in bargaining.

One way of reading the table is to assume that we can allocate as follows: we start out by asking how to spend the first billion dollars and then continue with each of the remaining eleven billion. Given the opportunity, the rational policy maker or citizen should spend the first billion on highways because it will provide him with 80 units of marginal utility as against 60 units if he spent it on dams. His second billion should go to highways, too, for the same reason—72 units as against 60 units. The third billion, also for highways, gives 64 as against 60 units. The fourth billion, however, goes into dams because the marginal utility (60 units) is greater than for highways (56 units). And so the rational citizen or policy maker would go on down the table calculating each expenditure in terms of its relative marginal contribution. At the end he would have allocated $5 billion to highways and $7 billion to dams. At the last expenditure the marginal returns should be the same for both uses; 48 units each, as Table XIV-1 shows.

This was a nice neat solution to a textbook problem; in real life it could be done by a dictator or expert without consulting the people. Of course, democracies do not permit that but even if they did it would still pose serious practical computational problems. How do we measure utility and marginal utility? Where do these figures come from? We would, in fact, encounter exceptional difficulty in deriving such figures for any individual let alone a large society. We make up these figures for expository purposes to show how rational men ought to operate. But a general rule can be formulated. *Try to allocate resources in such a manner that the greatest total utility from combined uses will be maximized. It will be maximized whenever the marginal utilities of the two uses are equalized.*

In the above illustration we assumed not only that we could measure utility but also that we were dealing with one person or a society in which all men agreed on the same utility rankings of the two goods—highways and dams. Obviously, neither condition obtains in the United States. Few citizens agree about the relative worth of highways and dams because they derive differing amounts of satisfaction from their use. Even if we could construct utility curves for each one, how could they be summed into a public policy? How can such diverse preferences be summarized into a public budget?

Lower-Order Efficiencies

The very general and abstract definitions of efficiency advanced thus far make a great deal of logical sense. They are not, however, very practical or operational criteria for legislators, administrators, and voters, because they are neither sufficiently specific nor measurable. One should not conclude, therefore, that achieving greater efficiency in the public sector is impossible. In the first place, each of us as individuals can decide for ourselves whether the public sector is adequate to meet our demands. Second, each of us as individuals can decide whether existing compositions of public budgets meet our approval. We cannot decide whether the entire system is efficient for all but only for ourselves as individuals.

It is equally important to remember that efficiency criteria can be developed and applied consistently at lower levels of governmental operations. These lower levels are concerned with the concrete daily allocations made by the operating agencies of government. At these lower levels engineering and economic techniques are possible for achieving maximal results from given outlays of funds or achieving given levels of public service or performance at the lowest cost. Most members of government deal with these practical kinds of problems even though many public services are difficult to measure as forms of output. Commonplace examples are everywhere. Police, for instance, are able to measure the effectiveness of their work by a variety of indicators, including the percentage of crimes solved, number of crimes prevented, accident rates, extent of riot injuries, and so forth. Also, public health officials might wish to measure the efficiency of their programs by comparing the incidence of various diseases with different preventive programs. Flood control officials can check damage effects, or count the number of floods prevented; likewise they might wish to measure the amount of electricity produced against the cost of dams and other facilities. Educational instruction in high schools can be evaluated in terms of the school's rate of graduation, the success of students in being admitted to colleges, their eventual career successes, and cost per pupil. Each of these examples suggests that various measures can be devised relating the input of resources and the output of valued services or goods. These assist officials and voters in both measuring existing levels of efficiency and achieving higher levels of performance.

A variety of disciplines and skills developed during and since World War II contribute to greater achievement of efficiency in all walks of life. These skills, tools, and occupations are variously known as "systems analysis," "operations analysis," and "cost/benefit analysis." The basic tools were developed in conjunction with electronic computers and, for complex problems, have become inseparable from these devises. Originally used for war strategy, the tools more recently were applied with considerable publicity and some success in the Defense Department under MacNamara. Still more recently they have been extended to other departments and programs under the label of "planning-programming-budgeting." Whatever the label, tool, or level of analysis the purpose is to attain more efficiency in public activities.

COST/BENEFIT ANALYSIS: URBAN RENEWAL

Urban renewal and many other domestic programs have been subjected to cost/benefit analysis in order to assess existing programs and to evaluate proposals for future programs. The basic idea is to discover all the costs and benefits of each alternative and select the best program. This complicated process is illustrated in Figure XIV-4, an oversimplified tabular presentation of the es-

FIGURE XIV–4

Cost/Benefit Preliminary Worksheet

EXPECTED OUTCOMES	ALTERNATIVES		
	Existing system	B	C
Number of public buildings			
Number of commercial buildings			
Number of residential apartments			
Number of displaced householders			
Number of displaced businesses			
Number of new employees			
Total gross business in dollars			
Wages and salaries			
Assessed valuation of property			
Taxes for local government			
Cost of property acquisition			
Proceeds from sale of property			
Parking facilities			

sential elements. The table might better be termed a preliminary "worksheet" for the analyst prior to computing the actual calculations of expected costs and benefits. Each of the expected outcomes in the left column is checked against each proposal and the existing system to determine the effects of the alternative proposals on that item.

Because the items we have included are essentially quantitative, we can assign a number to each for comparison. When the values are not quantitative, the analyst has incommensurables and intangibles to measure in terms of costs and benefits. These non-quantifiable values abound in the work of governments, and some of them are shown in the worksheet in Figure XIV-5. This tabulation allows the analyst to identify expected beneficiaries and cost bearers. This sort of analysis at least makes the comparisons explicit for policy makers and citizens—a pronounced gain over past procedures.

Even in areas that permit a considerable amount of quantitative assessment, such as water resource use, mistakes are made at a fairly high rate. One critic claims that about half the 150 projects he studied did not meet minimal requirements of efficient

FIGURE XIV-5

Cost/Benefit Estimate Worksheet

ALTERNATIVE USES OF THE RESOURCE	Expected benefits		Expected beneficiaries		Expected costs		Expected cost-bearers		Political feasibility	
	Short run	Long run	Short run	Long run	Short run	Long run	Short run	Long run	Politicians	Voters
Existing system										
B										
C										

operation.[9] But Congress, in adopting these projects in 1960, did not employ a sophisticated cost/benefit analysis so it is unfair to criticize the analyst.

It is true that one of the more important deficiencies of this type of system analysis stems from its nonpolitical orientation, because the worksheet has no room for political costs and benefits. But we have included them in our illustration, Figure XIV-5. Logrolling is not concerned with economic efficiency; it is concerned with political success of politicians and the provincial interests of their constituents. The gain from adopting an inefficient water control project in one state may be a highly efficient highway project in another.

MILITARY OPERATIONS

Our previous example illustrated some of the difficulties in attaining efficiency in domestic programs; our present example is offered in contrast because it clearly shows the greater probability and perhaps ease in specifying the criteria of success or performance. In many military situations effectiveness can be measured by a host of indicators; the kill ratio in Vietnam, for example. The number of targets destroyed in a bombing operation can be related to costs in money or lost planes and personnel. Whatever criteria of effectiveness are used it is possible, in principle and often in practice, to make fairly precise comparisons of alternatives.[10] The air force attempts to make precise comparisons of various aircraft performances while the infantry subjects their weapons to careful analysis. The worksheet of the military analyst can often assume a more mathematical appearance as suggested in Figure XIV-6 where effectiveness is related to cost.

Effectiveness can be indicated by such measures as the number of targets or enemies destroyed, reductions in productive capabilities, reduced morale, prisoners captured, land occupied, captured supplies, and the like, while cost can be measured in terms of our losses or the monetary expenditures of each option. Some analysts claim it costs us at least $110,000 to kill one North Vietnamese. Calculation of this figure can be justified, but only if the analyst chooses convenient but highly misleading indicators of success and woefully inaccurate estimates of costs inflicted on

[9] Robert H. Haveman, *Water Resources Investment and the Public Interest* (Nashville, Tenn.: Vanderbilt University Press, 1965).
[10] Charles J. Hitch and Roland N. McKean, *The Economics of Defense in the Nuclear Age* (Cambridge, Mass.: Harvard University Press, 1960).

FIGURE XIV–6

Hypothetical Cost-Effectiveness Ratios in War

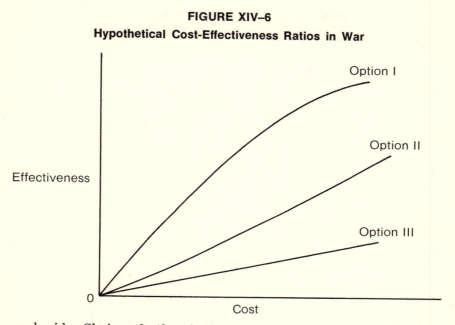

each side. Choice of other indicators can give equally misleading figures to support opposing views.

Political Obstacles to Efficiency

Despite our sophisticated tools of analysis and a strong commitment to efficiency norms the American people are unable to attain any remarkable degree of efficiency in the public sector. This failure may not be particularly upsetting if we rank other values higher than efficiency; for those who value principles of economy, however, the loss is more disturbing. In addition to the analytical difficulties we have just considered, a major reason for this condition is a fundamental political obstacle—the institutions we have chosen for making our fiscal choices.

We do not fully understand the precise impacts of our political institutions on fiscal choices, and on efficiency in particular, but we do understand some of them.[11] Let us assume the major element in efficiency is the federal budget and the political process. Many

[11] See Buchanan, *Public Finance in Democratic Process* (Chapel Hill, N.C.: University of North Carolina Press, 1967), and Carl S. Shoup, *Public Finance* (Chicago: Aldine Publishing Co., 1969).

incoming Presidents promise great changes in our priorities and the achievement of greater economies. They are in for a considerable shock if they believe their own promises.

FORMULATION OF THE BUDGET

Formulation of the federal budget to allocate resources is a highly intricate and delicate process involving nearly everyone in the federal government. At least eighteen distinct major stages within the executive branch take place over a period of at least nine months. The process begins in March of each year and culminates in January when the President submits his budget to the Congress.[12] The Congress then proceeds through at least thirteen different phases or stages in considering the budget and the accompanying budget messages of the President. These proceedings, like those already completed in the executive branch, are marked by many hearings, debates, conflicts, competition, and bargaining activities. By July the Congress will have a budget bill to send back to the President for his signature or veto. After monies have been appropriated funds are made available to the operating agencies for their use. Continuing control over expenditures is exercised by both the Congress and by executive agencies such as the General Accounting Office and the Bureau of the Budget.

Although this enormously involved process complicates the management of resources and increases the bargaining costs of producing policies, it also provides everyone who feels affected with an opportunity to be heard. But protest may be futile, for despite the incredible attention budgets receive they are not very amenable to alteration at any level of government. Let us see why at the federal level.

CONTROLLABILITY OF THE NATIONAL BUDGET

A major reason for this immutability of budgets—to the extent that even our Presidents cannot alter them, is that many funds are relatively uncontrollable; that is, vast numbers of programs and dollars are so obligated that an incoming President cannot alter either in any appreciable degree. He is a prisoner of our institutions, power structures, previous policies and laws. By

---

[12] An excellent yet highly readable account is that of Aaron Wildavsky, *The Politics of the Budgetary Process* (Boston: Little, Brown & Co., 1964). A most useful flow chart of the budget-making process is appended in pages 194–99.

one estimate, only 52 percent of the budget is "relatively control-lable." Suppose an incoming President wants to enact his own budget. Table XIV-2 shows what he might face in terms of reshaping the priorities:[13]

TABLE XIV-2
Controllability of the Federal Budget, 1969

Amount of control	Percentage of funds controlled	1969 budget (in millions)
No control over		
Farm Credit Administration	0	$ 535
Export-Import Bank	0	608
Railroad Retirement Board	0	1,082
Treasury Department	0	15,410
Post Office	0	920
Civil Service Commission	3	3,799
Department of Health, Education and Welfare	12	51,370
Department of Labor	12	4,836
Somewhat more controllable		
Department of Transportation	26	6,525
Defense (Civil)	26	1,307
Veterans Administration	30	7,790
Agriculture	38	7,530

The above table merely lists the agencies and the amounts of con-trollable or uncontrollable funds; it does not include or specify certain untouchable programs. In that category, the 12 programs in Table XIV-3 accounted for over $85 billion from a total budget of slightly more than $200 billion in 1969.[14]

If a President who is reputed to be the world's most powerful democratic leader cannot reshape more than 52 percent of the federal budget, how can expenditures ever be significantly real-located to achieve greater economies? Even within the theoreti-cally controllable part of the budget we find additional constraints that have little to do with the institutions of fiscal choice. Defense is the single biggest item in the federal budget. It is not realisti-

[13] Murray T. Weidenbaum, "Institutional Obstacles to Reallocating Government Expenditures," in Robert H. Haveman and Julius Margolis, eds., *Public Expenditures and Policy Analysis* (Chicago: Markham Publishing Co., 1970), pp. 232–45.

[14] Weidenbaum, Murray T., "Institutional Obstacles," p. 241.

TABLE XIV–3

Committed Budget Funds

Program	1969 Budget (in millions)
Social Security trust funds	$37,670
Interest on the public debt	15,200
Public assistance	5,765
Veterans' pensions and compensation	4,654
Highway grants to the states	4,650
Unemployment insurance	4,095
Civil service retirement payments	3,626
Farm price supports	3,362
Military retirement pay	2,275
Project Apollo	2,133
Medicare (Treasury contribution)	1,360
Railroad retirement payments	1,064
TOTAL	$85,000

cally controllable to any great extent given the attitudes of Americans, the existence of potential and real enemies, and an industrial-military complex with an interest in the maintenance of a high level of expenditures. But there are other reasons why the budget is uncontrollable even over domestic activities.

How is it that certain items or activities have gained a privileged legal position in our national budgets and priorities? Other expenditures that are equally important or perhaps more important have not been as successful in isolating themselves from annual review. Does bargaining theory shed any light on the problem? How? If not, why?

Why is the President constrained in the legal sense? Previous commitments of Congress are the chief source of limitation since the Congress appropriates the monies. Trust funds such as the Old-Age, Survivors', and Disability Insurance program; numerous permanent appropriations including interest payments on the debt, fixed charges such as veterans' pensions, and partially completed programs or projects such as bridges, roads, dams, and the like, are so enacted that they must be completed—half a bridge is of little value. Each of these types of expenditures is built into budgets and is relatively uncontrollable, and the President must simply honor the commitments. He will have to seek savings and control elsewhere.

A Moral on Efficiency

The term "efficiency" is somewhat like the concept "public interest" in that nearly everyone is for whatever may be meant by the term. Imagine the reception a national leader would receive if he announced that he was for greater inefficiency in national life! Although such a popular concept would seem to be very useful, it is not useful at all unless it is properly understood. Accordingly this chapter has a threefold moral: (1) There is no such thing as high-level efficiency; (2) There is a lower-level of efficiency in operations that is technically meaningful and should be accorded a high ranking in our values; and (3) The limitations on achieving greater rationality or efficiency in resource management are profound and not readily altered because collective choice, no matter what the institutions, does not lend itself to highly efficient choices.

Exercises in Analysis

THE SUPPLY OF PUBLIC GOODS

Summaries of various theories of the supply of public goods were presented on pages 304–6, above, to illustrate how three well-known and able theorists differ on how and why we are allocating our resources. On the basis of these summaries indicate whether Buchanan, Downs, and Galbraith think the following goods are overproduced, underproduced, or are in optimal supply. Explanations are also in order.

Public Goods
Interstate freeways
Secondary education
Municipal swimming pools
Defense
Low-cost public housing
Medical care
National parks
Police protection

ALLOCATING A FEDERAL GRANT

Suppose that a local city council were to be made the recipient of a $100,000 grant to be used for the following purposes: (1) secondary education, (2) public health, (3) promoting local business, (4) rebates to the taxpayers. If the council were solely interested in efficiency it would prepare and compare marginal returns on each dollar spent on each activity and allocate in such a manner that these marginal returns are equalized. Is this technically possible? Perhaps the city council could hire a consulting firm that would estimate the amount of "good" that each one thousand dollars would produce for each of the activities. Thus the experts might claim that each thousand dollars spent on education might see another four students through another grade of school, or they might say that because of the law of diminishing marginal productivity that as more was spent on education a smaller number of students could be financed after a certain point. They might claim that a certain number of persons could benefit in certain ways from each additional thousand dollars devoted to medical aid. The same logic would guide the estimates of each of the other services.

Devise your own estimates of the marginal returns for each service and prepare a trade-off table in which you show how many student-years of education you are prepared to trade for how many medical patients, additional dollars of local business, and tax rebates. In short you are placing marginal values on different people and different services you would like to see provided in the community. Your final tabulations should show how much money you would allocate to each activity or service. Compare and consult with others.

Suggested Readings

Churchman, C. West. *The Systems Approach* (New York: Dell Publishing Co., Inc., 1968).

Dorfman, Robert, ed. *Measuring Benefits of Government Investments* (Washington, D.C.: The Brookings Institution, 1965).

Krutilla, John V. and Eckstein, Otto. *Multi-Purpose River Development* (Baltimore, Md.: Johns Hopkins University Press, 1958).

McKean, Roland N. *Efficiency in Government Through Systems Analysis* (New York: John Wiley & Sons, Inc., 1958).

————. *Public Spending* (New York: McGraw-Hill Book Co., 1968).

Novick, David, ed. *Program Budgeting* (Cambridge, Mass.: Harvard University Press, 1965).

Schultze, Charles L. *The Politics and Economics of Public Spending* (Washington, D.C.: The Brookings Institution, 1968).

Smith, T. Arthur, ed. *Economic Analysis and Military Resource Allocation* (Washington, D.C.: Office, Comptroller of the Army, 1968).

Chapter XV

INCREASING INDIVIDUAL WELFARE

If our Declaration of Independence and the Preamble to the Constitution are representative of continuing opinion, Americans believe that governments are instituted to serve the people by providing justice, order, happiness, tranquility, and welfare. These noble ends, none of which was defined or is ever fully attained, have meaning only in terms of individual satisfactions. In more contemporary language, each of us attempts to acquire more or perhaps even maximize our shares of income, wealth, status, security, affection, and power. Maximizing means getting as much as we can within the limitations of our resources, our tastes or preferences, and the prices we must pay for acquiring more of these desired goods. Each of us places a somewhat different value upon each of these goods. One citizen may prefer income to power, while another seeks more power and a third aspires for social status. It is important to remember that we can become satiated with each of these goods and that as we acquire more of them the added value of each increment is apt to decline. The rate at which this occurs is different for different persons and different goods— we cannot claim that a single rate obtains for all people and all goods. This fact enables us to exchange, since the basis of exchange is a differential valuation of goods. Further, the fact that we value increments at a decreasing rate prevents us from being insatiable and therefore demanding on other people. If this law of diminishing marginal utility did not apply we would truly enter a state of nature or war of each against all others. Since no one could ever be fully satisfied we would be in endless conflict over the distribution of scarce resources and the welfare they provide. Man may be selfish but there are limits to his self-aggrandizement.

If we were saints, or if there were no scarcities of resources, we would have no problem; this chapter would not have been written. But since we are less than saints and there are resource constraints, even in America, we must face up to the problems of achieving more welfare or the betterment of our lives and be concerned with the distribution of that welfare. We think it is possible to produce more welfare and achieve better distributions than have prevailed.

In defining welfare in this chapter we do not, of course, mean payments made to "welfare cases"; that is, people with no visible means of support. Instead we use the term to refer to subjective states of individuals. A person's welfare is said to have increased if he says he is happier than he was in the past. A person's welfare has decreased if he claims that he is less happy or is unhappy. We want more people to be happier.

What makes a man happier? Or, what will increase his sense of welfare? The answer to this question is not simple. If we believe the psychologists and psychoanalysts, many Americans are unhappy. Certainly these practitioners are making a good deal of money trying to increase the welfare of their clients. Whether Americans are happier or better-off than other peoples is exceedingly difficult to say because we cannot compare national or individual states of welfare or happiness, except in the case of obvious material well-being. Nor can we compare states of misery; can you claim, for example, that your toothache is worse than your roommate's? Although this seems impossible to decide surely we can distinguish between a happy and an unhappy person. And that really is all we need to do in formulating public policy. Let us agree to transfer as many citizens from the unhappy category to the happy category as we can.

Components of Individual Happiness or Welfare

It is often the case that those who look hardest for happiness are the least happy, simply because that most precious commodity remains in short supply for them. If the basic elements of happiness are affection, respect, power, and material goods and services, they are rarely acquired without money. Although money in itself does not guarantee happiness, it is certainly a generalized means or resource for acquiring other elements of welfare. This is not to say that making individuals richer will automatically make them happier, but only that more money can usually make life somewhat easier, particularly at the lower-income levels. In accordance with the law of diminishing marginal utility, the more one acquires the less important each additional dollar becomes.

Common sense strongly suggests that a man's welfare is based on achieving what he regards as his *just share* of income, status, power, wealth, security, and affection. Most of us go through life seeking additional quantities of at least one of these components of our happiness. They are not easily acquired because they are costly and because all are partially dependent upon the choices and actions of others. Social or professional status, for example, can only be achieved in relation to others and with their consent. Their evaluations are finally dependent upon our own choices and actions. We can earn a good or bad reputation by our actions. If we acquire a good reputation, it may be accompanied by higher status. Social interdependence obviously shapes the distribution of happiness in society, and political systems can influence these distributions. That is our present interest. How can we increase our own individual welfare and how can we achieve better distributions for all?

The Distribution of Income

One of the most important and controversial questions in political philosophy and modern social science concerns the extent to which men should treat one another equally (or unequally). Although we cannot expect to resolve the question scientifically, we can be fairly analytical, reasonable, and detached in our search for a policy position. First, we must state that we are concerned with the problem of economic equality, not simply with courtesy in daily social life. In other words, we want to take a position on how governments ought to treat citizens in terms of their respective incomes. Should government take from some and pay others? If so, who should pay and who receive how much and how? In earlier times, when the government did not influence or manage as much of our income as it does today, we did not have to be much concerned with these issues. Today, however, the benefits our governments distribute constitute a substantial portion of everyone's income—in some instances all of that income. First let us clarify some alternative principles on which income and benefits, more generally, can be distributed. There are at least three possibilities: equal shares (complete equality) ; distribution according to services rendered ; and distribution according to needs.

EQUAL SHARES

When socialist thinkers and some religious philosophers contend that all men should be treated equally, they almost always hold, among other things, that their incomes should also be equal. Whatever national income is produced, they say is to be divided among the population so each would receive an equal share during each pay period. Equal shares is not always clearly defined. For some writers it is based on absolute equality; for others equal pay for equal work.

The basic idea underlying this rule of distribution is the fundamental notion that all share equally in being human; this basic humanity is regarded as more significant than any differences or distinctions. Because all are human, all are thought to be equally capable of enjoying satisfactions engendered by income. This assumption is of considerable consequence in the actual analysis of achieving greater equality as well as in defending the idea as an ideal. We will return to it shortly when we discuss the extent to which equalization should take place.

Except among small, voluntary groups complete income equality has rarely been instituted and has never been practiced for very long. In America, complete income equality seems a very remote possibility, because most Americans believe that merit should be the chief criterion in the distribution of income. Capitalist and Protestant ethics have firmly entrenched the norm in our economic system's operations.

If complete equality were somehow instituted, problems would surely arise concerning the justness of the distributions— particularly from those who feel they contribute more to society than others do. If men cannot affect the size of their incomes they will probably alter the size of their contributions by working less and less hard for whatever they receive in income. In short, income restrictions would have some negative effects on incentive that would have detrimental economic consequences. This is not to say that movement in the direction of greater income equality makes men lazier; there is no evidence to that effect in this country. High income earners who pay out more than 50 percent of their annual incomes in taxes do not work fewer hours nor serve with less dedication.

DISTRIBUTION ACCORDING TO SERVICES RENDERED

Under our more or less private enterprise market system individuals are rewarded according to the services they provide *as evaluated by others*. Highly-valued services yield high incomes, but those who provide less-highly-prized services compete with more people and usually earn less money. The size of one's income depends upon the scarcity of the skill and the demand for it. As might be expected, those who earn high incomes are in accord with this distributive system. Those who receive less, however, hope and sometimes work for the reform of the system. They want the government to pursue policies that will distort the initial distributions of the economy and redistribute income from better-off members to those who are worse off.

The distribution of income in 1967 is tabulated in Table XV-1. If complete equality prevailed everyone in every fifth of the population would receive the same shares of income. As these figures show, however, the distribution is rather skewed or unequal. Many think it desirable to moderate the degree of inequality in the direction of greater equality. We must not, however, underestimate the political difficulties inherent in such a change.

TABLE XV–1
Distribution of Income, 1967

Families	Share of income
Lowest fifth	5.4%
Second fifth	12.2
Third fifth	17.5
Fourth fifth	23.7
Highest fifth	41.2
Top 5 percent	15.3

Source: U.S. Bureau of the Census, *The Statistical Abstract of the United States, 1969* (90th ed., Washington, D.C.: U.S. Government Printing Office, 1969), p. 322.

DISTRIBUTION ACCORDING TO NEED

Marxism is the best known of the philosophies that have argued that all men should be rewarded on the basis of their "needs" and not their contributions or their status in life. Their position necessarily assumes not only that all men have *needs* but also that these needs can be *identified* and *listed* in some *order* of importance. While the argument has powerful emotive connotations its empirical and policy implications are far less convincing. Nevertheless, most societies, including our own, make provision for supplying income based on need. We may honor marketplace principles of rewarding merit and we may make even more use of market rhetoric but we also have extensive private philanthropic aid as well as public aid for the needy. No society could operate with a clear conscience if it did not recognize the existence of the needy and make provision for them. The question, then, is not whether to base rewards on merit or need but what kinds of merit, what kinds of need, and to what extent should they be honored.

First let us define the difficulties of this position philosophically and scientifically. If these pages are being read by a member of a political science class, perhaps he can experiment in class by asking his classmates for their personal lists of needs and relative importance. It is doubtful that he will find extensive agreement on either problem. Because food will surely be viewed as essential, nutrition will no doubt be rated in first place. How much agreement will be found concerning levels and types of nutrition? Should the government guarantee gourmet meals for all? Should it provide only flour, milk, potatoes, and other basic but starchy items? Meeting men's physical needs appears to be within the capacity of all highly industrialized societies; we can provide the necessities of life—food, clothing, and shelter. How can we go about it?

Some theorists have maintained that man also has social and psychological needs including affection, respect, skill, wealth, equality, self-esteem, self-realization, belonging, and the like.[1] What ordering should be attributed to these needs? What if psychological needs of some are in conflict with the health or safety of others? Finally, if a hierarchy of social needs can be established, what role should government play in their realization? Can government insure minimal needs of affection, respect, or self-esteem? How?

Provision of these social needs presents a different and more difficult problem than provision of physical needs. Governments, no matter how powerful, cannot force one person to love or respect another. They may, however, be able to provide some of the

---

[1] See Harold D. Lasswell and Abraham Kaplan, *Power and Society* (New Haven, Conn.: Yale University Press, 1950), and James C. Davies, *Human Nature in Politics* (New York: John Wiley & Sons, Inc., 1963).

conditions under which people come to treat (if not regard) each other as well as themselves. We know that poverty produces anti-social behavior considered undesirable by the more affluent. We know, too, that poverty frequently yields low self-esteem and even self-hatred, destructiveness, and hopelessness. Governments cannot suddenly reverse these tendencies by fiat, but they can foster programs to reform the basic conditions that produce them. Governments cannot overnight make the selfish into humanitarians, nor can they remake the degraded into self-respecting, proud, cultured people. But a government can, through its leadership and resources, inspire and enable men to eliminate the misery that exists.

Three Distributive Norms

All this is merely preliminary to the statement of our norms of public policy. Government must analyze the need preferences of citizens and recognize the deficiencies of some labor markets. Needs should then be classified. The more basic needs that governments can assist in meeting include food, clothing, and shelter. Higher needs include such goods as respect, affection, sense of belonging, rectitude, and the like. These are needs that governments cannot easily provide but that they should recognize when planning and implementing policy programs. No person should be permitted to go hungry, ill, poorly dressed, or inadequately sheltered. For these reasons alone our governments should pursue policies that increase our national income or national product. These material needs depend on increasing national income as our population grows and our standards of what constitutes adequate diet, shelter, and clothing rise. Accordingly, we state these premises for government action:

1. *No citizen will have his more basic wants ignored while others have less basic ones honored.*

2. *No citizen should have his less urgent needs cared for before his more basic needs.*

3. *Government should pursue policies that are designed to increase national income and employment of all resources (land, labor, and capital).*

To What Extent Should Income Be Equalized?

Money income is one of the most precious assets we can command; that is why Americans strive to acquire more of it. For the most part our incomes are decided in the marketplace, but some of the income of most people is decided upon and/or provided by governmental policies. Our original market incomes are either increased or decreased as a result of public expenditures, taxation, and control. This sometimes occurs because the government has consciously decided to redistribute income. It more often occurs because some policies the government pursues in order to accomplish other goals have these incidental side-effects. In any case, our concern here is whether a government ought to redistribute income. In fact, government does redistribute income by providing better market advantages for those already advantaged.

Those who feel they will be deprived will resist the idea of equality through political transfers, but respectable defense of such policies can be made. Income, like all commodities, is capable of generating satisfactions (utility).[2] Normally, more income generates a greater total amount of satisfaction. (See Figure XV-1.) Note that the curve (1-a) rises as income increases but—and here one must look closely—it does so at a decreasing rate; that is, as income increases more satisfaction is provided but each additional dollar provides less satisfaction than the previous one. Thus, the increase proceeds at a decreasing rate. The steeper the curve the greater the rate of increase in total satisfactions; the flatter the curve the lesser the rate of increase. The slope of the total utility curves determines the shape of the marginal utility curve (1-b) since the latter depicts the rate of change in total satisfactions. The marginal utility curve is of crucial significance in the argument for a redistribution of income, for this reason: if an individual has a great deal of money the worth of his last dollar is apt to be far less than in the case of a person with very little money. Some economists have suggested that if this is true we should take away some of the "surplus" money from the rich and give it to the poor, thus increasing the total amount of satisfaction in the society. The vast increase in satisfactions for the poor will more than overcome the marginal losses of the rich. We can visualize this much better with the aid of a marginal utility curve.

[2] More detailed treatments of income and its redistribution by government may be found in nearly all intermediate economic theory texts.

FIGURE XV–1

a. Total Utility Curve of Income

b. Marginal Utility Curve of Income

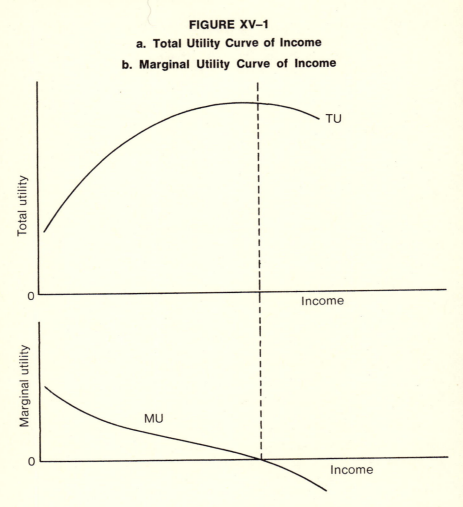

We have drawn a hypothetical marginal utility curve in Figure XV-2 (the shape is sneakily designed to prove our point) to show that the loss in satisfaction resulting from an income reduction for a high-income person (from R to R₁) is less than the gain incurred (from I to I₁) by the lower-income recipient from that same amount of money. Total satisfaction, as one can see by the shaded areas, has been increased by the transfer of income.

Taking income away from the rich and giving it to the poor not only poses political problems but creates some basic theoretical difficulties in the argument for income redistribution. For one

FIGURE XV–2

Redistribution of Income and Welfare

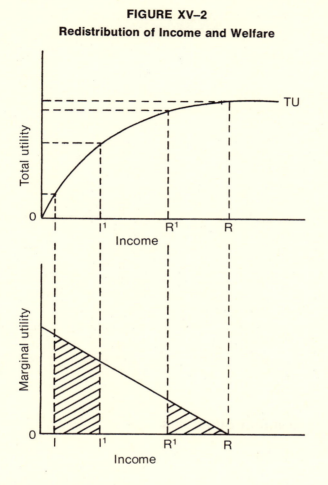

thing, the argument is based on the idea that we can actually compare the satisfactions of one person with the sacrifices of another; that is, that we can say that income has the same meaning to a rich and poor man. That is equivalent to our saying that my injury is more painful than yours, or that one student gains more satisfaction from a drink than another. Many modern economists have rejected the idea that we can make these "interpersonal utility comparisons," and therefore a main support of the argument for redistribution is destroyed.

But that is not the only difficulty in the argument for transferring income. Even if we make these comparisons among individuals we still face the practical problem of drawing their marginal utility curves; but in fact we do not really know the worth of money (its marginal utility) for individuals. Introspection tells us that people seem to behave and choose as though they were following a negatively-sloped (downward to the right) curve of marginal utility. This information is hardly sufficient to decide how much income to take from whom and to give to whom. While many citizens want to believe that it is not unreasonable to ask a man with a million dollars to give up one thousand in order to improve the life of a man who has less than a thousand, such a generality does not solve the problem in theory.

We cannot reasonably consider income redistribution without noting its side effects. For example, if we want to further equalize incomes, we should be concerned about its effects on employment, incentives to work, prices, economic growth, equity, and the allocation of resources. Transferring income may be a good thing in itself or in the interests of equity but may have disastrous consequences for the other goals we value. Perhaps severe equalization might impede the growth of the national income, thereby producing a situation opposite to the intended one in which everyone is equal but less well off. Professional economists will have to decide which of these side-effects is most likely. It is enough for us to note consequences that politicians must take into account when formulating income policy.

Rules for Granting Subsidies

With more than $8 billion being spent on federal subsidies, alone, the question of whether subsidies should be paid is almost academic; they are not about to be removed from the national budget. The question of whether to expand the number of subsidies, by how much, and to whom are still open policy questions. Some subsidies may even disappear as the original purposes for which they were used disappear. In any event, policy makers must think about subsidies because people will always demand them. Some rules or cautions for policy makers can be advanced on these matters.

1. *The burden of proving that a subsidy is needed should rest upon the advocate.* Skeptical policy makers should be entitled to know both the reasons for and expected consequences of any subsidy advocated. Too often, legislators have resorted to logrolling

practices without regard for the substantive elements of subsidies. Vigorous questioning should attack the most ingenious arguments proponents can devise. Opposing policy makers should be sufficiently skilled and informed to question every claim on the taxpayers for special privilege.

2. *No subsidy should have the effect of making the rich richer.* Many of our subsidy programs, in agricultural programs (cotton, wheat, tobacco) ; oil and gas policies; and shipping on the high seas are designed to give monetary gain to politically powerful individuals and groups. In addition, the tax exemptions we reviewed in Chapter V can be considered subsidies for the wealthy and for those in the process of becoming wealthy. Since these persons already have enormous advantages there is little reason for making them cumulative at the expense of less-well-off citizens. Unfortunately, these massive subsidies to the rich are less well publicized than the small ones we pay to the poor and needy.

3. *Subsidies are recommended whenever they serve to overcome serious disadvantages that are not the responsibility of the subsidized.* Victims of industrialized society such as the disabled, aged, helpless young, injured veterans, and the worker who becomes obsolete by change, need some kind of assistance to sustain life. Under this same justification we favor subsidizing certain minority groups who have never had an equal opportunity to prepare themselves for employment, and who would otherwise be exploited. Blacks, Mexican-Americans, and Indians are the major groups involved in these historic injustices. They must be provided with compensatory resources to escape the dire and miserable state forced upon them. Their increased productivity will serve to end their subsidies in the long run.

4. *A subsidy is justifiable whenever some widespread need is not met by the free marketplace.* Subsidies for some farmers are justifiable under some conditions. Farmers (real ones), can frequently be caught in a cost-price squeeze that is ruinous unless some aid is forthcoming. Agricultural markets have certain peculiar features that encourage production and drive down prices. Since the farmer's services are indispensable and his markets beyond his immediate control he should be regarded as a suitable applicant for subsidization. Whenever other needed members of society find themselves in a similar set of conditions they too should be subsidized. To what extent they should be subsidized is the crucial political question. Its economic consequences are too extensive to be considered or resolved here.

Guidelines for a More Equitable Tax Burden

We have seen how difficult it is to devise rules or norms for the distribution of resources and benefits; we will now see that it is equally difficult to devise appropriate norms for sharing burdens. Again, the problem is one of choosing among criteria that are in basic conflict. Should we be more interested in the amount of revenue needed by government or in the amounts the citizens will have to pay? Should our contributions be based on "ability to pay" or on the "benefit" principle? In either case, how much should we levy on which citizens?

No society relies on a single set of consistent principles in allocating burdens. Every society, including our own, employs a wide variety of principles or norms; many are inconsistent when viewed from any single perspective. We make use of benefit principles as well as the ability to pay. We also use quite different rates; some are proportional, some regressive, and others progressive, as we saw in Chapter V.

THE BENEFIT CRITERION

Intelligent voters and policy makers should favor the benefit approach in public finance, especially when (1) they wish to emphasize the voluntary element either in the choice of public goods or in the relationships of the individual with his governments and (2) they wish to make those who benefit from a service pay for its continuance.[3] In other words, market standards are applied to citizen-government relationships. More specifically, one should employ the benefit approach whenever benefits are considerable and whenever they redound to the benefit of a specific, identifiable group. Ready use of the benefit principle cannot be made when the goods are indivisible. Since we do not know who benefits how much from these public goods and services, we simply cannot tax on these grounds. Occasionally, indirect measures of benefit can be used. For example, in taxing motorists and truckers on the basis of their gasoline usage and imposing differential license fees government attempts to relate taxes paid to benefits received. Similarly, public utilities charge on a user-fee basis.

---

[3] An excellent treatment of the different bases for taxation is contained in John F. Due, *Government Finance: Economics of the Public Sector* (Homewood, Ill.: Richard D. Irwin, Inc., 1968), Chapters 13–16.

The great problem with making this principle the basis of all taxation is the indivisibility of benefits. The principle, therefore, should only be used where it is feasible, assuming there are no other major adverse consequences. Any service that can be distributed to specific persons is divisible; it can and may be usefully administered by user fees. Thus, it is possible to charge the users of parks, postal services, highways, and bridges, but not to price and ration national defense. Police protection might be considered divisible but is too inconvenient to administer on a fee basis. This suggests another criterion: administrative feasibility or cost. If collection of the fees costs more than they bring in, there would seem to be little sense in the fee system. No one wants to call the fire department and negotiate the rates on fire fighting when his house is burning down. If the firemen fail to save the house would he get his money back? On the other hand, some user fees are both administratively feasible and convenient, such as tolls on bridges and highways, postage for post office service, and fees for use of the swimming pool. The nature of each of these activities is such that the user should pay because he is the immediate beneficiary. The most important exception to this rule occurs when users are primarily low-income individuals. In this case some other financing may be necessary including the possibility of graduated fees. Some universities are now considering graduated tuition fees based on family income.

ABILITY TO PAY

If a taxation system cannot be based on purely beneficiary principles we might want to consider what is known as the ability-to-pay principle. Ability to pay can be defined in different ways but Americans typically think of income, property, or a combination of both as the major measures of a citizen's capacity to make contributions to the state. The idea is that the more resources a citizen commands the easier it is for him to sacrifice a larger portion to the government. Besides the concepts we discussed above in the contexts of redistributing income and the marginal utility of money, there is an additional rationale for this principle. Those who have more money or property probably derive more governmental services; they have more to lose by not paying the government to protect them and their advantages.

This principle is used chiefly in our income tax and property tax laws—the more you have, the greater the tax. Ability-to-pay principles have some severe limitations as sources of revenue, means of redistributing income, and as revenge politics. In the first instance, even if all the income of the top 5 percent of the income recipients were confiscated it would not provide our governments with a large enduring source of revenue. The vast amounts of revenue governments require must be substantial, dependable, and replaceable. Our governments must turn primarily to the bulk of income earners in the middle class. While "soaking the rich" has considerable appeal for the majority of voters, the size of redistributed gains would be small.

In any case, the causes of low incomes and earning power must be overcome on their own grounds. Most of our social problems have their causes in other factors and conditions than the current unequal distribution of income. *Creating* more income and seeing that it is better distributed is a better solution than assuming a zero-sum situation and encouraging men to do battle over shares of a fixed amount. Some scholars are hopeful that the degrees of inequality are diminishing. Simon Kuznets, an internationally known scholar of the problem, claims that the decline in the shares of the upper groups from 1939 to 1949 was striking and unmatched anywhere else.[4] Recent changes are not as clearcut but the rate of change toward equality seems to have slowed down since 1950. The causes of diminution of income inequality are not readily identified, but it does not appear that our taxation policies have been major forces. The chief causes are probably impersonal forces operating within the economy along with expenditures policies of governments, especially at the national level. One policy implication is that those interested in greater equality should restructure or reform the economy and propose better expenditures policies.

Exercises in Analysis

VOLUNTARY CONTRIBUTIONS TO GOVERNMENT

The maintenance and support of our society need not be considered as burdensome as we have perhaps made it appear. Instead we are hopeful that means can be devised that enable

---

[4] Simon Kuznets, *Shares of Upper Income Groups in Income and Savings* (New York: National Bureau of Economic Research, Inc., 1953), pp. xxxv–xxxvii.

citizens to contribute their resources in far greater and more rewarding ways. We can better tap these resources, however, if we make our society and its political system more valuable to individuals, so that they will want to contribute voluntarily because they believe in and value America. They will view government as "we" rather than as "they," and no citizen will consider his government the "enemy."

We need not wait for government to discover these possibilities. Citizens are already at work. Many examples are at hand. In Eugene, Oregon, a city of about 70,000, the Department of Parks and Recreation now has a volunteer staff of more than 400 assistants in its many programs. More than 1,400 volunteers, both young and old, serve some 55 community agencies that are mostly private organizations doing community work. The national student volunteer program estimates that 250,000 college students contribute their time, energies, and imagination to community activities. The state of Washington has recently established a small volunteer program to assist state agencies.[5] At present most of the volunteers work for the Department of Public Assistance; others do corrections work and assist in expanding employment security. Several city police forces work with private citizens not only to acquaint them with police activities but also to promote meaningful law and order. Citizens traditionally volunteer for fire protection.

School children assist in reforestation programs of the government by planting trees under the supervision of foresters. Proposals for a modernized version of the Civilian Conservation Corps are annually introduced in Congress, with growing support. The Peace Corps and its domestic counterpart, VISTA (Volunteers in Service to America), have tapped the allegiances and ideals of college youth and others. In earlier days citizens volunteered to build public buildings; perhaps they will again.

What other forms of service might be instituted and made politically acceptable? How can volunteers be induced to join and continue to serve? Remember our cost/benefit analysis and explanations of human behavior. What kinds of personal costs are to be expected? How much of what sorts of rewards are required to overcome the costs? Who is in the best position to volunteer? Why? Who would find it difficult? Why? How much good would various services be for the community?

[5] Dale Nelson, "Washington Coordinates Efforts of Volunteers Aiding Institutions," *The Oregonian*, April 13, 1970, 12.

A WORLD TAX

Under a proposal before the United Nations in 1970 everyone in the world would pay a sales tax on certain home appliances and luxury items to assist the poor countries. The tax would be levied at the rate of 0.5 percent of the purchase or retail price and would be collected by the authorities of each nation. Each nation would also have the right of choosing the development organizations they want to have the money. These organizations would come from a list supplied by the United Nations.

Would the American people accept such a tax scheme? Who might be opposed? In favor? Why? Would an international income tax do any better? Why was a sales tax chosen?

DISTRIBUTION OF MEDICAL SERVICES

Shortages of medical facilities, personnel, and care are much publicized facts of American life. They need not be detailed here in order to appreciate the allocative problems that would arise if suddenly, tomorrow, a cure were announced for any fatal disease such as cancer, heart disease, coronary thrombosis, or emphysema. Suppose such a cure were discovered. In view of the lamentable shortages of medical resources and the inevitable demand to be cured who should be treated and in what order of priorities? Should the young be given priority? Males? Females? Mothers? How can we formulate rules to govern distribution? Should wealth, income, or contributions to society be a factor? Should the cost of the treatment be included as a criterion so that the less expensive cases are cured before the more costly? With these few suggestions, devise rules or criteria for the distribution of cures for one or more of the fatal diseases. Defend your ordering. Which ordering will be most feasible in political terms?

Suggested Readings

Buchanan, James M. *The Public Finances* (Homewood, Ill.: Richard D. Irwin, Inc., 1965).

Hirsch, Werner Z. *The Economics of State and Local Government* (New York: McGraw-Hill Book Co., 1970).

Shoup, Carl S. *Public Finance* (Chicago: Aldine Publishing Co., 1969).

Chapter XVI

ACHIEVING POLICY ENDS

If governments were consistently effective and efficient there would be no need for this chapter. But they are not; the record of failures is long, and failure, especially persistent failure to achieve noble or even mundane objectives, can be highly dangerous in an idealistic nation. Daily experience and newspaper headlines give evidence that governments sometimes set goals that are impossible to achieve or that can be achieved only at great real costs to society. These recent headlines serve as examples:

Juvenile Dept. 'Regressing'

Meat Control Plan Drags

39 States Not Meeting
Requirements of Welfare Law

Enforcing of New Law Bogs Down,
Stirring Uproar in Coalfields

Ironically, at times we benefit from government ineptitude and failure, especially when they affect our own freedom, pocket-book, and status. Those who enjoyed hard liquor during the 1920s no doubt profited from governmental failures to implement the Volstead Act. Most of the time our governments are vastly more effective but rarely do they operate at full efficiency.

Cases in Failure

The following case studies in failure raise some questions about government controls. Later we will consider various reasons for success and failure.

MISUSE OF CITIZENS' BAND RADIO

A bizarre exception exists in a modern industry that is carefully controlled. It is a flourishing $65 million business in complete violation of federal law.[1] Some 3 million Americans are involved and some 15,000 more are added each month to the total who make use of the Citizens' Band radio. The Citizens' Band was originated in the 1950's to enable the untrained operator to make use of two-way radios in his car or boat, on the farm, or any place else, as a convenience. The enormous appeal of the idea was not expected, but once these radios became popular, business encouraged their sale. The FCC has made no effort to attempt to regulate the broadcast policies, so use has become chaotic. Although the band was intended to be reserved for business use it has become a recreational and amusement device. Even the emergency band is clogged with idle, personal chit-chat, especially of teenagers and young children. Electronics manufacturers openly advertise—a further violation of the federal law.

In diagnosing this or any failure we must devote some attention to the motives of the ordinary citizen, the businessman, and the controlling agency. We must also look into the nature of the activity and the regulation that was designed to control it. Then we should inquire into the agency's resources for control. Finally, we can ask why so many patriotic people who otherwise believe in "law and order" violate this law without a second thought.

WELFARE PROGRAMS AND THE ELIMINATION OF POVERTY

From the welfare recipient to the conservative businessman, almost everyone believes that existing welfare programs are in a mess. They are an insult to the recipients and do not make able-bodied people productive. They are extremely burdensome for local governments, since their costs are rapidly rising. Finally, they are a continuing source of conflict.

About 10 million people out of a population of more than 200 million currently receive some form of welfare payments.[2] Almost

---

[1] Jack Gould, "Citizens Band Radio Being Misused: Many Laughing at Law," *Eugene Register-Guard*, December 1969, 11.

[2] U. S. Bureau of the Census, *Statistical Abstract of the United States, 1969* (90th ed., Washington, D.C.: U.S. Government Printing Office, 1969), p. 296.

half of these are children and another 1.5 million are mothers of preschool children. Two million are aged, 728,000 are disabled, and 80,000 are blind. About 500,000 are able to work.

We should qualify this criticism by admitting that these programs do provide some measure of relief to all these unfortunate individuals. We do wish, however, to cite a major program with multiple goals whose respective achievement is highly questionable. The criteria of success are by no means self-evident. We do not agree on what the various welfare programs are designed to achieve, and this criticism is not valid without some knowledge of the goal(s). Thus, the welfare programs of the nation may not eliminate poverty, if that is their goal, but they may succeed in relieving certain types of misfortune. Who would deny assistance to the blind? Who would claim that innocent children of fatherless families are not worthy of support? In reviewing the welfare programs, then, we must identify the misfortunes they cover, the recipients, how much assistance is given, and what, if anything, could or should be added or substituted that would accomplish the same ends.

The welfare activities of governments, like many other of its activities, are always studies in *partial* achievement in the overcoming of problems. As partial achievements they are also partial failures. Not only must goals be kept in mind but some well-defined criteria of success are necessary to enable measurement of how well we have done. As the welfare example shows, these criteria are neither easily devised nor likely to be equally acceptable among all people.

REGULATION OF INDUSTRIAL SAFETY

From the point of view of businessmen government often seems to be all powerful and very effective in controlling business activities. Yet some impressive failures have been logged by government in its attempts to achieve its own declared goals of regulating business.

Countless students of industry have claimed that regulatory agencies do not do their jobs well. For example, thousands of industrial firms, especially in the mining industry, violate safety regulations with impunity. While inspectors discover hazards in more than 90 percent of the factories they enter, only about one percent of the companies held responsible are ever called to formal account and barely one in a thousand is ever punished.[3] Perhaps many of these are minor infractions that are not likely to be consequential for safety, but it is also a fact that more than 14,000 workers are killed each year on the job and more than 2 million sustain disabling injuries.[4] Although the loss from accidents is said to be ten times the loss from strikes, we pay far more attention to reducing the number of strikes and strike days than to preventing accidents.

CRIME AND CRIMINAL JUSTICE

Our next instance of failure is a continuing one, involving one of the most basic functions of government: the control of crime. Our nation has one of the highest crime rates in the world —no matter how crime is defined and measured. In 1965, for example, more than 2.78 million crimes were noted in the *Uniform Crime Reports for the United States, 1965*. Of all these crimes, relatively few are finally solved and the criminal prosecuted.[5] In 1965, for example, only 727,000 arrests were made, suggesting that unpunished committal of a crime is a fairly safe possibility in the United States. No complaints were issued for 290,000 of those arrested. For only 177,000, formal accusations and detention ensued. After various types of court proceedings such as bench trials, trial by jury, and guilty pleas, sentences were issued for 160,000 of the accused; 35,000 went to jail, 56,000 were put on probation, 63,000 were sentenced to prison, and 6,000 were left unsupervised.

We are not suggesting that putting people in jail is a desirable end in itself. We are saying that (1) police are unable to solve a very large percentage of the crimes committed, (2) many arrests are erroneous, and (3) the justice and penal systems are efficient neither in meting out justice nor in reducing crime.

[3] Ralph Rugaber, "Thousands of Violations but Few Penalties," *The Oregonian*, January 9, 1970, p. 27.

[4] Rugaber, "Thousands of Violations." Also see the brilliant analysis set forth by Rand Guffey, "Mine Safety Furor: Enforcing of New Law Bogs Down, Stirring Uproar in Coalfields," *The Wall Street Journal*, June 25, 1970, 1, 13.

[5] Above figures were derived from Alfred Blumstein and Richard C. Larson, "A Systems Approach to the Study of Crime and Criminal Justice," in Philip M. Morse, ed., *Operations Research for Public Systems* (Cambridge, Mass.: The M.I.T. Press, 1967), p. 166.

FEDERAL WELFARE STANDARDS AND STATE NONCOMPLIANCE

At the date of this writing (1970) some 39 states have failed to comply with many requirements concerning the rights of welfare recipients prescribed by the Department of Health, Education and Welfare and by the Supreme Court.[6] While some of the violations are minor and have little impact on the nation's needy, many are major departures or violations. These standards have been in effect for several years. They pertain to who may receive how much aid and protect some individuals against being cut back or removed from programs. Whereas the South resists federal standards concerning racial integration they are the most compliant with respect to the welfare standards. Red tape is supposed to have caused some of the noncompliance problem but outright opposition is a fact in many states.

This problem of noncompliance is interesting in that one level of government (the states) is resisting another level (the federal government, especially the Supreme Court, and the Congress). How can we explain noncompliance by a unit of government? Some leading questions: What is the nature of the activity being resisted? What resources of the several states enable resistance? Does the federal government have any resources to implement standards? What resources, if any, are available to the Supreme Court to back its own decisions?

Conditions of Effective Control

The best of social goals are worthless without effective implementation. Better governmental performance inevitably includes a concern for improving the effectiveness of its controls, including the necessary negative controls over the behavior of at least some citizens. While the study of governmental control is not far advanced we do know some things from experience. We know that countless programs have not worked well because the controls were inadequate for the task; in fact, the task could not be reasonably achieved because certain conditions were either unknown or ignored by the leaders of the day. Such failures include the prohibition of liquor during the 1920s; antitrust laws; racial

[6] G. C. Thelen, Jr., "U.S. Welfare Law Crackdown Pledged," *Eugene Register-Guard*, April 3, 1970, 7–A.

integration in schools, particularly in the Southern states; control of firearms during the 1960s; regulation of Citizens' Band or shortwave radios; elimination of prayers in public schools; and misuse of valuable resources to enforce unenforcible laws in daily police work.

FOUR CONDITIONS OF FAILURE

These failures in public policy suggest that the sources of failure are to be found in four conditions attending the controls:

1. A vast number of people whose behavior is to be altered;
2. A considerable alteration in expected behavior from previous behavior;
3. Importance of the existing forms of behavior or ways of doing things;
4. Inadequate rewards for compliance and penalties for noncompliance.

In brief, the amount of difficulty a government encounters in sponsoring control is a function of the *scope of the proposed change, the numbers of the population to be controlled,* and *the significance of the controlled acts to those being controlled.*

The Prohibition Amendment to the Constitution was doomed to failure because it demanded too much from too many people in an area of valued activity—drinking. The same may be said of integration efforts in a number of institutional arenas of our national life. Men and women do accept a vast array of controls over their lives, but most controls do not demand major changes in daily patterns of living and most can be adequately defended as rational and necessary. For example, most of us obey traffic regulations because we can see and appreciate the value of these controls *if all others are also controlled.* The costs of compliance are viewed as appropriate, given the expected benefits or the avoidance of costly consequences. Persons who value religious institutions, however, do not see social value in prohibition of prayer in the schools; indeed, they see it as a considerable loss. To expect a Supreme Court decision to immediately alter or prevent such a fundamental form of behavior is unrealistic.[7] Prayer is a crucial

[7] See the special issue of the *American Behavioral Scientist,* 13 (March–April 1960) entitled "Law and Social Change" for several excellent treatments of the conditions under which law can influence behavior. A more detailed listing of our four conditions of control as they pertain to the Supreme Court is offered in that issue by Jack B. Grossman, "The Supreme Court and Social Change," 545–46.

ritual to many of our citizens, and we should not be surprised to see them resist these controls effectively.

Large numbers of citizens who feel similarly aggrieved can become a powerful force against government. Each citizen can gain courage in the knowledge that others agree with him. Few men have the courage and resources to stand alone against public opinion. Perhaps that is why totalitarian states attempt to isolate men and break down their bonds of affection and support. Commonly held values, norms, and opinions are among the most powerful forces in a society; a government that would counter them must recognize them as such. In some situations, large numbers of people will sacrifice traditional ways and even material self-interests. Such circumstances are rare, however, and cannot be depended upon in day-to-day governmental administration. Conditions of war, especially a popular war, are normally considered a legitimate demand for dramatic change and sacrifices. Americans generally honored such demands during World Wars I and II, but even then certain controls did not work well. Profiteers, for example, may be found under all conditions, and sellers of illicit goods never seem to lack buyers.

In general, an administrator should expect that programs can best be implemented whenever small numbers of citizens are involved; changes in their behavior are minimal; and the changes will not involve fundamental beliefs, values, or behavior. Whatever the configuration of these elements, the administrator must also employ an appropriate and sufficient balance or mix of inducements for compliance or, conversely, penalties for noncompliance. Inducements may include monetary and psychic rewards; penalties may include loss of income, status, convenience, personal liberty, and the like. In a democracy it is probably wiser to emphasise positive rewards for compliance. Although negative sanctions cannot be ruled out, it may be difficult to avoid inflicting undue harm. In economic terms we should balance the marginal gains from penalties with their marginal costs in order to achieve optimal results.

The next consideration regarding both penalties and rewards is deciding which are appropriate and in what quantities. The wisest choice seems to be to expand their varieties and gradations. The more a particular behavior is desired the greater must be the rewards for compliance or the greater the costs of noncompliance, or both. Of course the government must consider the net costs of compliance; if the same level of compliance is attained by two different methods the cheaper one should be used. If the same expenditure results in different levels of compliance the higher one should be selected. Whenever finer variations are possible the government should apply the marginal calculus; that is, ask whether an additional expenditure will produce sufficient additional compliance to warrant the added costs of supplying rewards or imposing penalties. In terms of appropriateness, controls should be designed in such a manner that the "punishment fits the crime." The death penalty, for example, is obviously too severe a penalty for a traffic violation or operating a Citizens' Band radio; indeed most traffic violations should not even entail jail sentences if fines serve as adequate deterrents. In designing controls, the only objective should be control of behavior, not revenge or reprisal. Retribution is a primitive act, and not a proper function of government. Unfortunately public officials, governments, and citizens have chosen on far too many occasions to exercise their punitive wills and anger against others. The Volstead Act prohibiting liquor production and distribution was surely inspired by hatred and revenge as were the infamous Palmer Raids of the 1920s. The McCarthy era of the early 1950s was another. Repression of the blacks by both citizens and governmental officials is undoubtedly the worst current example. The so-called "relocation" of Japanese-Americans during World War II was surely the hastiest and worst conceived control we have ever instituted for it was not only unnecessary but immoral by our own standards.

It is wise to remember that few wish to be controlled; whenever we desire to control others we might imagine ourselves in their position and assess the consequences before we act. In fact, the rational planner ought always to consider the possibilities of self- or private control. Not infrequently, groups will attempt to police their own members in order to ward off more drastic government control. And market solutions to our problems are a distinct possibility.

ATTITUDINAL CONDITIONS FOR EFFECTIVE CONTROL

The effectiveness of governmental controls rests to a significant degree on the attitudes of those to be controlled. Citizens of a democracy have the capacity to resist and subvert even the best of controls if they see them as unjustifiable or as imposing undue constraints and deprivations. Administrators would do well to include citizen views in the design of controls. Our limited information on this matter has led to a few generalizations that can serve as focal points for analysis; some of these propositions are listed here without further discussion since each is relatively self-explanatory. The following generalizations describe conditions that facilitate government controls:[8]

1. A widespread belief that the policy and control are necessary (for example, a draft during a world war).

2. Confidence in the reasonableness of the control.

3. A widespread belief that the policy control was selected in a legitimate way by legitimate policymakers.

4. A widespread belief that one may profit from the control.

5. Assurance that noncompliance will be punished.

6. Support of prestigious members of society, or, more particularly, the segment of the population to be controlled.

7. Awareness that those who are about to be controlled were effective participants in designing the controls.

8. A conviction that the controls are to be applied only so long as they are necessary or an emergency is met.

9. Assurance that appeals for equity can be made and are effective.

10. Knowledge that controls have been designed to cure widespread abuses of privilege.

Basic Questions for Administrators

Suppose we adopt the perspective of the government administrator. We will assume, for the moment, that policy objectives have been provided by Congress but the means of implementation remain to be decided upon. If one were put into a position of responsibility in designing legislation or having to administer the program he would want to shape the means and the ends so that the latter could be accomplished as quickly, completely, and easily as possible.[9] How do we proceed to design an effective program of action? We might ask a series of questions in such a manner that appropriate answers are more likely to be provided.

---

[8] This listing is based on a discussion by James E. Anderson, *Politics and the Economy* (Boston: Little, Brown & Co., 1966), pp. 93–101.

[9] Bertram M. Gross discusses these matters with fine insight in "Activating National Plans," in J. R. Lawrence, ed., *Operational Research and the Social Sciences* (London: Tavistock Publications, 1966), pp. 449–82.

1. What do we wish to accomplish?
2. What obstacles will we encounter?
3. What resources will be available?
4. What are our policy options?
5. Can we estimate the probabilities of various payoffs for each option?
6. Are the alternatives politically feasible?

The listing of these basic questions in the above order does not mean that leaders ask questions in that precise sequence but it does suggest that they eventually pose similar questions even if in other language. They should be asked, however they are stated. Let us see why.

WHAT DO WE WISH TO ACCOMPLISH?

If priority in time and importance must be attached to our list of inquiries undoubtedly this one would have first place. The answers to all others are dependent upon the response to this single question. Effective means cannot be designed if goals remain unknown. Put in this manner the comment seems banal; still, it is astonishing how often politicians and administrators launch into solutions for problems that have not been defined or analyzed in terms of the objectives.

Consider a commonplace issue in local government: traffic control. Everyone thinks that traffic ought to be controlled, but for what purposes? Possible answers include (1) reducing the possibilities of accidents, (2) facilitating the flow to get drivers to their destinations more rapidly, (3) diverting traffic into business areas, and (4) diverting traffic from residential areas. Each of these ends is, in itself, laudable for someone. But each end may not be consistent with each of the other goals; in this event, different means are required to resolve the problem or achieve the stated goal. For example, to reduce fatal accidents it may be desirable to slow traffic, but expediting the flow of vehicles might require facilities that permit greater speeds. In other cases, goals may be complementary such that the increased capacity to achieve one goal may facilitate achievement of others. Thus, directing traffic away from residential areas may mean directing it toward the business district and increasing the possibilities of sales by merchants.

Our advice, therefore, is to clarify and distinguish goals as much as possible and to select those goals that are most compatible with others. In other words, be sensitive to the side-benefits of each proposal. If additional goals can be achieved at little or no additional expense, so much the better. It is a fact of life, however, that the more goals sought the greater the probabilities that conflicts will arise among them.

WHAT OBSTACLES WILL WE ENCOUNTER?

For opposite reasons, both the supporters and the opponents of any policy are interested in identifying the obstacles to implementation. In fact, a great deal of political action results from the efforts of interested persons in noting and assessing obstacles to be overcome or bypassed. Those who expect to profit from a proposed change usually attempt to minimize the roadblocks; those who expect to be hurt tend to inflate the number and size of these obstacles. In both cases the interested parties may be imagining roadblocks where there are none or overlooking real difficulties that ought not to be minimized or ignored. In a more general sense, conservatives tend to be unduly sensitive to the money costs while radicals appear equally insensitive to constraints on change.

All policy alterations encounter problems. Such impediments include two general classes of hindrances: (1) beliefs, values, norms, and interests of the citizenry; and (2) the objective state of society at any particular point in time. The first class of obstacles or potential obstacles pertains to the citizens themselves and their subjective lives in particular. The values Americans hold are such that they encourage some types of policies but inhibit or prevent others from being successfully administered. As a highly idealistic, materialistic, achievement-oriented, and patriotic nation we tend to prefer policies that can be rationalized or defended in those terms and opposed to policies that are not as easily justified by these widely accepted symbols and reasons. Our welfare policies have been vitally shaped by these values and norms. A guaranteed annual income has not, until recently, won much favor because such programs do not seem in accord with deeply felt and widely accepted notions of economic justice, personal ambition, and achievement. Such orientations are, in fact, obstacles to the reform of our welfare system and they have prevented substantial change for many decades.

An able politician will either attempt to reform the welfare policies by rationalizing them in terms of legitimate verbal symbols or he will achieve his ends by small incremental changes that go largely unnoticed by the general public. When President Nixon advanced his reform proposals for welfare in 1969 he did not tell the American people he wanted to "subsidize" the poor; rather, he said he wanted to give everyone who wanted to work the opportunity and favored "family supplemental incomes." President Nixon had to justify his reforms in such a way as to minimize the opposition of his more conservative supporters. He did so by identifying himself with their values and norms but at the same time proving the need for reform. His reforms were then couched in language that pleased members of both groups—those who believed in welfare and those who were opposed. In a sense the President recognized an obstacle to change but sought to alter and minimize that obstacle by an artful selection of phrases and ideas.

The norms by which Americans live may even obstruct the effective achievement of widely shared goals. The fast and effective control of inflation, for instance, may well be deterred by the fact that most Americans rebel against wage and price control. Failure to adopt these controls may be quite rational for they are costly, but under some circumstances such controls may be well worth the added costs. Devotion to traditional norms and the conventional wisdom has its own costs in coping with a changing world; the failure to improve and adopt new means of control often means the destruction of still more cherished values. The city administrators of Portland, Oregon, for example, recently hired a group of "hippies" when it discovered they were better able to control activities in a city park than uniformed police were. Constant questioning of tradition is a wise activity for administrators.

It is unwise to assume that policy makers can proceed without active opposition to their designs. Many an otherwise able administrator, having laid what he regarded as well-designed plans, is shocked to discover that he has opponents who not only will not cooperate but will actively oppose seemingly unexceptional policy changes. For example, he may hire a big-city professional police chief to head a small-town police force on the assumption that he can simply move in and professionalize the force because everyone including the officers value a highly professional force. He may be very surprised to discover that his careful plans are opposed by some of the force, some of the citizens, and a few of the politicians. He must cut back on goals and plan for a much longer and more costly period of reform. Had he known that making the police or any agency more professional levies its own costs, he might not have launched such audacious plans so suddenly upon an unsuspecting city. Less revolutionary changes might have been handled more successfully. This bit of "scenario" is commonplace across the United States. The drive for efficiency is costly and often unwise. The lesson: expect opponents to arise. The moral: reduce opposition numbers and influence by co-opting them if possible; that is, inducing the leaders to join your side by assigning them responsibilities.

WHAT RESOURCES WILL BE AVAILABLE?

To attempt to attain noble goals without adequate resources is to produce frustration and disappointment among both the supporters of a plan and its administrators. Such a broad generalization requires further specification of what is entailed in resource mobilization and allocation to particular activities. It should be said at the outset that when an agency begins its work it does not need all the resources of labor, leadership, skill, knowledge, capital, motivation, land, and organization it will eventually need. Paradoxically, if the resources for full-scale action were instantly available some would be wasted. No organization can make immediate and efficient use of vast resources, particularly when new goals or experimental means are being tried under high uncertainty. Our overnight mobilization for World War II was replete with gross inefficiencies.

Administrators who are skillful and motivated can overcome enormous resource limitations by ingenious temporary solutions. After success becomes visible, resources are usually made more available. Politicians tend to support successful endeavors (after they prove themselves) and are apt to reward the already successful administrator. Therefore, one should not panic or become immobilized by current shortages of resources. Substitutes and more efficient use of existing labor and materials are always possible.

WHAT ARE THE POLICY OPTIONS?

Once goals have been set and resources are known, the administrator or politician is in a position to begin considering and choosing the actual means by which compliance will be induced or sought. While the choice may be difficult, the alternatives are fairly clearcut. A combination of means can comprise direct or indirect rewards for compliant behavior and/or direct or indirect imposition of penalties or sanctions for failure to comply. Thus,

TABLE XVI–1

Means of Influencing Citizens

Means	Number	Percent
Economizing (subtotal)	163	57.6%
1. Possessing, maintaining, managing materials assets	19	6.7
2. Direct production of goods and services ..	7	2.5
3. Buying of resources or of goods already manufactured	15	5.3
4. Subsidizing, granting free welfare	34	12.0
5. Contracting	34	12.0
6. Lending	15	5.3
7. Paying of services, of insurance re-payments, of loans, social security, bonds, deposits	18	6.4
8. Selling	18	6.4
9. Borrowing and associate management ...	3	1.1
Informing (subtotal)	95	33.6
10. Educating, publicizing, persuading	55	19.5
11. Studying, planning, researching, prototype development	27	9.5
12. Inspecting, investigating	9	3.2
13. Conferencing, consulting, negotiating	4	1.4
Directing (subtotal)	26	9.2
14. Promulgating rules	5	1.8
15. Ordering individuals, companies, groups ..	2	.7
16. Hearing, trying, sanctioning	2	.7
17. Human organization and management	9	3.2
18. Coercing, guarding, compelling, restraining	3	1.1
19. Licensing, patenting, copyrighting	3	1.1
20. Taxing	2	.7
TOTAL	283	100.0

Source: Adapted from Alfred A. de Grazia, "A Classifiable Inventory of Faceted Operations of Government," *Hearings before The Subcommittee on Executive Reorganization of the Committee on Government Operations,* United States Senate, 90th Congress, 2nd Session, Washingon, D.C.: U.S. Government Printing Office, 1968, 618.

the controller has a mix of four basic instruments to select from. Which one to choose depends upon a variety of factors including (1) the goal selected; (2) availability of resources; (3) expected costs and benefits; and (4) the moral traditions of the controllers and controlled. Since we are discussing these four considerations throughout this chapter there seems little point in elaborating upon them at this juncture.

Instead, it may prove useful to note the balance of controls actually used by our federal government. Fortunately one scholar, Alfred de Grazia, has provided us with an interesting compilation of such instruments, after surveying a total of some 283 programs or activities of the federal government. His purpose was to classify what he termed the "means of influencing clientele"; that is, those persons subject to the activities or controls.[10] He compiled 20 discrete means; they are categorized in Table XVI–1 under the labels of *economizing, informing,* and *directing.* Economizing (rewarding) is by far the most frequently employed means (in 57.6 percent of cases) and directing the least popular means (in 9.2 percent of cases). These figures need not remain constant; during wartime or severe financial depression one should expect the directing category to increase. The 20 means of control can be further subdivided into a great variety of practices but that hardly appears important in this context. In any case, our governments have not been unimaginative in devising ways of implementing their policies, but all too often they have failed to choose the best ones for handling particular difficulties.

CAN WE ESTIMATE PAYOFFS OF OPTIONS? (Social and Political Consequences)

An essential calculation or estimate all planners must make consists of comparing the likely payoffs of alternatives. Some of these comparisons are relatively simple, especially when estimating technological returns, but many that involve the behavior of people are not so easily calculated, and must be highly conditional. Consider this policy problem: Suppose a President wishes to slow inflationary forces and ultimately attain a more stabilized price system.[11] His Council of Economic Advisors will provide him with a variety of policy alternatives that must be assessed in terms of their economic consequences or payoffs and their political feasibility and consequences. One need not understand much of either field to know that the estimation of both economic and political payoffs must be uncertain. But let us make this more concrete. A President might have the following possible options:

1. Increase taxes.
2. Cut expenditures.

[10] See citation accompanying Table XVI–1.
[11] A lucid discussion of inflation is offered by Amotz Morag, *On Taxes and Inflation* (New York: Random House, 1965).

3. Increase costs of borrowing.

4. Institute direct controls on wages and prices.

5. Persuade people to restrain certain market behaviors.

6. Make certain structural changes in the economy that will increase productivity.

7. Freeze wages, prices, dividends, and profits on a temporary basis.

8. Devise price guidelines to be self-administered by members of the economy.

9. Institute immediate full control over all elements of the economy.

With these options before him a President must decide, usually on the basis of conflicting advice from his advisors and outside consultants, how successful each of these means might be individually (or in combination) in halting or reducing inflation. These are the purely economic consequences. Although economists are presumed to have considerable expertise to apply to these questions they may still strongly disagree about (1) which conditions prevail; (2) which option should be employed; and (3) what degree of success is expected for any and all options. Four of these options are listed in Table XVI–2. We have considered in this table the political feasibility and consequences of each. In any policy decision, however, a President and his consultants would also have to consider economic conditions and consequences.

ARE THE ALTERNATIVES POLITICALLY FEASIBLE?

Presidents are elected, and therefore will have some concern for the political implications of any policy—that is, the immediate feasibility of a program and the effect it would have on his re-election and his party's. Estimating these factors is complicated by the fact that he must really decide the political effects of economic success or failure.

Each option will produce results that please some voters and make others unhappy. Halting inflation may seem a universal public good but actually some people profit from rapidly inflated prices. Wage earners may be able to stay ahead of inflation because employers are more willing to make wage increases. Realtors and debtors stand to profit from inflationary periods. Other groups clearly do not profit from inflation. The creditor, the person on a fixed income, the house buyer, and the consumer in general, are all penalized when prices rise rapidly. A President must,

TABLE XVI–2

Some Anti-Inflationary Options: Prevailing Conditions, Feasibility, and Consequences

Options	Political feasibility	Expected political consequences
1. Sharp decrease in federal spending.	Difficult during a congressional election year.	Depends on program being cut but opposition may be expected from the benefitted, support from those opposed to the program.
2. Stiff tax increase.	Difficult during any election year.	Depends on type and size of increase. Income tax increases would be least supported. Excise tax on luxury most supported.
3. Cajoling Federal Reserve Board into tightening credit restrictions.	Easiest course.	Will be opposed by those who want easy credit, such as borrowers, retail merchants, and manufacturers.
4. Direct controls over wages and profits.	Most difficult except during a dire crisis such as full-scale war.	Likely to be opposed by both business and unions.

therefore, make some estimates of the amount of economic benefit and costs each group will sustain and how they will respond the next time they attend an election. Our knowledge of voter responses to economic policies and conditions is incomplete and somewhat undependable but it would seem that those who become dissatisfied are most likely to respond at the polls. Those who have benefitted do not always appreciate the connection between their success and governmental policies. In any event, the politician is forced to calculate the marginal gains and losses in votes at subsequent elections for his advocacy of policies. His calculations are usually rough and ready, as we observed in Chapters VI and IX.

One dilemma with poignant possibilities concerns the choice faced by a leader who must decide between a policy with proven short-run political appeal but little durable social gain and one with long-run social benefit but little immediate political popularity. Control policies having only long-run benefits but immediate high costs create these dilemmas. Leaders who opt for the long run good usually do not have a long political life; it remains for posterity to recognize their worth.

Our analysis has the promise of anticipating problems and crises with the expectation that something can be done to prevent or at least reduce their frequency and severity. As all politicians know, the unexpected is the most expected characteristic of their jobs—the least expected outcome is likely to be the most probable in real life. Administrators and politicians must be prepared to choose from among the less optimal options under unfavorable conditions.

Crisis Conditions and Public Choice

Government officials may be aware of impending crises because similar crises have occurred elsewhere. Indeed, such crises have probably been occurring for some time and have attracted much attention from the media; they have become a staple conversational topic among leaders. Yet the incidence of a crisis in one's own city always seems remote to most policy makers. Since policy makers typically find themselves confronted with a major crisis precisely when they do not expect one they may be quite unprepared to handle it. Why should this be? The normal mental sets of our policy makers when confronted with crisis—whether provoked by dissidents or by natural disaster—combine with the following elements to create typical crisis behavior: uncertainty; conflicting demands; decentralized decision making; constraints of time; inadequate resources or training for crisis control, and inadequate leadership. A brief discussion of these elements follows:[12]

UNCERTAINTY

Precipitation of a crisis is normally in the hands of others or of nature. Officials then are put in the initial position of having to react rather than assume the initiatives. Needless to say, no ra-

[12] For a detailed treatment see Allen H. Barton, *Communities in Disaster* (Garden City, N.Y.: Anchor Books, 1969).

tional leader of a planned forthcoming riot will disclose his timing. At best, the official can depend only upon inadequate intelligence concerning the motivations, resources, strategies, and
tactics of the dissidents. Since most local and state officials are not
accustomed to treating their citizens as enemies they are usually
not well informed about them. Officials, usually white, dealing
with blacks they have never really known or understood, are a
good case in point. Another is "establishment" officials coping
with youthful dissenters. However, some uncertainty—possibly
hostility—prevails between officials and all citizens because differences in status and power often preclude sympathetic understanding. And, of course, the larger the constituency the greater
the possibilities for uncertainty. In New York City, for example,
the mayor must deal with a population of more than seven million
while a President must concern himself with over two hundred
million people.

CONFLICTING DEMANDS

Every emergency or crisis affects different citizens differently. As a result each develops different demands and expects officials to do different and usually incompatible things. For example, in many cities and towns unexpected natural disasters have
devastated valuable property and taken many lives. Officials in
these localities must make instant, crucial decisions about whom
to help and in what order. A few years ago, the city of Eugene,
Oregon, was confronted with the most severe snowstorm in its history. The city was without snowplows and other snow removal
equipment. Officials substituted earth removal equipment and then
had to decide in what order areas and streets would be plowed.
The downtown area received highest priority and many citizens
complained about the lower orders because they felt their demands
were more pressing than those of other citizens. When the crisis
was over the local media publicized many complaints, recriminations, and second-guessing on the allocation of relief. Because a
modern city is a highly interdependent system the ordering of priorities under crises and inadequate resources is of the greatest
political and social importance.

Since Americans tend to value equality this ordering process
becomes a trying choice. Generally, the solution is temporarily to
forget equality and proceed in terms of the functional importance

of people and their activities. Thus, a city mayor may declare an emergency and seek federal and state aid. He may also declare that (1) communications media must be kept open; (2) certain necessities of life must be met first, including the delivery of milk and food to the aged and the newborn, those on the verge of starvation, and hospitals; and (3) only those who serve as police and firemen may use the streets. Curfews may also be ordered. The intent is to keep the basic processes of a social system in operation so that the necessities of life may be supplied.

Generally, disasters serve to unite people and make their mobilization by the government easier and more effective. A common natural plight seems to rub out certain social and economic distinctions, at least for the short run. When a crisis lasts longer than people can tolerate it, however, it may strain relationships, especially when differential burdens are experienced. The demand for equalized sharing of burdens is apt to be very high during an emergency. One task of leadership is to show that such equality is indeed a reality.

DECENTRALIZED DECISION MAKING

Many an executive official has been blamed after a riot, a war, a demonstration, or a natural disaster for not having handled the situation with greater ease, more success, fewer costs, and the like, as though he could have accomplished all these objectives simultaneously. In addition to all the other situational constraints encountered by a policy maker, one of the more important is our decentralization of authority and power. No single official can oversee everything and command others to do what he wants them to. Normally, the lines of authority are multitudinous, vague, complex, and occasionally in conflict; inefficiency is one result. Numerous policy makers must be consulted for every decision, and both formal authority and personal status are involved.

Since more rather than fewer officials must be included more considerations are entered into each choice and because more officials participate greater time is consumed in arriving at critical decisions. Officials, not infrequently, disagree over who has responsibility for what during the emergencies. Intense recriminations may take place after the event as each party to the handling of the situation blames others for inadequate or wrong actions.

Post mortems however, rarely prepare officials for more effective administration in the future.

CONSTRAINTS OF TIME

An emergency or crisis is by definition an unexpected event of a relatively brief duration. That means officials are usually taken by surprise and must respond without sufficient time to devise alternative strategies that can be systematically and thoroughly analyzed and assessed. If a riot should break out in a ghetto the mayor of the city must quickly learn where, who and how many citizens are involved, what they are doing, how many police and firemen he can send into the area, how they should conduct themselves, and how to contact the leadership of the riot if there is such leadership. All these bits of information and decisions must be made under the intense pressure of limited time. A mayor cannot sit back and idly contemplate his wisest course of action; instead he must act on the basis of an intuitive understanding of the situation. Hopefully, his intuition is that of a wise and sane man who knows how to act without going through the torture of a systematic examination of everything that should and could be studied under ideal circumstances.

Decisions may be good decisions, in general, but if they are ill-timed they can be worse than bad decisions or none at all. Being precipitous is as bad as coming in too late with too little or too much. Unfortunately, we rarely know how to estimate timing and even post mortems can rarely settle the question of what would have been better timing. Governments make serious errors in the timing of both fiscal and monetary policies even though some of our soundest knowledge is in precisely these areas. Imagine, then, the problem of optimal timing without adequate information and theory under conditions of crisis accompanied by violence.

INADEQUATE TRAINING FOR CRISIS

Most governmental decision making, particularly at lower levels, is of a routine sort demanding no specialized training or preparation. Crisis, however, interrupts this routine and causes entirely new problems. These problems require novel choices for which the typical official has had little if any formal training and probably inadequate experience on the job. American colleges and universities do not really train men to be public officials and most certainly do not prepare them for emergencies. Whereas businessmen can take college courses in how to make decisions under varying conditions of risk and uncertainty, we do not teach decision courses to aspiring politicians in political science departments. If anything, we teach them to expect stable situations and interpret them in terms of legal definitions.

Even if we did prepare officials in school and on the job we still would face a difficult problem; that problem stems from the fact that we can generalize about typical situations but not about how to handle unique instances. We can write books about the most common elements in emergency periods but cannot predict the exact configuration of these various elements in any specific future case. As each emergency has some common elements so each has its unique combination. Only the responsible, informed person on the scene can begin to estimate the dimensions of the matter and he is bound to be only partially correct. Unfortunately, we find that men prefer learning from experience. This tendency traps them in obsolescent ways of responding to new conditions. As generals always seem to want to fight the last war over again, and coaches want to repeat a victorious game, so politicians seem to treat each new emergency as if it were an exact replica of the previous one. But no two are ever identical. The problem is knowing which elements remain similar and which have been altered and how.

Perhaps the most important lesson to be learned from this analysis is that the policy maker must develop a certain frame of reference or set of premises that enable him to respond to unexpected emergencies so that he can treat them as normal political events. In short, emergencies are to be expected. Politicians should not treat crises as abnormal or as necessarily bad or evil. Keeping options open and keeping cool to avoid reacting out of anger are goals to strive for. Policy makers should also be wary of advice from angry persons.

LEADERSHIP DURING NATURAL DISASTERS

With these general considerations in mind we can now set forth some more specific guidelines or decision premises for leaders who may one day have to cope with disaster such as a tornado, flood, landslide, major fire, or the like. These disasters are rather different from the man-made crises involving conflict and violence we will consider in the next section. Since some of these premises have been alluded to we will simply list them and leave discussions to readers.

1. Some people will act in wild and disordered ways but most will manage to retain their sanity and search for leadership and means of recovery.

2. Cooperation is contingent on the perceived possibilities of success; expect some people to pursue their own ends and safety regardless of others.

3. Most people's first concern will be with their families.

4. People will expect the government to organize reconstruction.

5. Expect new leadership to arise; some will be competitors.

6. Expect some people to loot and take advantage of confusion and lack of control.

7. Expect complaints and back-biting after the height of the disaster.

8. Expect to make mistakes, anger people, and waste resources.

Confrontation Strategies for Government

We know that American governments have rarely been able to avoid confronting new groups making new demands. What remains to be explained is what these governments have done in response and what they ought to do. Normally, governments have several strategic options, although particular situations may restrict them somewhat and encourage the adoption of one or some particular combination rather than another. The obvious options include: forcible repression; gimmickry in policies; co-optation of leadership, policies, and issues; genuine reform of policies; and genuine inclusion in policy making.

FORCIBLE REPRESSION

To exercise force on deviants or rebels is an attractive strategy for far too many impatient people; that is why we must include the option in the American setting. Repression is particularly appealing to citizens and leaders who happen to hate the values and goals of those in rebellion. To stamp out the movement is viewed as a kind of final solution to a frightening challenge. And the fact is that force can be a highly successful deterrent under some circumstances; so long as the conditions persist the strategy works. For example, blacks in the Southern states have been forcibly controlled with great success for 300 years. Indians have been forced into reservations and controlled for close to a century. Other groups have been successfully controlled in lesser ways and for shorter periods of time including most ethnic populations from southern and eastern Europe.

That repressive control should be employed, often in brutal forms, is hardly unexpected even in a democracy. First, all polities including democracies rest on a monopoly of ultimate coercion. Second, majorities may vote to control minorities and in fact have done so. Third, most men have the psychological capacity within themselves to dominate and even maim or kill others. Few men are born pacifists. When sorely tried by rebellions, riots, revolts, and the like, government leaders find it relatively attractive to attempt repression as a solution to their problems. Under some conditions repression is a highly rational choice; under others it may be irrational as public policy but highly satisfying psychologically.

Forcible repression works best when success is guaranteed; that is, the population to be repressed is (1) smaller than those who repress; (2) ignorant; (3) lacking in resources to support organized resistance; (4) composed of members who can be isolated and demoralized; and (5) led by those who can be socialized or frightened into passivity. Each of these "substrategies" serves to reinforce one or more of the others thus guaranteeing the failure of resistance. Powerful governments can cow populations into subservience, but they must maintain a continual show of strength and be willing to use their power without shame or fear of the victims. If the oppressor loses enthusiasm for the task he will be found out by the oppressed. And that is the beginning of the end.

Certain limitations to the use of force can be ignored by a government only at a high cost. To repress deviants costs the oppressor as well as the oppressed. In the first place, opportunity costs are incurred that prevent the government from providing more goods and services even if for only its own supporters. As we saw in Chapters II to V the opportunity costs of national defense and police protection are very high. Such sums could be devoted to curing the domestic ills that beset our society and cause alienation and rebellion. These sums might also have been used to further subsidize the advantaged.

A second, less tangible cost is also incurred by the controllers in the form of unhealthy mental responses. We have learned from our studies of political systems that totalitarianism can cause men to become paranoid; that is, excessively suspicious and fearful of everyone and their motives. The drain of paranoia must be immense even if it cannot be readily converted into dollars and cents. Mutual suspicion consumes energies and time, and men who live in fear are less productive than those who do not.

GIMMICKRY IN POLICIES

An attractive short run strategy for a politician beset by crisis or opposition is to invent policy gimmicks that appear to be substantive solutions to outstanding problems but are, in fact, little more than popular phrases and extremely short-run solutions. Such courses are attractive because they seem to resolve problems cheaply and to pacify demands, yet they really work only in the interests of those whom the politicians wish to benefit. (As with contracts, one must read the fine print to discover the gimmicks.)

Whether a particular policy is gimmickry is not always easy to detect. Policy, after all, is rarely a clearcut statement about alternatives, but consists instead of innumerable actions, statements from diverse sources, inactions, laws, executive orders, budgetary allocations, and the like, which in total suggest general directions rather than specific choices. Gimmickry may dominate in one of these areas but not others. When President Nixon decided to begin withdrawing troops from Vietnam during 1969 he engaged in a bit of gimmickry. He had to satisfy "hawks" that he neither was leaving precipitously nor was defeated, yet he had to comply with the demands of doves to withdraw; at the same time he had to consider the strategic impact of the withdrawal on many factions: his allies, the North Vietnamese, the Viet Cong, and the South Vietnamese government. While figures on the withdrawal of troops were juggled and concealed, confusing statements were issued to satisfy the intensely conflicting demands of interested parties. Just how many of these confusing stands and actions will be adjudged as political gimmickry remains to be decided in the hindsight of historical studies. Another prevalent example of gimmickry may be found in most tax reform legislation. The appearance of equity and justice almost always conceals innumerable loopholes and exemptions inserted for the benefit of those who are powerful enough to have such exemptions enacted into law.

Gimmickry has the high costs of all short-run solutions; because problems are not effectively resolved they reappear in the future to do greater damage. How soon they will reappear no one knows. Each President, city mayor, or state governor must cope with the consequences of his predecessor's gimmicks. About the only satisfaction he can derive is the bitter knowledge that his own successors will inherit his short-run options and their unfortunate results. Fake solutions are sometimes impossible to avoid but we believe they should be adopted only as a last resort.

CO-OPTATION OF ISSUES, LEADERS, AND POLICIES

One of the oldest and often most successful strategies for a government is co-opting the leaders of the opposition into "responsible" positions within the government. Co-optation means diverting the loyalties of a leader to another group. By doing this a government accomplishes at least two important goals: the opposition is weakened by the departure of its leadership and the government's own position is strengthened by support gained from the opponents. If the co-optation is not too flagrant cooperation and harmony may replace or reduce conflict.

President Truman co-opted the famous and powerful isolationist Republican Senator Arthur H. Vandenberg of Michigan at the conclusion of World War II to support America's continued activist role in world politics, a role which Republicans at that time did not support and indeed had opposed prior to the war. Senator Vandenberg served to make this interventionist role acceptable to Republicans; as a reward he was given a powerful voice in shaping these policies. Every President attempts some co-optation, as he must if he is to govern. At present, Presidents and others try to co-opt black leaders to cool off racial tensions. In an earlier day Republicans attempted to co-opt labor leaders as Democratic leaders now co-opt business leaders. Of course, some opposition leaders will refuse to be co-opted if they suspect that they will not be consulted on major policies but will be used to justify choices made by others. Both co-opted and co-opter have tough decisions to make in establishing and maintaining relationships. If the co-opted becomes disillusioned he may blast the government for failing to follow his advice and thereby invite or encourage his followers to be doubly suspicious of promises made by the government. On the other hand, the co-opter has the problem of justifying the presence of the opposition in his ranks; the more fanatic loyalists will resent the loss of a position and the acceptance of policy advice of which they do not approve.

The extent to which one should co-opt probably depends upon one's margin of victory in winning office and one's margin of continued support by the public. A politician who barely wins ought to co-opt more than one who wins by substantial margins. In the latter case, because solid support has been shown the opposition need not be consulted as much as when one wins by a bare majority or plurality. Recent Presidential experience suggests that those who won by a wide margin, like Eisenhower, did little co-opting; those who barely won, including Truman, Kennedy, and Nixon, have done much more. As popularity polls record dips in Presidential popularity one may expect him to be seen more frequently courting the opposition. Whenever controversial policies are being decided Presidents often attempt to co-opt a famous opposition leader to be chairman of a study group or commission.

Leadership co-optation is only one form; another is the co-optation of issues and policies. All governments engage in this practice, sometimes with great skill and highly effective results. President Nixon, for example, captured the initiative from the liberal Democrats when he co-opted some of their views on welfare reforms and environmental control as did President Eisenhower whenever he pursued liberal Republican policies. Stealing issues and policies is hardly restricted to American politics or even other democratic nations. Students of the Soviet Union have shown how the successors of Stalin have all co-opted the issues and policies of their erstwhile opponents. In brief, one should keep an eye on the doings of the opposition for they frequently hold the key to future happenings and choices.

GENUINE REFORM

The last two strategies enumerated above have a certain suspicious ring to them and with good reason; they are essentially dishonest whereas the first and the present one are highly honest choices. A government confronted with disaster, crises, or sharp challenges may and can adopt genuine reforms in policy and procedures. Governments which fail or refuse to bend will not last long. Whenever evidence suggests that disparities exist, that injustices have been committed, or that existing processes do not work a government should recognize the situation and set out to produce better results. Politicians need not always publicly admit they have been wrong but their actions can surely suggest that they know it. Given the large floating independent vote in this country a government is foolish not to pursue reforms that can deal more effectively with problems. If insistent and intense minorities make their demands felt for reform a rational politician will make some honest effort to learn of the possibilities before things get out of control. Since most men are not hyperactive in politics one must assume that whenever they do become so it must be for good reasons. The conservative politician should always show the vitality of the status quo by a willingness to make reforms which serve to strengthen the ongoing system and thereby prevent eventual revolution. All great conservatives have shown this capacity to reform at the right time.

Exercises in Analysis

ACHIEVING RACIAL INTEGRATION

Suppose you were invited by government leaders to advise on achieving more racial integration and at as low a cost as possible. Suppose further that these leaders, say, a Congressional Committee, asked you to provide advice on the order in which various areas of racial integration be broached by federal law. Let us assume that the following issues are to be ranked on a scale ranging from the least costly (objectionable to whites), to the most costly and therefore most likely to be widely and intensely resisted: The right to vote, the right to register, classroom integration in higher education, marriage, pre-marital sex, private housing, equal job opportunities, public school desegregation, and use of public facilities.

How would you rank these several areas? Why? In constructing a cost/benefit sheet try to identify and measure these factors: opposition to each proposal, their numbers, likely political responses, supporters, and their most probable responses. Make an estimate of the political feasibility of each proposal. Consider too, the time lags involved in achieving integration.

GRADUATED FINES

Sweden, Denmark, and Finland operate graduated fine systems in which the same violation of a law will produce a quite different fine depending upon the income of the violator.[13] West Germany plans to institute the same system in 1973, while Belgium is now considering the matter in Parliament. The exact amount of the fine is specified in a fine schedule but the defendant's ability to pay is decided upon by the prosecutor, defense lawyer, and the tax inspector. The plan in Belgium would have the fine of a poor drunkard who insults a policeman set at $16, the minimum, while a rich man who commits the same offense would pay $320. A Socialist Minister of Justice introduced this plan in collaboration with a wealthy member of the Christian-Democrat Party.

Is such a control politically feasible in this country? Who would support it? Why? Who would oppose it? Why? How do you feel about the plan? If you do not like it, why not? Could it be modified to win your approval? How? One leading Belgian newspaper editorialized that if this plan were to be adopted (early 1970) "one must be consistent and make intellectuals pay more because they know laws better than those who did not go to school . . . ." Is this a consistent extension of the main principle? Why? How shall "intellectualism" be measured? Will intellectuals, who support equality, support the plan?

CONTROLLING CRIME

Crime is a major undertaking in the United States that obviously is worth a great deal to the criminal world. The cost to others, including victims, is terrible. Government also incurs staggering costs as it struggles to control the problem. In 1968 some 4.4 million crimes were reported to the police; these crimes claimed more than 2 million victims and resulted in nearly 5.5 million arrests.[14] In 1965, as much as $21 billion was involved. The attempt to control crime has become highly expensive; more than 4,566 public agencies and 458,000 police contended with offenders and

---

[13] "Measures Would Let Poor Pay Smaller Fines than Rich," *Eugene Register-Guard*, April 8, 1970, 7A.

[14] Various figures from U.S. Bureau of the Census, *Statistical Abstract of the United States, 1969* (90th ed., Washington, D.C.: U.S. Government Printing Office, 1969), pp. 137; 144–45.

TABLE XVI–3

Crime and Public Expenditures

Year	Number of offenses (in thousands)	Percent increase	Expenditure for law enforcement (in millions)	Percent increase
1960	2,015		$3,349	
1962	2,214	___%	3,800	___%
1964	2,755	___%	4,222	___%
1966	3,264	___%	4,903	___%

Source: U.S. Bureau of the Census, *Statistical Abstract of the United States, 1969* (90th ed., Washington, D.C.: U.S. Government Printing Office, 1969), pp. 137, 145.

crime at a cost to the taxpayers of more than $3.3 billion in 1967. More than $8 million were spent in 1966 for police protection and judicial and corrections work—more than $25 per capita.

With this background, consider whether we are making any gains in either reducing crime or reducing the costs of fighting it. Table XVI–3 provides some basic facts. By making some simple calculations you will be able to learn the percentage increase in reported crimes as well as the public expenditure for each crime reported and the percentage of increase in that figure. Unfortunately it is impossible to provide any reliable figures on the benefits of police protection so we cannot really perform a cost/benefit analysis. We could attempt to estimate costs to the victims and determine whether those costs are increasing, decreasing, or remaining constant as we spend varying amounts to control crime.

Suggested Readings

Chamberlain, Neil W. *Private and Public Planning* (New York: McGraw-Hill Book Co., Inc., 1965).

Etzioni, Amitai. *The Active Society* (New York: The Free Press, 1968).

Packer, Herbert L. *The Limits of the Criminal Sanction* (Stanford, Cal.: Stanford University Press, 1968).

Report of the National Advisory Commission on Civil Disorders (Washington, D.C.: U.S. Government Printing Office, 1968).

Sharkansky, Ira. *Public Administration* (Chicago: Markham Publishing Co., 1970).

Steiner, George. *Government's Role in Economic Life* (New York: McGraw-Hill Book Co., Inc., 1953).

Chapter XVII

IMPROVING THE CONDITIONS FOR CHOICE

Democracy involves the citizens and the government in the making of choices. If we value this expression of our personal preferences and the effective use of scarce resources we should want to improve the conditions under which our collective decisions must be made. In previous chapters we detailed a great variety of "rationality aids" for formulating policies, choosing strategies, and making election choices, but in those chapters we accepted the existing basic framework of public choice in this country. In this chapter we will make some general suggestions for improving that very framework to facilitate choice at both the individual and collective levels, and to permit those choices to be more intelligent than our present arrangements allow. (If review is desired at this point, the reader may refer to Chapter VII. Much of what was said there is applicable to our present problem.) One last qualification: the proposals we will make suggest directions of reform rather than catalogs of detailed particulars.

Collective Choice and Bargaining

According to the theory we have developed collective choice is achieved through political bargaining. Policy makers and policy consumers (citizens) achieve their personal satisfactions through bargaining with one another over the allocations of resources between the public and private sectors, allocations among various public goods, distributions of those goods, and allocations of the inevitable burdens. The offering of support on a contingency basis is the means by which the entire process is conducted. In order to gain something, something must be offered in turn. This latter offer is the cost or price of the former gain.

The theory of political bargaining suggests that at least a rough approximation of the tastes and preferences of the nation is found. We learned, however, that many citizens do not participate effectively and that others are prevented from doing so, thus limiting the approximation of their preferences. We learned, too, that the political process of bargaining contains other shortcomings or imperfections including external costs, limited and maldistributed information, unequal distributions of the resources of bargaining, free riders, many immobilities and time lags. Each of these imperfections manifestly harms certain citizens and benefits others; each imperfection tends to distort the overall efficient allocation of resources. Because of the latter we do not, as a nation, realize all the value we might otherwise. A great many illustrations of these costs or consequences of imperfections in the political markets or polity were detailed throughout the text. We need only cast an eye about us, however, to observe some of these consequences: pollution, unrepaired streets, electrical power shortages, overcrowded school rooms, depleted natural resources, underpaid public servants, insufficient parks and other recreational facilities, woeful public transportation, and many other poverties of the public sector.

The intricate unseen hand of bargaining in government is likely to malfunction simply because it is so intricate yet is required to accomplish so much; our ideals demand much of the bargains and institutions within which they work. Whenever the system does not function properly, that is, whenever the balance of costs and benefits perceived by people who do not receive adequate representation prevails our democracy has failed to that extent.

In these remaining pages we attempt to show how the bargaining process can be improved by aiding the voters, politicians, and the institutions of bargaining so that greater rationality can be attained.

Improving the Situation of Voters

We can encourage rational choice among voters by a number of methods. Some of these methods constitute major reforms in the political process; other reforms are minor. A perfectly rational voter is one who is sufficiently informed that he knows his own goals or preferences and can rank them in order, is aware of alternative public policies as they relate to his preferences, and has some grasp of the expected benefits and costs to himself and society of these alternatives. How can we improve his command over these elements of choice?

Voters can be made more aware of their preferences in a number of ways. The most immediate one is for politicians and other leaders to be more explicit than they usually are about the interests involved in public issues. Currently, interest groups perform a highly useful function in this area, for they do attempt to detail the consequences of public policy for their membership. Their work, however, is not adequate. A longer-range reform would introduce the function to public education, so that students would be provided with information relating to their own self-awareness and political interests. Our civics courses should be instructing the young in the realistic pursuit of their interests. If this development came about it would foster many mutually profitable exchanges among intelligent politicians and voters. Above all, it would give voters an urgently needed new view of self-interest and the public interest.

Successful alteration of the basic perception of politics would create an even greater need for reform in the immediate arena of choice of the voter. When voters are in the throes of voting decisions they must have alternative parties, candidates, and policies from which to choose. This requires more competition in many more states so that voters do have to select between two more meaningful opposites. More candidates, representing a wider spectrum of positions, are needed if any degree of choice is to be achieved. We do not need unrealistic extremes for they promote drastic and unstable alterations of public policies that not only complicate the administration of government but complicate the voter's choices as well. They require far more information. Acquiring this information increases the voter's decision-making costs and may even dissuade him from making any choice at all. Less drastic alternatives, therefore, have more of both social and individual utility.

Another institutional improvement concerns the referendum, a special type of election. When voters are asked to pass on such specific proposals as school bonds, taxes, rates and bases, constitutional revisions, voting age requirements, and the like, they should have conveniently available as much pertinent information

as possible. Useful information concerning the estimated consequences could surely be published in some suitable form and displayed at the election stations. If the consequences are controversial each party could be asked to summarize its estimates briefly
so voters would have a clear picture of the possible significance of
their votes. In budgetary referenda the information could also include simplified versions of previous budgets. In expenditures referenda the proposed means of financing should always be included.
Such information may cause voters to vote against the issues, leading to undersupplies of public goods. They would, however, soon
recognize their own responsibility. In any case, they should be
aware of the cost/benefit nexus, regardless of the practical consequences.

Participation should be encouraged because it is a rational
choice whenever a citizen can *visibly affect significant outcomes*.
Unless both conditions obtain there is little point in encouraging
active participation and still less point in condemning voters for
not being political. One of the major contentions of this book is
that we should keep the political sector of society (and therefore
of our individual lives) as small as possible—subject to the limitations of private institutions and choice detailed in Chapter XIII.

But Americans hold many elections, and the citizen must study
a great deal of information if he attempts to achieve perfect rationality as a voter. Very early in the game he must learn that
attention and emotions must be carefully allocated to meet the
time available. We do not favor abolition of elections or artificial
remaking of our party system in order to simplify the task of the
voter. Rather, we prefer keeping our present system because it
offers more opportunities for *those who want to express their
preferences*. We should never coerce voting or other forms of
political participation; political action should always be an individual act of choice. Those who do not wish to participate place a
higher value on other activities and goals; that should be their
right. The common assumption that men have some innate desire
to participate in politics and are prevented from doing so by either
venal men or bad institutions is much overdone. We can and
should try to lower the costs of participation, but we cannot assume that political activity can be made costless, as we pointed out
in our discussion of the inverse relationship between external
costs and decision-making costs.

Some reformers would no doubt attempt to reduce decision-
making costs by instituting a strong two-party system, but they

forget or overlook the extraordinary external costs that would be incurred as the winning party assumes office, particularly if the margin of victory were small. Our present system induces the winning party to bargain constantly with the loser since the federal structure and separation of powers in our system always ensure that no one wins everything and no one loses everything. The benefits of drastically simplifying the task of the voter and encouraging participation are often exaggerated because the opportunity costs of political action are assumed to be zero.

The Citizen as Consumer of Public Services

Even though many of us do not vote, all of us consume public services and are the objects of governmental controls. If we are to act as reasonable men in pursuit of our own interests, we should want to improve our services and make controls as convenient as possible. We should require government to inform the citizenry on the availability of services and the conditions of their distribution, that is, whether they are sold or are free for the asking. This might be accomplished in a variety of ways, but some kind of advertising is called for; perhaps each agency of government could publish its services in the local newspapers once a year or more often. Inexpensive paperback editions listing major services could be prepared and sold on regular newsstands. As it now stands, Americans have limited information about the availability of governmental goods because word-of-mouth seems to be the only vehicle of information.

With more information, the demand for public goods would increase. Voters would find it in their own interests to attend elections and insure that demands be more fully met.

The Citizen as a Holder of Rights

Our roles as subjects of control can stand a great deal of reform. Each citizen ought to be fully informed as to his individual rights regarding all others—particularly in his relationship to government. The further use of ombudsmen is highly commendable, as is establishment of civilian review boards over activities that have close relationships with ordinary citizens. Continued employment of public hearings is a must at all levels of government, and they should be conveniently scheduled so those who have interests in the issues can attend them. Traveling Congressional committees, and any other means that bring the government into more frequent and informal contact with citizens is to be encouraged, even though they may increase the cost of operations. Public defenders should be more available to meet the desperate need for low-cost legal aid among the disadvantaged. They are, unfortunately, most likely to encounter difficulties with governments.

The quality of that aid and of our court system in general needs immeasurable improvement, both in capacity to handle more cases more expeditiously and in terms of the qualities of justice meted out; currently there is too much of a "class" ring to them. Although the liberal rulings of the Supreme Court in recent years have improved the situation of the poor the wealthy still seem to come out better when and if they go to court. Equality before the law should not be a cliché. Our judges should be responsive officials imbued with a deep sense of humanity and equity. These judges would profit from efficient processing of their case loads. In addition, we should resist the intrusion of government into our personal lives, especially intrusion based on the use of wiretapping and secret files of unevaluated testimony, accusations, rumors, and the like. Certain governmental agencies are alleged to be gathering this kind of evidence on an ever larger scale.[1]

Unfortunately, many citizens support the increasing power of government and intrusion in the personal lives of others. During the Great Depression of the 1930s the common man supported the interference of government into economic affairs to control big business; today he supports the police activities of government to control the expressive behavior of student activists, hippies, professors, and blacks and other racial minorities. Civil liberties are not always popular, as some reporters recently discovered when they presented the Bill of Rights to the Constitution for the approval of ordinary American citizens. The freedoms represented therein were viewed suspiciously, as these responses clearly suggest: "Be careful who you show that kind of antigovernment stuff to, buddy"; and, "Somebody ought to tell the FBI about this sort of rubbish."[2]

---

[1] Ben A. Franklin, "Files Being Compiled on 'Persons of Interest,'" *Eugene Register-Guard,* July 5, 1970, 7–B.

[2] "Polls Finds Man-On-Street Won't Sign Declaration of Independence Copy," *The Oregonian,* July 5, 1970, 11.

Since government is the single most powerful institution in modern life the importance of the Bill of Rights cannot be over-estimated. Perhaps school children should learn to recite it rather than the Pledge of Allegiance. Parenthetically, we might wonder who would support and who oppose such a practice.

Making Politicians More Responsive and Responsible

With this concern for improving the situation of the voters by making their job somewhat easier, we suggest that the job of the politician be made more difficult. He must be made accountable to the people he serves for his actions and policies. These conditions are not intended to punish him, but to enable him to be more responsive and responsible. To be responsive is to act as if he cares about the demands and expectations of voters; to be responsible is to exercise some intelligent judgment concerning those demands.[3] Obviously, the two norms are in at least partial conflict. So we seek some means of enabling both the individual politician and politicians collectively to improve their performances. Some offices should emphasize responsiveness while others should emphasize responsibility. In our system, federalism and separation of power are designed to further both these ends and should be maintained in as strong a condition as possible. Legislatures, for example, divide their attention between these two norms in the sense that the House is usually more responsive while the Senate is usually more responsible. The difference in terms of office tends to provide or allow a different choice in the matter. Longer terms permit greater responsibility while shorter terms encourage responsiveness. Hopefully, some workable compromise results. Different types of local government further one or the other of these norms; the city manager form, for example, tends to stress responsibility, while the elected strong mayor form probably stresses responsiveness.

While a number of institutional reforms would facilitate achievement for these norms perhaps the most important is creating a more competitive party system. A politician who wishes to win elections must act carefully. If in, he has to defend his record; if out, he must promise better performances.

[3] See also Herbert J. Spiro, *Responsibility in Government* (New York: Van Nostrand Reinhold Co., 1969).

IMPROVING COMPETITION

To improve competition among politicians we must first lower entry barriers and costs for those who wish to challenge incumbents. Our existing system, especially at the state and national levels, is far too expensive to encourage new competitors, and its requirements are far too complex. Any reform should be designed to ease and simplify requirements, short of permitting lunatics to compete. One way of easing financial burdens would be for government to share a portion of the campaign costs; another would make it profitable for the ordinary citizen to contribute to the party of his choice. The latter can easily be encouraged by permitting income tax deductions for political contributions.

Institutional reforms can profoundly shape behavior but ultimately voters must discipline politicians as consumers discipline sellers in competitive markets. Politicians will "run scared," because they respect the opinions of voters. And that requires voters to become more sophisticated about making demands yet understanding the dilemmas this creates for the politician. The best way to lose out in allocative struggles is to remain ignorant of them; the best way to insure one's just share is to understand the allocative implications of public choice.

IMPROVING EXCHANGE

While each of us is encouraged to protect his own interests, each must also realize that doing good for himself requires him to offer some good to others. Because our politicians are the major agents or bargainers in this process, it is to our joint interest to provide appropriate institutional conditions for seeking out and concluding successful agreements. Our political culture provides both discouragements and encouragements for bargaining; we need to reorient our beliefs and values from those that inhibit exchange to those that facilitate it and induce us to seek mutually profitable arrangements. On the one hand Americans deride compromises as "deals"; on the other hand they give grudging recognition to the necessity of compromise. Our hostility toward bargaining does not provide a favorable environment for politicians or for citizens who make demands on politicians. Once more, the educational institutions have a special responsibility in reorienting our views.

To the extent that our political institutions encourage politicians and others to take adamant, uncompromising stands and pursue zero-sum strategies, political exchange is discouraged. To encourage exchange we need political markets or institutions that lead men to behave as if mutually rewarding exchanges are possible, as our notion of "winners" and "losers" does.

Most important, we should equalize distribution of political resources in order to permit bargainers the capacity to reward others as well as the capacity to resist unjust solutions or trades. The best sort of rewards or goods for exchange benefit others positively. They are not unilaterally based on the withdrawal of threats and negative sanctions, as in an "exchange" between robber and victim. This kind of exchange is not desirable because the robber says, in effect, "You can remain unhurt or alive if you will give me your money." The victim has no choice. We do not want this type of forcible exchange in the political system. We neither want powerful groups exploiting the weak, as in many distributive issues, nor do we want the disadvantaged groups blackmailing others into agreements. Unfortunately, the disadvantaged now see no alternatives to disruption and blackmail. Hopefully, admission to society will proceed more rapidly so that concrete useful exchange can replace the current exercises of threat and violence.

Our political institutions generally encourage exchange, but at a price. The price is increased decision-making costs including time, increased confusion, and partially conflicting and unsatisfactory settlements. These costs are inevitable, although their precise amounts should be cut whenever possible.

Some Problems to be Solved

Improving the rational potential of citizens is viewed here as possible only incrementally and on a trial and error basis. Our eventual objective is simply to improve whatever potential a citizen has for advancing his own goals. The writer does not share the view of those who seek to convert every citizen into some kind of calculating machine. This new voter, in this view, would be confronted with sharply drawn policy alternatives advocated by highly disciplined political parties who can be expected to enact all their proposals when elected to public office. Such reforms seem unrealistic for a number of reasons. First, they require human beings who are unlike any the writer has ever encountered. Second they are not remotely possible under existing political conditions, because they entail exorbitant costs for most people, particularly the politicians. Finally, their social costs appear much higher than most reformers realize, because they substitute conflicts for the workable compromises that are apt to be more reflective of our diverse values. Substitution of the clear-cut alternatives being proposed by reformers would inevitably make the costs of losing much greater, encouraging losers to challenge outcomes as well as the processes that produce them. But voters in democracies need more rather than fewer positive-sum choices to serve and unite them, and to make political decisions less crucial in their daily lives. Political scientists like to stress the importance of government, as we did in the first chapter, but most problems and concerns should be left to private persons. There are no magical solutions to be derived from converting private choice into public choice. When the externalities are significantly increased public processes should prevail, but we must not minimize the importance of increased decision costs for individuals or the more indirect costs of increased animosities. Unfortunately, these latter costs tend to accumulate across issue lines making exchange more elusive—perhaps impossible.

Advocacy of workable compromises—the politics of accommodation—is not apt to enlist legions of devoted followers but it does have the value of building upon institutions that have already proven their long-term worth. Our possession of such resources ought not to be taken lightly, inasmuch as most societies have not been able to institutionalize workable democratic procedures. There are only about 20 successful democracies, while the number of really successful large-scale democracies can be counted on the fingers of one hand. What seems so remarkable is our having any democracy let alone the oldest continuous one in history. That so diverse a people spread over so large an area should have managed to produce stable representative institutions is one of the more splendid political achievements of mankind.[4]

Democracies are not hardy plants, and many more have died than have survived. We do not know how much conflict of what types can be adequately handled by different systems, but logic and considerable historical evidence suggest that democracies cannot be expected to cope successfully with continuous basic conflicts.[5] Some issues must be more or less resolved in order that oth-

---

[4] For a contrasting view see Thomas R. Dye and L. Harmon Zeigler, *The Irony of Democracy* (Belmont, Calif.: Wadsworth Publishing Co., 1970).

[5] See Harry Eckstein, *Division and Cohesion in Democracy* (Princeton: Princeton University Press, 1966): Arend Lijphart, *The Politics of Accommodation* (Berkeley: University of California Press, 1968).

ers may be considered and fought out. Needless to say, the more diverse, frequent, and intense the conflicts the less likely are workable compromises. We have seen how Arrow's Paradox illustrates the difficulty of achieving consistent public policies when voters disagree. While we cannot rule out disagreements if people have them, surely we can devise institutions which permit at least sufficient agreement to enable the game to continue.

Political Alternatives

We do not expect to find total agreement with the analysis of public choice we have presented, with the directions of reform we have proposed, or even with our basically sympathetic evaluation of American democracy. The range of views opposing these issues is extensive, but two schools of thought that have emerged should command our immediate attention. One is basically reformist in nature; the other is essentially revolutionary. The first may be said to constitute the liberal version of how our system ought to operate if we would only adopt a few institutional reforms. The other view wants to completely demolish the entire system and reconstruct it along far more leftist lines. Most political scientists adhere to the reformist tradition while the revolutionaries appear chiefly centered among students, some radical nonstudent groups, and a few other individuals.

THE LIBERAL REFORM

It is not easy to portray accurately a school of thought that prides itself on not being totalitarian in ideology. Such is the case with the reformers. Still, one can identify a nucleus of ideas and reforms. They include the substitution of a national Presidential primary for the present party nominating system; strengthening of Presidential power over policy making and party activities; reducing the influence of Congress and its seniority system; abolition of the Electoral College; and a variety of lesser institutional reforms at all levels of government.[6] The purposes of

---

[6] A good summary and critique of the reform school is offered by Nelson W. Polsby and Aaron B. Wildavsky, *Presidential Elections* (2d ed., New York: Charles Scribner's Sons, 1968), Chapter 5.

these proposals include a desire to rationalize the political system; to provide for voters more clear-cut alternatives and a more responsive and responsible set of governments. Preservation of the two-party system is also an important goal of the reformers.

Students who wish to look into these proposals at greater length should consult the suggested reading at the end of the chapter. They might also like to work out the consequences of one proposal—that of substituting primaries for the present system; this exercise, along with some others, is at the end of this chapter. More challenging, however, is the New Left.

THE NEW LEFT: PARTICIPATORY DEMOCRACY

A school of thought that has been developed by the New Left during recent years is usually labelled "participatory democracy" by its adherents.[7] The New Left maintains a perspective on America that is critical of our institutions, especially the political. Their perspective is far more critical than is conventional reform. It is probably more critical than any since the Marxists of the 1930s. Because the nature of individual commitment is highly emotional the animosities of this school are far more articulated than is its program of action. They do hold, however, that current institutions do not permit the people to have an effective voice in government. "The people" include the poor minorities as well as students. The values, norms, interests, and life style of the people, they maintain, are constantly being suppressed by a "silent majority" of middle class and the rich led by the Establishment and implemented by the police. The United States is viewed as a repressive, international imperialist regime, destined for eventual forcible overthrow by the people. Poverty and racial discrimination, the crucial evils of the system, are inevitable given the values and interests of the Establishment. The rhetoric is crude and powerful, and although the supporters are few in number their militancy is intense. This revolutionary vanguard has been able to command enormous attention in the media, largely because of its willingness to resort to violence.

Precise prescriptions of institutional reform and policy redirection of the New Left are hard to identify. Behind the rheto-

[7] For a variety of more or less radical diagnoses and prescriptions, see: Maurice Zeitlin, *American Society, Inc.* (Chicago: Markham Publishing Co., 1970); and Robert Theobald, ed., *Social Policies for America in the Seventies: Nine Divergent Views* (Garden City, N.Y.: Doubleday & Co., Inc., 1969).

ric, however, one discovers some guiding prescripts. Surprisingly, these prescripts have some parallels with ideals held by the Right and even some found in this book. The basic ideals and policies appear to include (1) a decentralized, individual choice, which they call "doing your own thing"; (2) use of open meetings and rather continuous public gatherings at which the people collectively make decisions; (3) intense and expressive involvement in public affairs; (4) redistribution of income and wealth; (5) greater equality among all peoples; (6) extensive retrenchment from foreign involvements, particularly those that concern the efforts of radicals to overthrow fascist regimes; (7) a distrust and hostility toward public and private bureaucracy; (8) a fondness for charismatic revolutionary leaders.

Similarities to the traditional right include emphasis on individual choice, decentralized decision making, and suspicion of bureaucratic ways. And, although they share some values with traditional Marxist and Socialist thought, the New Left does not favor bureaucratic administration of the economy. Apparently, opinion on this issue is divided; some New Leftists claim they want socialism rather than capitalism, but there is no clear statement of this economic position. In theory, the workers would probably install participatory democracy in each firm and industry. How they would adjust their decisions to accord with the interests of consumers and other firms and to meet other market demands is not clear.

A number of the ideals also appear contradictory raising the question of trade-offs and opportunity costs. For example, if business bureaucracy is viewed with distrust, how would large-scale production and distribution be accomplished? If individual expression—"doing your thing"—is valued, how can we justify the enormous amount of public choice that the system would require? If highly expressive behavior is valued how could passionate disagreements be worked out? In all these dilemmas one must sacrifice one value for another at some rate or other. And, worse, how does one devise institutions for carrying out the manifestos? How do traditional American institutions fit into the picture?

While it is relatively easy to deride this image, it should not be taken lightly. Regardless of the institutional implications and contradictions the criticisms of our institutions and practices are often cogent. Demand for greater humaneness in superorganized society must have a powerful appeal. The New Left's desire for increased democratization of private institutions and organiza-

TABLE XVII–1

Some Hypothetical Changes in Rules

Institutions or rules	Expected gains and gainers	Expected costs and bearers	Political feasibility
Direct national presidential primary			
Four-year terms for Congressmen			
Simultaneous election of senators and President			
Abolition of seniority rule in Congress			
Repeal of 22nd Amendment to the Constitution			
Require TV debates between Presidential candidates			
Compulsory voting (fine for not voting)			
Abolition of counties			
National referendum on keeping the Bill of Rights in Constitution			
Regional governments to replace states			
Abolition of judicial review by Supreme Court			

tions makes a great deal of sense, for the quest of democracy toward these ends is never fulfilled.

Exercises in Analysis

INSTITUTIONAL CHANGES

Those who have finished this book should have a somewhat better understanding of the impact of our political institutions and processes on our daily lives and should, therefore, be in a better position to assess the potentialities and costs of altering our basic rules of the game. On that basis, here is a problem: Table XVII-1 is a presentation of various hypothetical institutions or rules of the game. Consider these rules in terms of (1) their potential advantages or benefits and costs and (2) their respective political feasibility. Complete the tabulations. To add sophistication and realism to your assessment, include some consideration of the short-run as distinct from the long-run advantages, disadvantages, and feasibility. In addition, estimate or determine which groups will profit most and which least from such institutional alterations for that affects the feasibility of change. Furthermore, what constitutes an advantage for one group may be a serious disadvantage for another since institutions or rules are never neutral in their effects.

ENCOURAGING POLITICAL PARTICIPATION

Suppose that you have been asked by one of our major parties to devise a program for encouraging legitimate political participation among certain groups of citizens. Further suppose that you have accepted the cost/benefit calculus employed throughout this book and wish to apply it in the development of the program. What sorts of appeals would you use for each group in Table XVII-2? Perhaps it should be noted that no citizen falls exclusively into any one of these groups. In shaping incentives for participation, take account of possible contradictory roles and, therefore, incentives. Thus, a person who is a young American Indian career military man could respond to three different types of incentives or appeals but which one will be most and least sensible to him? At certain times his being an Indian will be most important; at other times being a professional soldier may count most.

TABLE XVII–2

Group Appeals for Political Participation

Group	Cost of nonparticipation	Benefits of action
Low-income blacks		
Pensioners		
Women		
21–26 year olds		
Career military		
American Indians		
Southern low-income whites		
Primary school teachers		
Union members		
Agricultural workers		

The political strategist confronts a difficult problem when he attempts to discover the balance of roles and commitments among the potential voters.

Suggested Readings

Bolling, Richard. *House Out of Order* (New York: E. P. Dutton & Co., 1965).

Burns, James M. *The Deadlock of Democracy* (Englewood Cliffs, N.J.: Prentice-Hall, Inc., 1963).

Clark, Joseph. *Congress: The Sapless Branch* (New York: Harper & Row, 1964).

Davidson, Roger H., Kovenock, David M., and O'Leary, Michael K. *Congress in Crisis: Politics and Congressional Reform* (Belmont, Calif.: Wadsworth Publishing Co., Inc., 1966).

de Grazia, Alfred. *Republic in Crisis* (New York: Federal Legal Press, 1965).

Peirce, Neal R. *The People's President* (New York: Simon & Schuster, 1968).

Polsby, Nelson W. and Wildavsky, Aaron B. *Presidential Elections*, (2d ed., New York: Charles Scribner's Sons, 1968).

GLOSSARY

This glossary, intended only as a convenience for readers, lists some of the more fundamental and frequently-used concepts in this book. While many of the terms are familiar as economic language they are probably much less understood in the context of political analysis. The definitions provided here are as simple as precision will allow and the goals of political inquiry make mandatory. Discussion of the terms in the body of the text is more extended, as one might expect.

Ability to pay. A principle of taxation based on the idea that taxpayers should pay taxes in accordance with the size of their income and/or their wealth.

Bargaining. A means of exchange in which the terms of settlement are within the control of the partners to the exchange.

Benefit principle. A principle of taxation based on the idea that taxes should be levied according to the benefits derived from governmental services.

Bargaining costs. Expenditures of time, energy and money to influence collective decisions.

Budget, public. A financial plan for the operations of government.

Coalition. Persons or organizations having certain complementary goals and who cooperate to achieve them.

Competition. Mutual seeking of a scarce value by two or more persons.

Conflict. Incompatible goals.

Cost. That which is given up in order to achieve something.

Cost benefit analysis. Systematic estimation of the relative benefits and costs of alternative public policies.

Criterion. A standard by which performance is measured.

Earmarking. Allocating specific taxes to specific governmental activities.

Efficiency. A ratio of inputs of resources and output or performance.

Efficiency, optimal. The greatest output given the input of resources or least resources given the output.

Exchange. The reciprocal transference of benefits.

Externality. Benefits gained or burdens incurred for which one is not responsible.

External cost. Burdens sustained by persons other than those who created the cost.

Federalism. A means of organizing a polity in which at least two levels of government rule the same people and each level has some autonomy to make public policy.

Free riders. Beneficiaries who do not pay or share in the costs of producing their benefits.

Government. A specialized organization having authority to enact and administer public policies.

Gross national product (GNP). The total value of all final goods and services in a nation during any year.

Incremental. Describing small changes in value or amount.

Ideology. A system of beliefs, values, and norms concerning the state of society and its reorganization.

Indifference curves. Combinations of two goods that yield equal satisfaction or are equally preferred.

Institution. A means of doing something that is at once widely accepted as right and that, if violated, usually leads to sanctioning the "wrongdoer."

Interest group. A formal organization which pursues at least some of its goals by attempting to influence public policy through political activity.

Marginal cost. Added costs entailed by increased activity.

Marginal utility. The added satisfaction derived from increased use of a good or activity.

Market. An institution that enables buyers and sellers to exchange goods and services.

Norm. A prescription of behavior.

Opportunity cost. Benefits or gains forgone or lost as a result of adopting a particular course of action.

Paretian optimality. A state in which it is not possible to make one person better off without making someone else worse off.

Polity. A subsystem of society that makes collective decisions and has a legal monopoly of power to enforce those decisions in that society.

Power. The capacity to shape the behavior of others.

Private goods. Those goods which, when consumed, diminish the supply available to others.

Public goods. Those goods which can be consumed by some persons without diminishing the supply available to others.

Public policy. A proposed or adopted course of action of a government.

Rationality. The capacity to choose appropriate means for the realization of one's goals.

Role. A set of norms that defines an activity in terms of what should and should not be done by the person fulfilling the position.

Strategy. A general plan of action containing instructions concerning what to do in every contingency.

Subsidy. A financial gain or aid provided by a government.

Tax. A compulsory payment for the support of government and its activities.

Uncertainty. Unknown probabilities of events.

User fees. Direct charges for governmental services.

Utility. Capacity of a good to produce satisfaction.

Zero-sum game. A situation in which the gains of the winners are exactly equal to the losses of the losers.

INDEX